The Evolution of European Competition Law

The Evolution of European Competition Law

Whose Regulation, Which Competition?

Edited by

Hanns Ullrich

Professor of Law, European University Institute, Firenze, Italy

ASCOLA COMPETITION LAW
The First ASCOLA Workshop on Comparative Competition Law

Edward Elgar
Cheltenham, UK • Northampton, MA, USA

Published by
Edward Elgar Publishing Limited
Glensanda House
Montpellier Parade
Cheltenham
Glos GL50 1UA
UK

Edward Elgar Publishing, Inc.
136 West Street
Suite 202
Northampton
Massachusetts 01060
USA

A catalogue record for this book
is available from the British Library

ISBN-13: 978 1 84542 701 6
ISBN-10: 1 84542 701 7

Typeset by Cambrian Typesetters, Camberley, Surrey
Printed and bound in Great Britain by MPG Books Ltd, Bodmin, Cornwall

Contents

List of contributors   vii
Foreword   viii

I INTRODUCTION

Introduction   3
Hanns Ullrich

II STRATEGIC COMPETITION POLICIES? US–EU CONFLICTS AND CONVERGENCE

 1 Foundations of competition policy in the EU and USA:
    conflict, convergence and beyond   17
    Clifford A. Jones
 2 Strategic competition policy: a comment on EU competition
    policy   38
    Wulf-Henning Roth
 3 Revision of the new Technology Transfer Block Exemption
    Regulation: convergence or capitulation?   53
    Mark R. Patterson
 4 The evolution of European competition law and the Italian
    Autorità Garante della Concorrenza e del Mercato   71
    Giuseppe Tesauro

III CONTROLLING RESTRICTIONS OF COMPETITION

 5 Vertical agreements: 4 years of liberalisation by regulation
    n. 2790/99 after 40 years of legal (block) regulation   85
    Denis Waelbroeck
    Comments
    Wolfgang Kerber   111
    Roger Zäch   121
 6. Cooperative networking: bridging the cooperation–concentration
    gap   126
    Maria Manuel Leitão Marques and Ana Abrunhosa

v

Comments
Andreas Fuchs   157
Daniel Zimmer   166
7   Mergers in the media sector: business as usual?   170
Laurence Idot
Comments
Peristera Kremmyda   191
Ulf Bernitz   197
8   Abuse of market power: controlling dominance or protecting
competition?   201
Laurence Boy
Comments
Peter Behrens   224
Eleanor M. Fox   233

IV   APPROACHING COMPETITION BY REGULATION

9   Regulating towards what? The concepts of competition in
sector-specific regulation, the likelihood of their realisation and
of their sustainability, and their relationship to rendering public
infrastructure services   241
Christian Kirchner
Comments
Kurt Stockmann   256
Fabiana Di Porto   263
10 Competition, regulation and system coherence   274
Joël Monéger
Comments
Jens Fejø   291
Paul L. G. Nihoul   300

V   CONCLUSION: THE NEW THINKING

11 Efficiency claims in EC competition law and sector-specific
regulation   313
Damien Geradin
Comment
Gustavo Ghidini   357

Index   363

Contributors

Ana Abrunhosa, Faculdade de Economia, Universidade de Coimbra
Peter Behrens, Fakultät für Rechtswissenschaft, Universität Hamburg
Ulf Bernitz, Juridiska Fakulteten, Stockholms Universitet
Laurence Boy, Faculté de Droit, Université Nice-Sophia Antipolis, Nice
Fabiana Di Porto, Facoltà di Giurisprudenza, Università LUISS, Roma
Jens Fejø, Handelshøjskolen i København, Copenhagen
Eleanor M. Fox, New York University School of Law
Andreas Fuchs, Juristische Fakultät, Universität Osnabrück
Damien Geradin, Département de Droit, Université de Liege
Gustavo Ghidini, Facoltà di Giurisprudenza, Università LUISS, Roma
Laurence Idot, Département de Droit, Université Paris I, Paris
Clifford A. Jones, University of Florida, Levin College of Law, Gainesville
Wolfgang Kerber, Wirtschaftswissenschaftliche Fakultät, Philipps-
    Universität, Marburg
Christian Kirchner, Juristische Fakultät, Humbolt Universität, Berlin
Peristera Kremmyda, European Commission, Brussels
Maria Manuel Leitão Marques, Faculdade de Economia, Universidade de
    Coimbra
Joël Monéger, Département de Droit, Université Paris-Dauphine, Paris
Paul L. G. Nihoul, Faculté de Droit, Université Catholique de Louvain,
    Louvain-la-Neuve
Mark R. Patterson, Fordham University, School of Law, New York City
Wulf-Henning Roth, Rechtswissenschaftlicher Fachbereich, Rheinische
    Friedrich-Wilhelms Universität, Bonn
Kurt Stockmann, ehem. Bundeskartellamt, Berlin/Bonn
Giuseppe Tesauro, Facoltà di Giurisprudenza, Università La Sapienza, Roma
Hanns Ullrich, Law Department, European University Institute, Florence
Denis Waelbroeck, European Legal Studies Department, College of Europe,
    Bruges
Roger Zäch, Rechtswissenschaftliches Institut, Universität Zürich
Daniel Zimmer, Rechtswissenschaftlicher Fachbereich, Rheinische
    Friedrich-Wilhelms Universität, Bonn

Foreword

On 12 and 13 November 2004, the first workshop of the Academic Society for Competition Law (ASCOLA) was held at the European University Institute, Florence. Thirty-nine academics from Europe and the USA met to discuss 'The Evolution of European Competition Law – Whose Regulation, Which Competition' at a conference which had been organized by the Institute's Chair of Competition Law and of Intellectual Property Law in cooperation with the Osservatorio di Proprietà Intellettuale, Concorrenza e Comunicazioni of the LUISS University of Rome. This volume contains the papers and invited comments that have been presented for discussion; the vivid discussion among all participants remains their academic souvenir.

The workshop was multilingual, both formally and informally. Two contributions, which originally were in French, and have been published as such, spontaneously were presented in English at the workshop: they are reproduced here in English translation.* But all contributions, except of course those by native English language authors, had to undergo a minimum of linguistic revision. Paul Harvey and Katherine Worthington, researchers of the Institute's Law Department, and Mel Marquis, visiting fellow, have sacrificed their talent and time to this revision work, and, in addition, have brought their research skills to finalizing the contributions stylistically and formally. By setting up a fully detailed index Agnieszka Machnicka, also a researcher at the Law Department, provided the access code to all the information contained in the many contributions. Anna Coda Nunziante has, beyond her secretarial duties, taken care of the proper form of presentation of the contributions while preserving their stylistic diversity.

The authors and the editor owe all of them sincere gratitude.

Hanns Ullrich
Florence, June 2005

---

* See *infra* chapters 7 and 8.

PART I

Introduction

Introduction

Hanns Ullrich

I   THE PROGRAMME

1   A Subjective Approach

The choice of 'The Evolution of European Competition Law' as the topic for the first conference of the newly established Academic Society for Competition Law was obvious enough. The interpretation, implementation and application of the rules of competition of the Treaty of the European Community (Art. 81 et seq. EC-Treaty) have undergone and continue to undergo profound changes, and they do so under American intellectual, industrial and political influence. An association with a predominantly European membership – inside and outside the European Union – but which looks across the Atlantic and seeks (and has) members there, probably may begin with a self-assessment of 'our' law. However, the nature and the narrow framework of a workshop – more had never been intended – required a rather selective and allowed a quite subjective approach. Thus, rather than to propose a re-examination of the modernization of enforcement[1] or of merger control reform[2] on the basis of a comparison with its US counterparts as suggested by predecessor projects of comparative competition law,[3] the letter of invitation

---

[1]   Council Regulation 1/2003 of 16 December 2002 on the implementation of the rules on competition laid down in Article 81 and 82 of the Treaty, OJEC 2003 L 1, 1; Reg. 1/2003 has been implemented by a number of Commission Notices and Guidelines, all published in OJEC of 27 April 2004, No. L 101, at pp. 43 et seq., 54 et seq., 65 et seq., 81 et seq., 97 et seq.

[2]   Council Regulation 139/2004 of 20 January 2004 on the control of concentrations between undertakings (the EC Merger Regulation), OJEC 2005 L 24, 1; Commission Regulation 802/004 of 7 April 2004 implementing Council Regulation 139/2004 on the control of concentration between undertakings, OJEC 2004 L 133, 1; see also the Commission Notices in OJEC of 5 March 2005, Nr. § 56 at p. 24 et seq. (simplified procedure), 32 et seq. (referral to national authorities).

[3]   H. Ullrich (ed.), *Comparative Competition Law: Approaching an International System of Antitrust Law*, Baden-Baden 1998; R. Zäch (ed.), *Towards WTO Competition Rules*, Berne 1999; J. Drexl (ed.), *The Future of Transnational Antitrust – From Comparative to Common Competition Law*, The Hague 2003.

to contributors of papers and to their commentators deliberately was based on my personal perception of the trends and reasons underlying the evolution of European competition law. This made me ask by way of a sub-title: 'Whose regulation, which competition?'

2 Trends in the Community's Competition Policy

There are several overlapping and interdependent trends that characterize the evolution of European competition law.

(i)   One such trend is the shift in focus of competition policy, and, consequently, of the practical importance of the various areas of development and enforcement of the law. Privatization, de- and re-regulation of national public infrastructure sectors (telecommunications, air and railway transportation, energy) have not only allowed the Community to expand its regulatory competencies so as to largely overshadow reservations of Member States' powers as implied in Art. 86 EC-Treaty. Rather, it has established a broad new field of regulatory competition law[4] which does not merely complement but rather has become an equal counterpart of the law against restraints of competition, and indeed may even be a rival body of law.[5] Control of industrial concentration through mergers, acquisitions and joint ventures, ever since its belated introduction,[6] has attracted more interest than control of contractual or otherwise concerted practices of restricting competition. This holds true both as regards administrative concern and political focus. In this regard, it suffices to compare the modes of control (ex ante/ex post) and the allocation of competencies between the Community and the Member States as provided for, on the one hand, by Regulation 1/2003 with respect to Art. 81 EC-Treaty and, on the other, by Regulation 4064/89, now Regulation 139/2004 as regards merger control.[7] Whilst there may be

---

[4]   For an overview see E.J. Mestmäcker, H. Schweitzer, *Europäisches Wettbewerbsrecht*, 2nd edn, Munich 2004, 21 et seq.; Bundeskartellamt, *Marktöffnung und Gewährleistung von Wettbewerb in der leitungsgebundenen Energiewirtschaft*, available at http://Bundeskartellamt.de/wDeutsch/download/pdf/AKK02.pdf; summary in WuW 2003, 497; as regards telecommunications more specifically A. Bavasco, 'Electronic Communication: A New Paradigm for European Regulation', 41 *CML Rev.* 887 (2004).

[5]   See *infra* Part IV, in particular the comments by P. Nihoul on Chr. Kirchner, p. 300 et seq. with references.

[6]   Council Regulation 4068/89 of 21 December 1989 on the control of concentrations between undertakings, OJEC 1989 § 395, cm. OJEC 1990 § 257, 14.

[7]   References in footnotes 1, 2 and 6 *supra*; as to the workload of the

good reasons for the differences of approach, these pertain less to the legal or economic nature of the transactions in question than to the politico-economic importance attributed to them.[8] Even within the field of application of Art. 81 EC-Treaty the focus of control has been limited essentially to horizontal arrangements, and then mainly to hardcore cartels, leaving industrial cooperation largely unattended, if not privileged.[9] Cooperation may, indeed, reach high market shares or, at least, need not be exposed to competition by more than two or three other groups.[10]

(ii) This redefinition of the fields with which competition policy is concerned of course has its nuances[11] and tends to favour various forms

---

Commission in both areas (after modernization of enforcement, which aimed precisely, *inter alia*, at a more or less equal workload, see Commission, 'Report on Competition Policy 2004', SEC (2005) 805 final of 17 June 2005 at I.E (p. 56 et seq.), II D (p. 96 et seq.).

[8] As regards differences of structural impact by concentration and by cooperation respectively these are generally overestimated: specialization, joint production, selling or purchasing, cooperative research and development do and are intended to reallocate resources in a no less irreversible way as it occurs in the case of mergers. (See also Commission, 'Guidelines on the application of Article 81(3) of the Treaty', OJEC 2004 L 101, 97 at no. 45.) EU (like German) competition policy does tend to level off the cartel/concentration gap by raising the threshold for control of cooperation rather than by lowering the thresholds for concentration control (see critically J. Schmidt, A. Fritz, 'Pro und contra Konzentrationsprivileg: Die unterschiedlichen Wirkungen von Kartellen und Fusionen auf Wettbewerb und Effizienz', in J. Kruse, O.G. Mayer, (eds) *Festschrift E. Kantzenbach* (Baden-Baden 1996), p. 119 et seq. The reason is presumably the problem of political acceptance of merger control by both industrial circles and governments relying on them.

[9] Compare, in the first respect, the different definition of safe harbours for, on the one hand, horizontal restraints (20%–25% combined market share according to Commission Regulation No. 2658/2000 (Art. 4) for specialization agreements and No. 2659/2000 (Art. 4) for joint research and development, No. 772/2004 (Art. 3(1)) for technology transfer agreements), and, on the other, for vertical restraints (30% individual market share according to Commission Regulation No. 2790/99 (Art. 3) for vertical restraints generally, No. 772/2004 (Art. 3(2)) for technology transfer agreements); for the enforcement focus on hardcore cartels see Commission, 'Report on Competition Policy 2004', *supra* n. 7, at p. 7, 29 (Box 3); for the generous treatment of cooperation of all kinds see Commission, 'Guidelines on the application of Article 81 to horizontal cooperation agreements', OJEC 2001 L 3, 2 at no. 3 et passim; H. Ullrich, 'Competitor Cooperation and the Evolution of Competition Law: Issues for Research in a Perspective of Globalization', in J. Drexl (ed.), *supra* n. 3, p. 159 et seq. (sub II A2).

[10] See Commission, 'Guidelines on horizontal cooperation agreements', *supra* n. 9, at nos. 36, 51, 71, 105, 134, 168, Commission, 'Guidelines on the application of Art. 81(3)', *supra* n. 8 at no. 116.

[11] Thus, for example, Art. 4 Commission Regulation 2790/1999 of 22 December 1999 on the application of Article 81(3) to categories of vertical agreements and concerted practices, OJEC 1999L 336, 21 outlaws a number of traditional hardcore

of market regulation. One such form is self-regulation by market actors. It seems to be the logical result of a looser antitrust regime which puts much trust in market control of private arrangements. An example of this is, when broad block exemptions of vertical agreements[12] or technology transfer agreements[13] leave the configuration of systems of distribution or of licensing, which before had been subject to a structured legal framework,[14] to determination by the parties; that is typically to collective negotiations of model agreements between a manufacturer or an assembler and the distributors of products or suppliers of components.

Other examples of private regulation of competition by collective action are presented by standardization;[15] by the exploitation of TV or radio and merchandizing rights by sports associations as well as by their practices of recruiting or transferring sportsmen/women and of admitting brokers,[16] by the joint establishment of Internet market places, and

---

restrictions (resale price fixing, attribution of territorial exclusivities, albeit with considerable reservations; Commission Regulation No. 1400/2002 of 31 July 2002 on the application of Art. 81(3) of the Treaty to categories of vertical agreements and concerted practices in the motor vehicle sector, OJEC 2002 L 203, 30, seeks to loosen the grip of automobile manufacturers over distributors (comp. S. Vezzoso, 'On the Antitrust Remedies to Promote Retail Innovation in the EU Car Sector', ECLR 2004, p. 190).

[12]   See Commission Regulation 2790/1999, *supra* n. 11, and the contribution by D. Waelbroeck, 'Vertical agreements: 4 years of liberalisation by regulation n. 2790/99 after 40 years of legal (block) regulation', and the comments by W. Kerber, R. Zäch, Chapter 5 of this volume, at pp. 85 et seq.

[13]   Commission Regulation No. 772/2004 of 27 April 2004 on the application of Article 81(3) to categories of technology transfer agreements, OJEC 2004 L 123, 11 as compared to the Commission's predecessor Regulation 240/96 of 31 January 1996 on the application of Article 85(3) to certain categories of technology transfer agreements, OJEC 1996 L 331, 2; and see Commission, 'Evaluation Report on the Transfer of Technology Block Exemption Regulation Nr. 240/96 of December 2001' (available at http://europa.eu.int/comm/competition/antitrust/technology-transfer/en.pdf).

[14]   Frequently denigrated as a 'straight jacket' approach, but also defended as providing not only legal certainty, but also some backing in cases of unequal bargaining power in licensing negotiations, see M. Lejeune, 'Die neue europäische Gruppenfreistellungsverordnung für Technologietransfervereinbarungen', CR 2004, 467 at pp. 472, 475.

[15]   Commission, 'Guidelines on horizontal cooperation agreements', *supra* n. 9, at nos. 169, 172 favours standardization resulting from procedures involving substantial parts of the industry concerned or 'all competitors', apparently as an alternative to standardization by (semi-) official organization, ibid. at no. 162.

[16]   See recently CFI of 26 January 2005, case T-193/02, Piau/Commission, WuW E EU-R 881; Commission of 19 January 2005, case DG Comp/C-2/27.214, Deutsche Bundesliga, WuW EU-V 1041; of 23 July 2003, case comp./C 2-27389-UEFA Champions League, WuW E EU-V-889; Commission, 'Report on Competition Policy 2004', *supra* n. 7, at nos. 84 et seq., 92 et seq.

by the various types of mass-exploitation of intellectual property through pools[17] or collecting societies.[18] Their common feature is the group-wise internalization of at least some elements of the markets in question, and the institutionalization (typically due to more or less soft intervention by the competition authorities!) of some neutralization mechanism regarding the exercise of collective, in fact frequently, absolute market power.[19] By contrast, the admission of many forms of industrial cooperation, such as teaming agreements, joint research and development or purchasing, is, at least in the more important cases, based on and satisfied by the mere existence of group competition.[20] The common denominator, however, is the reversal of the role of competition: it is not the conditions of competition which determine the opportunities and limits of the market for individual enterprises, but it is the individual actors which, by joining forces or action, redefine their conditions of competition and, therefore, the market opportunities available to them.

(iii) Such reliance on private self-regulation and reversal of the role of competition may ultimately invite competition authorities to apply methods of regulatory control under Art. 81 EC-Treaty. Examples are the imposition of mechanisms of power neutralization, of duties of non-discrimination and of mandatory access.[21] Whilst this may be only a means of last resort limiting the leniency of the antitrust regime established by a reinterpreted

---

[17]   See Commission, 'Guidelines on the application of Article 81 of the EC Treaty to technology transfer agreements', OJEC 2004 L 101, 2 at no. 210 et seq.

[18]   See recently Commission of 8 October 2002, case COMP/C-2/38.014, JFPJ 'Simulcasting', OJEC 2003 L 107, 58; Commission, 'Report on Competition Policy 2004', *supra* n. 7, p. 85 (Box 4); Commission, 'The Management of Copyright and Related Rights in the Internal Market', COM (2004) final sub 3., 3.4.

[19]   As regards standardization Commission, 'Guidelines on horizontal cooperation', *supra* n. 9, at nos. 163, 172 requires openness, transparency and representativeness of the standardization process; as regards technology pool building Commission, 'Guidelines on technology transfer agreements', *supra* n. 17 at no. 230 favours pools based on an institutional framework ensuring objectivity and transparency (for a critique see H. Ullrich, 'Patentgemeinschaften', in A. Fuchs et al., (eds), *Festschrift U. Immenga*, Munich 2004, 403, 423 et seq.; as regards sports rights, open and transparent licensing procedures (auctions) are considered to be countervailing remedies, see references *supra* n. 16 and ECJ of 27 September 2004, case C-470/02 P, EBU/ Commission, OJEC 2004 C314, affirming CF1 of 8 October 2002, case T-185/00, Métropole Télévision (M6)/Commission, Rep. 2002 I 3808.

[20]   See also *supra* n. 10.

[21]   See n. 19 *supra* and references therein; for open access to the use of standards Commission, 'Guidelines on horizontal cooperation', *supra* n. 9, at nos. 169, 174 et seq.; for access to pooled technology Commission, 'Guidelines on technology transfer agreements', *supra* n. 17, at nos. 224, 226, 231.

Art. 81 EC-Treaty, a trend towards the application of prescriptive regulatory remedies more typically characterizes the enforcement of Art. 82 EC-Treaty. Concern for safeguarding whatever potential for competition exists aside of the market dominating enterprises, as expressed in the formula of a specific responsibility for maintaining residual competion,[22] becomes the point of departure for requiring dominant enterprises, particularly those controlling information markets, to open access to opportunities for more competition on adjacent markets or with complementary and even with diversified products.[23]

The 'philosophy' underlying this prescriptive approach seems to be borrowed from the justification for (re)regulation of liberalized/ privatized sectors where incumbent monopolists are subject to obligations to share assets with or to open market opportunities for both enterprises operating on adjacent markets and/or enterprises serving the same market. However, the origins of the problem and the basis for their solution are different. Re-regulation typically addresses problems of restructuring historically or naturally monopolistic markets by simulating competition-like constraints for the incumbent monopolist and by seeking to establish a basis for competition to begin on its market and/or on those markets which actually or potentially exist up- or downstream or which are or may be adjacent. By contrast, Art. 82 EC is not concerned with challenging the dominant position as such, but only with its 'abuse'. Nevertheless, if it is relied upon as a basis precisely for issuing regulatory remedies in the interest of, *inter alia*,[24] market expansion in all directions, vertical or horizontal, then the reason must be that the efficient satisfaction of consumer welfare interests generally cannot be left to the control of a market dominating enterprise. Whatever the latter's merits, and notwithstanding the procedural ex post perspective,

---

[22] See ECJ of 13 February 1979 case 85/76, *Hoffmann-La Roche v. Commission*, Rep. 1979, 461 at 541 (no. 91); of 11 December 1980, case 31/80, *L'Oréal v. De Nieuwe Amck*, Rep. 1980, 3775 at 3794 (no. 27); of 9 November 1980, case 322/81, *Michelin v. Commission*, Rep. 1983, 3461 at 3511 (no. 57), 3514 (no. 70); CFI of 30 September 2003, case T-203/01, *Manufacture Française des Pneumatiques Michelin v. Commission*, Rep. 2003 II 4071 at no. 97, and see also ECJ of 26 November 1998, case C-7/97, *Oscar Bronner v. Mediaprint*, Rep.1998 I 7791 at 7830 (no. 38): exclusion of 'all competition'.

[23] See ECJ of 6 April 1995, cases C-241/91 P and C-242/91 P, *RTE and ITP v. Commission*, Rep. 1995 I 743 at p. 824 (no. 56); ECJ of 29 April 2004, case C-418/01, *IMS Health v. NDC Health*, WuW E EU-R 804 at no. 40 et seq.

[24] Public interest concerns may inform the competition analysis, see J. Haracoglou, *The Duty to Deal in Biopharmaceutical Industry: A Follow-on Innovation Perspective*, EUI PhD-thesis Florence 2005.

the likelihood, or possibly even only the risk, of forgoing future welfare gains, which renewed or reinforced competition promises, is unacceptable as a matter of maintaining a minimum of political and legal control over the competition system.

3   A Strategic Orientation of Competition Policy?

(i)   The overall trend then is not simply a 'liberalization' of the scope, application and enforcement of the competition rules, but the operationalization of a deliberate strategy of realizing, in the interest of international competitiveness,[25] the utmost of what the market may yield up to the limits of its working competitively.[26] Such a strategic approach,[27] whilst not always made explicit, is equally at the root of the recent revision of the concentration test in merger law, even though it may conflict with the aim of maintaining control over private market dominance.[28] It may also be used to achieve objectives other than exclusively economic ones via the operation of the market, albeit within narrow limits.[29] The novelty of this strategic orientation, however, lies less in the instrumentalization of the competition system for general or specific political goals, since this, in a way, may be implied in the role the Treaty assigns to the system of undistorted competition, or at least in the rival concepts of competition existing in economic and political theory. Rather, the novelty is in the rigour with which the strategic change is put into operation, precisely

---

[25]   See Commission, 'Report on Competition Policy 2004', *supra* n. 7, at p. 6 et seq., Commission, 'A Pro-active Competition Policy for a Competitive Europe', *COM* (2004) 293 of 4 April 2004.

[26]   In this respect see Commission, 'Guidelines on the application of Art. 81(3) of the Treaty', *supra* n. 7, at no. 105 is less revealing than at nos. 108, 114, 116, and, at any rate, is not as telling as the 'Guidelines on horizontal cooperation', *supra* n. 9

[27]   The term is used here in the traditional sense with no connotation of domestic favouritism, see also H.-W. Roth, 'Strategic Competition Policy – A Comment on EU Competition Policy', this volume Chapter 2, at p. 38.

[28]   Art. 2(2) (3) Regulation 139/2004 (the EC Merger Regulation), *supra* n. 2, whilst intended to allow a more flexible test of possible anticompetitive effects than the former dominance test (Art. 2(2) (3) Reg. 4064/89), in particular as regards non-dominant mergers, will also allow an 'efficiency defence' for mergers formally resulting in market dominance, see Recital 29 Reg. 139/2004, and for a discussion S. Mandhuit, T. Soames, 'Changes in EU Merger Control: Part 2', ECLR 2005, 75, 77; F.E. Gonzales Diaz, 'The Reform of European Merger Control: Quid Novi Sub Sole?', 27 (2) *World Competition* 177, 185 et seq. (2004); A. Pappalardo, 'Evolution récentes du contrôle des concentrations', *J.T. (Droit eur.)* 2004, 204, 207 et seq.

[29]   See Commission, 'Guidelines on Horizontal Cooperation', *supra* n. 9, at no. 179 et seq. regarding environment protection; for a broad discussion see C. Townley, *Article 81: Putting Public Policy in its Place*, EUI PhD-thesis Florence 2005 (to be published).

because the pursuit of the goal of increased international competitiveness is an invitation to emulate the political rival's way of market regulation.[30]

Such rigour may have become more easily acceptable since the political, economic and legal environment of competition policy in the EU has changed considerably since the 'early days'. In particular, whilst due to EU enlargement and risks of recidivism of market actors, market integration remains a primary concern,[31] protection of individual freedom and prevention of bargaining imbalances has in part lost political support,[32] just as, for another part, it may have won sufficient recognition in general contract law or related rules of law.[33]

(ii) However, strategic rigour also has its price. There has been an alignment of Member States' competition law with the rules of competition of the Community, as required by Art. 3 Regulation 1/2003. Whilst on the face

---

[30] As regards reform of merger control the discussion always and explicitly turned around the US-model of Sect. I Clayton Act, see M. Burgstaller, *Marktbeherrschung oder 'Substantial Lessening of Competition'*, WuW 2003, 726; and in depth U. Denzel, *Materielle Fusionskontrolle in Europa und den USA*, Baden-Baden 2004, 68 et seq.; the claim is now made that a 'truly European solution' has been found, see Gonzales Diaz, *supra* n. 28, 27 (2) *World Competition* at p. 188 (2004). Whilst modernization of enforcement has many different roots, in its result it looks very much like a copy of the US system adapted to European needs (and with a number of imperfections), see C. Jones, 'A New Dawn for Private Competition Law Remedies in Europe? Reflection from the US', in Cl.-D. Ehlermann, J. Atanasiu (eds), *European Competition Law Annual 2001: Effective Private Enforcement of EC Competition Law*, Oxford 2003, 95 et seq.. The Commission's Guidelines on Horizontal Cooperation or on Technology Transfer, loc. cit., both are rather close to their US counterparts, see as regards the latter H. Ullrich, *Patentgemeinschaften*, *supra* n. 19, at p. 412 et seq.

[31] See Commission, 'Report on Competition Policy 2004', *supra* n. 7, at p. 7, and note that under both Art. 81, 82 EC-Treaty and Art. 2(2) (3) Reg. 139/2004 the criterion of legality is the 'compatibility with the common market'.

[32] This seems to be particularly true for the basic assumption that individual freedom is a precondition of competition that is put in peril whenever enterprises, by concertation or by concentration, reduce not so much their own freedom but that of the other actors on the market, see E.J. Mestmäcker, H. Schweitzer, *supra* n. 4, at pp. 72, 80. The 'neutralizing mechanisms' mentioned *supra* n. 19 seem to bring back some of this idea of freedom, but miss the point: it is not fairness within a group that counts, but freedom from that group.

[33] One example are national rules against unfair competition, which Art. 3(3) Reg. 1/2003 expressly exempts from the Community's claim for priority of its competition rules, see Recital 9 Reg. 1/2003, the contribution by L. Boy, 'Abuse of market power: controlling dominance or protecting competition?', and the comment by P. Behrens in Chapter 8 of this volume, see also H. Ullrich, *Anti-Unfair Competition Law and Anti-Trust Law: A Continental Conundrum?*, EUI Working Papers, Law No. 2005/01.

of it this has been a matter of saving transaction costs for enterprises or of creating legal uniformity and certainty, most Member States have fallen into line by themselves. Merger control always was based on the one-stop-shop principle, and national enforcement zeal outside the hard-core areas is not to be feared. Thus, the imposition of mandatory uniformity is really a matter of maximizing the effects of the overall strategic orientation of Community competition policy.[34] In fact, it also implies a transfer of power. Member States, whilst retaining their legislative competence in competition matters, have lost control over its substance. They are, as a matter of law, bound to fully and closely follow whatever direction is given to the Community's competition policy. That is, up to one ill-defined limit:[35] the control of market power. Indeed, by reserving Member States' power to adopt or apply 'on their territory stricter national laws, which prohibit or sanction unilateral conduct engaged in by undertakings', Art. 3(2,2) Regulation 1/2003 not only allows Member States to lower the thresholds of intervention but also to develop their own concepts of abuse of market power.[36] Thus, again, sovereign control over the exercise of private market power becomes the hard core of any competition policy.

(iii) Ultimately, Art. 3(2,2) testifies to the difficulties of establishing in practice a stringently conceived competition policy. However, claims for the centralization of competition policy and to a reserved national domain are not so much based on different views of the objectives of competition policy. There is a basic, albeit differentiated consensus that consumer welfare should have priority even if additional objectives may

---

[34] Art. 10, 11, 15, 16 Reg. 1/2003 enable the Commission to impose the Community's political choices in everyday practice of decentralized enforcement; but see H.-W. Roth, this volume, Chapter 2, sub. 7.

[35] Art. 3(2) Reg. 1/2003 uses the distinction between concerted practices and unilateral conduct as the connecting factor for the Community's claim to priority of its competition policy. This means that not only does the conduct of enterprises, whose dominance may result from lawful mergers, come under national control, but also all practices which fail to meet the contract/concertation-test of Art. 81, such as recommended prices, quantitative supply limitations etc.; see F. Wagner von Papp, *Empfiehlt sich das Empfehlungsverbot?* WuW 2005, 379, 380 et seq.; A. Klees, *Europäisches Kartellverfahrensrecht mit Fusionskartellverfahren*, Cologne 2004, 69 et seq., 73 et seq.

[36] See Recital 8 Reg. 139/2003; the second proposition follows from the basic rule that enterprises enjoying absolute market power may hardly be treated less strictly under national law than enterprises possessing only relational market power. However, the matter is not settled, since the Community's policy under Art. 82, which is about to be redefined, risks being compromised by divergent national rules, see H. Ullrich, *Anti-Unfair Competition Law, supra* n. 33, sub. I 2.

legitimately be pursued. Rather, such claims are based on divergent concepts of which competition will best serve these objectives and be socially acceptable.[37] In part, these relate to a technical understanding of the operation and potential of the process of competition, as becomes apparent in controversies over how much residual competition is enough to check existing market dominance or how much competition is required to allow transition from regulatory to antitrust control. More generally speaking, however, they relate to the question of whether and how individual freedom should be guaranteed as a prerequisite to effective competition or, conversely, how protection should be afforded against the exercise of market power (as well as the extent of that protection). These are both matters about which the Community itself seems to worry when it asks for institutional or procedural safeguards against otherwise accepted group action[38] or when it favours the – rather ambivalent – establishment of countervailing power.[39] Could it be that this is no more than the last point of resistance against a total turn-around from the original defence against the cooperative or concentrative creation of private control over the market to public control merely of generally accepted market power? If so, this move would seem to be a rather desperate one for a Community that is not yet politically powerful.

II   THE WORKSHOP

Since these technical and societal aspects of a competition system are just as interrelated as they are interdependent with the definition of the objectives of competition policy, it is no surprise that the contributions to the workshop collectively demonstrate a much more differentiated picture of the evolution of EU competition policy than has been suggested here as a subjective working hypothesis. They do so by dealing with a number of topics, which have been selected and proposed by me with no less subjectivity, and certainly with no attempt to achieve comprehensiveness.[40]

---

[37]   A point which I have argued in more detail in H. Ullrich, 'L'ordre concurrentiel – Rapport de synthèse – ou "Variations sur un thème de Nice"', in *L'ordre concurrentiel – Mélanges A. Pirovano*, Paris 2003, 663; see also B. McDonnell, D. Farber, 'Are Efficient Antitrust Rules Always Optimal?', 48 *Antitrust Bull.* 807 (2003).

[38]   See *supra* text at n. 19.

[39]   See ECJ of 15 December 1994, case C-250/92, *Gottrup-Klim v. DLG*, Rep 1994 I 5641 at p. 5687 (no. 32); Commission, 'Guidelines on Horizontal Cooperation', *supra* n. 9, at no. 116, 134.

[40]   Thus, unfortunately, the changing interpretation and application of Art. 86(2) EC-Treaty, however relevant in the workshop's context, could not be dealt with nor

The title of the first session was aimed at a politically provocative comparison with US antitrust law as the model law for EU reforms, and the rival in regulatory competition, if indeed there is such a competition. Clifford A. Jones,[41] and W.-H. Roth[42] approach the subject from different angles, and M. Patterson[43] illustrates divergences between the systems by the recent example of the antitrust treatment of licensing transactions. Modernization of the enforcement of the EU competition rules has kindly been taken up as a subject and presented in the perspective of practice by G. Tesauro,[44] then president of the Italian Autorità Garante della Concorrenza e del Mercato.

Vertical restraints were the point of departure for a revision of competition policy in both the US and the EU. D. Waelbroeck's, W. Kerber's and R. Zäch's different contribution and comments[45] show that the law in this area, far from being settled, may need to be developed. But in what direction?

Horizontal agreements cover too many types of practices to be dealt with by one paper. They may not have been sufficiently analysed under the antitrust laws as regards, on the one hand, the interplay of networking and economic globalization, and on the other, the relationship between antitrust control of cooperation and of concentration. By an extensive factual and legal examination, and by broad complementary comments, M.M. Leitao Marques, A. Fuchs and D. Zimmer contribute to filling this gap.[46]

Nor is merger law a subject that can be examined in a meaningful way by one paper alone. The limits of an economics based standard of control might be reached when asking the question of whether media concentration may be assessed in the same terms as are mergers and acquisitions in any other business area, or whether additional or alternative criteria, possibly even a (sector-) specific procedure, need to be applied. L. Idot as the author of the report P. Kremmyda and U. Bernitz as commentators were guarantors of a lively discussion.[47]

An even more controversial discussion was bound to arise from the report of L. Boy on a proper Continental reading of Article 82 and from the comments by E. Fox and P. Behrens.[48] It foreshadowed the controversies

---

could the application of Articles 10(2), 3(g), 81, 86 EC-Treaty to state involvement in cartelization/anti-competitive self-regulation be examined. The programme simply would have become too full.

[41] *Infra* Chapter 1.
[42] *Infra* Chapter 2.
[43] *Infra* Chapter 3.
[44] *Infra* Chapter 4.
[45] *Infra* Chapter 5.
[46] *Infra* Chapter 6.
[47] *Infra* Chapter 7.
[48] *Infra* Chapter 8.

which are likely to arise as soon as the Commission publishes its new Guidelines on its reading of Article 82, a draft of which is expected by the end of 2005.

Using a non-conventional systematic approach, the analysis of Art. 82 had deliberately been placed after the discussion of merger control and before the examination of competition-oriented market regulation so as to make the conceptual links and systemic contradictions between competition law and (re-)regulation of potentially competitive markets for infrastructure services more visible. This new counterpart of competition law merited much attention, as its raison d'être of ensuring an optimal as well as some universal supply of '*services publics*' by way of, on the one side, imposed and, on the other, invited competition, raises the question whether it really is based on the same idea of competition which the antitrust laws protect. In a welfare economics, efficiency oriented perspective, the answer seems to be obvious enough. But the contributions by C. Kirchner and J. Monéger as well as the comments by K. Stockmann, F. Di Porto and by J. Fejø and P. Nihoul respectively seem to suggest that the law of (re-)regulation is still in too much of a state of flux to allow for a satisfactory answer at present.[49]

Instead of a conclusion D. Geradin gives an account of what efficiency claims mean in both EU competition law and sector specific regulation.[50] G. Ghidini[51] in his final remarks introduces a number of additional value criteria into what otherwise might appear to be tantamount to a normative impoverishment of competition law.

Having been entrusted by Ascola with the main responsibility for the organization of the workshop, and as editor of the publication of the papers and written comments, which have been contributed to it, my sincere thanks go to all their authors. Their spontaneous and generous participation was at the heart of the success of the workshop as an academic meeting, and so was the spirit of frank and vivid discussion which all the participants brought to Villa Schifanoia. I am deeply indebted to all of them.

---

[49] *Infra* Chapters 9 and 10.
[50] *Infra* Chapter 11.
[51] *Infra* Chapter 11.

PART II

Strategic competition policies? US–EU
conflicts and convergence

1. Foundations of competition policy in the EU and USA: conflict, convergence and beyond

Clifford A. Jones*

I INTRODUCTION

The theme of this volume revolves around the evolution of European competition law, and the following chapters examine diverse aspects of the underlying rationales, goals and objectives of competition policy and some specific doctrines in an expanding European Union and a globalizing economy. The objective of this chapter is to provide some introductory American perspectives on this evolution and in the process to consider some of the ways in which American antitrust and European Union competition policy at times have both diverged and converged. While it would be wrong to treat this evolution purely as a reflection of current events, one cannot help but consider the political, economic and possible strategic implications of some of the present debate.

The European Union has for a substantial period of time endured weak economic growth and high unemployment generally as well in the 'euro-zone', the twelve Member States which at present comprise the participants in the Third Stage of Economic and Monetary Union, the single currency (euro).[1] The Treaty of Amsterdam (1997) brought with it a Growth and Stability Pact designed to make economic and job growth major EU goals along with the price stability envisaged for the euro. In 2000, the Lisbon European Council pronounced the EU's 'Lisbon Strategy', an ambitious goal for the European Union 'to become the most competitive and dynamic knowledge-based economy in the world, capable of sustained economic growth with more and better

---

*   J.D. (Okla.), M.Phil., Ph.D. (Cantab), Lecturer, Frederic G. Levin College of Law, University of Florida, USA. He may be reached at jonesca@law.ufl.edu.
[1]   At the time of writing the euro-zone participants are Germany, France, Italy, Spain, Portugal, Greece, Finland, Austria, Belgium, The Netherlands, Luxembourg and Ireland.

jobs and greater social cohesion'.[2] In early 2005, the five-year (mid-term) assessment of progress toward the goals of the Lisbon Strategy, was sufficiently negative that the Commission called for more realistic objectives and in particular called for a 're-launching' of the Lisbon Strategy, with more priority given to economic growth and less to social and environmental issues. The link between the proposed increased emphasis on broad economic growth and international competitiveness objectives of the EU and competition policy was made explicit by the new (2004–2009) Competition Commissioner Neelie Kroes, who noted that:

> As President Barroso told the Parliament yesterday, the Commission has identified jobs and growth as the most urgent challenges facing Europe today. We have set this question at the very heart of what the Commission hopes to achieve over the next five years. Our agenda will be focused on actions to help the Union and the Member States drive up productivity and create new jobs.
> . . .
> I am convinced that competition policy is of fundamental importance for the future of the partnership for growth and jobs. . . . That is the role of competition. Competition drives competitiveness, growth and productivity. An effective, well-managed competition policy is both a pre-requisite and a key tool for delivering the Lisbon agenda.[3]

The explicit linkage between competition policy, economic growth and international competitiveness might have been expected in the USA but seems to represent some shifting in historic European attitudes toward principles of competition and their place in the post-World War II social market economy. It may be useful to keep this in mind as we briefly return to some original principles of antitrust on both sides of the Atlantic.

II　PHILOSOPHICAL AND CULTURAL HERITAGE

There is wide agreement that contemporary antitrust has its origins in the US Sherman Anti-Trust Act (1890), and some of the thinking behind that seminal statute remains even now in the USA, though it has evolved greatly even in its original home. A brief look at antitrust through the rear-view mirror may contribute to an understanding of where we may be going in an increasingly (so far) globalizing world as well as where we have been. Antitrust is an inter-disciplinary combination of at least law, economics and politics, and at times disconcertingly reveals the stamp of history, philosophy and perhaps geogra-

---

2　　See Lisbon European Council, 23 and 24 March 2000, Presidency conclusions, available at http://ue.eu.int/ueDocs/cms_Data/docs/pressData/en/ec/00100-r1.en0.htm.

3　　N. Kroes, Speech to the EMAC Open Meeting of Coordinators, Brussels, 3 February 2005, available on Commission's website.

phy when least expected. This brief look also reminds us how little many of the same arguments have changed over the decades and in some cases even centuries of business regulation.

An American look which may surprise[4] Europeans encountering it for the first time is found in one of the works of Corwin Edwards,[5] one of the drafts-men of the competition code intended as part of the ill-fated Havana Charter of the still-born International Trade Organization. Edwards, in remarking on the post-war surge in antitrust legislation outside the USA noted the differ-ences from US legislation in 'purpose, content, and spirit':[6]

> There are differences in attitudes toward private economic power, the grant of broad discretionary authority to governmental bodies, the place of morality in economic affairs, the importance of freedom of contract relative to freedom of trade, and the emphasis to be placed on distributive justice as compared with enhanced productiv-ity. These differences reflect dissimilarities in cultural, moral, and political history – that is, in the cultural inheritance. Cultural difference appears to be more significant than contemporary dissimilarity in economic structures, processes and interests.

Edwards described European society over centuries as having accepted 'hier-archies of power' which were 'accredited by history' and reflecting little distrust of concentrated power, in a 'spirit that contrasts sharply with American distrust of both powerful business and powerful government'.[7] As an example of how these differences in attitude have been significant in the development of European approaches toward regulating businesses, Edwards offers the follow-ing discussion of European concepts of distributive justice and favoring equal-ity of opportunity over pure productivity, which deserves to be quoted at length:

> Public policy toward restrictions is focused upon fairness in dividing what the econ-omy produces rather than enlargement of the product. Fairness as to prices, as to avail-ability of supplies, and as to access to markets is the point of attention. This fairness has two aspects. First, it includes fairness between supplier and customer, both as to the height of prices and as to the availability of supplies. Second, it includes fairness between one supplier and another as to access to markets and as to discrimination in terms of access. Though these goals are moral, they are usually described as economic. They are so in the sense that they identify fair conduct by the nature of the economic relationship that it establishes rather than by the motives of the participants. But they are not economic in the sense that the preferred courses of action have been chosen because they yield the largest practicable aggregate economic product.[8]

---

[4]   The surprise may be that an American noticed any differences between Europe and the USA.

[5]   C. D. Edwards, *Control of Cartels and Monopolies: An International Comparison*, Dobbs Ferry, NY 1967.

[6]   Ibid., at 15.

[7]   Ibid., at 16.

[8]   Ibid., at 22–3.

Edwards' discussion finds echoes in Giuliano Amato's interesting and thoughtful monograph[9] thirty years later, when he notes that of European nations only Britain had 'cultivated the competitive economy', but that the Continental cultures:

> were not only statist, but also favourable to co-operation among (national) firms rather than to mutual competition. In traditionally *dirigiste* France, and in Germany and Italy with their delayed [industrial] development, State protectionism, publicly owned firms, exclusive rights for public, and private, firms and consortia among private firms were common ingredients in the guidance of the economy. That a totalitarian regime like the Italian fascism of the 1930s could go so far as providing for an obligatory consortium for all the firms in a sector when that met with the majority desire of the firms in that sector may seem incomprehensible to someone who has grown up in the culture of the Sherman Act. But in the European culture, it was merely an extreme form of a rooted principle, that the cartel was one of the positive manifestations of private associationism and of the freedom of trade: all the more positive if the cartel was operating with an eye to definite objectives of public interest and approved by public organs.[10]

These excerpts of a now somewhat distant period of antitrust serve to remind us that at root in the USA antitrust has sought to control economic power. In the USA, there is also a strong suspicion of governmental power that may even now not exist in much of Europe. Europe's antitrust history reflects confidence in governmental power not found in the USA and a tolerance of economic power that probably exceeds that found in the USA. Amato captures it well in his statement of the democratic dilemma:

> Here, then, is the dilemma. How can private power be prevented from becoming a threat to the freedom of others? But at the same time, how can power conferred on institutions for this purpose be prevented from itself enlarging to the point of destroying the very freedoms it ought to protect?

> In a democratic society, then, there are two bounds that should never be crossed: one beyond which the unlegitimated power of individuals arises, the other beyond which legitimate public power becomes illegitimate. Where do these two bounds lie? . . . It is a fact that within liberal society itself one of the key divisions of political identity . . . is between these two sides: the side that fears private power more, and in order to fight it is ready to give more room to the power of government; and the side that fears the expansion of government power more, and is therefore more prepared to tolerate private power.

---

    9   G. Amato, *Antitrust and the Bounds of Power: The Dilemma of Liberal Democracy in the History of the Market*, Oxford, 1997.
    10   Ibid., at 39–40.

That was so in the argument between federalists and republicans in the first years of life in the USA and is today between Republicans and Democrats in the same country. And it is very much so in the division between left and right in Europe, once the layer of Marxism that bore down so much on it in previous decades is scraped off. . . . The study of antitrust law indeed helps to understand the arguments of each, and to perceive the vitality and meaning of the dilemma that has marked liberal democracy ever since it has existed, and has always run through antitrust law itself.[11]

A comment from The Netherlands in 1980 expresses very much a nostalgic longing for the good old days of respectable cartels in Europe:

And now I expect, but I sincerely do not hope, that this second time that Western civilization is seriously endangered since the eighth century when Rome crumbled under the victorious Islam, that the second time will bring to light that the Sherman Act and Article 85 are luxuries, the fundamental errors of which are not felt in a fast-growing economy but that they are an obstacle to a society which should be based on solidarity and regard for others. In my country, before the [former Article] 85 [now 81] men on horseback came galloping in, we did not speak about competitors; we spoke about 'colleagues'. I feel that we shall have to face the oncoming economic war not with *competitor competitori lupus*, but with the concepts I just evoked – solidarity and regard for others.[12]

At least among government competition authorities in Europe, the tolerance and respect for cartels seems to have largely been reversed. This has occurred gradually over time since the Second World War, as is chronicled in Harding and Joshua.[13] When former (1999–2004) European Commissioner for Competition Mario Monti spoke of cartels as 'cancers on the open market economy'[14] and Director-General for Competition Philip Lowe commented that 'we have only touched the tip of the iceberg in terms of our attack on cartels',[15] it is clear that a major shift in social and economic culture has occurred in the direction of the longstanding US antipathy toward cartels.[16]

---

[11] Amato, *supra* note 9, at 3–4.

[12] F. Salomonson, quoted in C. A. Jones, *Private Enforcement of Antitrust Law in the EU, UK, and USA*, Oxford, 1999, p. 28.

[13] C. Harding, J. Joshua, *Regulating Cartels in Europe: A Study of Legal Control of Corporate Delinquency*, Oxford, 2003.

[14] Harding, Joshua, *supra* note 13, at 277.

[15] *Interview with Philip Lowe, European Commission, Director General, DG Competition*, found at http://www.eupolitix.com/EN/Interviews (Sept. 25, 2003).

[16] C. A. Jones, 'Sleeping With The Enemy: Tales of Yankee Power, Globalization, and the Transformation of Economy by Cartel in the European Union', 36 (5) *Geo. Washington Univ. Int'l. L. Rev.* 1263, 1268–9 (2004), reviewing C. Harding, J. Joshua, *supra* n. 13.

Attitudes toward cartels notwithstanding, this does not automatically signal abandonment of some of the European concepts of 'economic' goals described by Corwin Edwards, as was expressed in the European Council's Laeken Declaration of December, 2001:

> The European Union is a success story. For over half a century now, Europe has been at peace. Along with North America and Japan, the Union forms one of the three most prosperous parts of the world. *As a result of mutual solidarity and fair distribution of the benefits of economic development,* moreover, the standard of living in the Union's weaker regions has increased enormously and they have made good much of the disadvantage they were at. (emphasis added)

In contrast to the European cultural heritage, the USA's response to the rapid industrialization occurring after the US civil war (1865) was fear of the economic power of the infamous Standard Oil and other trusts.[17] The Sherman Antitrust Act (1890) reflected a 'hatred of monopoly', which Letwin notes was 'one of the oldest American political habits'.[18] The public 'found the trusts to be a growing and intolerable evil'[19] and Congress responded by passage of the statute. The American States had a history of enforcing antitrust laws even prior to the adoption of the Sherman Act,[20] and the now internationally famous treble damage remedy[21] ironically was modeled[22] on the (imported) treble damage provisions of the English Statute of Monopolies 1623.

The origins of US antitrust policy were thus political in the sense that they were driven by popular demand to which Congress responded. By the Presidential election of 1888, antitrust laws were planks in the political platform of all four then-major political parties.[23] The history of the statute reflects such a diverse variety of objectives that it is difficult to say with any certainty beyond a certain point exactly what goals Congress had in

---

[17] Clifford A. Jones, *Private Enforcement of Antitrust Law in the EU, UK, and USA*, Oxford: Oxford Press, 1999, pp. 6–8. The leading histories of the Sherman Act include H. B. Thorelli, *The Federal Antitrust Policy: Origination of an American Tradition*, Baltimore 1954 and W. Letwin, *Law and Economic Policy in America: The Evolution of the Sherman Antitrust Act*, New York 1965.

[18] Letwin, *supra* n. 17, at 59.

[19] W. H. Taft, *The Anti-Trust Act and Supreme Court*, New York 1914, p. 2. Taft was a former federal judge, President of the United States, and later Chief Justice of the United States.

[20] Hans B. Thorelli, *supra* n. 17, at 155.

[21] 15 U.S.C. § 15.

[22] Thorelli, *supra* note 17, at 213. Even more ironically, some 65 different English enactments once provided for double, treble, or quadruple damages. *BMW of North America, Inc. v. Gore*, 517 US 559, 580–81 (1996).

[23] Thorelli, *supra* n. 17, at pp. 150–51.

mind.[24] Waller has suggested that 'if there ever was such a thing as a true history of the Sherman Act, it has long been shrouded in the majestic but imprecise language chosen by Congress', and that 'any discourse about the proper meaning and interpretation of the Sherman Act today is a rhetorical exercise in favor of a normative vision about the importance and definition of competition'.[25]

What we can say with some confidence is that Congress did not have in mind the allocative efficiency and narrowly defined consumer welfare objectives attributed to it by Bork. The ink was barely dry on Alfred Marshall's neoclassical *Principles of Economics* (1890) when the Sherman Act was adopted and it defies even the most normatively-based legislative history to conclude that such principles informed the Congressional deliberations which had begun the year before. Antitrust in the USA has always reflected a political content, as has been noted by Pitofsky and others.[26] Moreover, the influence of economic analysis in US antitrust judgments does not date only from the mid-1970s cases such as *GTE Sylvania*,[27] but may be found in earlier examples, such as the cross-elasticity of demand analysis found in the famous *Cellophane* case.[28]

III   EXPORTING COMPETITION POLICY: FROM DEPRESSION TO WORLD WAR

The early history of US antitrust law and policy reflects a primary concern for the domestic market and an initial reluctance to intervene in foreign anti-competitive arrangements.[29] At times, even the American commitment to

---

[24]   See, generally, Thorelli, *supra* n. 17; R. H. Bork, *The Antitrust Paradox: A Policy at War with Itself*, New York 1978; R. J. R. Peritz, *Competition Policy in America 1888–1992: History, Rhetoric, Law*, Oxford 1996, pp. 9–26; R. H. Lande, 'Wealth Transfers as the Original and Primary Concern of Antitrust: The Efficiency Interpretation Challenged', (1982) 34 *Hastings L. J.* 67; E. M. Fox, 'The Modernization of Antitrust: A New Equilibrium', (1986) 66 *Cornell L. Rev.* 1140.

[25]   S. Weber Waller, 'Neo-Realism and the International Harmonization of Law: Lessons from Antitrust', 42 *Kansas L. Rev.* 557, 577 (1994).

[26]   R. Pitofsky, 'The Political Content of Antitrust', 127 *U. Pa. L. Rev.* 1051 (1979). See Fox, *supra* n. 24.

[27]   *Continental TV, Inc. v. GTE Sylvania, Inc.*, 433 US 36 (1977).

[28]   *United States v. E.I. Dupont de Nemours & Co.*, 351 US 377 (1956). (Cellophane).

[29]   See, e.g., *Am. Banana Co. v. United Fruit Co.*, 213 US 347 (1909) (Sherman Act inapplicable to foreign conduct); *United States v. Sisal Sales Corp.*, 274 US 268, 275–76, (1927) (Sherman Act applies so long as some of defendants' conduct occurred in US and affected domestic commerce); *United States v. Aluminum Co. of Am.*, 148 F.2d 416, 443–44 (2d Cir. 1945) (Sherman Act applies so long as foreign conduct intended to and did affect commerce in the United States) [hereafter, *Alcoa*].

rigorous domestic competition wavered. During the First World War (1917–18) the antitrust laws were essentially inoperative if not formally suspended as a result of wartime mobilization. Between the wars, Herbert Hoover, first Secretary of Commerce and later President, experimented with 'associationalist' schemes then popular in Europe, effectively rationalizing cartels, until the election of Franklin D. Roosevelt in 1932. Roosevelt initially tried the same approach in the National Recovery Act of 1933, until it was declared unconstitutional by the Supreme Court. Roosevelt then reversed field, and antitrust was revitalized with the appointment of Thurman Arnold as chief of the Antitrust Division in 1937.[30]

The closest the US Supreme Court have come to recognizing permissible 'crisis cartels' was the decision to legitimize a joint coal-selling arrangement during the Depression in *Appalachian Coals*.[31] However, the case is considered an aberration that was effectively overruled in *Socony*.[32]

The Allied occupation of Germany following World War II included a decartelization plan. When the 'Schuman Plan' for the creation of the European Coal and Steel Community (1952–2002), precursor to the current European Community and European Union, was presented to US Secretary of State Dean Acheson on 7 May 1950, Acheson's first reaction was the fear that the plan was a clever cover for a 'gigantic European cartel'.[33] Although Acheson's concerns were satisfied, and the plan went forward, the history of cartels in Europe to that point would have supported Acheson's initial reluctance.[34]

---

[30] A. A. Foer, R. H. Lande, *The Evolution Of United States Antitrust Law: The Past, Present, and (Possible) Future* 11 (1999), available at www.antitrustinstitute.org. See generally, Rudolph J. R. Peritz, *Competition Policy in America: History, Rhetoric, Law*, Chapter 3 (rev. edn 2001).

[31] *Appalachian Coals, Inc. v. United States*, 288 US 344 (1933).

[32] *United States v. Socony-Vacuum Oil Company*, 310 US 150 (1940).

[33] D. Acheson, *Present At The Creation: My Years In The State Department 383* (1969). D. Dinan, *Ever Closer Union?*, Houndmills and London 1994, p. 23. Acheson feared objections by the Antitrust Division, which took a dim view of cartels controlling essential war material in light of then recent experience with the powerful cartelized German economy.

[34] Acheson's reaction to the Schuman Plan for the ECSC was not without basis: '[T]he ECSC then substituted a supranational system of extensive public management. Part of the latter entailed the ability of the new supranational body, the High Authority [later the Commission], to require conformity with arrangements reminiscent of a conventional business cartel. Article 58 of the ECSC Treaty enabled the High Authority to impose production quotas in response to crisis conditions or decline in demand. Article 61 allowed the High Authority to fix maximum and minimum prices. Article 63 enabled the High Authority to specify conditions of sale. To that extent the ECSC organized coal and steel producers into a kind of public cartel.' Christopher Harding and Julian Joshua, *Regulating Cartels in Europe: A Study of Legal Control of Corporate Delinquency*, Oxford, 2003, p. 94. Competition rules were added to the ECSC Treaty.

In Europe, cartels were seen favorably as engines of industrial development driving the economic growth of Europe, especially in Germany.[35] Indeed, cartels were respected economic institutions, and economy by cartel was the rule in Europe prior to 1945.[36] Harding and Joshua have reviewed some of the literature on the behavior of cartels in Europe and paint a broad and detailed picture of cartel history from private systems of transnational trade regulation to government-encouraged market stabilization, to the compulsory cartelization in Nazi Germany, to international commodity agreements. This history helps to explain why the culture of competition represented by American antitrust has never been as completely accepted in Europe. The history of German and other European cartels is recounted in some detail by Harding and Joshua.[37] The first vigorous antitrust enforcement in Europe and particularly in Germany was carried out under the Allied decartelization plan beginning in 1947 and expanding in scope in 1950 shortly before the ECSC Treaty was agreed.[38]

The Department of Justice's (DOJ) interest in international cartels increased with the appointment of Thurman Arnold, and the growing revelations of pre-war cartels (in which some American firms participated)[39] gave impetus to more intense scrutiny of the international conduct of firms[40] and new efforts to export antitrust laws to foreign nations. The existence of international cartels and their support of, *inter alia*, Nazi Germany even prompted US President Franklin Roosevelt to suggest curbing them through the United Nations.[41]

After the war, the US pressured its European allies such as the UK[42] and Australia and the recently defeated Japan[43] and Germany to adopt antitrust

---

[35]   See generally, C. Trebilcock, *The Industrialization of the Continental Powers 1780–1914* (1981).

[36]   H. G. Schröter, 'Cartelization and Decartelization in Europe, 1870–1995', 25 *J. European Econ. Hist.* (1996), pp. 129, 137. See also, Jones (1999), *supra* n. 14, pp. 23–8.

[37]   Harding, Joshua, *supra* n. 13, at 63–82, and for developments in other European countries, pp. 84–113. See also, Trebilcock, *supra* n. 35 and Schröter, *supra* n. 36.

[38]   Harding, Joshua, *supra* n. 13, at 86–7.

[39]   T. Freyer, 'Antitrust and Bilateralism: The US, Japanese, and EU Comparative and Historical Relationships', in C. A. Jones, M. Matsushita (eds), *Competition Policy in the Global Trading System* 3, The Hague 2002, pp. 14–15.

[40]   See, e.g., W. Berge, *Cartels: Challenge to a Free World*, Washington, DC, 1946. Berge was head of the Antitrust Division of the Department of Justice.

[41]   Letter, President Roosevelt to Secretary of State concerning cartel policies, 6 September 1944, reprinted in Harding, Joshua, *supra* n. 13 at 61–2.

[42]   See generally, T. Freyer, *Regulating Big Business: Antitrust in Great Britain and America, 1880–1990*, Cambridge 1992, pp. 234–68.

[43]   J. O. Haley, 'Harmonized Rules, Peculiar Laws: Recent Developments in Japanese Law', in Roger Zäch (ed.), *Towards WTO Competition Rules* (1999), pp. 137, 140.

laws. Japan (under occupation) was the first to do so, adopting its Anti-Monopoly Act (AMA) in 1947. In the UK, the Sherman Act prohibition model was rejected in favor of an 'abuse' system under the Monopolies and Restrictive Practices (Inquiry and Control) Act 1948, which required the approval of Parliament before any remedy (limited to injunction) could be ordered.[44] This 'puny infant' according to one MP was radically altered and essentially supplanted by the Competition Act 1998, which adopted the prohibition approach and text of the EC Treaty's Articles 81 and 82.

In Germany, the shift from collaboration between the Nazi government and use of private cartels as a vehicle for forced labor and then extermination of the Jews was heavily influenced by a group of lawyers and economists at the University of Freiburg, which was known as the Freiburger Ordoliberalen.[45] The post-war German Cartel law was introduced into the Bundestag by Fritz Böhm, a lawyer and Member of the Bundestag who was one of the leaders of the Freiburg School.[46]

The German Cartel Law did not take effect until 1958 and followed in time the signing of the aforementioned ECSC Treaty and its broader counterpart, the European Community Treaty (EC). Monnet described the antitrust provisions of the ECSC Treaty: 'For Europe, they were a fundamental innovation: the extensive anti-trust legislation now applied by the European Community essentially derives from those few lines in the Schuman Treaty.'[47] The competition provisions of the EC Treaty[48] closely follow the ECSC Treaty and bear the substantive imprint of the Sherman Act derived from their American ancestry.[49] Moreover, the gradual expansion of the European Community has thus carried with it to many more countries the competition rules derived from Robert Bowie's 'few lines in the Schuman Treaty'.[50]

---

[44] Jones (1999), *supra* n. 17, at 36–39.

[45] Amato, *supra* n. 9, at 40–42. See also, Jones, *supra* n. 17, at 24.

[46] Amato, *supra* n. 9, at 42.

[47] Jean Monnet, *Memoirs* 352–3 [Richard Mayne trans.] (1978). Compare Article 65 ECSC with Article 81 EC. Monnet noted that the drafter of the Treaty provisions, Robert Bowie, was a 'young Harvard professor . . . who was said to be the leading expert on US anti-trust legislation, which the Americans applied as rigorously as morality itself.' Ibid.

[48] Treaty Establishing the European Economic Community, Mar. 25, 1957, 298 UNTS II [hereinafter EC Treaty].

[49] Bowie's American text was 'reworked into "European idiom" by Maurice Lagrange', later Advocate General to the European Court of Justice. Harding and Joshua, *supra* n. 13, at 95. Hence, the language differs from the Sherman Act but lays down the same substantive principles as developed in the US case law.

[50] The later EC Treaty version of Section 1 reflects a substantive summary of judicial authority under the USA Sherman and Clayton Acts, put into 'European idiom' by Maurice Lagrange: *Article 81 EC, ex 85.*

From the 'Six' in 1952 (France, Germany, Italy, Belgium, The Netherlands, Luxembourg) to the addition of The United Kingdom, Ireland and Denmark in 1973, Greece (1981), Spain and Portugal (1986), and Austria, Sweden and Finland (1995), the European Community now stands at 25 in number. The 1 May 2004 addition of Poland, The Czech Republic, Malta, Cyprus, Latvia, Estonia, Lithuania, Slovak Republic, Slovenia and Hungary brings the total to 25 countries in which EC competition law is directly applicable and directly effective.[51] Moreover, 1 May 2004 was the effective date of the new EC Competition Regulation 1/2003 ('Reg. 1'),[52] which substantially revises EC

---

1. The following shall be prohibited as incompatible with the common market; all agreements between undertakings, decisions by associations of undertakings and concerted practices which may affect trade between Member States and which have as their object or effect the prevention, restriction or distortion of competition within the common market, and in particular those which:

(a) directly or indirectly fix purchase or selling prices or any other trading conditions;

(b) limit or control production, markets, technical development, or investment;

(c) share markets or sources of supply;

(d) apply dissimilar conditions to equivalent transactions with other trading parties, thereby placing them at a competitive disadvantage;

(e) make the conclusion of contracts subject to acceptance by the other parties of supplementary obligations which, by their nature or according to commercial usage, have no connection with the subject of such contracts.

2. Any agreements or decisions prohibited pursuant to this Article shall be automatically void.

3. The provisions of paragraph 1 may, however, be declared inapplicable in the case of:

– any agreement or category of agreements between undertakings;

– any decision or category of decisions by associations of undertakings;

– any concerted practice or category of concerted practices;

which contributes to improving the production or distribution of goods or to promoting technical or economic progress, while allowing consumers a fair share of the resulting benefit, and which does not:

(a) impose on the undertakings concerned restrictions which are not indispensable to the attainment of these objectives;

(b) afford such undertakings the possibility of eliminating competition in respect of a substantial part of the products in question.

[51] Edwards, *supra*, note 5, at 323–4, notes that the EEC (now EC) Treaty competition rules were 'substantially stronger' than those of the member states at the time, and described the experience of the member states: 'Whereas laws to curb restrictions had national roots in France, Germany and the Netherlands, repressive legislation had not existed in Belgium, Italy and Luxembourg prior to EEC, and in 1965 still did not exist in the latter two countries. Belgium and the Netherlands had experimented during the depression with mandatory cartelization, and Italy and Germany with Fascist or Nazi forms of state control.'

[52] Council Regulation (EC) No 1/2003 of 16 December 2002 on the implementation of the rules on competition laid down in Articles 81 and 82 of the Treaty, OJEC L 1, 4.1.2003.

competition law with the first major (non-merger) procedural (and substantive) changes in the last forty-plus years. Between the EU Member States, candidate countries (Romania, Bulgaria, Croatia, Turkey, and perhaps soon the Former Yugoslavian Republic of Macedonia and the Ukraine), other countries which have signed association agreements, and the EFTA/EEA states, more than 30 countries now or soon will apply EU competition rules.

Although many of these countries adopted antitrust rules, they did not always enforce them aggressively.[53] In the post-*Alcoa* world of the effects doctrine, increasingly aggressive US antitrust enforcement began to create friction with some of our closest allies and greatest trading partners. The Canadian provinces of Ontario and Quebec enacted the first blocking statutes in response to the US investigation in the late 1940s into the Canadian paper industry.[54] In the 1950s, Canada reacted negatively to a US investigation into a Canadian radio and television patent pool designed to exclude US manufacturers from the Canadian market,[55] and in the 1970s the uranium litigation[56] created perhaps even greater conflict.[57] In 1976 Canada enacted an important competition law which has in some respects brought it closer to the US model.

The uranium litigation was apparently the impetus for the UK's adoption of a blocking statute, the Protection of Trading Interests Act 1980, which essentially prohibited UK courts from compelling the production of UK-located documents, assisting in the enforcement of treble damage judgments, and provided that UK nationality defendants could 'claw-back' from the assets located in the UK of foreign companies any excess over actual damages in a

---

[53]   Portions of the following draw on C. A. Jones, 'Exporting Antitrust Courtrooms to the World: Private Enforcement in a Global Market', (2004) 16 (4) *Loyola Consumer L. R.* 409.

[54]   C. Stark, 'Improving Bilateral Antitrust Cooperation', in Jones and Matsushita, eds, *supra* n. 39 at pp. 83, 84.

[55]   See *Zenith Radio Corp. v. Hazeltine Research Inc.*, 395 US 100, 89 S.Ct. 1562, 23 L. Ed. 129 (1969).

[56]   See, e.g., *In re Uranium Antitrust Litigation*, 617 F.2d 1248 (7th Cir. 1980), where the court considered issues raised by the governments of Australia, Canada, South Africa and Great Britain as to whether the district court could proceed in a case brought by Westinghouse Electric Corporation alleging antitrust violations against 26 foreign and domestic uranium producers. Plaintiff's antitrust action against 12 foreign and 17 domestic corporations engaged in various aspects of uranium industry obtained final default judgments as to liability against nine defaulting defendants in the United States District Court for the Northern District of Illinois, Eastern Division, and also obtained injunctions prohibiting various defaulting defendants from transferring funds out of the United States without approval by the Court upon 20 days' prior written notice. See also, *Rio Tinto Zinc v. Westinghouse Electric Corp.*, [1978] AC 547, [1978] All ER 434, HL.

[57]   See Stark, *supra* n. 54.

judgment obtained abroad. The target was clearly US antitrust treble damage actions, although the statute does not explicitly say so.

Among the most bizarre procedural sagas was the Laker antitrust litigation in the 1980s, involving Sir Freddie Laker, a principal in Laker Airlines, a low-cost trans-Atlantic carrier which failed, allegedly due to a conspiracy among other airlines (including British Airways, Sabena, and others) and banks to exclude Laker Airlines from the market. A multitude of diverse litigation ensued in which Laker filed suit in the US under the Sherman Act,[58] Midland Bank filed suit in the UK to keep Laker from continuing his suit in the US, and obtained an injunction to that effect from the UK Court of Appeal,[59] but a similar order in favor of British Airways was reversed by the House of Lords.[60] The private cases ultimately settled, and the US government discontinued its criminal grand jury investigation against British Airways and others on diplomatic grounds at the request of the UK Prime Minister.

Since these frictions, the DOJ has concentrated on negotiating international antitrust enforcement cooperation agreements with foreign countries and now has agreements with Germany, Australia, Canada, the European Union, Brazil, Israel, Japan and Mexico. These agreements indicate among other things that tensions related to extraterritorial enforcement of US antitrust law have eased somewhat as other jurisdictions have become more cognizant of the need for antitrust enforcement. Moreover, since the EU has adopted something akin to the USA's 'effects' doctrine,[61] what once seemed to be unjustified extraterritoriality on the part of the USA has become more internationally accepted. However, in the recent *Empagran* decision,[62] the Supreme Court narrowly interpreted the extraterritorial reach of the Sherman Act to deny foreign purchasers the right to bring private treble damage actions in the US against the Vitamins Cartel in part based on comity concerns raised by the governments of Germany, the UK, Ireland, the Netherlands, and others in amicus

---

[58] E.g., *Laker Airways Ltd. v. Sabena, Belgian World Airlines*, 731 F.2d 909 (D.C.Cir. 1984).

[59] *Midland Bank plc v. Laker Airways plc*, [1986] QB 689, [1986] All ER 526, CA.

[60] *British Airways v. Laker Airlines*, [1985] AC 58, [1984] 3 All ER 39, HL.

[61] See the '*Dyestuffs*' case, Case 48/69 etc *ICI v. Commission* [1972] ECR 619, [1972] CMLR 557 (economic entity doctrine); '*Woodpulp*' Cases 114/85, etc *A Ahlström Oy v. Commission* [1988] ECR 5193, [1988] 4 CMLR 901 (Community implementation doctrine); and *Gencor v. Commission*, Case T-102/96 [1999] ECR II-753, [1999] 4 CMLR 971 (merger jurisdiction).

[62] *F. Hoffman-La Roche Ltd. v. Empagran S.A.*, 542 US 155, 124 S.Ct. 2359, 159 L.Ed.2d 226, 72 USLW 4501, 2004 WL 1300131 (2004). The Court of Appeals opinion is found at *Empagran S.A. v. F. Hoffman-Laroche, Ltd.*, 315 F.3d 338 (D.C. Cir. 2003).

briefs. Ironically, neither the EU nor the EC filed an amicus brief, and it is questionable whether the Member State submissions were appropriate in light of Community law.[63] However, the *Empagran* decision does not prevent foreign plaintiffs from bringing actions if their injury is causally related to injury to the US market.

IV   EU COMPETITION AND US ANTITRUST IN A GLOBALIZING ECONOMY

1   Convergence: Economics in EU Competition Policy

The story of US antitrust over the last thirty-plus years has been the rise in the importance of neoclassical price theory economics in the formulation of antitrust doctrine under the influence of the 'Chicago school' of economics. Although it has now been somewhat tempered by the rise of 'post-Chicago' thinking in antitrust, even under the latter approach allocative economic efficiencies and consumer welfare remain very influential in guiding the interpretation and application of US antitrust law. The Chicago school's narrow conception of the goals of antitrust and the limited circumstances in which the government should intervene have in turn been informed by 'Post-Chicago' thinking about game theory and analysis of strategic behavior by firms. These developments have been chronicled in many works[64] and will not be addressed in detail in this chapter. It is expected that following essays will discuss the influence of these developments on certain substantive areas of EU competition rules. However, because EU competition law and policy appears

---

[63]   See C. A. Jones, 'Foreign Plaintiffs, Vitamins, and the Sherman Antitrust Act After *Empagran*', (7/8) *Eur. L. Reporter* (2004), pp. 270, 275: 'More importantly, given that the German courts have refused compensation to private plaintiffs in Germany on the grounds that the vitamins cartel was not explicitly directed at particular plaintiffs, the German position may well be inconsistent with its obligations to the EC. This provision of German law was declared in conflict with EC law as long ago as *Factortame III*. Moreover, since Community competition policy is allocated to the Commission, it would have been more appropriate for the Commission to present the position on behalf of the Member States rather than individual Member States doing so. One might read some of the Member State amicus briefs as assuming EC competition law and the doctrine of supremacy of EC law did not exist or already alter the sovereignty of the Member States in this area' (citations omitted).

[64]   See, for example, Foer, Lande, *supra* n. 30; the excellent selection of essays found in A. Cucinotta, R. Pardolesi, R. Van den Bergh, *Post-Chicago Developments in Antitrust Law*, Norwood, MA and Cheltenham, UK, 2002; J. E. Kwoka Jr., L. J. White, (eds), *The Antitrust Revolution: Economics, Competition and Policy*, Oxford, 4th edn 2004; and R. Greaves, (ed.), *Competition Law*, Burlington, VT, 2003.

to be increasingly influenced to some degree by these economic developments, it appears worthwhile to discuss briefly the general impact on the
convergence of the two systems.

It is readily apparent from the earlier discussion of the differences between
historical European culture as related to competition and American competition culture that Chicago school thinking would not be expected to be received
fully or uncritically in Europe. At the same time, post-war Europe was
attracted by the example of the powerful competitive US economy[65] and
European business and governmental leaders were told by the American
government that 'there was an intimate connection between American productivity and the intensity of competition in American industry. This statement
was repeatedly endorsed in public reports by groups of businessmen who were
sent to the United States to find out if American methods could be used to
expedite European reconstruction'.[66] However, it was only later (1970s) that
Chicago school thinking began to influence American antitrust, and the
European Community's important goal of market integration, among other
differences, suggested that any influence of the Chicago school would be less
than complete.[67]

The Commission at least has over the last several years attached increasing
importance to economics in their competition analysis and decisions. Brussels
practitioners have told me of the Commission's increasing use of economic
tools even when formal Commission policy documents had not yet made this
apparent. This is undoubtedly the result of several factors including the
appointment (1999–2004) of Mario Monti, an economist, as Commissioner
holding the competition portfolio, the scrutiny of the Court of First Instance
and reversal of some high profile Commission decisions which might have
been bolstered by more economic analysis, and an increasing concern with the
competitiveness (or lack thereof) of the European economy, and perhaps
others. As noted above, the increased economic and competitive economy
focus has been made manifest in the Lisbon Strategy, which seeks to make the
EU 'the world's most competitive and dynamic knowledge-based economy'[68]
by 2010.

For example, in its *Pro-active Competition Policy Communication*, the
Commission noted:

---

[65] Jones, *supra* n. 17, at 24–5.

[66] Edwards, *supra* n. 5, at 11.

[67] B. Hawk, 'The American (Anti-Trust) Revolution: Lessons for the EEC?',
[1988] (9) *ECLR* 53.

[68] See Commission, 'Communication From The Commission: A pro-active
Competition Policy for a Competitive Europe', COM(2004) 293 final (Brussels,
20.4.2004).

Another common theme of the new regulatory competition framework is the
stronger emphasis on economic analysis. Competition policy is adapting to recognize both the teachings of modern economics and the constantly evolving dynamics of markets and the necessary industrial development of Europe. Economic
analysis is central because competition policy shapes fundamental economic decisions on investment, consolidation, pricing, and thereby economic performance. It
shifts the focus firmly to the economic effects of firm behaviour or of government
measures. It helps more generally identify the circumstances in which characteristics such as high profits and substantial market shares are signs of market power.[69]

For example, when the modernization 'package' came into force on 1 May
2004, then-Commissioner Monti noted with respect to the new Merger
Regulation[70] that

> The package of reforms reinforces the principle of the 'one-stop shop' review for
> mergers that have an impact in more than three Member States, clarifies the
> Commission's powers, provides better guidance as to those mergers that are likely
> to be challenged and *increases the level of economic analysis* and the internal
> checks necessary to ensure that our decisions are fair, sound and based on solid
> facts.[71]

More particularly, the new Merger Regulation and accompanying
Guidelines[72] expressly authorize consideration of ('proven') efficiencies as
justification for challenged mergers, which is much more in line with US
merger thinking. The Commission noted:

> As a result of its recent review of the Merger Regulation, the Commission
> concluded that there were compelling reasons to give more explicit consideration to
> efficiencies in merger control than in the past. Mergers may allow companies to
> reorganize their activities or bring together complementary capabilities in ways that
> induce them to compete harder and thereby counteract the negative effects on
> competition and in particular the potential harm to consumers that a merger might
> otherwise have.

> The Commission's new Guidelines on the assessment of horizontal mergers there-
> fore specify that the Commission intends to carefully consider substantiated effi-
> ciency claims in the overall assessment of a merger, and that it may decide, as a
> consequence of the efficiencies that the merger brings about, a merger does not

---

[69]   Ibid., at 7.
[70]   Council Reg. (EC) No 139/2004.
[71]   M. Monti, *Competition Policy Newsletter*, Special Edition, 2004, at p. 1.
(emphasis added).
[72]   Council Regulation (EC) No 139/2004 of 20 January 2004 on the control of
concentrations between undertakings (the EC Merger Regulation). Guidelines on the
assessment of horizontal mergers under the Council Regulation on the control of
concentrations between undertakings no. C 31, 5.2.2004, p. 3. OJEC L 31, 5.2.2004.

significantly impede effective competition. The Guidelines specify that various types of efficiencies can be taken into account, in particular cost savings in production and distribution but also efficiency gains in the sphere of R & D and innovation, which could lead to new products to the benefit of consumers.

The Guidelines outline a more modern economics based approach to efficiencies that allows the Commission to better distinguish the mergers that harm competition from those that bring more competition.

A similar approach is identified with respect to the Art. 81 EC block exemption regulations, as to which former Commmissioner Monti said, 'We have replaced all the old legalistic block exemption regulations (i.e. regulations granting antitrust immunity to types of agreements or agreements common in a given industry) with *a new generation of block exemption regulations and guidelines which embody a more economic approach*'.[73] Other concrete indications of formal policy are the appointment of a Chief Staff Economist and other economist staff for use in major cases[74] and emphasis on the consumer welfare[75] aspects of competition policy, as noted by the Director of DG-Competition, Philip Lowe,

> We are trying to develop a systematic approach to priority setting, which makes us take a conscious decision in the competition field as to what the effects of a certain problem are on *consumer welfare* . . . If there has been more emphasis in the past on complaints, and complaints from competitors rather than consumers, we will now be putting the emphasis more on the benefits for consumers. More competition delivers the best deal for consumers.[76]

The Commission is now speaking with some of the semantics of the Chicago School, although it is not yet clear whether decisions of the Commission or judgments of the European courts will be consistent with Chicago or even post-Chicago thinking. So far, for example, the ECJ and CFI have not followed Chicago theory in demanding proof of recoupment before finding predatory pricing,[77] and this has been criticized as inconsistent with economic theory and the goal of market integration.[78]

---

[73]   Monti, *supra* n. 71 (emphasis added).

[74]   P. Lowe, *Competition Policy Newsletter*, Special Edition, 2004, p. 3.

[75]   It is doubted that the term 'consumer welfare' used both by Mr. Lowe and Robert Bork has quite the same meaning.

[76]   Lowe, *supra* n. 74 at 3 (emphasis added).

[77]   Case 62/86 *AKZO v. Commission* [1991] ECR I-3359 and Case T-83/91 *Tetra Pak International SA v. Commission* [1994] ECR II-755.

[78]   R. J. Van den Bergh, P. D. Camesasca, *European Competition Law and Economics: A Comparative Perspective* (Antwerp-Groniggen-Oxford, 2001), pp. 303–5.

One can say that in its announcements and policy instruments, the Commission apparently has brought Community competition law into greater convergence with US law as influenced by Chicago and post-Chicago, although the details vary. Much remains to be seen as some of these changes are quite new. One area which the Commission has not yet reformed is Art. 82 (abuse of dominant position), although this may happen soon. Another previous area of conflict has been the emphasis in the USA on private enforcement compared to the European administrative approach. This, too, will now receive attention from the Commission and is likely to lead to legislation designed to encourage private litigation. As then-Commissioner Monti stated recently:

> To try to make the possibility of private enforcement of competition law more of a reality, the Commission is currently looking at the conditions under which private parties can bring actions before the courts for breach of the Community competition rules. At the end of last year I commissioned a study in this area, the final results of which were published on DG Competition's website in September of this year. The study found that private competition actions in Europe are 'totally underdeveloped'. On the basis of the study, work has begun in DG Competition on the drafting of a Green Paper on the encouragement of private enforcement of EC competition law.[79]

2   Conflicts: Boeing, GE/Honeywell and Microsoft

The three best known instances of recent 'conflict' between US and EU competition enforcers involved *Boeing/McDonnell-Douglas*,[80] *GE/ Honeywell*,[81] and some would say, *Microsoft*. The Boeing/McDonnell-Douglas merger was passed by the FTC, even though it appeared to raise competitive concerns, because the FTC concluded essentially that McDonnell-Douglas was such an ineffective competitor that competition was no worse off if Boeing acquired it. In Brussels, the Commission appeared ready to prohibit the merger on the grounds that the acquisition would lead to a strengthening of Boeing's dominant position, but approved it at the eleventh hour after Boeing agreed to significant conditions. Politicians used their special skills to

---

[79]   Speech of Commissioner Mario Monti, *Competition for Consumers' Benefit*, Competition Day, Amsterdam, 22.10.2004, p. 6. Available at http://europa.eu.int/ comm/competition/speeches/text/sp2004_016_en.pdf

[80]   See the FTC decision, *In the matter of The Boeing Company/McDonnell Douglas Corporation*, 5 CCH Trade Reg. Rep. (CCH) [Transfer Binder 1997–2001], & 24, 295 (July 1, 1997); for the Commission decision, see *Boeing/McDonnell-Douglas*, Case IV/M.877 OJEC L 336/16 (8 December 1997).

[81]   *General Electric/Honeywell*, Commission Decision, Case COMP/M. 2230, 3 July 2001.

make matters worse; then-US Vice-President Al Gore threatened a trade war if the merger were blocked and Commissioner Karel Van Miert threatened that if Boeing went ahead with the merger without EC approval, the Commission would impose prohibitive fines on Boeing and perhaps seize Boeing planes flying into Europe. A direct conflict was avoided due to Boeing's concessions. One wonders, though, whether under the new Merger Regulation the outcome in the Commission would have been any different. In particular, absent the concessions made by Boeing, would the Commission have prohibited the merger under the new regulation as it seemed poised to do under the old regulation?

In *GE/Honeywell*, the conflict was not avoided. Although the US and Canada had approved the merger, the Commission prohibited the merger based on the conclusion that GE's financial strength and vertical integration into aircraft purchasing, financing and leasing combined with Honeywell's strength in various product markets such as corporate jet engines, avionics and non-avionics products would quickly result in creation of true dominant positions in Honeywell's products.[82] Again, consider whether the result in the EU would have been any different under the new Merger Regulation with its recognition of 'proven' efficiencies. It seems unlikely.

Microsoft of course was not a merger case, but in Europe, an abuse of dominant position case and in the USA a monopolization case. It is not so much a conflict as a situation in which the US (in the end via settlement) and the Commission imposed different remedies for different conduct. On 24 March 2004, the European Commission announced[83] its long-awaited decision in proceedings against Microsoft which had been ongoing for about five years. According to the Commission, Microsoft had abused its dominant position in PC operating systems in infringement of Art. 82 EC by (1) deliberately restricting interoperability between Windows PCs and non-Microsoft workgroup servers; and (2) tying its Windows Media Player (WMP), a product with which it faced competition, with its Windows operating system, in which it holds a global 95 per cent market share. Because of the duration and ongoing nature of Microsoft's infringements and the size of its European turnover, the Commission imposed the largest single company fine in its history, €497 million, or approximately $612 million. However, this is less than 1 per cent

---

[82] G. Drauz, 'Unbundling GE/Honeywell: The Assessment of Conglomerate Mergers Under EC Competition Law', 2001 *Fordham Corp. L. Institute* 183, 192 (2002).

[83] Rapid Press Release No. IP/04/382 (24 March 2004). The full text of the decision may be found on the Commission's website, Commission Decision of 24.03.2004 relating to a proceeding under Article 82 of the EC Treaty (Case COMP/C-3/37.792 Microsoft), Commission Document C(2004) 900 final.

of Microsoft's cash on hand, so even this historically remarkable fine is not material to Microsoft.

The most significant remedy imposed by the Commission may be its two conduct remedies: requiring Microsoft to market a version of Windows without the tied media player and requiring Microsoft to disclose its Application Programming Interfaces (API) to other firms, for a reasonable remuneration, so as to enable them to make their non-Microsoft server software properly interact with the Windows operating system. Microsoft has appealed, although its efforts to obtain a stay pending appeal were rejected by the Court of First Instance.

This followed the US settlement with Microsoft on remand after the US Court of Appeals had affirmed findings of monopolization under the Sherman Act Section 2, reversed other findings, reversed the District Court's order breaking up Microsoft and remanded for new trial on the remedies to be awarded.[84] The settlement included requirements of nondiscriminatory licensing of certain software protocols, prohibitions on retaliation against customers who use competitive products, and requirements that Microsoft permit access to competitors' middleware products.

No direct comparison of these cases equivalent to the comparison in the merger cases can be made. The earlier US case was directed at conduct with respect to different products, although both cases found that Microsoft had monopoly power (in the US) with respect to personal computer operating systems or a dominant position (in the EU). The Commission's action took into account the results achieved in the USA and avoided direct duplication of targeted conduct on the grounds that the USA had already dealt with certain problems. While the Commission's remedy, assuming it withstands judicial review, is more severe than that imposed by settlement in the USA, it is also imposed with respect to different conduct. It would be wrong to characterize this as a conflict, but some observers had suggested that the EU should not have imposed a more burdensome remedy than did the US government, although the basis for this argument is unclear.

V   CONCLUSION: BEYOND MODERNIZATION

The history of Community competition rules and US antitrust laws reveals both convergence and divergence in the past and promises some of the same for the future. The EU's modernization packages seem to bring the EU closer

---

[84]   *United States v. Microsoft Corporation*, 253 F. 3d 34 (D.C. Cir.), *cert. denied*, 534 US 952 (2001).

to current USA concepts of competition and economics, but that has yet to be confirmed. There are substantially more countries which will apply the EC style of competition law in the future than will apply the Sherman Act. The interesting question is whether the present interest in Europe concerning application of more economics-based doctrines of competition policy will persist, and perhaps more importantly will it spread to other countries who do not now apply it? If so, will economics-based antitrust principles draw other antitrust jurisdictions closer to the US approach as well, notwithstanding that their competition legislation is based on the European approach?

The common conditions facing the USA and the EU in a globalizing world raise the question of what competition policy best serves their respective citizens and economies as well as the other roughly 90–100 countries which have adopted competition laws in some form. As we ponder what global and international competition policy and enforcement regimes should look like, we must keep in mind that if the EU and USA, the two most experienced and active antitrust jurisdictions in the world, cannot come to substantial agreement in harmonization of their competition laws, then what hope is there for the rest of the countries with competition laws? The answer must be that if the EU and the USA can co-exist with differing competition rules, then so can the rest of the world. The challenge of international antitrust enforcement will likely have to be met without uniform laws. It remains to be seen whether it will or can be met by textually different laws which converge in practical application based on common underlying principles of economics.

2. Strategic competition policy: a comment on EU competition policy

Wulf-Henning Roth*

I   INTRODUCTION

The title of this chapter presupposes that the European Union may be on its way to developing a strategic competition policy – perhaps in the way that it has pursued strategic aims in the application of its antidumping regulations.[1] Viewed from this perspective, the *Boeing*,[2] *Honeywell*,[3] and *Microsoft*[4] cases could be analysed as examples in which the Commission attempted to fight the market power of US-American champions on the European market, thereby protecting European based competitors. Whether and to what extent the Commission has pursued such a strategic aim could only be verified on the basis of an in-depth analysis of the decisions taken, and of the perhaps hidden considerations behind the decisions. This goes beyond what could be done in a comment.

There is another aspect to the topic of 'strategic competition policy' that I would prefer to deal with: in its Communication of April 2004 on 'A proactive Competition Policy for a Competitive Europe',[5] the Commission linked the reform and enforcement of European competition policy with the 'Lisbon strategy' to make the EU 'the world's most competitive and dynamic knowledge-based economy by 2010'. One of the major characteristics of the new regulatory competition framework that has been set up in the last five years is the stronger emphasis on economic analysis.[6] This characteristic feature raises

---

* Professor Dr. iur., L.L.M., Rheinische Friedrich-Wilhelms Universität Bonn.
1 See, e.g., Wessely, *Das Verhältnis von Antidumping- und Kartellrecht in der Europäischen Gemeinschaft*, München 1999.
2 Commission decision of 30 July 1997, OJ 1997 L336/16.
3 Commission decision of 3 July 2001, OJ 2004 L48/1. For comment, see, e.g., Holland, 'Using Merger Review to Cure Prior Conduct: The European Commission's GE/Honeywell Decision', 74 *Col.L.Rev.* (2003), p. 74.
4 Commission decision of 21 April 2004, C (2004) 900 final.
5 COM (2004) 293.
6 See, e.g., Commission Notice, Guidelines on the applicability of Article 81 of the EC Treaty to horizontal cooperation agreements, OJ 2001 C3/2, paras 27–30;

the question whether and to what extent the 'more economics-based approach' turns out to be an explicit or implicit choice not so much in favour of an economically enlightened enforcement of competition law, but rather in favour of fostering 'European champions' in the world of global competition and, as such, can be viewed as a strategic choice taken and pursued by the Commission (and, perhaps, fostered by other Community institutions).[7]

Such a strategic choice would correspond to developments that are said to have taken place in the United States twenty years ago. As one (European) commentator has observed:

> one might have to see the adoption of economic efficiency by American cartel authorities as the main goal of antitrust rules in the broader context of the American economic situation. It might not be a total coincidence that this particular choice took root during the Reagan administration. Equally it might not be a coincidence that this goal – resulting in a more permissive view regarding large companies – was accepted in a time of increasing international competition. The political choice taken was to revitalize the economic power of American companies on world markets.[8]

If we compare this statement with a citation from the Communication of the Commission of 20 April 2004, we will discover obvious similarities, at least if we take a quick look: 'As a principal factor behind increased innovation and growth in productivity, effective competition between firms in the enlarged internal market must be seen as one of the key elements of a successful strategy to build up a competitive Europe and reinvigorate the Lisbon Strategy.'[9]

In the following, I would like to comment briefly on a number of questions that are related to the topic of this chapter: the bases and implications for a 'strategic competition policy' pursued by the European Union. For the purpose of the following brief comments I would like to define 'strategic competition policy' as a policy that goes beyond merely shaping a favourable environment for competition by fostering an attractive infrastructure (in all its dimensions) and sustaining innovation and technological development, and conceives and uses competition law as an instrument to assist European competitors on world markets.

Communication from the Commission, Notice – Guidelines on the application of Article 81 (3) of the Treaty, OJ 2004 C101/97, paras 5, 48–72, etc.; Guidelines on the assessment of horizontal mergers under the Council Regulation on the control of concentrations between undertakings, OJ 2004 C31/5, paras 14–57.

[7] See Mestmäcker, Schweitzer, *Europäisches Wettbewerbsrecht* § 3 para. 82, 2nd edn München 2004, where the authors speculate that the new competition policy may have indirectly been inspired by industrial policy considerations promoted by the Member States.

[8] Bouterse, *Competition and Integration – What Goal counts?*, Boston, 1994, p. 43 and fn. 21, with further references.

[9] COM (2004) 293, p. 5.

II   THE GOALS OF EUROPEAN COMPETITION POLICY

Let us first turn to the constitutional foundations. The starting point for a discussion of the goals of competition policy should be Article 2 EC, in which the ultimate goals of the European Community are articulated: 'a harmonious, balanced and sustainable development of economic activities, a high level of employment and of social protection, . . . a high degree of competitiveness and convergence of economic performance'.

To reach these ultimate goals, the Community pursues the policies described in Article 3, which include, among others, 'a system ensuring that competition in the internal market is not distorted', 'the strengthening of the competitiveness of the Community industry', and 'the promotion of research and technological development'. The Community, in pursuing its economic policy is, according to Article 4(1) EC, bound by the 'principle of an open market economy with free competition'. The ultimate goals and means, as described in Articles 2 and 3 EC, have to be taken into account when we inter-pret the major provisions of the Treaty.[10] They are an important starting point for a teleological interpretation of the provisions on competition policy in the EC Treaty and the EC Merger Regulation. It is generally accepted that the goals described in Article 2 EC may conflict with one another, and that there is no absolute priority of one goal or of a specific policy. Whether the promo-tion of research and development is pursued by way of competition or, in contrast, by allowing restrictions of competition, is a matter to be decided by interpreting the relevant Treaty provisions.

Thus, the EC Treaty, by its reference to 'a high degree of competitiveness', opens the road to achieving this end by adopting a competition policy stress-ing rivalry and the competitive process,[11] but it may also attain this end by supporting – at least in an indirect manner – European champions to help them compete on the global level.[12] The point I would like to make is simply this: The EC Treaty does *not* hinder the Community institutions from pursuing a *strategic* competition policy.

---

[10]   Mestmäcker, Schweitzer, *supra* n. 7, § 3 Rz. 62.

[11]   Communication from the Commission – Notice – Guidelines on the applica-tion of Article 81 (3) of the Treaty, OJ 2004 C101/97, para. 105.

[12]   This is what the Commission may have in mind in its Communication, COM (2004) 293, p. 2: 'A pro-active competition policy is characterised by: – improvement of the regulatory framework for competition which facilitates . . . efficient economic restructuring throughout the internal market.'

III LOOKING BACK . . .

The Community, and especially the Commission, have always pursued, with more or less rigour, a strategic competition policy. To state the obvious: European competition law from its beginning pursued the goal of integration. The creation of the common market was, however, not only a political goal but also an instrument to strengthen European industry. The Commission, in its Competition Reports, starting in the 1970s, conceived competition policy, oriented towards market integration, as an instrument for 'raising the competitiveness of Community industry'.[13]

We should, moreover, remind ourselves that the call for harmonization has been inspired by the assumption that it serves productivity and fosters economies of scale, thereby increasing the competitiveness of European industry. This position has been restated in the Commission's Communication of 20 April 2004: 'A competitive and open internal market provides the best guarantee for European companies to increase their efficiency and innovative potential.'

The Commission has, from the 1970s on, viewed competition policy and industrial policy as *complementary means* on the way to a 'technology Community'.[14] Therefore, it should not come as a surprise that the Commission, on the same day that it published its Communication on 'Pro-active Competition policy' in April 2004, also published a Communication on 'Fostering structural change: an industrial policy for an enlarged Europe'.[15] Lacking any competences for an industry policy in the 1970s and 1980s, the Commission's position did not exert a great influence.[16]

However, when we look to the decisions taken by the Commission with regard to exemptions from Article 81(1) EC, we find some traces indicating the pursuit of an industrial policy. In the *Carbon Gas* case, the Commission granted an exemption stating that the agreement contributed to the development of alternative energy sources and the reduction of the dependence on foreign oil supplies.[17] And in the decisions taken in the 1980s with regard to the chemical industry, the aims of reducing structural overcapacity, supporting

---

[13] *Thirteenth Report on Competition Policy* (1984), point 11.
[14] *Fifteenth Report on Competition Policy* (1986), points 13, 225.
[15] COM (2004) 274.
[16] See Sauter, *Competition Law and Industrial Policy in the EU*, Oxford 1997, pp. 57 ff., 116. For a description of the legal foundations, the history and the aims of European industrial policy, see Hellmann, in von der Groeben, Schwarze (eds), *Kommentar zum Vertrag über die Europäische Union und zur Gründung der Europäischen Gemeinschaft*, vol. 3, Art. 157, 6th edn, Baden Baden 2003.
[17] OJ 1983 L376/19.

structural change, and increasing the competitiveness of the industry were the central basis for the exemptions granted.[18]

The Commission has always stressed its position that vigorous competition is a *key driver for competitiveness*, and, accordingly, competition policy has a key role to play in ensuring that EU industry remains competitive.[19]

The point to be stressed is the following: whatever we think of the 'more economic analysis approach' that has gained so much importance in recent times,[20] we should keep in mind that – in a nutshell – European competition policy has always been conceived, at least by the Commission, in a somewhat strategic manner to serve the industrial development of the European industry – either by relying on the advantages of the competitive process or by exempting restrictive agreements on the basis of Article 81(3) EC.

IV   INTERPRETING ARTICLE 81 EC

The question that one might pose is whether the 'more economic approach' to which the Commission has recently turned to is nothing but a *camouflage* for pursuing a strategic competition policy. In the following I would like to argue that, far from such a contention, the Commission's new approach – in its general thrust (although not necessarily in all its details) – seems to come much closer to the case law of the European courts than its former practice. In this regard I would like to make three points.

(i) As a starting point we should remind ourselves of the fact that the approach of the Commission in applying Article 81 EC has for a long time met with strong criticism, especially from academic quarters.[21] It has been argued that the overbroad and somewhat formalistic interpretation of Article 81(1) EC by the Commission has not been and cannot be based on a solid theory of the notion of a 'restriction of competition'. In contrast to the approach taken by the Commission, a restriction of competition cannot be inferred from the terms of a contract, but rather has to be analysed with regard to specific market conditions.[22] It has often been stated that the overbroad application of Article 81(1) EC has been based on a fundamental *misconception*[23] of the term

---

18   See the analysis by Bouterse, *supra* n. 8 at 57.
19   *Twenty-fifth Report on Competition Policy* (1995).
20   See the references *supra* n. 6.
21   See, e.g., Bright, 'EU Competition Policy: Rules, Objectives and Deregulation', 16 *Oxford J. of L. Studies* (1996), p. 535; Whish, *Competition Law*, 5th edn, London, 2003, p. 106 (with further references in fn. 244).
22   Whish, *supra* n. 21, at p. 117.
23   Hildebrand, *The Role of Economic Analysis in the EC Competition Rules*, 2nd edn, 2002, p. 184.

'restriction of competition', which is rather an economic concept. The reason why the Commission has too often and too easily assumed that a restraint on the *commercial freedom* of action of the parties involved results in a 'restriction of competition'[24] may find one explanation in the simple fact that the Commission pursued the goal of getting hold of as many cases as possible in which *market integration* was endangered in order to deal with them on the basis of Article 81(3) EC.[25] In a 1997 conference at the European University Institute, there was unanimous agreement that a change in the analysis of Article 81(1) EC was therefore called for.[26]

Another reason for this approach (which, rightly or wrongly,[27] has also been described as the 'German approach', relating to § 1 GWB) may have been the attempt to attain *legal certainty* with regard to the notification requirement. For the parties involved it may seem to be easier and more convenient just to examine individual clauses in a given contract in order to decide whether a notification is required, rather than to indulge in an economic analysis of whether a restriction of competition is likely to ensue. However, with Regulation 1/2003 now in place,[28] such a formalistic approach cannot be justified on this basis any longer. Moreover, it has long been argued that a restriction on the commercial freedom of the parties is neither a necessary nor a sufficient condition for assuming a restriction of competition.[29] Richard Whish has described the Commission's approach to Article 81(1) EC as 'lazy thinking'.[30] Finally, the way in which the Commission devised the group exemption regulations – based on the formalistic 'list' approach – met with

---

[24]   See Bright, *supra* n. 21, at pp. 537–8 with an analysis of the case law; Faull, in *European Competition Law Annual 1997 – The Objectives of Competition Law* (1998) p. 506.

[25]   Hildebrand, *supra* n. 23, at p. 185, argues 'that the Commission was seeking to maximise the number of cases about which it receives detailed information through the notification process'.

[26]   See *European Competition Law Annual 1997 – The Objectives of Competition Law* 498 (1998) (Whish summarizing the discussion).

[27]   Under traditional § 1 GWB analysis, a restriction of commercial freedom had to have an appreciable impact on the relevant market conditions. See Möschel, *Recht der Wettbewerbsbeschränkungen*, München, 1983, para. 185; Huber, Baums, in *Frankfurter Kommentar zum Kartellrecht*, Bonn, 1993, § 1 GWB paras 127–47 (restriction of commercial freedom) and paras 373–405 (impact on market conditions). With regard to vertical restraints, the former § 18 GWB (which is § 16 GWB today) has always been applied in a non-formalistic, 'economic' fashion, requiring the proof of a substantial negative impact on competition or market access.

[28]   OJ 2003 L1/1.

[29]   Faull, *supra* n. 24, p. 506.

[30]   Whish, in *European Competition Law Annual 1997 – The Objectives of Competition Law* (1998), p. 496; *cf.* Whish, *supra* n. 21, at pp. 117–18.

much criticism for their lack of consideration for the economic impact of the agreements.[31]

(ii) Even more importantly, the Commission's basic philosophy in applying Article 81(1) EC did not seem to be in accordance with the case law of the Court of Justice and the Court of First Instance. Both courts have applied a much less formalistic approach than the Commission ever pursued. Already back in 1966, the Court, in *Maschinenbau Ulm*, stated that Article 81 EC cannot be interpreted as introducing any kind of advance judgment with regard to a category of agreements determined by their legal nature.[32] In order to consider a clause to be prohibited by Article 81(1) EC

> by reason of its object or effect, it is appropriate to take into account in particular the nature and quantity, limited or otherwise, of the products covered by the agreement, the position and importance of the grantor and the concessionaire on the market for the products concerned, the isolated nature of the disputed agreement or, alternatively, its position in a series of agreements, the severity of the clauses intended to protect the exclusive dealership or, alternatively, the opportunities allowed for other commercial competitors in the same products by way of parallel re-exportation and importation.

In *Metro I*, dealing with a selective distribution agreement, the Court held that a restriction of competition can only be based on an analysis of the 'nature and intensiveness of competition . . ., dictated by the products or services in question and the economic structure of the market',[33] taking into account the kind and quality of the products, the number and size of the producers, the preferences of the consumers, and the existence of a 'variety of channels of distribution adapted to the peculiar characteristics of the various producers and to the requirements of the various categories of consumers'.[34] And *Delimitis*[35] stands out for the proposition that distribution agreements have to be analysed to determine whether their effect is to substantially impede market access. In this regard, a full blown analysis of the relevant market is called for: the number and size of the producers present on the market, the degree of saturation of that market (the market share) and customer fidelity to existing brands,

---

[31]   Green Paper on Vertical Restraints in EC Competition Policy, COM (96) 721, Executive Summary, No. 37; Lane, *EC Competition Law* 128 (London 2000); Hildebrand, *supra* n. 23, at p. 251.

[32]   Case 56/65, *Société Technique Minière v Maschinenbau Ulm*, judgment of 30 June 1996, [1966] ECR 235, 248.

[33]   Case 26/76, *Metro v Commission*, judgment of 25 October 1977, [1977] ECR 1875, para. 20.

[34]   Ibid.

[35]   Case 234/89, *Delimitis v Henninger Bräu*, judgment of 28 February 1991, [1991] ECR I-935, para. 20 ('inaccessible').

that is, the conditions under which competitive forces operate on the relevant market.[36] Moreover, besides analysing the existing distribution contracts to assess whether their effect is to impede market access, the Court calls for an examination of whether there are other possibilities for a new competitor to enter the market, such as acquiring a competitor with an established distribution system, the acquisition of outlets, and the existence of wholesalers not tied to producers.[37]

It is obvious from the case law that, in the application of Article 81(1) EC, there is an important difference between the notion of a restriction of economic freedom and a 'restraint of competition'. It is simply *not sufficient* to show that individual parties (either those involved in the agreement or third parties) are restricted in their economic freedom. Nor is a restriction of commercial freedom a necessary *prerequisite* for a restraint of competition, as may be inferred from the case law concerning information exchanges.[38] The Court, in a number of judgments, has held that (irrespective of whether we have a horizontal or a vertical agreement or concerted practice), in the application of Article 81(1) EC, 'account should be taken of the economic context in which undertakings operate, the products or services covered by the decisions of those undertakings, the structure of the market concerned and the actual conditions in which it functions'.[39]

The Court of First Instance has more than once referred to this economic approach to Article 81(1) EC,[40] applying it, for example, to a joint venture concerning rail night services.[41]

Summing up this point, I would like to submit that, in as far as Article 81(1) EC (in the interpretation of the European courts) requires an 'economic approach' to the notion of 'restriction of competition', we should not attribute to the Commission a 'strategic' competition policy when it just follows the demands of the Treaty.

(iii) The Commission has reacted to the criticism launched against the formalistic approach of the group exemptions by introducing market share

---

[36] Ibid., para. 22.

[37] Ibid., para. 21.

[38] Case T-35/92, *John Deere v Commission*, judgment of 27 October 1994, [1994] ECR II-957; Case 7/95 P, *John Deere v Commission*, judgment of 28 May 1998, [1998] ECR I-3111.

[39] Joined Cases C-180/98 to C-184/98, *Pavel Pavlov v Stichting Pensioenfonds Medische Specialisten*, judgment of 12 September 2000, [2000] ECR I-6451, para. 91.

[40] Case T-112/99, *Métropole télévision (M6) v Commission*, judgment of 18 September 2001, [2001] ECR II-2459, para. 76; Case T-65/98, *Van den Bergh Foods v Commission*, judgment of 23 October 2003, para. 84.

[41] Joined Cases T-374/94 etc., *European Night Services v Commission*, judgment of 15 October 1998, [1998] ECR II-3141.

criteria.[42] The Commission proceeds on the assumption that certain categories of agreements should be exempted as long as the parties involved have not assumed a certain degree of market power. This approach – though still somewhat formalistic in its sole reference to a certain percentage of market share – reflects the 'economics-based approach' which assesses the impact of agreements or concerted practices on the relevant market'.[43] Again, I would like to submit that the insertion of market share criteria into the group exemption regulations has been an overdue and a long-awaited reaction of the Commission that should not be interpreted as a move towards a 'strategic' competition policy. It might, however, be an open question whether the Commission has introduced market shares which may be considered as being too generous.

V   IMPLICATIONS OF THE MORE ECONOMIC APPROACH

It seems to be obvious that the application of a more economic approach to Article 81(1) EC will prove to be much more burdensome for the Commission in terms of the need for human resources. The Commission has more than once announced that it will (therefore) concentrate its efforts on combating those agreements and concerted practices that are most obnoxious to consumer welfare.[44] We therefore have to expect fewer enforcement activities on the part of the Commission with regard to less important agreements, which will be left for the national competition authorities to take care of.

Agreements that do not restrict competition in an *appreciable* manner are not covered by Article 81 EC. The Commission, in its latest 'Notice on agreements of minor importance' of 2001,[45] has been quite generous in extending the relevant thresholds (for market shares) for non-appreciable horizontal and vertical restraints of competition, with the exception of the so-called hard-core restrictions. These thresholds will probably exempt most agreements among small and middle-sized companies from the application of Article 81(1) EC.

---

[42]   Art. 3(1)(2), Commission Regulation 2790/1999, OJ 1999 L336/21; Art. 4, Commission Regulation 2658/2000, OJ 2000 L304/3; Art. 4, Commission Regulation 2659/2000, OJ 2000 L304/7; Art. 3, Commission Regulation 772/2004, OJ L123/11.
[43]   See, e.g., Recital 5, Commission Regulation 2658/2000, cited in the previous footnote.
[44]   Commission, White Paper on Modernisation of the Rules Implementing Articles 81 and 82 of the EC Treaty, OJ 1999 C132/1. *Cf. also* the White Paper on Regulation 4056/86 on the application of the EC competition rules to maritime transport, Commission programme [2003/COMP/18], proposing the withdrawal of the *ex lege* exemptions.
[45]   OJ 2001 C368/13.

Moreover, in its 'Guidelines on the applicability of Article 81 of the EC Treaty to horizontal cooperation agreements',[46] the Commission goes beyond these thresholds to rely on market power as the relevant test to be applied to horizontal cooperation agreements (except for hard core cases). The Commission, thereby, seems to be on the way toward bringing the preconditions for an application of Article 81(1) EC closer to the criteria relevant for merger control. This approach seems to be highly questionable as a policy decision (for going too far in relaxing the relevant standards) and as a legal approach to Article 81(1) EC: market power is not the relevant test under that provision.[47]

Be that as it may, the relaxation of antitrust enforcement with regard to horizontal agreements could be viewed as an attempt by the Commission to pursue an active industrial policy to help smaller and middle-sized companies to increase their efficiency and potential. Competition policy is thus used as an instrument of industrial policy to drive the competitiveness of European companies (*vis-à-vis* companies from outside). However, this policy is double-edged: increasing the competitiveness of smaller and medium-sized companies may tend to improve the competitive process on the European market as well.

VI EFFICIENCIES

One may wonder whether the Commission is giving 'efficiencies' a new role to play in European competition law and thereby pursuing strategic aims.

(i) To restate the obvious: ever since its inception, European competition policy has protected competition 'as a means of . . . ensuring an efficient allocation of resources'.[48] This is what the prohibition of Article 81(1) EC is aiming for. Moreover, the first condition of Article 81(3) EC – 'improving the production or distribution of goods or to promoting technical and economic progress' – introduces an efficiency defence as far as *productive* (in its widest sense) and *dynamic* (innovative) efficiency gains are concerned (economies of scale, economies of scope, and so on).[49] The Commission Guidelines on the application of Article 81(3) of

---

46 OJ 2001 C3/2.
47 See Mestmäcker, Schweitzer, cited *supra* n. 7, § 10 No. 24.
48 Communication from the Commission – Notice: Guidelines on the application of Article 81 (3) of the Treaty, OJ 2004 C101/97, para. 13.
49 *Cf.* Whish, *supra* n. 21, at p. 152 (introduced as 'a narrow view' of Article 81(3) EC).

the Treaty[50] give a fair description of how the competition authorities and the courts should apply this condition. And the second condition of Article 81(3) EC – 'allowing the consumers a fair share of the resulting benefit' – should be interpreted as alluding to the notion of *allocative* efficiency. It is therefore fair to say that *efficiency analysis* has been with us as part of European competition law right from the beginning.

(ii)   What is new is that an efficiency defence has now been introduced into European merger control. To be sure, the newly adopted Merger Regulation[52] has been changed with regard to the substantive standard by introducing the 's.i.e.c.' criterion ('significant impediment to effective competition'), but beyond that the original text has been preserved. There is no express reference to efficiencies except for the provision in Art. 2(1)(b) ECMR according to which the appraisal of a merger should also take into account 'the development of technical and economic progress' by the merger, 'provided that it is to the consumers' advantage and does not form an obstacle to competition'.

The 'Guidelines on the assessment of horizontal mergers',[52] however, explicitly refer to an efficiency defence. This reference is not based on Art. 2(1)(b) ECMR, but on Recital 4 of the Merger Regulation, which refers to the ultimate goals of the EC Treaty defined in Article 2 EC. Reorganizations are to be welcomed to the extent that they are 'capable of increasing the *competitiveness of European industry*, improving the conditions of growth and raising the standard of living in the Community'.[53]

Traditional EU merger law was criticized[54] for the somewhat paradoxical treatment of the efficiency defence in European competition law:[55] efficiencies had to be analysed and used in the application of Article 81(3) EC, but an efficiency defence appeared to be foreclosed when two companies merged.

---

50   OJ 2004 C101/97, paras 48–72.
51   Council Regulation 139/2004 of 20 January 2004 on the control of concentrations between undertakings, OJ 2004 L24/1.
52   Guidelines on the assessment of horizontal mergers under the Council Regulation on the control of concentrations between undertakings, OJ 2004 C31/5.
53   Ibid., paras 76–84 (emphasis added).
54   It has also been argued that the formulation in Article 2(1)(b) appears to be rather odd: it seems to allow a defence relating to productive efficiencies only if there are no anticompetitive consequences. But if there are no such consequences, the merger has to be declared compatible with the common market anyway – and there is no need for the efficiency 'defence'. See Van den Bergh, 'Modern Industrial Organisation versus Old-fashioned European Competition Law', [1996] *ECLR* 75, 86.
55   Amato, *Antitrust and the Bounds of Power*, Oxford 1997, p. 80. *Cf. also* Whish, *supra* n. 21, at p. 155.

The Guidelines on horizontal mergers, by introducing the efficiency defence, obviously react to this kind of criticism. It is submitted that this criticism, however, has overstated the case. According to the fourth condition of Article 81(3) EC, the efficiency defence may only be applied if the companies concerned are not in a position to eliminate competition in respect of a substantial part of the products concerned. Article 81(3) EC thereby acknowledges that the ultimate aim of European competition law is to protect the competitive process, and that short-term (productive) efficiency gains may be outweighed by long-term losses resulting from the absence of competition.[56] In some contrast, according to Article 2(3) of the old Merger Regulation, a decision to declare a merger to be incompatible with the common market could only be taken if market dominance was created or strengthened. The argument could be made that, under such market conditions, we may no longer rely on the competitive process to work effectively. Accordingly, the much debated asymmetry[57] between Article 81(3) EC and the Merger Regulation is less obvious than has been claimed.

The introduction of the efficiency defence into European merger law by the Guidelines could easily be justified if under the new Merger Regulation of 2004 (ECMR) the relevant standard of 'significantly impeding effective competition' indeed meant what, at least at first sight, it seems to suggest. That is, that a merger may be declared to be incompatible with the common market even in cases where the merging companies will not yet attain a dominant position in the relevant market. Indeed, if Article 2(3) ECMR applies in situations where the competitive process may become weakened, but is still working in an effective manner, we have a case *comparable* to Article 81(3) EC, fourth condition, in which efficiencies may justify a merger. However, Recital 25 of the ECMR of 2004 explains the new 's.i.e.c.' test as applying (only) with regard to mergers in *oligopolistic market structures* where the test is meant to extend 'beyond the concept of dominance, *only* to the anti-competitive effects of a concentration resulting from the *non-coordinated* behaviour of undertakings which would not have a dominant position on the market concerned'. It is submitted that the application of the efficiency defence could make economic sense in this case, but we have to admit that the Guidelines in no way limit the efficiency defence to that setting:[58] the efficiency defence is applicable irrespective of the market power of the merged entities. In paragraph 84 of its Guidelines, the Commission states (correctly) that '[t]he incentive on the part

---

56   Commission, 'Guidelines on the application of Article 81 (3) of the Treaty', OJ 2004 C101/97, para. 105, referring to losses incurred by rent seeking, misallocation of resources, reduced innovation and higher prices.
57   But see Whish, *supra* n. 21, at p. 155.
58   Guidelines, *supra* n. 52, at paras 76–84.

of the merged entity to pass efficiency gains on to consumers is often related to the existence of competitive pressure from the remaining firms in the market and from potential entry'. The Commission then goes on to state that it will have to make sure that 'the claimed efficiencies are . . . likely . . . to be passed on, to a sufficient degree, to the consumer'. And it then concludes that '[i]t is highly unlikely that a merger leading to a market position *approaching that of a monopoly*, or leading to a similar level of market power, can be declared compatible with the common market'. The Guidelines on horizontal mergers (obviously on purpose) omit (in this respect) any reference to the traditional main test in European merger control, that is, the test of the creation or strengthening of the dominant position which the Merger Regulation of 2004 still uses as a decisive criterion.[59] We may conclude therefrom that the Commission also intends to apply the efficiency defence in cases where a dominant position is either gained or strengthened. What is missing in the Guidelines on horizontal mergers is a clear statement by the Commission that 'the protection of rivalry and the competitive process is given priority over potentially pro-competitive efficiency gains' – a statement that we find in the Guidelines on the application of Article 81(3) of the Treaty.[60]

Accordingly, an argument could be made that the Guidelines on horizontal mergers attempt to rewrite Article 2 ECMR without changing its wording. However, such an argument would overlook the fact that the Merger Regulation of 1989, in its Article 2(2)(3), contained the requirement that the creation or strengthening of the dominant position should *result* in *significantly impeding effective competition*. One could have argued that the latter requirement was more or less a statement of the consequences of the first, but the Court of First Instance, in more than one judgment,[61] made it clear that the application of Article 2(2)(3) required a two-stage test with the consequence that dominance alone should not suffice to block a merger. The old Merger Regulation therefore gave some leeway to the Commission to declare a merger compatible with the common market even in cases of market dominance, for example when the strengthening of dominance was only insubstantial or where the strengthening would be only temporary. In those cases, Article 2(1)(b) ECMR 1989, with its reference to productive (and dynamic) efficiencies, already gave a basis for efficiency considerations. The proviso contained

---

[59]   See Recital 26.
[60]   OJ 2004 C101/97, para. 105.
[61]   Case T-5/02 – *Tetra Laval v Commission*, judgment of 25 October 2002, [2002] ECR II-4381, para. 120. See also Case T-342/99 – *Airtours v Commission*, judgment of 6 June 2002, [2002] ECR II-2585, paras 58 and 82; Case T-310/01 – *Schneider Electric v Commission*, judgment of 22 October 2002, [2002] ECR II-4071, paras 321 and 380.

in Article 2(1)(b) 'and does not form an obstacle to competition' had to be read in the light of Article 2(2)(3) with its criterion of significantly impeding effective competition.

The introduction of an efficiency defence in the Guidelines on horizontal mergers finds its basis in Recital 29 of the ECMR of 2004, where it is stated that it is possible that the efficiencies of a merger 'counteract the effects on competition, and in particular the potential harm on consumers, . . . and that, as a consequence, the concentration would not significantly impede effective competition'. This statement is obviously based on the case law of the Court of First Instance, which represents a reasonable interpretation of the old Merger Regulation. It is submitted that this development in European merger law (which should not be attributed to the 'more economic approach' as such) opens the door to some *strategic* considerations by the Commission. Stressing the point that a merger may create productive and dynamic efficiencies, the Commission finds itself in a position to enhance the competitiveness of European industry by promoting European champions.

VII   CONCLUSION

(i)   We have argued that the Commission, from the 1970s on, has conceived of competition policy as an instrument complementary to its industrial policy, and that it has used its powers in the field of competition policy to ensure and increase the competitiveness of European industry. At the same time, the Commission has always stressed that competition is the best guarantee for competitiveness. As long as the Commission is duly guided by this insight, stressing the importance of the *competitive process*, the 'pro-active competition policy' seems to be on the right track. Although, as I have argued, a strategic competition policy may find its ultimate justification in Article 2 EC, the new legal framework for competition set up in the last five years gives only a restricted leeway for such a policy.

(ii) Enhancing European champions by the simple non-application of competition law will work in the field of *mergers*. However, the same result may ensue if the standards of proof[62] under Article 2 ECMR are set by the European Courts in such a manner that the Commission will only seldom have a chance to win a case[63] or that it will have to invest

---

[62]   See Bailey, 'Standard of Proof in EC Merger Proceedings; A Common Law Perspective', 40 *Common Market Law Review* (2003), p. 845.

[63]   With regard to 'convincing' (economic) evidence, see Case 12/03 P, *Tetra Laval v Commission*, judgment of 15 February 2005, paras 39–44 (especially with

so many human resources in a single merger case that a broad-scale enforcement will no longer be feasible.

(iii) As far as the application of Articles 81(1) and 81(3) EC is concerned, the direct applicability of Article 81(3) EC will restrict the margin of appreciation that the Commission has enjoyed up to now. Although the Commission may still be able to pursue strategic goals on the basis of Articles 9 and 10 of Regulation 1/2003, the concurrent jurisdiction of national courts will probably lead to an increased use of the preliminary reference procedure under Article 234 EC, and thereby to an increased juridification of the relevant criteria of Article 81(3) EC. In this regard, it is worth mentioning that the Guidelines on the application of Article 81(3) of the Treaty totally ignore (public policy oriented) justifications other than those listed in Article 81(3) EC, thereby rejecting a position that has been described as a 'broader approach' to Article 81(3) EC.[64] Indeed, the taking into account of the *Querschnittsklauseln* (Articles 6, 127(2), 152(1), 154(2), etc.)[65] might be possible for an administrative body which is attributed considerable discretion (or power of appraisal/margin of appreciation)[66] in the application of the relevant criteria. As from now on national courts will have to autonomously apply Article 81(3) EC, only legal (justiciable) and not political standards can be employed.[67] In the long run, as far as Article 81 EC is concerned, European competition law may become less policy-oriented and more rule-oriented, notwithstanding the competences of the Commission attributed to it by Articles 9 and 10 Regulation 1/2003, thus restricting the scope for any strategic competition policy to be pursued.

---

regard to future developments). For a brief analysis, see Seeliger, Grave, 'Neue Machtverteilung in Europas Fusionskontrolle', *Frankfurter Allgemeine Zeitung* No. 45, 23 February 2005, p. 23. See also the Order of the President of the Court of First Instance of 22 December 2004 in Case T-201/04 R, *Microsoft v Commmission*, paras 326 et seq. and 396 et seq.

64 Whish, *supra* n. 21, at p. 152.

65 For their relevance, see, e.g., Mestmäcker, Schweitzer, *supra* n. 7, § 3 paras 63–64 and § 13 paras 75–77. See also Jones, Sufrin, *EC Competition Law* (Oxford, 2001), p. 191; Gasse, *Die Bedeutung der Querschnittsklauseln für die Anwendung des Gemeinschaftskartellrechts* (Frankfurt am M., 2000).

66 For a discussion of that topic, see Bailey, 'Scope of Judicial Review under Article 81 EC', 41 *Common Market Law Review* (2004), pp. 1327, 1337; Monti, 'Article 81 EC and Public Policy', 39 *Common Market Law Review* (2002), p. 1057.

67 See Mestmäcker, Schweitzer, *supra* n. 7, § 13 para. 77.

3. Revision of the new Technology Transfer Block Exemption Regulation: convergence or capitulation?

Mark R. Patterson*

I INTRODUCTION

It is generally believed that European competition law is becoming both more similar to US antitrust law and more based on economics.[1] Indeed, former Commissioner Monti has stated that changes in both of these directions were goals when he led the Commission.[2] Professor Jones outlines some of these

---

*   Professor of Law, Fordham University School of Law, New York. I am grateful to Eleanor Fox, Mel Marquis, and the other participants at the First Ascola Workshop on Comparative Competition Law for helpful comments and to Nic Snow for valuable research assistance.
    [1]   See, e.g., Speech by Charles A. James, Assistant Attorney General, Antitrust Division, US Department of Justice, *Antitrust in the Early 21st Century: Core Values and Convergence*, US Mission to the European Union, Brussels, 15 May 2002, http://www.useu.be/Categories/Antitrust/May1502JamesAntitrust-Speech.html (discussing convergence of US and EC antitrust law); Commission Evaluation Report on the Transfer of Technology Block Exemption Regulation No. 240/96, COM(01) 786 final [hereinafter TTBE Report], at 5 ('The recent reforms of the EC competition rules in the field of vertical and horizontal agreements have signified a shift from a legalistic and form-based approach to a more economic and effects-based approach'), available at http://europa.eu.int/comm/competition/antitrust/-technology_transfer/en.pdf.
    [2]   Speech by Mario Monti, *The New Shape of European Competition Policy*, Competition Policy Research Center, Tokyo, Japan, 20 November 2003, http://jpn.cec.eu.int/home/speech_en_Speech202020November202003.php ('When I was appointed Competition Commissioner four years ago, one of my main objectives was an increased economic approach in the interpretation and enforcement of European competition rules.'); Speech by Mario Monti, Antitrust in the US and Europe: A History of Convergence, General Counsel Roundtable, American Bar Association, Washington, DC, 14 November 2001, http://europa.eu.int/rapid/start/cgi/guesten.ksh?p_action.gettxt=gt&doc=SPEECH/01/540%7C0%7CRAPID&lg=EN (referring to past EC–US convergence and stating that 'further efforts are needed and on both sides of the Atlantic we are deeply committed to this process'). In another speech, Commissioner Monti characterized the shifts toward US law and economics as one.

changes in his chapter, placing them in the context of his overall discussion of the evolution of US and EC competition law.[3]

My goal in these comments is much narrower: I will consider just one recent set of changes in European law. In April 2004, the Commission promulgated a new Technology Transfer Block Exemption Regulation (TTBER), with accompanying Guidelines.[4] The new TTBER relies to a greater extent than did the former TTBER on market share measures, and in this respect and others, it is said to be more based on economics.[5] Furthermore, the new TTBER is said to resemble more closely US antitrust law as it is applied to intellectual property licensing.[6]

The final versions of the TTBER and Guidelines incorporate significant changes from draft versions[7] that were offered for comments by the Commission, and it is the changes between the draft and final versions on

---

Speech by Mario Monti, *The New EU Policy on Technology Transfer Agreements*, Ecole des Mines, Paris, 16 January 2004 [hereinafter Monti TTBER Revision Speech] ('It only means that we will implement a similar general economic approach to all agreements under Article 81, underpinning the importance that economic arguments and considerations should have in a competition assessment and in line with the general competition policy approach of our main trading partners.').

    [3]   C. A. Jones, 'Foundations of competition policy in the EU and USA: Conflict, convergence, and beyond', this volume, Chapter 1.

    [4]   Commission Regulation 772/2004 on the application of Article 81(3) of the Treaty to categories of technology transfer agreements, OJ L 123/11 (2004) [hereinafter Final TTBER]; Commission Notice: Guidelines on the application of Article 81 of the EC Treaty to technology transfer agreements, OJ C 101/2 (2004) [hereinafter Final Guidelines].

    [5]   Monti TTBER Revision Speech (speaking about the revision of the TTBER and stating that 'we will implement a similar general economic approach to all agreements under Article 81').

    [6]   See, e.g., R. Gilbert, *Converging Doctrines? US and EU Antitrust Policy for the Licensing of Intellectual Property*, University of California, Berkeley, Competition Policy Working Paper No. CPC04-44, available at http://papers.ssrn.com/sol3/papers.cfm?abstract_id=527762, at 12 ('The TTBER and the accompanying guidelines go a long way toward harmonizing antitrust policy for licensing arrangements between the US and the European Union.'); P. Lowe, L. Peeperkorn, *Singing in Tune with Competition and Innovation: The New EU Competition Policy Towards Licensing* 26, Fordham Corporate Law Institute Thirty-first Annual Conference on International Antitrust Law & Policy (October 2004, 'The new TTBER and Guidelines bring about an important degree of convergence between EU and US competition policy towards licensing agreements.').

    [7]   Draft Commission Regulation on the Application of Article 81(3) of the Treaty to Categories of Technology Transfer Agreements, 2003 OJ (C 235) 11 [hereinafter Draft TTBER]; Draft Guidelines on the Application of Article 81 of the EC Treaty to Technology Transfer Agreements, 2003 OJ (C 235) 17 [hereinafter Draft Guidelines].

which I will focus.[8] The comments on the draft TTBER seem to have had considerable influence, with Commissioner Monti indicating that several of the changes were prompted by the comments.[9] The comments, in turn, relied frequently on claims that the changes they proposed would bring EC law into line with US law or would make the TTBER more economically supportable.[10]

I will suggest here that for some issues it is not clear that the changes from the draft to the final TTBER are economically justified. I will focus on three such issues: the selection of the time at which it should be determined whether firms are competitors, the treatment of field-of-use restrictions, and the treatment of reciprocal running royalties. I chose these issues because each was the subject of numerous comments that appeared to influence the Commission, yet the comments offered little in the way of economic support.

II DETERMINATION OF COMPETITOR STATUS

In the draft TTBER, firms were defined as 'competing undertakings' if they were actual competitors in the relevant technology market or if they were actual or potential competitors in the relevant product market.[11] Whether the firms were competing undertakings determined, in turn, which license restrictions were hardcore restrictions that would make the block exemption inapplicable. This reflected the general view of the regulations that restrictions between competitors are more dangerous than similar restrictions between non-competitors.

A number of commentators objected to this aspect of the regulation on the

---

[8]   My focus is actually even narrower, focusing on three of the particular changes adopted by the Commission. For a more comprehensive review of the changes, see E. Vollebregt, 'The Changes in the New Technology Transfer Block Exemption Compared to the Draft', 25 *ECLR* (2004), p. 660.

[9]   See *infra* text accompanying notes 14, 44, and 49.

[10]   See, e.g., Joint Comments of the American Bar Association's Section of Antitrust Law, Section of Business Law, Section of International Law and Practice and Section of Intellectual Property Law on Draft Commission Regulation on the Application of Article 81(3) of the EC Treaty to Categories of Technology Transfer Agreements and Draft Commission Notice on Guidelines on the Application of Article 81 to Technology Transfer Agreements 23 ('The Sections wish to point out that the treatment of vertical nonprice restrictions as hardcore infringements, albeit with enumerated exceptions, differs from the treatment of these license terms under US law, where a showing of adverse competitive effects is necessary for the condemnation of these terms.'), available at http://europa.eu.int/comm/competition/antitrust/technology_transfer_2/15_aba_part2_en.pdf [hereinafter ABA Comments]; *infra* text accompanying notes 30 and 40–43.

[11]   Draft TTBER, art. 1(h).

ground that the status of firms might change over time.[12] The specific concern of these commentators was that firms could enter into a license agreement when they were non-competitors but later become competitors. As a result, some license restrictions that were not hardcore restrictions at the time the firms entered into the license could later become hardcore restrictions, making the block exemption inapplicable.

Apparently in response to these comments,[13] the final TTBER was revised to apply the non-competitor list of hardcore restrictions '[w]here the undertakings party to the agreement are not competing undertakings at the time of the conclusion of the agreement but become competing undertakings afterwards.'[14] Moreover, the final TTBER provides that in those circumstances the non-competitor list 'shall apply for the full life of the agreement unless the agreement is subsequently amended in any material respect'.[15]

Despite the commentators' concerns and the Commission's response, the draft approach seems the correct one. If the firms are in fact competitors, the fact that they once were non-competitors seems no reason to apply a narrower list of hardcore restrictions. Indeed, in this case the Commission seems to have adopted an approach that the US antitrust agencies have rejected. The US agencies' Antitrust Guidelines for the Licensing of Intellectual Property state that '[t]he status of a licensing arrangement with respect to the safety zone may change over time'.[16] The fact that the parties may have made investments in reliance on their original status is handled in the US in a different way, as discussed below.[17]

Nor do the comments to which the Commission responded offer convincing justifications for treating competitors as non-competitors. On the contrary, consider the scenario suggested by GlaxoSmithKline:

Given that the draft TTBER requirements have to be met throughout the duration of

---

[12]   See, e.g., Pharmaceutical Research and Manufacturers of America, Comments on Proposed Changes to EU Technology Transfer Block Exemption Regulation 4, available at http://europa.eu.int/comm/competition/antitrust/technology_transfer_2/29_pharmaresearch_part2_en.pdf; GlaxoSmithKline Comments on the Draft Commission Regulation on the Application of Article 81(3) to Technology Transfer Agreements ('TTBER') 3, available at http://europa.eu.int/comm/competition/antitrust/technology_transfer_2/13_glaxo_en.pdf [hereinafter GlaxoSmithKline Comments].

[13]   Monti TTBER Revision Speech.

[14]   Ibid.

[15]   Final TTBER, art. 4(3).

[16]   US Department of Justice & Federal Trade Commission, Antitrust Guidelines for the Licensing of Intellectual Property § 4.3 (April 6, 1995) 4 Trade Reg. Rep. (CCH) § 13.132.

[17]   See *infra* text accompanying note 24.

the agreement, it is possible that an agreement, which started out as an agreement between non-competitors, could cross over at a later stage into being an agreement between competitors (e.g. where at the time of signing the agreement, one of the parties has an early stage potentially competing compound, which should not be taken into account because of the high attrition rates for pharmaceutical compounds, but which some years later becomes a viable product). . . . Should an agreement change from one between non-competitors to one between competitors, restrictions which were permitted under Art. 4 (2) could then become hardcore restrictions, making the whole agreement void and unenforceable.[18]

Suppose that in the GlaxoSmithKline example the license arrangement was a cross-license of technologies, and that the cross-license specified the customers to whom the parties could sell the products produced with the technologies. In that case, the agreement would be reciprocal, and the allocation of customers would be a hardcore restriction for competitors[19] but permissible for non-competitors so long as it didn't restrict passive sales.[20] Yet under the final regulation, the parties would be treated as non-competitors even after the early-stage compound became a viable product. The result would be that the parties' customer allocation would continue in place, assuming that the competitor market-share thresholds are satisfied.[21]

It is true that the customer allocation would presumably apply only to the technologies that were part of the original license, so that the agreement would not restrict the customer to which the party with the late-entering product could sell that product so long as it was made only with its own technology. But as the Commission itself pointed out in the Guidelines, it might choose not to do so:

Once the licensee has tooled up to use the licensor's technology to produce a given product, it may be costly to maintain a separate production line using

---

[18]   GlaxoSmithKline Comments, at 3.
[19]   Final TTBER, art. 4(1)(c).
[20]   Final TTBER, art. 4(2)(b).
[21]   Interestingly, the final TTBER explicitly addresses only one difference between the treatments of competitors and non-competitors: the hardcore list. Commentators also expressed concern about how a change in status would affect the market-share thresholds. See GlaxoSmithKline Comments, at 3 ('As a result of becoming an agreement between competitors, the permitted market share thresholds plummet and the agreement could easily no longer be within the safe harbour, because the combined share would be over 20%.'). The final TTBER appears not to address this concern. See Final Guidelines, para. 31. It is possible that article 8(2), which provides a two-year grace period when market shares that initially were within one of the article 3 thresholds subsequently exceed the threshold, could be read also to preserve non-competitor market share status for two years when parties become competitors, but that does not appear to be a natural reading of that provision.

another technology in order to serve customers covered by the restrictions. Moreover, given the anti-competitive potential of the restraint the licensee may have little incentive to produce under his own technology.[22]

Alternatively, of course, the party with the early-stage product might simply cease development of that product upon entering into the license agreement. That would mean that the parties would remain non-competitors in fact, but it would not eliminate the anticompetitive harm.

Moreover, this effect seems likely to increase the incentive for parties to enter into agreements when they are non-competitors, in anticipation of the time at which they will become competitors. For example, as a patent approaches the end of its term, the patentee and a potential competitor might find it desirable to enter into an agreement restricting competition between them. Under the final TTBER, it appears that such an agreement would be treated as one between non-competitors. Moreover, the parties would have an incentive to make the term of their agreement quite long, because the TTBER accords them non-competitor treatment for the life of the agreement.

One might question whether these scenarios are really plausible. But similar problems have arisen in a number of US cases involving producers of brand-name and generic drugs. In these cases, the manufacturers of the brand-name drugs have entered into agreements with potential generic competitors that appear intended to keep the generics off the market. The point here is not that these agreements would be permissible under the TTBER – they probably would not be[23] – but that potential competitors can indeed have incentives to enter into agreements that will prevent actual competition between them. The final TTBER may have facilitated the ability to enter into such agreements.

None of this is to deny that the parties to a license agreement could have valid reasons for complaint if their status changed to that of competitors during the course of the agreement. In such instances, the parties may in fact have relied on their non-competitor status in entering into the agreement. But a more reasonable approach would seem to be that of the US agencies' Antitrust Guidelines for Collaborations Among Competitors:

> The Agencies assess the competitive effects of a relevant agreement as of the time of possible harm to competition, whether at formation of the collaboration or at a later time, as appropriate. However, an assessment after a collaboration has been formed is sensitive to the reasonable expectations of participants whose significant

---

22   Final Guidelines, para. 85.
23   See Final TTBER art. 5(2).

sunk cost investments in reliance on the relevant agreement were made before it became anticompetitive.[24]

To some extent, perhaps, the structure of the TTBER does not lend itself to this sort of flexible treatment, because the TTBER is a statement of the law, not just a statement of enforcement intentions, like the US guidelines. Moreover, as is discussed below, because the Commission has made clear that hardcore restrictions will be treated harshly, and has left itself little other option for taking a license out of the block exemption, the TTBER is not well suited to allowing the Commission the sort of flexibility provided by the US guidelines.

III   EXCLUSION OF FIELD-OF-USE RESTRICTIONS FROM THE LIST OF HARDCORE RESTRAINTS

The final version of the TTBER exempts field-of-use restrictions, even recip-rocal ones, within the TTBER's market-share thresholds, so long as the license does not restrict the licensor's own use of the technology.[25] The draft exemp-tion was narrower, in that all reciprocal field-of-use restrictions between competitors were hardcore restraints.[26] Comments, including those from the American Bar Association's Section of Antitrust Law, argued that all field-of-use restrictions should be block exempted, and the Commission softened its position. Commissioner Monti explained the justification for exempting reci-procal restrictions between competitors:

> On the one hand such a situation of reciprocal field of use restrictions, where both parties are restricted in the use of the other party's technology, creates the distinct risk of market sharing. However, this risk is less prominent in case of field of use restrictions than with reciprocal territorial or customer restrictions, as it is less likely that competitors withdraw completely from a particular product market.[27]

---

[24]   Federal Trade Commission & US Department of Justice, Antitrust Guidelines for Collaborations Among Competitors § 2.4 (2000).

[25]   The Guidelines indicate that *exclusive* reciprocal field-of-use licenses between competitors (i.e., those that restrict the licensor's own right to use the tech-nology) may be viewed as market allocations, which are hardcore restrictions under article 4(1)(c). See Final Guidelines, para. 181.

[26]   Draft TTBER, art. 4(c). Article 4(c) actually declared to be a hardcore restric-tion 'the allocation of markets or customers', and did not refer to field-of-use restric-tions explicitly. But article 4(c)(i) stated that non-reciprocal field-of-use restrictions were not to be included in that category, indicating that reciprocal field-of-use restric-tions *were* within article 4(c).

[27]   Monti TTBER Revision Speech.

It is unclear on what basis the Commission reached this conclusion. Although the ABA Comments offer a variety of theoretical justifications for allowing field-of-use restrictions, none of those justifications is focused specifically on reciprocal field-of-use licenses.[28] Therefore, they do not address the question of whether, for such reciprocal licenses, the dangers to competition may outweigh the benefits for innovation. This question is presented even more clearly in that the only cases that the ABA Comments cite are ones in which the courts concluded that such restrictions were used for allocating markets.[29]

The ABA Comments do offer this purportedly procompetitive example:

> For example, manufacturer A may license manufacturer B technology for use in making parts for B's products, but not to make parts for A's products, while B licenses A other technology with the restriction that A not use the technology to make parts for B's products; it is difficult to discern the competitive harm that may result from such restrictions, whereas the pro-competitive benefits are apparent.[30]

Contrary to the ABA's claim, it is quite easy to imagine anticompetitive harm from such an agreement. Suppose that A's technology provides more of an advantage than B's.[31] In the absence of the cross-license, it seems likely that A's advantage would spur competition, at least in producing parts for B's products, where A's technological advantage could help counter B's natural advantage as the original manufacturer. With the cross-license, though, it seems more likely that both A and B would confine their activities to the production of parts for their own products. That is, it seems likely that the result would be similar to that of exclusive reciprocal licenses, which the Guidelines indicate would be treated as hardcore restrictions.[32] Significantly,

---

[28]   See ABA Comments, *supra* n. 10, at 18–22.

[29]   See ABA Comments, *supra* n. 10, at 18–20 (citing *United States v. Crown Zellerbach Corp.*, 141 F. Supp. 118 (N.D. Ill. 1956); *Cutter Laboratories, Inc. v. Lyophile-Cryochem Corp.*, 179 F.2d 80, 92 (9th Cir. 1949); *Racal/Decca*, OJ L43/27 (1989)).

[30]   ABA Comments, *supra* n. 10, at 21 n. 36.

[31]   On this point, the ABA Comments state that '[i]n the context of reciprocal licensing, field-of-use licensing is much more commonly used when one party to the license agreement has a broader or stronger intellectual property portfolio than the other' ABA Comments, *supra* n. 10 at 19.

[32]   See Final Guidelines, para. 181; cf. *supra* text accompanying n. 21 (Final Guidelines discussion of incentives). Carl Shapiro, in his comments on the draft TTBER, rightly points out that nothing in the cross-license itself explicitly limits competition in this way. Carl Shapiro, EU Technology Transfer Draft Guidelines: Economic Analysis and Suggestions for Revisions, available at http://europa.eu.int/comm/competition/antitrust/technology_transfer_2/16_shapiro_en.pdf. The point is

this is exactly the result that Commissioner Monti cited as unlikely in explaining the inclusion of reciprocal field-of-use restrictions in the block exemption.[33]

As noted above, the cases cited in the ABA Comments were all ones in which the court found reciprocal field-of-use licenses illegal. This suggests that, at least in the US, from which most of these cases came, the legality of such arrangements is not clear. To be sure, the absence from the comments of cases upholding reciprocal field-of-use restrictions does not indicate that such instances do not exist. It might just be that procompetitive field-of-use restrictions are not challenged.

But it is worth noting that the law in the US does not encourage such challenges, even in cases in which the uses of field-of-use licenses are questionable. The Federal Circuit Court of Appeals, which in the US decides most patent cases, has said that field-of-use restrictions, so long as they 'relate[] to subject matter within the scope of the patent claims', are not subject to challenge.[34] This patent-law rule has been interpreted quite expansively,[35] so in recent years patent law has effectively foreclosed antitrust challenges to field-of-use licenses. As a result, to draw conclusions from US experience, or comments based on US experience, is problematic.

Moreover, a report[36] prepared for the Commission to assist in its review of the TTBER appears to recommend against the Commission's change. The view expressed in this report is that it is critical to determine whether the

---

not, though, that the license by its terms prevents such competition, but that its effect may make it less likely. Thus, although Shapiro may be correct that hardcore treatment is inappropriate for these arrangements if the Commission treats hardcore restraints as akin to *per se* illegal ones, it seems that it would also be inappropriate to exempt them. See *infra* text accompanying notes 52–59.

[33]   See *supra* text accompanying n. 27.

[34]   *Mallinckrodt, Inc. v. Medipart, Inc.*, 976 F.2d 700, 708 (Fed. Cir. 1992).

[35]   The most recent, and extreme, example was *Pioneer Hi-Bred International, Inc. v. Ottawa Plant Food, Inc.*, 283 F. Supp. 2d 1018 (N.D. Iowa 2003). In that case, Pioneer brought a patent infringement suit against resellers of its seed corn, who had purchased the corn from Pioneer's authorized dealers. In the court's view, Pioneer's initial sale of the corn to its dealers had been conditional, because 'its bag label restricted the uses for which the seed corn was sold to production of grain or forage'. Ibid. at 1034. Because the sale was conditional, the court said, it did not exhaust Pioneer's rights. And although the defendant's resales of the corn were in fact to farmers for the production of grain or forage, the court held that because the condition allowed only production for grain and forage, the 'license' granted by Pioneer did not include the right to resell. The result of this conclusion is that Pioneer was permitted to restrict its dealers to selling only to farmers, or to other authorized dealers.

[36]   Charles River Associates Ltd., *Report on Multiparty Licensing* (22 April 2003, available at http://europe.eu.int/comm/competition/antitrust/legislation/multiparty_licensing).

cross-licensed technologies are complements or substitutes. Because that determination is difficult, though, the report recommends that in general only zero-royalty, no-restriction cross-licenses should be permitted: 'Cross licences with royalties and other restrictions . . . should be allowed only if it can be reasonably proven that the technologies are complements.'[37] The Commission's change incorporated no such requirement.

IV EXCLUSION OF RECIPROCAL RUNNING ROYALTIES FROM THE LIST OF HARDCORE RESTRAINTS

The third example of a change is a change in the Guidelines only. The draft Guidelines were skeptical of reciprocal running royalties:

> Where competitors conclude an agreement providing for cross licensing and recip-rocal royalty payments based on the sales of the final product, the Commission will treat the arrangement as price fixing where the agreement does not lead to a signif-icant integration of complementary technologies. In the absence thereof the agree-ment is devoid of any pro-competitive purpose and does not constitute a bona fide licensing agreement.[38]

The approach described in the final Guidelines is quite different:

> Competitors can therefore use cross licensing with reciprocal running royalties as a means of co-ordinating prices on downstream product markets. However, the Commission will only treat cross licences with reciprocal running royalties as price fixing where the agreement is devoid of any pro-competitive purpose and therefore does not constitute a bona fide licensing arrangement.[39]

Once again, this change was advocated by the ABA Comments. They offer two basic procompetitive justifications for running royalties: valuation and

---

[37]   Ibid. at 75. The report appears to advocate this approach for all reciprocal licensing arrangements even though it also advocates a market-share-based safety zone, though it is not entirely clear on this point. On the one hand, it appears to advo-cate that the safety zone should apply even to cross-licensing arrangements. See ibid. at 43 (stating that the safety zone 'will allow firms with low markets shares [sic] to engage in exchanges and pooling of technology'). But the report also seems to reject a safety zone for royalty-based cross-licenses of substitute technologies. See ibid. at 74, 80 (proposing that cross-licenses be permissible only when they are of complementary technologies, involve zero royalties, or are for future technologies and satisfy certain other criteria).

[38]   Draft Guidelines, para. 77.

[39]   Final Guidelines, para. 80 (footnote omitted).

risk.[40] However, these two justifications are actually one. With regard to valuation, the ABA Comments state that '[t]he value of a license to a particular patent may depend on the extent to which the patented technology will be used over the life of the license, which may be highly uncertain', a problem that running royalties can solve through metering.[41] But uncertainty in valuation is what constitutes risk. This is made clear in the comments' explanation of risk allocation: 'A licensee may not be willing to pay a large lump sum royalty because of uncertainty as to the value of the technology or the prospects for the success of its product.'[42] That is, risk is based on uncertainty of valuation, so there is really only one justification offered.[43]

Nevertheless, the Commission repeats these 'two' justifications in support of its change:

> While recognizing that running royalties can be used for that purpose, it is now stressed in the revised guidelines that in most situations running royalties are a legitimate and efficient practice to determine the value of the license and a way to share risk between the parties. As you will see, we have taken account of this justified criticism and limit the hardcore treatment to running royalties used in cartels disguised as license agreements.[44]

Of course, the fact that there is really one justification, rather than two, for running royalties, does not mean that the single justification is not a perfectly valid one. But the justification as offered applies to running royalties generally, not particularly to reciprocal running royalties. Whether the additional anticompetitive danger of reciprocal running royalties is outweighed by the potential benefits of running royalties is not clear.

Moreover, the risk justification assumes that the patents in the cross-licensing situation at issue truly involve innovation for which a precisely calibrated and risk-sensitive incentive is required. This may not be the case in one of the more commonly cited instances of cross-licensing: the semiconductor industry. In that industry, empirical research suggests that patentees are not necessarily seeking returns on their particular inventions, but are often patenting in order to produce bargaining chips for cross-licensing negotiations.[45] In such

---

40   ABA Comments, *supra* note 10, at 12–14. The ABA also points to the ability to finance payments over time, but given the availability of loans, this is presumably a question of risk as well.

41   Ibid.

42   Ibid.

43   The ABA does acknowledge this to some extent, calling them 'related' reasons. ABA Comments, *supra* n. 10, at 13.

44   Monti TTBER Revision Speech.

45   W. M. Cohen et al., *Protecting Their Intellectual Assets: Appropriability Conditions and Why U.S. Manufacturing Firms Patent (or Not)*, NBER Working Paper

cases, it is not clear that valuation of the individual patents is even an issue that is a focus of the negotiations.

Interestingly, though, a recent article suggests that reciprocal running royalties may in fact be justifiable in certain circumstances. This article, by Stephen Maurer and Suzanne Scotchmer, investigates the advantages of, and need for, particular licensing arrangements.[46] One of the circumstances they consider is that of blocking basic and improvement patents. On the assumption that the goal of antitrust rules in the licensing context should be to allow the two patent owners to make the same profit as if one of them owned the patent – a goal they term profit-neutrality – they conclude that, with certain assumptions, reciprocal running royalties meet that goal. Their analysis applies specifically to *reciprocal* running royalties, unlike the justifications offered by the ABA Comments and apparently accepted by the Commission, but it is not mentioned by them.

In fact, the Commission provides no means for determining when reciprocal running royalties meet the stated condition that they be 'devoid of any procompetitive purpose'. Presumably the valuation-uncertainty justification will always be present, so it seems that there will always, or almost always, be *some* procompetitive justification. Perhaps the Commission proposes to challenge reciprocal running royalties where it concludes that there is little or no valuation risk, though it has not made that criterion explicit. Or perhaps the Commission might pursue a case, despite the Guidelines, even where a procompetitive justification is present, as long as the anticompetitive effects outweigh the procompetitive ones.

Aside from the absence of any specificity in the Guidelines, it also worth noting that once again, the multi-party licensing report prepared for the Commission makes a recommendation contrary to the Commission's ultimate position. Instead of reciprocal running royalties, the report recommends one-way payments: 'For example, rather than firm A paying firm B €10, and firm B paying A €8, A should pay B €2.'[47] Although the report notes that '[f]or this to work, it will need to be the case that there is some predictable relationship

---

7552 (February 2000); B. H. Hall, R. M. Ham, *The Patent Paradox Revisited: Determinants of Patenting in the U.S. Semiconductor Industry, 1980–94*, NBER Working Paper No. 7062 (May 1999); A. Jaffe, *The U.S. Patent System in Transition: Policy Innovation and the Innovation Process*, NBER Working Paper 7280, http://www.nber.org/papers/w7280. Interestingly, several of these articles have been cited by Luc Peeperkorn, who was one of the Commission officials responsible for the TTBER. See Peeperkorn, *IP Licenses and Competition Rules: Striking the Right Balance* 3–4, Ecole des Mines, Paris, 15–16 January 2004.

[46]   S. M. Maurer, S. Scotchmer, *Profit Neutrality in Licensing: The Boundary Between Antitrust Law and Patent Law*, NBER Working Paper 10546 (June 2004).

[47]   Ibid. at 76.

between sales and the payments that need to be exchanged',[48] such circumstances will sometimes be present, yet the Commission does not refer to the possibility of using that as an evaluative test.

V THE BURDEN OF PERSUASION

It is unclear what standard the Commission applied in making these three changes to the TTBER. In speaking about the revisions, then-Commissioner Monti said only that '[w]e have carefully read and analyzed all comments and have made substantial revisions to the draft proposals'.[49] This does not, however, indicate how persuasive the comments were required to be in order to prompt a change from the draft.

The question of the burden of persuasion is especially important given the Commission's characterization of hardcore restraints. The Commission stated that it classified restrictions as hardcore restrictions under the TTBER 'based on the nature of the restriction and experience showing that such restrictions are almost always anticompetitive'.[50] That is, the Commission treats hardcore restraints as presumptively illegal.[51]

In contrast, the standard for block exemption under Article 81(3) requires a strong showing of procompetitive effect. In the final Guidelines, the Commission restates this standard:

> [T]he agreements give rise to economic efficiencies, that the restrictions contained in the agreements are indispensable to the attainment of these efficiencies, that consumers within the affected markets receive a fair share of the efficiency gains and that the agreements do not afford the undertakings concerned the possibility of eliminating competition in respect of a substantial part of the products in question.[52]

These two standards yield a dramatic difference in legal treatment, particularly when the parties have low market shares (see Table 3.1):

Table 3.1   Impact of characterization as hardcore restraint under TTBER

	not hardcore restraint	hardcore restraint
below market-share threshold	exempt	almost always anticompetitive
above market-share threshold	case-by-case analysis	almost always anticompetitive

---

48   Ibid.
49   Monti TTBER Revision Speech.
50   Final Guidelines, para. 74.
51   Final Guidelines, para. 18.
52   Final Guidelines, para. 35.

All three of the changes discussed above had the effect, for parties with small market shares, of moving certain of their licensing arrangements from treatment as 'almost always anticompetitive' to exempt. Reciprocal (non-exclusive) field-of-use restrictions were removed from the hardcore list. The treatment of some competitors in fact was changed to that of non-competitors, thus resulting in the removal of some restraints from the hardcore category. And the Commission apparently determined to treat few or no reciprocal running royalty arrangements as price-fixing, thus removing them from the hardcore list as well.

As discussed above, the comments do not offer particularly compelling arguments for these dramatic changes. Indeed, even some of the comments that objected to the draft's treatment of these issues did not argue for exemption, but only for case-by-case analysis:

> Moreover, the guidelines confusingly provide an effects-based analysis for several of the hardcore restrictions, including reciprocal field of use provisions and running royalties in cross-licences between competitors. If the Commission deems an effects-based analysis appropriate for these provisions (which it is submitted is the correct approach), then they should be removed from the hardcore list. Otherwise, the mere labelling of these provisions as hardcore will deter businesses and their advisers from even considering including these types of provisions in licence agreements.[53]

In Carl Shapiro's thoughtful comments to the Commission, he focused specifically on the harsh treatment for hardcore restraints described in the Guidelines in advocating an individualized assessment for the restraints discussed above.[54]

---

[53]   Response of Ashurst Morris Crisp to the Commission's consultation in connection with the Proposed Technology Transfer Block Exemption Regulation and Guidelines, para. 1.13, available at http://europa.eu.int/comm/competition/antitrust/technology_transfer_2/39_ashurst_en.pdf. The problem is not one of 'mere labeling'. Although the Commission states that there is no presumption that agreements falling outside the block exemption will be prohibited by article 81(1), it appears that this is so only for agreements that fail to satisfy the terms of the exemption by falling outside the market-share thresholds. The Commission states specifically that 'when agreements contain hardcore restrictions of competition . . . it can normally be presumed that they are prohibited by Article 81'. See Final Guidelines, para. 37. See also Lowe, Peeperkorn, *supra* n. 6, at 25.

[54]   Shapiro, *supra* note 32, at 9–10; see also R. Gilbert, *Converging Doctrines?: US and EU Antitrust Policy for the Licensing of Intellectual Property*, Competition Policy Center Working Paper No. CPC04-44, University of California, Berkeley (2004) ('Including these restrictions in the hardcore list could be an acceptable compromise if the Commission were prepared to act flexibly to consider individual transactions and exempt hardcore restrictions when there are clear benefits.').

Of course, the commentators might have been advocating a case-by-case analysis only where the parties involved have market shares exceeding the threshold. In this context, it seems entirely reasonable for commentators to have objected to the inclusion of ambiguous practices in the hardcore list,[55] because these practices do not seem so clearly anticompetitive that they satisfy the Commission's own hardcore standard. But if the parties have low market shares, removing the practices from the hardcore categorization makes them exempt, and it is not clear that they satisfy the requirements of article 81(3), either. Indeed, the most that the same commentators say is that they 'believe that experience with these practices shows that they tend to enhance competition more often than they lead to competitive harm'.[56] That is not the article 81(3) standard.

Nor is the Commission's adoption of an exempt-condemned dichotomy for low-market-share restraints the approach taken in the US. Table 3.1 can be compared to the approach of the US IP Guidelines.

It might appear that the US approach as represented in the table differs little from the Commission's, but there are key differences.[57] First, although the 'facially anticompetitive' label plays a structural role somewhat similar to the hardcore restraint categories in the TTBER, the US label is more flexible. For example, with regard to reciprocal arrangements like those

---

[55]   For example, the ABA Comments say of the field-of-use license restrictions and running royalties discussed above that they 'cannot be said to have the restriction of competition as their normal object, and thus would appear not to merit the hardcore categorization as a matter of both sound competition policy and existing Community law'. ABA Comments, *supra* n. 10, at 11 n. 16. Some of the comments seem to assume, however, that this result is a product of EC law, not of the Commission's definition of a hardcore restraint:

[T]he Court of First Instance has held that agreements that do not have the restriction of competition as their purpose and aim may be found to infringe Article 81(1) only if a detailed market analysis shows that they have an anticompetitive effect. *European Night Services v. Commission*, Case T-374/94 at ¶ 136; *Delimitis v. Henninger Bräu AG*, Case C-234/89. Common licensing practices such as field-of-use license grants and running royalties cannot be said to have the restriction of competition as their normal object, and thus would appear not to merit the hardcore categorization as a matter of both sound competition policy and existing Community law.

Ibid. It is not clear that 'hardcore categorization' in fact has any status under Community case law.

[56]   ABA Comments, *supra* n. 10, at 11.

[57]   The differences discussed here relate to the basic nature of the US guidelines. There are also specific differences, such as the provision in the US Guidelines note that the applicability of the 'safety zone' may change over time. This presumably means that if the market shares of the parties increase, their license may come under scrutiny, even if the parties' shares were small when they entered into the license agreement.

Table 3.2   Impact of characterization as 'facially anticompetitive' under US
*   IP guidelines*

	restraint is not 'facially anticompetitive'	restraint is 'facially anticompetitive'
below market-share threshold or number-of-technologies test	agencies will not challenge '[a]bsent extraordinary circumstances'	*per se* or 'quick look' analysis
above market-share threshold or number-of-technologies test	rule of reason analysis	*per se* or 'quick look' analysis

discussed above, the agencies state that '[w]hen cross-licensing or pooling arrangements are mechanisms to accomplish naked price fixing or market division, they are subject to challenge under the per se rule'.[58] The US agencies therefore would not be precluded from challenging reciprocal field-of-use licenses or reciprocal running royalties as 'facially anticompetitive' in appropriate cases.

Second, and perhaps relatedly, although the US agencies state that they would not usually challenge low-market-share agreements that are not 'facially anticompetitive', they do state that challenge is possible in 'extraordinary circumstances'. This simply adds to the agencies' flexibility, even beyond that inherent in the 'facially anticompetitive' label. Perhaps the Commission could use the TTBER's Article 6 withdrawal provision to accomplish the same purpose, but that seems unlikely. Both Article 6 itself and the Guidelines' discussion of it focus on specific situations in which the article might be applied, and the fact that the Commission revised the TTBER to make certain practices exempt would make it difficult for the Commission to subsequently challenge the same practices.

Finally, and importantly, the US guidelines are merely a statement of the US agencies' enforcement policy, not a statement of law. Private parties are free to bring challenges to license restrictions, and courts are free to condemn them, despite the guidelines. To be sure, cases challenging agreements between parties with low market shares, if assessed under the rule of reason, are very unlikely to be condemned, and may be dismissed on summary judgment. On the other hand, there is in fact no requirement in the US of a significant market share for condemnation of an agreement under the rule of reason.[59] In the US, actual anticompetitive effects can be proof of market power, so agreements can be condemned even when the parties' shares are small.

---

[58]   US IP Guidelines § 5.5.
[59]   See M. R. Patterson, 'The Role of Power in the Rule of Reason', 68 *Antitrust LJ* (2000), p. 429.

To some extent, the source of the Commission's approach may derive from the 'gray list' provision in the former TTBER. In the former TTBER, the 'gray' license restrictions were those that were not block exempted yet were not hardcore restrictions; these restrictions could be notified to the Commission, and were then exempted if the Commission did not object.[60] In its evaluation report on the former TTBER, the Commission stated that 'it is clear that also the opposition procedure will have to be abolished and that the "grey" clauses must either be covered by the block exemption or treated as hardcore.'[61]

This seems the wrong approach, at least as the hardcore list is currently described. The only gain from the Commission's description of the hardcore restraints as presumptively anticompetitive – or 'almost always anticompetitive' – is that it perhaps deters some parties from using such restraints. That same guidance could presumably be provided simply by describing which restraints the Commission believes are presumptively anticompetitive. Then the 'hardcore' list could simply mean what it means formally, that such restraints are not exempted, and the Commission would not feel compelled to exempt competitively ambiguous practices to keep them off the hardcore list.

The one advantage of eliminating case-by-case analysis would appear to be certainty. Certainty does appear to have been a goal of the Commission in its revision of the TTBER. In announcing the change to determination of competitor status, Commissioner Monti said the change would 'seriously improve the level of legal certainty'.[62] One wonders, though, to what extent this is true where legal treatment depends on market share thresholds.[63] And one wonders also how much certainty is gained over the exemption provided

---

[60]   Commission Regulation (EC) No 240/96 of 31 January 1996 on the application of Article 85(3) of the Treaty to certain categories of technology transfer agreements, OJ L 31/2 (1996), art. 4.

[61]   Evaluation Report, para. 1(7). P. Lowe, L. Peeperkorn, *supra* n. 6, have said that '[b]y doing away with the white and grey lists of the 1996 Regulation, the straitjacket effect is avoided: whatever is not explicitly excluded from the block exemption is now exempted'. That actually describes only a re-fashioning, not a removal, of the straitjacket.

[62]   Monti TTBER Revision Speech.

[63]   See F. Fine, *New EU Rules for Technology Licensing: A Kinder Gentler Straitjacket?*, PLI Tenth Annual Institute for Intellectual Property Law (Sept. 2004); Pfizer Inc., Comments on Draft Commission Regulation on the Application of Article 81(3) to Categories of Technology Transfer Agreements and the Draft Commission Notice on Guidelines on the Application of Article 81 to Technology Transfer Agreements, available at http://europa.eu.int/comm/competition/antitrust/technology_transfer_2/2_pfizer_en.pdf (observing that '[f]ew, if any, US antitrust lawyers find [the analogous market-share-based safety zone in the US IP Guidelines] to be particularly useful').

by the *de minimis* notice, which already exempted low-market-share agreements, albeit at somewhat lower thresholds.[64]

VI CONCLUSION

Ultimately, then, the changes from the draft TTBER to the final version are neither clearly supported by economics nor in line with US policy. That is not to say that the new TTBER is not an improvement on the former one. The greater focus on economics and the somewhat less rigid structure are no doubt improvements.[65] But the changes from the draft version appear to capitulate to complaining commenters rather than to respond to convincing economic arguments.

One wonders, given this capitulation to industry commenters, whether the Commission might have been responding not so much to the particular comments, but to its reputation for being more harsh than the US on intellectual property owners.[66] In introducing the changes, Commissioner Monti said that the final TTBER was a 'regulation that will allow companies to do much more than ever before'.[67] That is no doubt true; whether it is desirable remains to be seen.

---

[64] Commission Notice on agreements of minor importance which do not appreciably restrict competition under Article 81(1) of the Treaty establishing the European Community (*de minimis*), OJ C 368/07 (2001).

[65] For a contrary view, see Fine, *supra* n. 63.

[66] See, e.g., Coudert Brothers, *Pitfalls in Intellectual Property Licensing in the European Union*, http://library.lp.findlaw.com/articles/file/00324/002645/title/Subject/topic/Antitrust%20and%20Trade%20Regulation_Vertical%20Restraints/filename/antitrustandtraderegulation_2_247 (1999) ('US companies licensing their intellectual property – patents, copyrights or confidential know-how ("IP") – for use in the European Union ("EU") need to be aware that the EU is not as receptive as the US to restraints in IP licenses or to simple refusals to license.')

[67] Monti TTBER Revision Speech.

4. The evolution of European competition law and the Italian Autorità Garante della Concorrenza e del Mercato

Giuseppe Tesauro*

I INTRODUCTION

The two turning points in the recent evolution of competition law are clearly the reform of the enforcement system of the Community law regarding agreements and abuse of dominant positions (the so-called modernization), and the reform concerning mergers. The modernization reform significantly affects the relationship between national and European enforcers of European law; both reforms have a bearing on the relationship between national and European competition laws. The merger reform also deals with a substantive issue, namely the standard of evaluation.

I would like to briefly recall the main characteristics of both reforms, from the perspective of national competition authorities (NCAs), and to underline some critical points. I will then make a few concluding remarks specifically focused on the impact of the reforms on the activity of the Italian Antitrust Authority.

II THE MODERNIZATION REFORM

Regulation 1/2003 sets out an extremely innovative reform of the enforcement system of Community rules relating to agreements and the abuse of a dominant position. The aim of the reform is to enable the Commission to concentrate on the most important cases and to implement a significant decentralization of the application of European competition law.

The four qualifying points of the reform are: the reduction of the enforcement

---

*   Presidente Autorità Garante della Concorrenza e del Mercato (retired), Professor at Università La Sapienza, Roma. The format of a free speech has been maintained.

activity of the Commission; the duty of national authorities and judges to apply Articles 81 and 82 EC; the relationship between national laws and European competition law; and the enforcement activity of NCAs.

1   The Reduction of the Enforcement Activity of the Commission

The reform introduces a *legal exception system* for the application of Article 81(3) EC, according to which agreements restricting competition caught by Article 81(1) are valid without a prior decision to that effect, provided they satisfy the conditions laid down in Art. 81(3). This is aimed at simplifying and reducing the administrative burden of the current notification system and prior authorization of agreements, decisions and practices prohibited under Article 81(1). The final goal is to allow the Commission to act more effectively and to allocate its resources better, concentrating on hard core cartels and other infractions with a significant Community interest.

To this end, Regulation 1/2003 significantly extends the tasks and powers of the Commission. Of great importance is, obviously, the power to adopt a decision imposing structural remedies to curb infringements. In addition, the power to adopt interim measures has been officially recognized. Moreover, the Commission can accept commitments and make them binding on the undertakings and, when the Community public interest so requires, it may act on its own motion to assess the inapplicability of Articles 81 and 82 to certain cases.

2   The Duty of National Authorities and Judges to apply Articles 81 and 82

The second basic feature of the reform is the *decentralized application* of Articles 81 and 82. In fact, the transition from an authorization regime to a legal exception regime makes it possible to depart from the previous monopoly held by the Commission in regard of the application of Article 81(3). This innovation is aimed at removing the main obstacle to a wider, more active involvement of national judges and competition authorities in the enforcement of Community law on restrictive agreements and concerted practices. In this regard, Article 3 of the Regulation is of particular importance, since it *requires* national judges and competition authorities to apply Community law to practices which may affect trade between Member States.

The fact that NCAs apply the same set of rules – Articles 81 and 82 – brings about one of the main innovations of Regulation 1/2003, the *horizontal interconnection* of national enforcement systems. Indeed, a network of authorities, all competent to apply European competition law, has been established. In this respect, the traditional limitation of the activity of national authorities within the national boundaries is superseded by the theoretical possibility that each authority may proceed against an infraction of European law, including those committed outside its own territory.

For this reason, Regulation 1/2003 regulates the interaction between the various enforcement centres and provides rules to determine the 'best placed' authority to intervene. In addition, NCAs may cooperate within the network by exchanging information and providing other forms of assistance in the conduct of investigations. Furthermore, the functioning of the network is ensured through mechanisms of *reciprocal control*, under the strict supervision of the Commission, to which I will return in a minute.

3 The Relationship between National Laws and European Competition Law

At the same time, Article 3 of Regulation 1/2003 introduces *de facto* the *exclusive* application of European competition law to agreements falling within the sphere of application of Article 81. In fact, Article 3(2) sets a *convergence rule*, providing that national authorities and judges may not under national law consider restrictive agreements to be illegal whenever they are lawful under Community law. This results in a codification, in a more extensive and radical form, of the *Walt Wilhelm*[1] principle, according to which agreements proscribed under European law should not be allowed under national law.

4 The Enforcement Activity of NCAs

Given the importance of their role as the main enforcers of European competition law, the powers and activities of the NCAs are subject to an extensive discipline.

Article 5 of Regulation 1/2003 introduces a sort of harmonization of the powers of NCAs when applying European law. It declares that NCAs should have the power to make a number of decisions, including those imposing interim measures and those accepting commitments offered by the parties.

Indeed, in order for the Commission not to have to proceed against a given infraction, it is essential that the national authorities are as effective as the Commission would have been. By the same token, when a national authority declines to exercise its competence in order to leave the enforcement to the best placed authority, it should be able to rely on the fact that the latter is entrusted with adequate enforcement powers.

In addition, Article 5 prescribes the circumstances in which an NCA should intervene and the decisions it should take. Particularly important for

---

[1]   ECJ of 13 February 1969, case 14/68, Walt Wilhelm, Rep. 1969, 1.

the functioning of the network is the possibility for an NCA to decline to proceed whenever another national authority has already instituted proceedings against the same infraction. Clearly, this provision aims at *concentrating* the competence to act in *one* enforcement centre, so as to minimize the risk of parallel proceedings. To the same end is the provision which allows the Commission to take over the disposition of the case whenever there is a disagreement on which authority is to be regarded as the best placed authority.

Certainly one of the most significant aspects of Regulation 1/2003, from the perspective of a national authority, is the definition of a principle of *horizontal and vertical cooperation*, which also amounts to a *system of reciprocal control*. With respect to the activity of the Commission, NCAs can exercise an *indirect* control. To this end, the role of the Advisory Committee has been reinforced. In particular, when called upon to express its opinion on a draft decision of the Commission, one or more Member States may request to give reasons for the positions expressed in the Committee's opinion. In addition, there is a duty on the Commission to 'take the utmost account' of the opinion delivered by the Committee and to inform it of the manner in which its opinion has been taken into account. The aim of the amendments introduced is to give NCAs a stronger influence on the enforcement activity of the Commission, as a 'compensation' for the loss of importance of their national laws. Therefore, the provision makes Commission decisions more transparent, compelling it to state the reasons for any position it may wish to take which differs from the opinion of the national authorities.

In addition, a completely new system of *direct control* is introduced with respect to the enforcement activities of NCAs. In fact, as a response to the delegation of powers to NCAs, the Commission acquires the means to oversee the uniformity and consistency of the decisions applying Articles 81 and 82. To this end, Regulation 1/2003 introduces a *binding* control of the Commission on NCAs. In particular, NCAs must inform the Commission of investigations undertaken by them, at the latest when they start proceedings according to Article 81 or 82. In addition, NCAs must transmit draft decisions, so as to allow the Commission to exercise control on the substantive assessment made. Where it considers it appropriate, the Commission may thus try to 'persuade' the national authority to change its analysis. In extreme cases, the Commission may take over the case, initiating proceedings itself, thus depriving the NCA of competence. It should be noted that, in such circumstances, the Commission actually also controls the application of national law whenever applied in parallel to European law.

Furthermore, a system of horizontal, *non-binding* control *between NCAs* has been introduced. In fact, within the network NCAs cooperate in many ways. In the first place, there might be a 'negotiation' regarding which authority should be competent to conduct a certain action, because it is deemed to be 'best placed'. Therefore, some authorities might give up their competence. As a counterpart to relinquishing competence, NCAs retain the power to request the Commission to schedule an Advisory Committee meeting in respect of the investigation conducted at a national level. In this way, NCAs may express an opinion on the case, albeit a non-binding one. In case of conflicts of opinion, any NCA within the Advisory Committee may ask the Commission to take over the proceeding.

5 A Few Remarks

The obligation of NCAs to directly apply Articles 81 and 82 of the Treaty is of great relevance. It finally solves the never-ending debate over such a possibility, which the Commission always excluded when it was not explicitly provided for by national law. However, the Commission's view appeared debatable and eccentric when related to the Community system considered as a whole, and especially when compared to the general principle of the application of Community provisions having direct effect and thus capable of being applied by national administrative agencies and judges. In fact, it is a central principle of European law that national judges and administrative agencies can and indeed must apply legislation having direct effect, and Articles 81 and 82 have never been an exception. This means that, following the well known scheme, these rules can be directly relied upon before national courts and that, in case of conflict between Community and national law, the latter must be disapplied. The issue poses no particular problem and, to that effect, judges have a further instrument of inquiry at hand, the preliminary ruling. Furthermore, Community law, in particular Article 9(3) of Regulation 17/62, as well as the consolidated case law of the Court of Justice, always explicitly assigned to national administrative agencies the power to apply Articles 81(1) and 82 of the Treaty in the absence of a Commission proceeding.

It is true, though, that compared to the typical model of Community legislation having direct effect, Articles 81 and 82 of the Treaty are somehow peculiar. Cases relating to anticompetitive agreements and abuses of a dominant position require a complex inquiring and technical assessment activity. Although this complex activity can be delegated to judicial review by national judges (who retain the advantage of the possibility to request a preliminary ruling), it could not just as easily be delegated to an administrative body having no specific competence and which has not been enabled to carry out such activity on the basis of an adversarial proceeding. On the contrary, when a national authority empowered to enforce competition rules does exist, there should never have been reasons to doubt its competence to apply Community competition rules having direct effect. This, regardless of the existence of an explicit authorization, makes no sense from the point of view of general legal theory either.

It is therefore important that Regulation 1/2003 finally moved towards what I consider to be a '*normalization*', rather a modernization of European competition law. The power and duty of judges and national competition authorities to apply Articles 81 (now in its entirety) and 82 should not, in itself, give rise to concerns regarding the uniform application of Community competition law. The concept of delegating the evaluation of agreements or abuses of dominant positions to national authorities is an aspect of decentralization already inherent in the fundamental principles of the EC Treaty. National administrations and judges are in fact the core of the decentralized application of all Community rules, and competition rules are no exception. Therefore, Article 81 being a rule like any other, I never saw any reason to fear its decentralized application by national judges, administrative authorities and, in particular, by antitrust authorities.

It cannot be denied that the reform has elicited some criticism. It has been pointed out that the practical consequences of the legal exception principle and of the decentralized enforcement of Article 81(3) are rather limited, given the fact that the number of notifications had already been reduced significantly. Indeed, undertakings were mostly already conducting self-assessment, thanks also to the introduction of a more economics-based approach in the assessment of alleged violations of Article 81(1) and the wide application of block exemptions. In exchange for such (limited) effects, Regulation 1/2003 significantly strengthened the Commission's powers and decision making role and imposed a sort of Community law hegemony. While this is clearly inspired by the need to adjust the system for the entry of ten new NCAs, which have less experience in antitrust enforcement and often are understaffed, more experienced national authorities conversely might 'suffer' from the reform. In fact, these more experienced NCAs are exposed to a 'negotiation' with other national authorities for jurisdiction in cross-border cases and to the risk of the Commission assuming competence. In addition, they are subject to the pervasive system of direct and indirect controls.

I believe that such criticisms lose sight of the quality and stability of the system. It cannot be denied, though, that some reason for concern might exist. What I consider to be most problematic is the lack of a procedural framework common to the different NCAs. Indeed, a substantial harmonization of national competition laws has taken place in a 'creeping' style, gradually taking Community legislation as a model for national laws. Conversely, the same has not (yet) happened with respect to procedural aspects. Hence the concern by undertakings that the differences in the procedural systems of Member States might, at least at the beginning, be problematic. Firstly, different regimes exist in terms of proceedings and investigative powers among the various national legislations – for instance, as to the extent of the investigative powers and the existence of a prior judicial control on the exercise by NCAs of their power. There are also differences with respect to the recognition of legal privilege, the extent of the participative rights of parties and complainants and the existence and characteristics of leniency programmes. In addition, sanctions of a different nature (that is, criminal versus administrative) and of different degrees of severity exist in the various countries. In this perspective, reallocation of cases among the network is not indifferent: the rules of procedure, the nature of the sanctions and the amount of fines to be imposed on undertakings become unpredictable; a risk of discrimination arises. Finally, the possibility of parallel proceedings, apart from posing issues of double jeopardy, increases the risk of contrasting decisions, which should induce the Commission to take over the case. It is therefore necessary to clarify the circumstances under which decisions by national authorities can be seen as 'contrasting' and therefore justifying the Commission's intervention.

From a more general point of view, this problem recalls the one which always characterized the European Community system as a whole. It is well known that national judges and administrative authorities are called upon to apply Community provisions on the basis of the national procedures existing in each Member State. This brings about two consequences. Firstly, there is a risk of diverging evaluations and outcomes in the application of the same Community rule. Secondly, at least in the mid- and long-term, the need arises for a centralized mechanism of judicial control to guarantee uniformity of the evaluation standards and of the level of protection of individual rights. Member States' autonomy in this regard has always been respected. On the other hand, the need to ensure a minimum degree of protection common to all national systems, in particular with regard to procedural rules, has always been clear. In this respect, the acknowledgement by the European Courts of a number of fundamental principles concerning the right to effective and full judicial protection is of the greatest importance. These principles include the rights of the defence in adversarial proceedings, the right to an impartial and adequately reasoned administrative decision and the right to a fair and reasonably short trial. Of equal importance are the principles according to which: (i) the protection of rights conferred by European law should not be less favourable when compared with the protection of similar rights provided under national law; and (ii) these mechanisms should not become excessively difficult or render it impossible to obtain full and effective protection.

In short, this is what we call a 'Community of Law', to underline that in the European Community the protection of individual rights is ensured through judicial control, to which the Community's institutions, Member States and individuals are all subject. In this respect, an intervention by the Court of Justice, determining, where necessary, the minimum standards of protection of individuals in applying Articles 81 and 82 under national procedural rules, would be desirable.

III THE MERGER REVIEW

As for merger reform, from the perspective of the NCAs there are two main points: the search for more refined criteria in allocating competence between national and European law and a new attitude in the economic analysis, more strategy-oriented and less bound to static/structural elements.

1 The Definition of the 'Best Placed' Authority

Within the merger control system, jurisdiction is allocated on the basis of turnover thresholds. This is a merely mathematical criterion, though, which does not take into account cases at the margin in which a merger falling within Community jurisdiction has effects mainly within one Member State, thus justifying an analysis by the NCA concerned according to national law. Likewise, mergers below the Community turnover threshold might affect competition in a supranational market, calling for a common analysis by the Commission rather than a split analysis by several NCAs, each applying its own law. To solve these problems, the Merger Regulation had cumbersome rules which made referrals particularly difficult, especially referrals to the Commission.

To overcome these difficulties, the Italian Antitrust Authority had a propulsive role in creating an informal network (the 'European Competition Authorities' – ECA[2]) between NCAs, which facilitates cooperation in applying the rules governing referrals from the NCAs to the Commission. As a result, for the first time since the Merger Regulation entered into force, several multi-jurisdictional mergers notified to a number of EU Member States were jointly referred to the European Commission. In addition, the Italian Authority pleaded with the Commission for more flexible and 'enterprise-friendly' rules in order to make the decision-making process concerning the opportunity of a referral more effective and to reduce the burden on parties that arise from the reallocation of competences between the national and the EC level.

As a result of the debate following the Green Paper on Merger Review and of the activities of the ECA network, the rules on referral have been substantially modified in Regulation 139/2004. Without getting into the technicalities of the procedural system defined, I would like to stress that the new rules introduce procedural correctives that render feasible the reallocation of jurisdiction to the 'best placed authority'. Where necessary, national and Community institutions therefore become interchangeable, similarly to the system defined by Regulation 1/2003. However, in the case of merger referral,

---

²   For more information see http://www.oft.gov.uk/ECA/About+the+ECA.htm.

such interchangeability also affects the legislation to be applied, and not only the enforcers.

In addition, one of the positive developments of the reform is that the new Merger Regulation has introduced a 'pre-notification' consultation process on competence, which significantly alleviates some of the economic burden on undertakings, which stems from the interaction – in terms of reallocation of competence – between European and national laws.

2   The Substantive Standard

The last years have been characterized by a significant debate, initiated by the Commission itself, on the opportunity of changing the substantive standard for merger review. Until the recent changes, the Commission could prohibit a concentration which might establish or strengthen a dominant position on the market, significantly hampering effective competition. The public debate centred on the opportunity of replacing the 'dominance' criterion, which is of a legal nature, with a 'substantial lessening of competition' test, more strongly centred on the economic analysis of the effects of the merger. Indeed, although the dominance test had already been expanded to apply to a collective dominance position, some commentators argued that a gap existed with respect to mergers that reduce competition through non-coordinated effects. In particular, in oligopoly settings, a merger between two competitors might lessen competition substantially as a whole in case there is little competition in the market, even though the merged entity could not be considered dominant. Therefore, according to some views, a substantial lessening of competition test would have facilitated the policy objective of prohibiting all anticompetitive mergers.

Critics of the reform pointed out the danger of abandoning the judicial case law developed during ten years of existence of Regulation 4064/89 and the advisability, from a systemic perspective, of maintaining the link to the market power of the undertaking, as is the case when assessing abuses. On the other hand, they stressed the flexibility of the notion of 'dominance', which had also been successfully applied to tacit collusion scenarios. The same criteria could therefore be adapted to the scenario of 'non-collusive oligopolies'. On the other hand, the speculative nature of this last statement justified the concerns of those favouring a change of the test. In fact, these opinions considered it unsatisfactory to rely only on the possibility that the European Courts *might* endorse such an extensive interpretation and preferred legislative change to creative judicial reasoning.

As you know, the Commission adopted a compromise approach, modifying the test so as to forbid those concentrations which could 'significantly impede effective competition in the common market or in a substantial part of it, *in*

particular as a result of the creation or strengthening of a dominant position'
(emphasis added). A European version of the SLC test has thus been introduced. In order to avoid too wide an application of the test, dominance has
been qualified as the typical case of a significant impediment of effective
competition. Apart from dominance, the new standard should be applied only
to the case of non-collusive oligopolies (recital 25 of Regulation 139/2004).

The possible consequences of such a change are currently subject to debate:
will it be significant or not; will there be an increase in the number of scruti-
nized mergers; will the Commission retain a higher degree of discretion or not;
will costs of predictability for the parties rise, and so on. I do not wish to get
into this discussion here; furthermore, it is still too early to evaluate the impact
of the changes. I would only like to say that, in my opinion, a correct economic
interpretation of the notion of dominance could already allow an analysis
based on the assessment of the elimination of important competitive
constraints and, therefore, of a substantial reduction of competition, regardless
of the position in terms of market share or of leadership. In other words, an
operator which has a competitor holding an equal or even higher position
might be considered as holding market power when, as a result of a concentration, he has attained such a dimension as to be able to reduce the competitive reaction of his adversaries, even if he does not himself hold a post-merger
leadership position on the market. Dominance should be interpreted as the
ability to influence prices, although taking into account competitors' reactions,
and to adopt strategies capable of maintaining prices higher than at competitive level. A concentration establishing or strengthening such power, even in
the presence of competitors with equally important market shares, can well be
considered as restricting competition.

If this interpretation were to be shared by other NCAs, it would reduce the
risk of uncertainties when reallocating jurisdiction between the Commission
and a Member State whose legislation is based on the dominance test.
Otherwise, the differences between many national laws and EC law might
constitute a problematic aspect with respect to referrals. In any event, I believe
that the Community model will impose itself in the mid-term, prompting, once
again, an indirect harmonization of national legislation.

IV FINAL REMARKS. THE REFORMS SEEN FROM THE ITALIAN ANTITRUST AUTHORITY

As regards the consequences for the Italian Antitrust Authority of the reforms
prompted by the Commission, I would like to underline that Italian legislation
allows the Authority to face these changes without great difficulties. In this
respect the farsightedness of the legislator in 1990 was of great help. Indeed,

the legislator shaped the national legislation on the Community model by imposing a teleological approach to the interpretation of the national provisions. As a consequence, from a substantive point of view, a more frequent application of Articles 81 and 82 will not alter the usual interpretation practice. This was, in any event, already based on a strictly economic approach even before the Community 'conversion' of the last years. Moreover, the Italian Authority has on numerous occasions already applied Articles 81 and 82. With regard to the decentralized application of Community competition rules, I would like to recall that the Court of Justice recently acknowledged the legitimacy of the decision of the Italian Authority, based on a general principle of Community law, to disapply national provisions which contravene Articles 81 and 10 of the EC Treaty.[3]

Nevertheless, it would be desirable to avoid uncertainties in the interaction between Community and national laws, for the substantive provisions of Italian Law no. 287/90[4] to conform to the new Community rules and for the Authority to be explicitly granted the same powers when applying national law as are granted to the Commission. I refer to the legal exception regime and the powers to grant interim measures, to conduct dawn raids to the same extent as the Commission, to impose sanctions on associations of undertakings and to apply national law in parallel with Community law.

As far as merger legislation is concerned, the new approach to non-cooperative oligopolies does not find us unprepared. Indeed, in 2002, in a decision regarding the merger between Sai and Fondiaria,[5] our Authority, while confirming the relevance of the establishment of a dominant position, already applied the notion of dominance to the case of unilateral effects in oligopolistic markets, by comparing it with the independence of behaviour which results from the power to unilaterally increase prices significantly. In this respect, the Italian Authority anticipated to a certain degree the changes which followed at the European level.

An amendment of the national antitrust law would nevertheless be desirable also with respect to mergers. Among the main reasons for this proposition is the fact that the Italian Authority is increasingly called upon to assess mergers which at first have been notified to the Commission. In doing so, it is subject to the restrictions imposed by a national procedure which allows only 45 days to reach a decision compared to the 4 months that may be used by the

---

[3] ECJ of 9 September 2003, case C-198/01, Fiammiferi/Autorità Garante del Mercato, Rep. 2003 I 8055.

[4] Of 10 October 1990, available at http://www.agcm.it/eng/E1.htm.

[5] Decision of 23 December 2003, case C 5422 B, press release available at http://www.agcm.it/agcm_eng/COSTAMPA/E_PRESS.NSF/VistaWWW?OpenView &Start=1&Count=30&Expand=4.

Commission. The consequences for the effectiveness of the decision-making process are obvious enough.

In addition, it would be important to bring Italian legislation into line with the Merger Regulation so as to allow all full function joint ventures to be assessed as concentrations. Indeed, according to Law no. 287/1990 joint ventures which are of a cooperative nature are considered to be agreements; therefore, according to Regulation 1/2003, they cannot be formally authorized. An amendment of the national law which extended the duty to notify all full-function joint ventures would therefore clearly favour the accomplishment of initiatives that require high investments and involve high risks.

By way of conclusion, I believe that the vitality of a complex and success-ful model of integration, such as the European Community, is measured also by its capacity to adapt to changing circumstances. In this respect, I consider the recent changes as very positive. Indeed, they give new stimulus to NCAs and to the Commission to adapt to the new framework in order to fully realize the significant potential offered by the network of authorities that has been established, and to protect the rights of undertakings. Certainly, both reforms open new and important perspectives not only for the application of European but also of national laws.

PART III

Controlling restrictions of competition

5. Vertical agreements: 4 years of liberalisation by regulation n. 2790/99 after 40 years of legal (block) regulation

Denis Waelbroeck*

I INTRODUCTION

On 1 June 2000 the new regulation on vertical restraints ('Regulation 2790/99')[1] entered into force and replaced the three former block exemption regulations applicable respectively to exclusive distribution, exclusive purchasing and franchise agreements. This new regulation initiated the first step in the Community's review and modernisation of its rules on competition. The aim was to simplify the rules and reduce the regulatory burden for companies, whilst ensuring a more effective control of vertical restraints implemented by companies holding significant market power.

The Commission claimed that the new rules embodied a shift from the more formalistic regulatory approach underlying the old legislation towards an increased emphasis on economics in the assessment of vertical agreements under the EC competition rules.

This new policy was designed to increase the companies' right to devise their contracts entirely to their own choosing as long as they have no market power, thereby removing the strait-jacket previously imposed on them by the former block exemption regulations.

Regulation 2790/99 therefore provides a safe harbour whenever the supplier has a market share below 30 per cent, under which he is free to agree any restriction he wishes, as long as his agreements do not contain so-called

* Partner, Ashtrust Brussels, Professor of EC Competition law at the Université Libre de Bruxelles and the College of Europe, Bruges. The author is grateful to David Mamane and Vanig Kasparian for their assistance in drafting the present report.

[1] Commission Regulation (EC) No 2790/1999 of 22 December 1999 on the application of Article 81(3) of the Treaty to categories of vertical agreements and concerted practices, [1999] OJ L 336/21, 29.12.1999.

'hardcore restrictions'[2] (nor indeed other restrictions enumerated in Article 5 of the Regulation, such as exclusivity clauses of excessive duration).

Above the 30 per cent market share threshold, vertical agreements are neither covered by the block exemption, nor automatically presumed to be illegal. They will therefore require an individual assessment under Article 81(3) EC if the agreement restricts competition. In such cases, companies are expected to assess on their own the possible consequences of their vertical agreements. The Guidelines adopted in 2000 ('Guidelines on Vertical Restraints'[3]) were intended to assist them in this assessment.

Four years after the entry into force of Regulation 2790/99 (as well indeed as the rest of the reforms including the whole modernisation package), it may be appropriate to attempt an appraisal of the new rules, in the light of the Commission's above-cited objectives. In doing so, I will first focus on the key characteristics of the system, that is the 30 per cent market share threshold and the hardcore restrictions. Thereafter it also seems worthwhile to consider briefly the appropriateness of the rules in the Guidelines for dominant companies and finally to discuss the possible merits and shortcomings of the new regime for agency agreements.

II GENERAL COMMENTS AS TO THE SYSTEM ITSELF AND THE MARKET SHARE THRESHOLD

As already explained, Regulation 2790/99 creates a 'safe harbour' for vertical agreements concluded by companies with a market share of less than 30 per cent. Above this threshold, vertical agreements – whilst not presumed illegal – will normally require individual examination.

The reform thereby aimed at combining the benefits of economic evaluation with concerns for legal certainty and enforcement efficiency. Ideally, an economic approach would have required an in-depth investigation of each and every individual agreement as against the market structure, and an evaluation and balancing of its pro-competitive benefits as against its potential anticompetitive costs. However, for obvious reasons of legal certainty and enforcement efficiency, this was not considered desirable. According to the

---

2   I.e. resale price maintenance, prohibition of passive sales for exclusive distribution agreements, restriction in a selective distribution system of active or passive sales by authorised distributors to end-users or other authorised distributors, preventing the supplier of components from selling these as spare parts to end-users or independent repairers.

3   Commission notice – Guidelines on Vertical Restraints, [2000] OJ C 291/1, 13.10.2000.

Guidelines on Vertical Restraints since, 'below the threshold of 30 percent the effects on downstream markets will in general be limited', a 'safe harbour' was justified below that level.

The market share threshold is intended to eliminate regulatory burdens from those firms that, to paraphrase Bishop and Ridyard, 'could not behave anti-competitively even if they tried'.[4] To this extent, it is undoubtedly a considerable advance, away from the formalistic approach and towards a more effects-based approach of competition law. The insertion of this criterion responds to criticisms made against the previous regulations which applied regardless of the market power of the parties concerned.

1 Shortcomings

a) General considerations

However, in the context of the present report, the first obvious question to be addressed is whether the right balance was found. In this regard, it is clear that any market share criterion is necessarily arbitrary to a certain extent (should the threshold be fixed at 30 per cent, 35 per cent or 40 per cent?) and provides in practice only imperfect guidance as to the real problems that agreements may in reality entail. Thus, some agreements might deserve scrutiny even below the thresholds, and nevertheless benefit from the exemption. Also, vice versa, above the thresholds perfectly innocuous agreements will be deprived of the legal certainty provided by previous group exemptions.

Moreover, market share thresholds are by nature always uncertain as they require a prior definition of the market – hardly an exact science – which is the reason for example why the concept of market share thresholds has been abandoned in most systems in merger control. In addition, the degree of market power can rarely be measured effectively by reference only to market share. If market shares are indeed generally indicative of potential market power, they can never be considered alone without taking into account several other indicators (such as the number of competing suppliers for the same products, the countervailing power of suppliers and purchasers, the availability of substitutes and product differentiation, barriers to entry and potential competition and the nature of the oligopolistic interaction between firms). In order to obtain a realistic appraisal of market power, such external factors ought normally to be taken into account.[5] For instance, in fast innovative areas the

---

[4]   S. Bishop, D. Ridyard, 'E.C. Vertical Restraints Guidelines: Effects-Based or Per Se Policy', [2002] *ECLR* 1, p. 35.

[5]   Several merger decisions adopted by the Commission demonstrate that market shares do not equal market power: in *Alcatel-Teletra* (Case IV-M042, 12 April 1991), a merger was allowed even though the combined market shares were 81% and

market share is liable to change very rapidly and is, therefore, no reliable indicator of market power.

These uncertainties and shortcomings which are inherent to any system based on market share thresholds may obviously be seen as the price to be paid for the legal certainty which the system otherwise affords to the companies concerned. Indeed it is unrealistic and excessively burdensome to expect a full-fledged economic analysis in each and every case. The need to find some sort of rough guidance in the law is all the greater since vertical agreements should normally give rise to competition concerns much less than horizontal agreements and since they are also much more frequent than horizontal agreements. The question arises, however, whether any more appropriate alternative system could have been conceived.

The most obvious question is in my view to examine whether the system should not – with regard to Article 81 EC – permit as a matter of principle all vertical agreements which do not contain hardcore restrictions, independently of the market share of the parties involved, and only apply a control under Article 82 EC in cases of dominance.

The major advantage of such a system in my view is that it would to some extent remove the burden for companies above the threshold to carry out on their own a complex assessment of their agreements under Article 81(1) EC and Article 81(3) EC. More legal certainty in this regard would be welcome, especially as since 1 May 2004 it has not been possible to notify agreements to the EC Commission for exemption. Moreover, the economic assessment required by the Guidelines on Vertical Restraints and the Article 81(3) notice[6] is demanding, and it is unlikely that many judges and parties will have the means or skills to undertake it adequately, thereby increasing the risk of lengthy, costly and uncertain litigation.

b) National laws

It would not be entirely unprecedented to have a system without a market share threshold where a prohibition is only possible in cases of abuse or in cases of hardcore restrictions, or alternatively where decisions are taken to withdraw the exemption *ex nunc*. It would be similar for instance to the current German system (as it is still in force before the enactment of the amendment of the German competition act[7]). According to the German Act in force, as I

83%. In *Rhône-Poulenc/SNIA* (Case IV-M206, 10 August 1992) the high degree of concentration was outweighed by the existence of rapid technology development.

    [6]   Commission notice – Guidelines on the application of Article 81(3) of the Treaty, [2004] OJ C 101/97, 27.4.2004.

    [7]   The German Act Against Restraints of Competition is due to be radically amended. With regard to the consequences on vertical agreements, see C. Bahr, 'Die Behandlung von Vertikalvereinbarungen nach der 7. GWB-Novelle', *WuW* 3/2004, p. 259.

understand it, vertical agreements are generally allowed, at any market share level, as long as they do not restrict a party in its freedom to determine prices or terms of business in its relations with third parties.[8] In addition, exclusive dealing agreements are not subject to a 'prohibition based system' but to a system of 'control of abuses' within which the cartel authority may declare agreements to be void and of no effect and may prohibit the implementation of new and similar commitments if it can be shown that competition is significantly impaired.[9] In other words, vertical agreements that do not contain restrictions on prices and terms of business are lawful until the cartel authority says otherwise.[10] There is no general requirement to show that such agreements above certain market share thresholds may benefit from an exemption.

A slightly different though nevertheless similar system applies in the UK.[11] Whilst the Competition Act of 1998 incorporated the wording of Articles 81 and 82 EC, vertical agreements were subsequently excluded from the scope of this Act by the 'Competition Act 1998 (Land and Vertical Agreements Exclusion) Order 2000'.[12] The reasons for doing so were mainly that the application of Article 81 EC to vertical agreements was strongly influenced by market integration concerns, which were not an issue within the UK, and that the national competition authority, the OFT, wanted to avoid a flood of notifications of agreements.[13] Therefore, vertical restraints are currently not considered in the UK under Chapter I of the Act (that is, the equivalent to Article 81 EC) unless they contain provisions on fixed or minimum resale prices. The only control is exercised under Chapter II of the Act (that is, the equivalent to Article 82 EC). In addition, the cumulative effects of vertical agreements in certain sectors can still be investigated,[14] and the OFT can always withdraw the antitrust immunity from a particular vertical agreement. Whilst it is currently considering repealing the order and aligning UK law with EC law (that is, applying Regulation 2790/99 directly to domestic agreements even where they do not affect interstate trade), this is still controversial. Indeed, it is feared that efficiency-enhancing agreements may

---

[8] Section 14 of the German Act Against Restraints of Competition.

[9] Section 16 of the German Act Against Restraints of Competition.

[10] However, there is according to Section 19(3) of the German Act Against Restraints of Competition a presumption of dominance above 33% market share.

[11] Within the process of modernisation, the UK will amend its domestic regime; *inter alia*, it will repeal the Verticals Exclusion Order SI 2000 No 310, which excludes vertical agreements from the Chapter I prohibition with effect from 1 May 2005.

[12] Verticals Exclusion Order SI 2000 No 310.

[13] R. Whish, *Competition Law*, 5th edn, at p. 646f.

[14] According to the market investigation provisions under the Enterprise Act 2002.

not be entered into whenever parties fear that it is too difficult to demonstrate efficiency gains to the competition authorities.[15]

2   A Proposal for Reform

Transposed into EC Competition law, such a system would entail removing the market share threshold in Article 3 of Regulation 2790/99 and exempting all vertical agreements, regardless of market shares, unless they contain certain hardcore restrictions or other excessive restrictions. Exceptionally, however, and as is currently the case in Regulation 2790/99:

- the benefit of the block exemption could always be withdrawn by the Commission (or indeed the national competition authority) in an individual case if the agreement has any effect that is incompatible with the conditions laid down in Article 81(3) EC (for example in the case of parallel networks of similar restraints);
- alternatively, special sector specific regulations could be adopted where specific and serious problems are identified[16];
- moreover, the behaviour of the contracting party could in any event always be scrutinised under Article 82 EC if one of the parties was held to be dominant, as is the case already today.

Such a system could in my view increase legal certainty for the firms entering into vertical agreements, by bridging the not inconsiderable gap between the 30 per cent threshold and true dominance, whilst retaining the possibility of intervening if there is a real competition problem.

One wonders indeed why one should set an arbitrary market share threshold if, as it is generally recognised, there is only a need to scrutinise vertical restraints in case of real market power and there is no need to care about restraints of firms which do not have large market power.[17] It is clear indeed that, as long as there is enough interbrand competition, it is unlikely that a vertical restraint could have a significant impact on competition.[18] If the objective of the 30 per cent threshold is thus to deal with concerns of true market power, that is dominance, it appears in my view most logical and coherent to use the obvious legal basis to that effect, that is Article 82 EC. In

---

[15]   D. Glynn, M. Howe, 'Distribution – Vertical restraints in UK and EU competition law', *Competition Law Insight*, July/August 2003, p. 14, at p. 17.

[16]   See Article 8 of Regulation 2790/99; see also the Motor Vehicle Block Exemption or the special rules in the UK on beer supply agreements.

[17]   M. Motta, *Competition Policy: Theory and Practice*, 2004, pp. 378–9.

[18]   S. Bishop, M. Walker, *The Economics of EC Competition Law*, 2002, p.169.

such a case, there is really no need for a market share threshold since – as is well-known – block exemption regulations do not prevent the application of Article 82 EC.[19]

Therefore I would tend to conclude that by setting the threshold at 30 per cent, the block exemption is unduly restrictive. Many agreements thereby escape the 'safe harbour' although they are in themselves perfectly innocuous from a competition law perspective. Moreover, removing the threshold would give more coherence to the system as not all restrictions of competition under EC Article 81 are an abuse under EC Article 82. For instance, only territorial exclusivities protecting a distributor against active sales from other distributors have so far never been regarded as abusive within the meaning of EC Article 82. Nevertheless, they do not benefit from the 'safe harbour' where the supplier has a market share above 30 per cent, although there is no compelling reason for them not to.

It seems to me that another advantage of abolishing the thresholds is that suppliers using independent resellers might as a result be penalised less compared with vertically integrated companies. Indeed, why, for example, should a franchise such as McDonald's be treated more severely than an integrated group which will operate in exactly the same way on the market? Provided certain hardcore restrictions are maintained (which may be justified by the fact that independent retailers are separate undertakings competing on the market; see below under 'Hardcore restrictions'), it is difficult to see any justification for depriving a non-dominant company of the safe harbour.

Is there any risk that this approach might induce the Commission and the national competition authorities to dilute the application of Article 82 EC in order to scrutinise vertical agreements to the largest extent possible (either by lowering the threshold of dominance or by extending the notion of abuse)? Or in other words, is there a need to prohibit certain clauses that are currently group exempt under the 30 per cent threshold as regards companies that are not dominant? In the past for instance tying agreements have been caught by Article 81 even below a dominance level.[20] Is there a risk also that the Commission be induced for example to develop the concept of abuse of collective dominance to bypass the Regulation in cases such as *Schoeller/Langnese Iglo*?[21] We do not think so, as the Commission or the

---

[19] CFI, Case T-51/89, *Tetra Pak Rausing SA v. Commission*, [1990] ECR II-309; ECJ, cases C-395/96 P, etc, *Compagnie Maritime Belge Transports SA v. Commission*, [2000] ECR I-1365.

[20] ECJ, Case 193/83, *Windsurfing International Inc. v. Commission*, [1986] ECR 611; Commission decision 79/86, *Vaessen/Morris*, [1979] OJ L 19/32, 26.1.1979.

[21] See Commission Decision 93/406 *Langnese-Iglo GmbH*, [1993] OJ 1993 L 183, p. 19 and Commission Decision 93/405 *Schöller Lebensmittel GmbH & Co KG*,

national competition authority always has the opportunity to take prospective measures by withdrawing the future benefit of the block exemption.

Alternatively, if this system is seen as too radical (which I think it is not) one might also consider a less radical change to Regulation 2790/1999 consisting of a differentiated approach identifying:

- Those clauses which are always unproblematic, even in cases of dominance and which therefore necessarily deserve an exemption and ought not to be subject to any market share threshold (such as open territorial exclusivities allowing passive sales);
- clauses which can be problematic above 30 per cent although the parties are not dominant (which under the current case-law would be the case for example for tying; one might also consider rules on most favoured customer clauses, stricter rules on exclusivities, and so on);
- clauses which should never benefit from a group exemption, even below 30 per cent (that is, the current clauses in Articles 4 and 5 of Regulation 2790/99).

III   HARDCORE RESTRICTIONS

The *Guidelines on Vertical Restraints* rightly recognise that rather than being *per se* restrictive, many vertical restraints serve procompetitive objectives. However, a limited number of clauses are nevertheless prohibited *per se*, even below the 30 per cent threshold.[22]

The treatment of the so-called 'hardcore restrictions' goes to the core of the question of competition policy towards vertical restraints. The policy towards vertical restraints has been subject to 'severe swings in intellectual and political fashion'[23] and little consensus of opinion on the question.

[1993] OJ L 183, p. 1, partly upheld in CFI, Case T-9/93 *Schöller Lebensmittel GmbH & Co. KG v Commission*, [1995] ECR II-1611 and CFI, Case T-7/93 *Langnese Iglo GmbH v Commission*, [1995] ECR II-1533. The distribution agreements of the two biggest suppliers for impulse ice cream on the German market were considered as a network of similar agreements having a cumulative effect that foreclosed the market. The Commission could in such a case have used the collective dominance theory, but instead the exemption granted by Regulation 1984/83 was withdrawn.

[22]   See also the '*de minimis* notice': Commission Notice on agreements of minor importance which do not restrict competition under Article 81(1) of the Treaty (*de minimis*), [2001] OJ C368/13, 22.12.2001.

[23]   D. Neven, P. Papandropoulos, P. Seabright, '*Trawling for Minnows: European Competition Policy and Agreements Between Firms*', Centre for Economic Policy Research, 1998, p. 17.

Basically, vertical agreements could be considered anticompetitive because they restrict the commercial freedom of the parties and may have effects on both *intrabrand* and *interbrand* competition. On the other hand, the argument has been made – in line with the Chicago school – that all vertical agreements ought *prima facie* to be regarded as procompetitive because there must be an offsetting efficiency justification if a manufacturer chooses a vertical restraint which limits retail competition.[24] Between these two extremes, mainstream economics would today argue that the procompetitive and anticompetitive nature of vertical agreements need more careful analysis to assess their actual effects.[25]

Generally, Regulation 2790/99 allows all restraints and exempts all agreements up to a market share threshold of 30 per cent, *unless the agreements contain one of the hardcore restrictions as set out in its Article 4 or a clause that contravenes its Article 5*. Therefore, a number of clauses are viewed as problematic, even below the 30 per cent threshold.

This in itself raises a number of questions. My first comment in that regard is that the very concept of 'hardcore restrictions' is problematic in economic terms because each case differs, and therefore the effects on competition need to be assessed according to the facts of each case at hand.[26] Indeed most 'vertical restraints can increase or decrease welfare, depending on the environment' and therefore rules of reason are clearly generally more appropriate from an economic point of view than *per se* illegalities.[27]

Finding that a contract which contains a hardcore restriction will in principle inevitably and entirely fall outside of the block exemption[28] is therefore probably excessively severe.[29] Moreover, the *Guidelines on Vertical Restraints*,[30] as well as the *Guidelines on the application of Article 81(3) of*

---

[24] See M. Hughes, 'The Economic Assessment of Vertical Restraints under UK and EC Competition Law', *ECLR* [2001], 22(10), p. 425.

[25] See D.W. Carlton, J.M. Perloff, *Modern Industrial Organisation*, 3rd edn, at p. 407 ff.

[26] S. Bishop, M. Walker, *The Economics of EC Competition Law*, 2002, p. 167.

[27] J. Tirole, *The Theory of Industrial Organisation*, 1988, at p. 188.

[28] See Article 4 of Regulation 2790/99 and para. 46 of the *Guidelines on Vertical Restraints*.

[29] See also ECJ Case 319/82, *Société de vente de ciments/Kerpen & Kerpen*, [1986] ECR 4173, at para. 11, which states that the consequence of nullity according to Article 81(2) EC 'applies only to those contractual provisions which are incompatible with article 85 (1) [now 81(1)]' EC.

[30] See para. 46 of the *Guidelines on Vertrical Restraints*: 'Individual exemption of vertical agreements containing hardcore restrictions is . . . unlikely'. See however also para. 62: 'Vertical agreements falling outside the Block Exemption Regulation will not be presumed to be illegal, but may need individual examination.'

the Treaty[31] state that it is normally not possible to exempt agreements which contain such hardcore restrictions. The mere fact of blacklisting certain clauses accordingly almost inevitably amounts to a *per se* prohibition of such clauses. In my view, this approach is overly prescriptive and difficult to justify from an economic point of view.

In the following sections, I will focus in particular on the two main hardcore restrictions as set out in Article 4 of Regulation 2790/99 – resale price maintenance and the treatment of territorial (or customer) restrictions – and will try to assess whether and to which extent they have been rightly singled out for *per se* prohibition or whether an alternative system might be advisable or not.

1   Resale Price Maintenance

Article 4(a) of Regulation 2790/99 excludes the application of the block exemption with regard to all agreements that lead to a 'restriction of the buyer's ability to determine its sale price'.[32] Maximum prices and recommended prices are however – rightly – allowed,[33] as long as they do not *de facto* amount to a minimum or fixed price as a result of pressure or incentives.

---

[31]   See para. 46 of the *Guidelines on the application of Article 81(3) of the Treaty*: 'severe restrictions of competition are unlikely to fulfil the conditions of Article 81(3). Such conditions are usually black-listed in block exemption regulations or identified as hardcore restrictions in Commission guidelines and notices. Agreements of this nature fail (at least) the two first conditions of Article 81(3). They neither create objective economic benefits . . . nor do they benefit consumers.'

[32]   Note the difference compared to the hardcore restrictions on pricing practices in vertical relationships in Regulation 772/2004 on the application of Article 81(3) of the Treaty to categories of technology transfer agreements, [2004] OJ L123/11, 27.04.2004. Article 4(2)(a) of Regulation 772/2004 prohibits 'the restriction of a *party*'s ability to determine its prices', which seems to be stricter than Regulation 2790/99 because also restrictions on the upstream party's ability on pricing are black-listed. This could be due to the fact that parties with blocking patents are considered to be non-competitors even though their final products might be competing.

[33]   See e.g. the following cases: CFI of 3 December 2003, Case T-208/01, *Volkswagen AG v Commission*, not yet officially reported: circulars and warnings were issued to dealers, telling them not to depart from the non-binding RRPs. The Commission considered this to amount to price fixing. The CFI quashed the decision on grounds of lack of evidence on acquiescence; Commission decision, *Nathan-Bricolux*, OJ [2001] L 54/1, see paras 86–90: the combination of maximum prices and the prohibition of discounts and rebates, amounted to the fixing of a resale price level; CFI of 13 January 2004, Case T-67/01, *JCB Service v Commission*, not yet officially reported: as there was no unequivocal evidence that the distributors were 'subject to a strict body of rules on retail prices' and that JCB's actions did involve coercion, it could not be concluded that there was a fixing of prices.

a) National laws

The negative approach towards price-fixing clauses can also be found in several national competition law statutes. Even national regulations that are very lenient towards vertical agreements such as those in the United Kingdom or Germany prohibit in general vertical price-fixing agreements.[34] Despite the discussion occasioned by the Chicago School on the subject,[35] the US has generally been hostile towards resale price maintenance ever since *Dr Miles v. John D Park*[36] in 1911. However the US still has a less strict approach than the EU. Indeed, the prohibition of resale price maintenance has often been criticised in the US for ignoring the underlying arrangement's economic purpose and effect on consumer welfare.[37] Judgments subsequent to *Dr Miles v. John D Park* tried to mitigate this situation, for example by permitting resale price maintenance if the retailers were agents[38] (as is indeed also the case in the EU) or by permitting an announcement not to sell to price-cutters (*de facto* price fixing) as long as buyers had access to alternative merchandise.[39] According to this approach (which applies the so-called *Colgate* doctrine) a supplier is allowed, as long as he does not do so in an agreement, to suggest a minimum or fixed resale price to his resellers and even to refuse to make further sales to

---

[34] See e.g. Article 4 of the UK Competition Act 1998 (Land and Vertical Agreements Exclusion) Order 2000 or Section 14 of the German Act Against Restraints of Competition.

[35] I. Lianos, *La transformation du droit de la concurrence par le recours à l'analyse économique: L'exemple du traitement des restrictions verticales par le droit communautaire et américain de la concurrence*, Strasbourg 2004, at pp. 842–3, with an overview of the relevant literature in footnote 4612.

[36] See *Dr. Miles Medical Co v. John D Park & Sons Co*, 220 US 373 (1911).

[37] R. Boscheck, 'The EU Policy Reform on Vertical Restraints – An Economic Perspective', World Competition (2000), Vol. 23, No. 4, pp. 3–50, at p. 21.

[38] *United States v. General Electric Co.,* 272 US 476 (1926).

[39] *United States v Colgate,* 250 US 300 (1919), reaffirmed by the Supreme Court in *Monsanto Co. v. Spray-Rite Service Corp.* in 1984, where the Court held that, 'independent action is not proscribed. A manufacturer, of course, generally has a right to deal, or refuse to deal, with whomever it likes, as long as it does so independently. Under Colgate, the manufacturer can announce its resale prices in advance and refuse to deal with those who fail to comply. And a distributor is free to acquiesce in the manufacturer's demand in order to avoid termination.' (*Monsanto Co. v. Spray-Rite Service Corp.,* 465 US 752 at 761 (1984)). However, a resale price maintenance agreement could be inferred if conspiracy to exclude could be proved, e.g. when an agreement with a price-cutting dealer was terminated based on complaints from non-discounting dealers. The plaintiff has to prove an agreement; this leads ultimately to double standards compared with horizontal price-fixing where the observation of conscious parallel behaviour is sufficient. See R. Boscheck, *The EU Policy Reform on Vertical Restraints – An Economic Perspective*, World Competition (2000), Vol. 23, No. 4, pp. 3–50, at p. 22.

any reseller that does not comply.[40] As long as such a refusal to deal is 'unilateral', whatever its motive, and even if the purchaser knows that if he does not comply with the supplier's policy his supplies will be cut off, it will not infringe Section 1 of the Sherman Act.[41] Although in the EC a decision of a manufacturer that constitutes unilateral conduct also escapes the prohibition of Article 81(1) EC, it is clear that the conditions are still stricter than under the *Colgate* doctrine. True, the mere expression of a unilateral policy of one of the contracting parties is not an agreement. However, genuinely unilateral measures, without express or implied consent, are to be distinguished from those in which the unilateral character is merely apparent because they received at least the 'tacit acquiescence' of the dealers. As soon as there is implementation in practice of a manufacturer's initiative, this can in itself establish acquiescence.[42]

b) Anti- and procompetitive effects

As is well known, the two main anticompetitive effects in relation to resale price maintenance are the reduction of *intrabrand* price competition, and the resulting risk of a reduction in *interbrand* competition which derives moreover from increased price transparency, thereby facilitating price collusion (whether tacit or explicit) at a horizontal level between manufacturers or distributors.[43]

---

[40]   B.R. Henry, E.F. Zelek, 'Establishing and Maintaining an Effective Minimum Resale Price Policy: A Colgate How-To', *Antitrust*, Summer 2004.

[41]   Gibson, Dunn & Crutcher LLP, *Antitrust Handbook*, 1997, pp. I–34.

[42]   ECJ of 3 December 2003, *Volkswagen AG v Commission*, Case T-208/01; Ibid., para. 54, citing ECJ of 18 September 2003, Case C-338/00 *Volkswagen AG v. Commission* Rep 2003 I 9189; ECJ of 6 January 2004, Joined Cases C-2/01 P and C-3/01 P, *Bundesverband der Arzneimittel-Importeure eV and EC Commission v Bayer AG*, Rep 2004 I 23. In *Bayer Adalat*, the Court stated that the existence of an agreement could be deduced from the conduct of the parties concerned. For an agreement within the meaning of Article 81(1) EC to be capable of being regarded as having been concluded by tacit acceptance, the mere manifestation of the will of one of the contracting parties was not sufficient, especially when the agreement was not at first sight in the interest of the other party. However, as soon as there is any compliance by the other parties, EC Article 81 applies. Furthermore, the *Guidelines on Vertical Restraints* state in para. 47 that resale price maintenance can be achieved by indirect means, e.g. by 'threats, intimidation, warnings, penalties, delay or suspension of deliveries or contract terminations in relation to observance of a given price level'. Therefore, it is clear that there is no equivalent to the *Colgate* doctrine in EC Competition law.

[43]   Guidelines on Vertical Restraints, paras 110–112. Reduced intrabrand competition is said to occur because the distributors will no longer be able to compete on prices (which amounts to a total elimination of intrabrand price competition). Ultimately consumers would then not be able to profit from lower retail prices, which might have occurred if the distributors could have competed on prices. The

There are also, however, positive aspects to be considered in connection with the imposition of a fixed or minimum price, which might justify its exemption in some cases:[44]

(i) Whilst it is clear that *intrabrand* price competition will be eliminated by imposing a fixed or minimum price, such price-fixing may also prevent 'free-riding' by retail price discounters on the pre-sales services and/or reputation of full price dealers.[45] This can be justified where one distribution outlet provides high quality services (for example showrooms, qualified sales staff and so on) on which customers then rely to buy at a cheaper discounter which does not provide these services and therefore is able to charge lower prices. A minimum price would take away the pricing advantage from the discounter and replace *intrabrand* price competition with competition on services. Minimum resale price maintenance can therefore sometimes be economically and commercially justifiable if certain conditions are fulfilled (free-riding on pre-sales, not after-sales services, new or complex products, high value of product, no possibility of imposing service requirements).[46] To be sure, in accordance with the *Guidelines on Vertical Restraints* one could argue, for example, that the 'free-riding' problem could be solved by using other – block exempted – restraints achieving the same result. Some inefficiencies and externalities caused by the 'free-riding' problem could for

---

Commission also presumes that less downward pressure on the price could have indirect effects on interbrand competition and result in a reduction of the latter. Moreover, resale price maintenance increases price transparency, which in itself could favour successful cartelisation. The monitoring and enforcement of a cartel can be simplified if all members of the cartel have price-fixing clauses in their distribution contracts. Furthermore, resale price maintenance will also favour tacit collusion. At a downstream level, it will have the effect of a horizontal pricing agreement between the distributors. This could act as a barrier to entry for discount stores. At the upstream level, resale price maintenance could reduce any incentive to deviate from a cartel as the resulting greater market transparency would make a deviation immediately visible.

[44] S. Bishop, M. Walker, *The Economics of EC Competition Law*, 2002, p. 167. In *Visa International*, the Commission itself for instance found that the so-called 'non-discrimination rule', which prevents a credit card company from charging his customers for the use of the Visa card and therefore which amounts to a form of resale price maintenance, was not even caught by EC Article 81 (although the Dutch and Swedish competition authorities had previously come to the opposite conclusions), Commission Decision 2001/782, *Visa International* [2001] L 293/24, 10.11.2001, at paras 54–58.

[45] See the overview 'Vertical Restraints as Responses to Supply and Distribution Problems' on page 5 of P.W. Dobson, M. Waterson, *Vertical Restraints and Competition Policy*, OFT Research Paper 12, December 1996.

[46] Guidelines on Vertical Restraints, para. 116(1).

instance be solved by exclusivity clauses,[47] or selective distribution (as far as they are exempted by Regulation 2790/99), but this restraint may, for practical reasons, not be a perfect substitute in all situations for resale price maintenance and it is therefore questionable that resale price maintenance should be *per se* prohibited in all cases.[48]

(ii)   In some sectors, for example the book trade, the argument has been made that resale price maintenance could allow publishers to increase their profits and therefore to cross-subsidise between high-volume books and other valuable books which would otherwise, without such a subsidisation, not be published because they would not be profitable.[49] It is to be noted that such a 'cultural exemption' has not been accepted by the Commission so far (and indeed the economic support for this argument appears doubtful as it is unclear that any increased profits will indeed be used for such philanthropic and cultural goals).[50]

(iii)   With regard to the risk of facilitating dealer or manufacturer cartels, such horizontal cartels are in any event subject to Article 81 EC and only their horizontal emanation should therefore be of concern. A vertical agreement which, hypothetically, could facilitate or induce a horizontal cartel is therefore not in itself illicit. If such a vertical agreement leads to efficiencies and increased welfare, then it should not be prohibited because it 'facilitates' a cartel at another level. In any event, serious arguments can be put forward against the effectiveness of using resale price maintenance for dealer or manufacturer cartels.[51] Indeed, there is empirical research in the US showing that there were only few documented cases of resale price maintenance being used to strengthen manufacturer cartels.[52]

---

[47]   Exclusivity clauses afford the distributor a local monopoly protecting it to a certain extent from price competition from others. See P.W. Dobson, M. Waterson, *Vertical Restraints and Competition Policy*, OFT Research Paper 12, December 1996, at fn. 9.

[48]   See P.W. Dobson, M. Waterson, *Vertical Restraints and Competition Policy*, OFT Research Paper 12, December 1996, at p. 9.

[49]   This is an interesting recognition of the interbrand effect of resale price maintenance.

[50]   Commission Press release IP/02/461 of 22 March 2002, *German book price fixing*: The Commission accepted an undertaking by the German booksellers' and publishers' association, which guarantees the freedom of direct cross-border selling of German books to final consumers in Germany, in particular, via the Internet. As long as this is possible, the Commission considers that the book price fixing in Germany does not appreciably affect trade between Member States.

[51]   R.H. Bork, *The Antitrust Paradox*, 1993, pp. 292ff.

[52]   M. Hughes, 'The Economic Assessment of Vertical Restraints under UK and EC Competition Law', *ECLR*, 22(10), pp. 424ff., at p. 429, citing Scherer and Ross, *Industrial Market Structure and Economic Performance*, 3rd edn, at p. 550.

c) Assessment

It is to be noted nevertheless that – as indicated above – the EU is not alone in its strict view as regards resale price maintenance. Most countries view resale price maintenance negatively although from a purely economic standpoint, it is fair to say that there is no conclusive view today as to how to deal with resale price maintenance. Depending on the case, resale price maintenance can be pro-competitive or anticompetitive. However, even when applying an effects-based approach, it is clear that in many cases competition will be hindered and that occasions when resale price maintenance is efficient are in practice rather rare.[53] Furthermore, resale price maintenance restrains intra-brand, as well as interbrand competition whilst other 'substitutable' restraints will only restrain one of them at the time.[54] Taking into consideration that the economic criteria to assess such restraints 'are still either too crude or too costly to apply to allow for efficient rules and a structured rule of reason',[55] it is difficult to argue that fixed or minimum prices should not be part of the hardcore list. However – and here the *Guidelines on Vertical Restraints* probably go too far – such clauses should not in my view be treated as if an exemption were inconceivable in any case. There are reasonable arguments that such restraints, assessed under an effects-based approach, can occasionally be considered as procompetitive.

2 Territorial (or Customer) Protection

Article 4 of Regulation 2790/99 also expresses the principle that market segmentation within the Community is undesirable. In practice, however, the protection against obstacles to market integration, to use the words of para. 103 of the *Guidelines on Vertical Restraints*, will often not be justified by consumer welfare or competition related concerns but by pure political objectives. Therefore, a conflict with the aims of efficiency and consumer welfare is inevitable.[56]

Due possibly to the specificities of the European set-up, case-law and Commission practice have, since *Consten and Grundig*,[57] regarded market integration as a major objective of EC competition policy as such, and repeatedly expressed the view that 'parallel imports enjoy a certain amount of protection

---

[53] S. Bishop, M. Walker, *The Economics of EC Competition Law*, 2002, at p. 165.

[54] Ibid., at p. 170.

[55] R. Boscheck, *The EU Policy Reform on Vertical Restraints – An Economic Perspective*, World Competition (2000), Vol. 23, No. 4, pp. 3–50, at p. 22.

[56] S. Bishop, M. Walker, *supra* n. 53, p. 167.

[57] ECJ, Cases 56 and 58–64, *Consten and Grundig v. Commission*, [1966] ECR 299.

in Community law because they encourage trade and help reinforce competition'.[58] At the same time, the economic arguments pointing to positive effects on competition of territorial restraints have so far been largely ignored.[59]

This is to be compared with US law which does not pursue any objective of market integration, and is much less concerned by vertical restraints that could partition the markets between the federal states. In the US, vertical restraints that give territorial exclusivities are not regarded to be *per se* problematic from an antitrust point of view.[60]

We will consider the following two situations in which territorial exclusivity may possibly be necessary to achieve an efficient distribution of the products and which may warrant therefore a more lenient approach than is currently the case:

a)   Market segmentation to prevent free riding

An excessively rigid view of territorial exclusivities ignores the fact that it will often be procompetitive to 'provide distributors with immunity from intra-brand competition that is necessary for important investments to be made'.[61] True, in addition to the rules in Regulation 2790/99, para. 119 (10) of the

---

[58]   ECJ, Case C-373/90, *Criminal proceedings against X*, [1992] ECR I-131, at para. 12.

[59]   See most recently e.g. the Commission's Decision of 16 July 2003 in Case COMP/37.975, *PO/Yamaha* rejecting the efficiency considerations put forward for limited territorial protection in a selective distribution agreement without even looking at the effect of the restrictions in question. Strangely in Case C-306/96, *Javico/Yves Saint Laurent Parfums* [1998] I-1983, the Court stated in paras 19 and 20 that an agreement which was giving territorial protection against parallel imports from a market outside the EC was not 'intended to exclude parallel imports and marketing of the contractual product within the Community', but was 'designed to enable the producer to penetrate a market', and consequently did not have as its object a restriction of competition.

[60]   See *Continental TV Inc. v. GTE Sylvania Inc.*, 433 US 36 (1977), where the Supreme Court decided that a vertical non-price restraint that was prohibiting sales outside a particular assigned territory, has to be considered under the *rule of reason*, and that insufficient intrabrand competition could be compensated by stronger interbrand competition. See also I. Lianos, *La transformation du droit de la concurrence par le recours à l'analyse économique: L'exemple du traitement des restrictions verticales par le droit communautaire et américain de la concurrence*, Strasbourg 2004, at pp. 856–7.

[61]   S. Bishop, D. Ridyard, 'E.C. Vertical Restraints Guidelines: Effects-Based or Per Se Policy', [2002] *ECLR* 1, p. 35. A distributor wishing to promote the launch of a brand in a new Member State incurs significant costs, which can only be recouped by the distributor by charging higher prices. Free-riders could take advantage of this by selling into this new market and by taking advantage of the investments of the local distributor by buying the products in other Member States in which the launch costs have already been recouped and the prices are, therefore, lower.

Guidelines on Vertical Restraints [62] provides that in case of the introduction of new products onto a different geographical market, it is not a restraint of competition, irrespective of market shares, to restrict both active and passive sales by direct buyers of the supplier which are located in other markets to *intermediaries* in the new market. Nevertheless passive sales to *end consumers* in the new market must always be permissible. Particularly given the large interpretation of 'passive sales' in connection with Internet-based business,[63] this will often be a real threat[64] and therefore the above paragraphs in the Guidelines provide only a very partial remedy.[65]

b) Market segmentation to take into account different market conditions

(i) Some market segmentation may also be necessary in view of the lack of homogeneity of today's Internal Market which may be due to a number of factors, such as different regulations (for example on reimbursement of pharmaceutical products), huge differences in taxes (for example on motor vehicles), differences in *per capita* income, and so on. This is more true than ever after the latest enlargement of the Union. The average *per capita* income in 2001 of the new Member States (excluding Cyprus and Malta) is only 23 per cent of the EU average at current exchange rates.[66] Given these huge differences, manufacturers have now to decide:

---

[62]   L. Peeperkorn, 'E.C. Vertical Restraints Guidelines: Effects-Based or Per Se Policy – A Reply', [2002] *ECLR* 1, p. 38

[63]   See para. 51 of the *Guidelines on Vertical Restraints*. It should be noted that the language(s) used on the websites do not play a role in deciding whether an Internet sale is active or passive. Only if the website is clearly targeted to customers/territories of other distributors, is it then no longer considered as passive selling.

[64]   In *B&W Loudspeaker Ltd*, Case Comp/C-3/37.709, Press Release IP/02/916 of 24 June 2002, the Commission scrutinised a distribution agreement which originally contained a prohibition on distant sales, including through the Internet. The Commission considered this to be a hardcore restriction (cf. para. 51 of the *Guidelines on Vertical Restraints*). However, qualitative service requirements regarding the website were admissible. On the other hand, in the German case *Depotkosmetik im Internet* (BGH Versäumnisurteil vom 04.11.2003, KZR 2/02) the German Federal Court (*Bundesgerichtshof*) rejected an application by an 'Internet-only' retailer who wanted to be supplied by a perfume wholesaler. In order to comply with Regulation 2790/99, the defendant allowed its retailer to make sales through the Internet as long as these sales did not exceed 50% of their turnover made in their brick-and-mortar shops. According to the Court, the defendant was allowed not to supply the Internet-only retailer.

[65]   Substantial cross-border sales of certain products might be effected via the Internet and, therefore, no effective protection would be possible for the penetration of a new market.

[66]   A. Lilico, D. Glynn, 'Price Discrimination – Virtuous price discrimination, pharmaceuticals, and parallel trade', *Competition Law Insight*, May 2003, p. 6.

- whether they adapt their prices to penetrate these new markets and consequently risk that these low-priced products will be subject to re-exports to the old Member States;
- whether they keep the prices in those States at the level of the old Member States, in which case they may not find many buyers for their products; or
- whether they decide not to distribute the products in these countries at all in order to prevent parallel trade which might well force prices down throughout the Community (either at the secondary level of sales to the consumer or more likely at the primary level of sales to the distributors, who will all be inclined to buy in the low prices countries to resell at the higher price in the other Member States).

Being excessively strict on market segmentation ignores the fact that from an economic point of view, it will often make sense to charge a higher price to a consumer group whose (marginal) 'willingness-to-pay' for the product is higher than that of others. In most cases, the total quantity will increase because of price differentiation, and this will be to the overall benefit of consumers.[67]

A *per se* approach ignores that there may be various efficiencies in some forms of segmentation. For example, was it really justified to impose a major fine on General Motors for introducing bonus payments limited to temporary promotion campaigns for selected car models that were slow-movers on the domestic market?[68]

(ii) Moreover, an excessively strict approach may also lead to unnecessary distortion. This is so particularly since an excessively rigorous approach to territorial segmentation may lead to alternative approaches by suppliers such as:

- Vertical integration (or agency): By integrating vertically, for instance by setting up their own distribution network or by serving the clients directly through the Internet (or alternatively by using agents), territorial protection can be achieved without infringing the law. Arguably however, there is no reason to encourage one form of distribution over another, particularly as there may be good reasons to prefer independent resellers to integrated resellers (or agents), as some products might not be suited for integrated distribution (or agency distribution), or as some

---

[67] P. Zweifel, R. Zäch, 'Vertical restraints: the case of multinationals', *The Antitrust Bulletin*, Spring, 2003, p. 271.
[68] See Commission Decision of 20 September 2000, *Opel*, OJ 2001, L59, p.1.

companies might not be able to integrate vertically by setting up their own distribution network (or to use agents).

• Unilateral actions: Another option for a supplier wishing to achieve market segmentation may sometimes be to unilaterally limit the quantities delivered to lower price markets in order to prevent the cheaper products from flooding existing markets. According to *Bayer Adalat*[69] such unilateral limitation can in some circumstances be admissible. However, this remains a risky exercise as Article 81 EC will apply as soon as there is 'tacit acquiescence', and it is difficult to foresee how the distributors will act and whether their behaviour will justify a finding of 'meeting of minds'.[70] Moreover, this case concerned pharmaceutical products, for which there were obligations to maintain national stocks in order to ensure the supply. For other consumer products this will not be the case and traders will be more inclined to engage in arbitrage between the different markets. Unilateral quantity limitations will, in this case, be of no use. Consumers in the low price Member States would ultimately be losing out if no restrictions are possible and decisions are taken not to supply goods in those States.

• Dual pricing: Finally, the manufacturer could try to apply a system of dual pricing and require the distributors to pay a higher price for products which will be exported to other Member States, but this system has been prohibited in the *Glaxo Wellcome* decision.[71] Subject to a still possible annulment of this decision by the EC courts, this route appears to be closed.

As a result, if there is no possibility of allowing for certain territorial exclusivities, a manufacturer could simply choose not to sell into a specific country or to sell at a higher price than he would have if he could have prevented parallel exports.

---

[69]   ECJ of 6 January 2004, Joined Cases C-2/01 P and C-3/01 P, *Bundesverband der Arzneimittel-Importeure eV and EC Commission v Bayer AG*, Rep. 2004 I 23.

[70]   Following the aforementioned judgment in *Bayer Adalat*, the Commission stated in its *Guidelines for the application of Article 81 EC to technology transfer agreements* (OJ [2004] C 101/2) that it still considers that quantity limitations could be an indirect means to restrict passive sales. They would not as such serve this purpose, but if further indicators were present (adjustment over time to cover only local demand, combination with an obligation to sell minimum quantities in the territory, differentiated royalty rates, etc.), it would consider them as 'agreements' within the meaning of Article 81 EC.

[71]   Commission Decision in Cases: IV/36.957/F3 *Glaxo Wellcome* (notification), IV/36.997/F3 *Aseprofar and Fedifar* (complaint), IV/37.121/F3 *Spain Pharma* (complaint), IV/37.138/F3 BAI (complaint), IV/37.380/F3 EAEPC (complaint), OJ [2001] L 302, p. 1; under appeal in Case T-168/01.

For instance in the case of pharmaceutical products, the new Member States will not be able, in the short- to medium-term, to pay the same prices as the 'old' Member States. Even as regards the 'old' Member States, there are huge price differences that are due not to the industry's own making but due to intervention by Member States so that normal conditions of competition do not prevail on this market. In those circumstances, some form of price differentiation may be desirable for those products. This is the more so as parallel trade will rarely lead to any advantage for the consumer.[72] A recent study by the LSE[73] has revealed that in the case of parallel trade in pharmaceuticals, the vast majority of benefits accrue directly to parallel importers and that savings for statutory health insurance organisations and patients were modest. The study revealed in particular that there was no measurable direct benefit for patients and that there was hardly any evidence for price competition or price convergence. This leads to the questioning of the main rationale for the prohibition of restrictions on parallel trade. It cannot be the goal of competition policy to merely provide business opportunities to parallel traders, whilst no real overall welfare advantage is noticeable. This seems to call for a re-evaluation of the policy on parallel trade, at the very least in certain sectors, such as the pharmaceutical industry.[74]

That this is so has been recently recognised openly by Advocate General Jacobs in his opinion in the *Syfait case*.[75] In this opinion, the Advocate General recognised that a pharmaceutical company, even if dominant, could refuse legitimately to supply a company engaged in parallel trade. In that market, he considered that it is the price differentials created by the intervention of the Member States that create the possibility for parallel trade.

As a result, normal conditions of competition do not prevail in that market. To require a dominant company to supply all export orders would in many cases impose a disproportionate burden, especially given the moral and legal

---

[72]   Lilico, Glynn, *supra* n. 66. The IP derogations in the accession treaties do not resolve all problems, as they only apply where product patent systems were non-existent or inadequate in the accession States before 1991.

[73]   Kanavos, Costa-i-Font, Merkur, Gemmill, *The Economic Impact of Pharmaceutical Parallel Trade in European Union Member States: A Stakeholder Analysis*, January 2004, LSE Special Research Paper. See also para. 133 of the Commission Decision in *Glaxo Wellcome, supra* n. 71, which makes the point that 'there is no proof that UK prices have gone or are likely to go down because of Spanish [parallel] imports'. This shows the absence of any benefits of such imports for the consumer or the national health system.

[74]   Ibid., pp. 15–16.

[75]   See opinion of Advocate General Jacobs of 28 October 2004 in case C-53/03, *Synetairismos Farmakopion Aitolias & Akarnanias – Syfait and others v. GlaxoSmithKline AEVE*, not yet officially reported.

obligations incumbent on that company to maintain supplies in all Member States. The Advocate General considered that a requirement to supply would not necessarily promote free movement or competition and could even harm the incentive for pharmaceutical companies to innovate, given the specific economic characteristics of the sector. If it can be shown that the only benefit of parallel trade is received by those in the distribution chain, there is no advantage to imposing on companies an obligation to allow parallel trade.

It remains to be seen whether the Court will follow its Advocate General and moreover how far such reasoning can be transposed to other industries.

On the other hand, it is undisputable that territorial protection is not in itself always harmless. In case of market segmentation, economies indicate that problems are unlikely if there is a high price elasticity of demand. In such a case, any attempt to increase prices will cause a sizeable reduction in the quantity demanded and it will therefore always be advisable to keep prices low. If consumers however have a low price elasticity of demand, the risk is greater that this territory becomes high-price territory if territorial exclusivity is granted.[76] In economic terms, the treatment of territorial exclusivities may therefore have to depend on elasticity of demand.

Taking into consideration the aforementioned arguments and facts, it seems to me that there are strong indicators that the current regulation and practice do not sufficiently take into account the positive aspects of territorial restrictions, at least not in some specific cases.

IV DOMINANT FIRMS

The next point that I would like to address briefly is that the *Guidelines on Vertical Restraints* appear to me to be excessively rigorous in so far as they exclude the possibility of exemptions for dominant undertakings. According to para. 135 of the *Guidelines on Vertical Restraints*, there is no possibility to exempt a vertical restraint entered into by a dominant undertaking if this restraint has appreciable anticompetitive effects (that is if EC Article 81(1) applies to it). The Guidelines base this particularly strict approach on the last condition of Article 81(3) EC, which states that an exemption is not possible if the agreement gives the undertakings the 'possibility of eliminating competition in respect of a substantial part of the products in question'. This however ignores the fact that the negative effects of vertical restraints can more often than not – even in the case of dominant companies – be offset by significant efficiencies.

---

[76]   Ibid.

In my view the aforementioned statement in the Guidelines therefore clearly goes too far. As stated by Bishop and Ridyard, an *a priori* ban would indeed 'fail to acknowledge that dominant firms have many of the same procompetitive rationales for implementing vertical restraints as non-dominant firms'.[77]

In his reply to this statement, Peeperkorn[78] argued that a dominant position would 'automatically imply' that not all of the four conditions of Article 81(3) are fulfilled. According to him, 'dominant undertakings should compete on the merit only and should avoid behaving anticompetitively'.[79] However, it is clear that even dominant undertakings should be allowed to compete, as long as this does not have any exclusionary or exploitative effect.[80] Therefore, they should also be able to get an exemption for vertical agreements if such agreements contain restrictions which have pro-competitive effects.[81]

This view has since been accepted in a number of cases by competition authorities. For instance in 2002, the Dutch Competition authority (NMa) published a decision on exclusivity clauses between *Heineken* (which supplies more than 50 per cent of draught pilsner to pubs in the Netherlands) and pubs/outlets to which it provided financial and commercial support.[82] Following a detailed assessment of the likely economic effects, the NMa found that enough outlets were available and that even the exclusively supplied outlets were contestable. Therefore, the exclusivity restrictions did not amount to a restriction of competition. The NMa thereby adopted a narrower and more economic approach than the EC Commission traditionally has.[83]

The Commission has since taken a similar approach with regard to

---

[77]   S. Bishop, D. Ridyard, 'E.C. Vertical Restraints Guidelines: Effects-Based or Per Se Policy', [2002] *ECLR* 1, p. 35, at p. 36.

[78]   L. Peeperkorn, 'E.C. Vertical Restraints Guidelines: Effects-Based or Per Se Policy – A Reply', [2002] *ECLR* 1, p. 38, at p. 39.

[79]   Ibid., at p. 41.

[80]   However, the CFI of 30 September 2003, case T-203/01, ruled in its *Michelin II* judgment that some pricing and rebate schemes would be abusive irrespective of their actual effect, not yet officially reported.

[81]   This had already been recognised by the ECJ in *Hoffmann-La Roche*, 85/76, 13 February 1979, Rep. 1979, 461 at para. 90, which stresses that exclusivity obligations *sensu lato* are prohibited for dominant undertakings 'unless there are exceptional circumstances which may make an agreement between undertakings in the context of Article 81 and in particular of paragraph (3) of that article, permissible'.

[82]   NMa decision of 28 May 2002, Case 2036, *Heineken – Horecaovereenkomsten*.

[83]   RBB Brief 04, 'Procompetitive Exclusive Supply Agreements: How Refreshing!', August 2002. This approach seems to be more in line with the CFI in Case T-374/94 etc., *European Night Services et al. v. Commission*, [1988] ECR II-3141.

Interbrew. After the beer producer amended its agreements, the Commission considered they would no longer appreciably restrict competition.[84] In order to achieve this, the exclusivity was limited to draught pils and the loan agreements could be more easily terminated. The Commission thus accepted serious non-compete obligations although Interbrew had a market share of 53 per cent.

More recently, the Commission also accepted an extended single branding obligation on petrol stations for Repsol in Spain, despite its 88 per cent market share.[85]

Interestingly, the *Guidelines on the application of Article 81(3) of the Treaty* seem to have changed the restrictive interpretation regarding the application of Article 81(3) EC to agreements with dominant undertakings. According to para. 106 of the *Guidelines on the application of Article 81(3) of the Treaty*, Article 81(3) EC should be interpreted to preclude any application to restrictive agreements 'that constitute an abuse of a dominant position'. This is materially different from the concept in the *Guidelines on Vertical Restraints* which excludes the possibility of applying Article 81(3) at all with regard to dominant undertakings as soon as there is a significant anticompetitive effect. The *Guidelines on the application of Article 81(3) of the Treaty* go on and state that 'not all restrictive agreements concluded by a dominant undertaking constitute an abuse of a dominant position'.[86] In a footnote,[87] the *Guidelines on the application of Article 81(3) of the Treaty* state that this is how para. 135 of the *Guidelines on Vertical Restraints* ought to be understood when it states that in principle restrictive agreements concluded by dominant undertakings cannot be excluded. This is also in line with the statement by the CFI in the *TACA* case,[88] which implied that there was a possibility for a dominant undertaking to get an exemption for its agreements. Thus, the position of the Commission seems to have changed and so does the interpretation which should be given to the *Guidelines on Vertical Restraints*.

---

[84]   Press Release, 'European Commission opens up Interbrew's Belgian horeca outlets to competing beer brands', IP/03/545.

[85]   See Notice pursuant to Article 27(4) of Council Regulation (EC) No 1/2003 (1) concerning *Repsol CPP SA*, [2004] OJ C258/7, 20.10.2004.

[86]   The Guidelines mention as an example a non full-function joint venture which is restrictive of competition, but which involves substantial integration of assets.

[87]   Footnote 92 of the Guidelines on the application of Article 81(3) of the Treaty.

[88]   CFI of 30 September 2003, Joined Cases T-191/98 and T-212/98 to T-214/98, *Atlantic Container Line AB and others v Commission*, at para. 1456, [2003] ECR II 3275.

V   AGENCY

My final comment concerns agency agreements. Paras 12 to 20 of the *Guidelines on Vertical Restraints* give new guidance with regard to agency agreements and certainly constitute progress when compared with the 1962 Notice,[89] and the case-law of the Court.[90] However, also here, it seems to me that the right balance may not have been fully reached yet.

Rightly, according to para. 13 of the *Guidelines on Vertical Restraints*, the determining factor for the application of Article 81(1) EC is 'the financial or commercial risk borne by the agent in relation to the activities for which he has been appointed as an agent by the principal'. Agreements fall outside Article 81(1) EC if the agent does not bear any, or bears only insignificant, risks in relation to the contracts concluded on behalf of the principal and in relation to market-specific investments for that field of activity.[91]

However, the Commission does not give any guidance on how to measure the 'insignificance' of a risk, for example whether this is only in relation to the particular contract, by reference to the absolute level of investment or by reference to the potential reward available to the agent.[92]

To be sure, in para. 16 of the *Guidelines on Vertical Restraints*, the Commission enumerates a non-exhaustive list of possible risks that could indicate that an agency agreement is to be considered 'non-genuine' and consequently falls within Article 81(1) EC. In so doing, however, the Commission has opted in my opinion for an excessively strict approach (almost any risk is sufficient to exclude the possibility of regarding the agreement as agency) so that a large number of agency agreements no longer qualify as 'genuine' agency.

In my view, some of the 'risks' mentioned by the Commission are not in reality at all relevant. To give an example, the contribution by the agent to transporting costs is not only common but also rather a question of cost allocation than of risk allocation. Why should an agent that receives a slightly

---

[89]   [1962] OJ 139, 24.12.1962, p. 2921.

[90]   See e.g. ECJ of 10 October 1987, Case 311/85, *Vereniging van Vlaamse Reisbureaus v Sociale Dienst van Plaatselijke en Gewestelijke Overheidsdiensten*, [1987] ECR 3801.

[91]   Para. 15 of the *Guidelines on Vertical Restraints*. This is in line with previous judgments by the ECJ. See e.g. the statement of the ECJ in para. 19 of *BKartA v VW AG and VAG Leasing GmbH*, Case C-266/93: 'Representatives can lose their character as independent traders only if they do not bear any of the risks resulting from the contracts negotiated on behalf of the principal and they operate as auxiliary organs forming an integral part of the principal's undertaking'.

[92]   M. Mendelsohn, S. Rose, *Guide to the EC Block Exemption for Vertical agreements*, 2002, p. 81.

higher commission whilst assuming responsibility for organising transport be in a materially different situation in competition terms from an agent receiving a slightly lower commission reflecting the fact that the principal is bearing the transport costs?[93] This argument can also be applied to other factors of cost mentioned by the Commission in this paragraph because certain costs that the agent should no longer be allowed to bear – if he is to be regarded as a true agent – would subsequently be reflected in the level of commission. This means that if the agent is no longer allowed to bear promotional costs for example, the principal will have to cover these costs, but reflect this reallocation in lowering the commission. This seems merely to be a question of cost accounting and ought not to have a real influence on the principal–agent relationship in competition terms.[94] With regard to promotional costs, it could also be inefficient to let the principal bear all costs in exchange for lowering the commission. Within a widespread network of agents, the latter will know the local markets much better and will be more efficient in promoting the products.

The consequence of such a broad list of risks could be that a lot of agreements that have initially been drafted as 'genuine' agency agreements risk now being – wrongly – considered as agreements that fall under Article 81(1) EC. In order to achieve an appropriate level of legal certainty and an appropriate assessment of agency agreements, it appears in my view reasonable to adapt the existing *Guidelines on Vertical Restraints* in order to allow a more effects-based assessment. All risks that merely constitute a cost allocation that could be reflected in the level of the commission for the agent should generally not be considered as risks that could trigger the qualification as 'non-genuine' agents.

The same could be true with other risks traditionally associated with agency, such as the *del credere* clauses. Other criteria, such as the need for the agent not to undertake any sector specific investments appear also excessively general.

Finally, one may wonder whether the requirement of 'integration' of the agent should be ignored totally henceforth even for clauses of exclusivity or non-compete. In my view, integration could justify such clauses even where the agreement bears certain limited risks.

VI CONCLUSION

Whilst, in general, the Regulation 2790/99 and the *Guidelines on Vertical Restraints* are welcome, especially due to their basic commitment to a more

---

[93] Ibid., p. 83.
[94] Ibid.

effects-based approach to the assessment of vertical restraints, there remain in my view doubts with regard to some points mentioned above.

Even though committed to an economic approach, some of the underlying concepts of Regulation 2790/99 and the Guidelines seem not to follow this path through. This is so particularly regarding the following points:

- With regard to the system as such and the market share threshold in particular, one may wonder whether the existence of Article 82 EC is not sufficient to deal with problems of market power and whether an additional market share threshold is really at all necessary.
- The 'hardcore restrictions' in themselves and their quasi *per se* prohibition ignores related efficiencies and appears therefore to be excessive. As shown above, there are good reasons in some cases to accept such restrictions.
- As regards dominant companies, it is interesting to note the Commission's own revised view on the treatment of the vertical restraints applied by such companies in the Notice on Article 81(3) as opposed to the *Guidelines on Vertical Restraints*.
- Finally, one may also advocate a review with regard to the treatment of agency agreements. It should in my view be possible to leave certain limited risks to the agent without necessarily recharacterising the agreement as a distribution agreement.

However, generally the system chosen seems to me to be adequate and workable although the introduction of relatively minor changes and adjustments in the light of what I have said above could be welcome so as to achieve a higher degree of legal certainty and coherence. Especially in the light of modernisation and decentralisation, such adjustments would be useful in order to secure a coherent and more logical and foreseeable application of the rules applicable.

Comment

Wolfgang Kerber*

1 INTRODUCTION

The enactment of Regulation 2790/99 on vertical restraints was – as Waelbroeck rightly emphasises – an important first step in the process of modernisation of European competition policy. It sought to take into account more the economic effects of vertical restraints and to enhance legal certainty and enforcement efficiency. In contrast to Regulation 1400/2002 on the motor vehicle sector, this general regulation on vertical restraints led to a liberalisation process. Waelbroeck's paper analyses the experience made with this regulation in recent years and suggests some specific and clear proposals for its improvement. At first glance, these proposals seem to be a logical next step in the development of the EU policy on vertical restraints. However, I do not agree with his statement that these proposals would only imply 'relatively minor changes and adjustments'.[1] On the contrary, I think they are far-reaching and raise additional fundamental questions about the overall architecture of European competition policy.

2 IS THE MARKET SHARE THRESHOLD OF 30 PER CENT TOO RESTRICTIVE?

Waelbroeck's first proposal is to abolish the market share threshold in the Regulation 2790/99. This would imply that all vertical agreements (except hardcore restrictions) are permitted, independently of the firms' market shares. As long as there are competition problems through vertical restraints, they should be solved by applying Article 82 EC (abusive behaviour by dominant firms).

   The economic analysis of the effects of vertical restraints, and therefore

---

*   Prof., Dr. rer. pol., Philipps-Universität, Marburg.
[1]   Waelbroeck, 'Vertical Agreements: 4 Years of Liberalisation by Regulation 2790/99 after 40 Years of Legal (Block) Regulation', in this volume, Chapter 5, sub. VI.

their assessment from the perspective of competition policy, is complex. On the one hand, a considerable number of efficiency arguments have been elaborated which show that vertical agreements can help to reduce various kinds of inefficiencies. The most important are inefficiencies due to double marginalisation, free-rider problems and other kinds of horizontal and vertical externalities within a vertical chain. On the other hand, economic analysis has also shown that vertical agreements can lead to a number of anticompetitive effects that reduce overall welfare (for example, facilitating collusive behaviour, leverage and foreclosure effects). These results imply that some kind of balancing between efficiency and the anticompetitive effects of vertical restraints might be necessary. Nevertheless, the most important factor for our discussion is that economic analysis shows that in most cases the welfare-reducing effects of vertical restraints depend on the degree of market power the involved firms have.[2]

This general insight was also the reason for the introduction of the market share threshold of 30 per cent in the Regulation 2790/99. It implies that any anticompetitive effects of vertical agreements of firms with market shares below 30 per cent will generally be so small that it can be presumed that they will be dominated by the welfare-enhancing efficiency effects of these vertical agreements (except hardcore restrictions). However, also beyond the 30 per cent threshold, vertical agreements can be permitted, if it can be shown that the efficiency effects are greater than any anticompetitive effects. In contrast, Waelbroeck's proposal implies that additionally all vertical restraints of firms between 30 per cent market share and the market dominance level should be permitted. Furthermore, even dominant firms should be permitted to use vertical agreements, as long as this behaviour is not abusive according to Article 82 EC. I would like to suggest reasons for being sceptical about this proposal.

Waelbroeck also emphasizes that there is a large gap between the 30 per cent threshold and market dominance. As a consequence, many vertical agreements of firms with a strong market position remain exposed to legal uncertainty. This would lead to a severe change in European competition policy in regard to vertical restraints. Can this change of policy be defended from an economic standpoint?

---

[2]   For surveys on the results of industrial economics in regard to the assessment of vertical restraints from the perspective of competition policy, see Scherer & Ross, *Industrial Market Structure and Economic Performance*, 3rd edn, Boston: Houghton and Mifflin, 1990, pp. 541–69; Katz, 'Vertical Contractual Relations', in Schmalensee & Willig (eds), *Handbook of Industrial Organization*, Vol. 1, Amsterdam: North Holland 1989, pp. 655–721; Bishop & Walker, *The Economics of EC Competition Law: Concepts, Application and Measurement*, 2nd edn, London: Sweet & Maxwell, 2002, pp. 153–71; Motta, *Competition Policy. Theory and Practice*, Cambridge: Cambridge University Press, 2004, pp. 302–409.

Waelbroeck argues (sub. II.2.) that:

> there is only a need to scrutinise vertical restraints in cases of real market power and (that) there is no need to care about firms which do not have large market power. . . . If the objective of the 30 per cent threshold is thus to deal with concerns of true market power, that is dominance, it appears in my view most logical to use the most obvious legal basis to that effect, that is Article 82 EC.

Waelbroeck is right that it is only necessary to be concerned with vertical agreements of firms with large market power but he wrongly equates 'large market power' with market dominance. The original quotation of Motta (2004, 377–8), who is Waelbroeck's reference with regard to 'large market power', is:

> Accordingly, there is no need to monitor restraints and mergers which involve firms with little market power. An efficient policy towards vertical restraints would grant exemption to all the vertical restraints of firms which do not have large market power. From the operational point of view, it would seem a good proxy to exempt firms with market shares below, say, 20–30% (as in the regime created in the EU . . .).

In contrast to the impression Waelbroeck gives in his text, Motta would not support his proposal to clear all vertical restraints up to the market dominance level. On the contrary, the market share threshold of the Regulation of 30 per cent is already at the top end of the recommended range of 20–30 per cent.

The main problem is that in most cases economic analysis shows that the size of anticompetitive effects of vertical agreements (both collusive and exclusionary effects) depends on the degree of market power. Therefore, anticompetitive effects also emerge in cases in which the firms have only moderate market power and because of this are far from market dominance. The crucial argument is not that vertical agreements of firms with only moderate market shares do not have anticompetitive effects, but that these welfare-reducing effects are smaller than in the case of firms with higher market shares.[3] As a consequence, vertical agreements of firms with 20 per cent, 30 per cent or 40 per cent can have anticompetitive effects but the probability that the efficiency effects of vertical agreements of firms with 20 per cent market share outbalance their anticompetitive effects is (on average) much higher than in the case of 40 per cent. In his proposal, Waelbroeck implicitly contends that in the range between 30 per cent and market dominance, the efficiency effects of vertical agreements will also on average outbalance the

---

[3]   See, for example, Motta, *supra* n. 2, at 354–6, where he shows in a model that the additional mark-up through strategic vertical restraints decreases with an increase in the number of the firms.

anticompetitive effects.[4] The industrial economics literature on vertical restraints does not support this contention. Additionally, firms with a market share of more than 30 per cent have the possibility of showing that the efficiency effects are greater than any anticompetitive effects. Although it implies some burden for the firms, this additional assessment will be relevant only for a few firms – in most cases only the leading firm in the market. One cannot see that this burden is really a big problem.

Independent of the question of the right threshold, the proposal to reduce the level of controlling vertical agreements to the question of whether these vertical restraints imply an abuse of market dominance, means a much more severe reduction of control. Indeed the difficulties of proving abusive behaviour of dominant firms are well known. Article 82 EC has always been considered as a cumbersome instrument of last resort, a kind of 'emergency brake' in competition policy for cases in which the main strategy of competition policy of preventing anticompetitive market structures and behaviour has failed. Therefore, we should be cautious in relying too much on the effectiveness of Article 82 EC.

In this context Waelbroeck also raises the question of whether it is appropriate that vertical restraints of dominant firms cannot be exempted according to Article 81(3) EC because this would not be compatible with the fourth condition for exemption, that the agreement should not give the firms the opportunity to eliminate competition. Waelbroeck himself favours a more flexible approach which would allow the balancing of procompetitive and anticompetitive effects even in the case of market dominance. He indicates that there might also be some inconsistency in the position of the Commission. Although I have much sympathy with the idea that dominant firms should also have the opportunity of using efficiency-enhancing vertical agreements, I am reluctant to endorse the idea of balancing procompetitive and anticompetitive effects in the realm of market dominance. This would be very close to the argument that mergers can also be cleared if the positive efficiency effects are larger than the anticompetitive effects. I would plead for a more cautious approach. Efficiency-enhancing vertical agreements of dominant firms should, indeed, be exempt if they have no significant anticompetitive effects. However, if there are significant anticompetitive effects then the danger of the reinforcement of the already dominant position of the firm should be seen as so important that this reinforcement of market dominance should not be balanced with efficiency advantages. Such an approach, which seems to be

---

4   In addition, he also implicitly contends that it is not worthwhile to make an additional differentiation in that range by balancing the positive and negative effects of vertical restraints.

compatible with the position of the EU Commission, emphasizes the preventive role of competition policy with regard to the emergence and strengthening of market dominance. Nevertheless, I agree with Waelbroeck that the possibility for dominant firms to use vertical agreements should not be overly restricted.

3 PER SE RULES VS. THE RULE OF REASON: SHOULD HARDCORE RESTRICTIONS BE ABOLISHED?

In his second proposal, Waelbroeck questions another of the main pillars of European competition policy regarding vertical agreements: the concept of hardcore restrictions. Regulation 2790/99 states that some kinds of vertical agreements are prohibited *per se*, independent from the market shares of the firms. By discussing resale price maintenance and territorial (or customer) protection, Waelbroeck argues that it cannot be shown from an economic point of view that these two types of vertical agreements always have anticompetitive effects. Indeed sometimes they can even be welfare-enhancing. Therefore, a rule of reason approach would be more appropriate. However, not only does Waelbroeck plead for a more differentiated treatment of resale price maintenance or territorial protection, he rather questions the concept of hardcore restrictions itself. Therefore, a more fundamental discussion of the problem of the rule of reason vs. per se rules is necessary.

If we ask whether resale price maintenance and territorial protection are always anticompetitive, then economic theory clearly confirms the argumentation of Waelbroeck that these vertical agreements are not welfare-reducing in all cases and that a number of cases can even be found in which they might have more positive than negative effects. Beyond this, economic theory can show that a policy which, for example, prohibits resale price maintenance *per se* but allows other vertical agreements, such as for example quantity fixing or vertical mergers, can lead to inconsistencies because, under certain conditions, the latter practices are substitutes for (and lead to similar effects to) resale price maintenance.[5] The crucial question is whether such an argument is sufficient for claiming that it is necessary to change from a prohibition *per se* to a rule of reason approach.

The application of competition rules can lead to type I and type II errors. A certain behaviour can be mistakenly allowed (type I error) or wrongly prohibited

---

[5] For the economic discussion on resale price maintenance, see Scherer & Ross, *supra* n. 2, at 541–58, and as part of a general discussion on vertical restraints Motta, *supra* n. 2, at 302–78.

because in fact it is not anticompetitive (type II error). The more differentiated the competitive assessment of business behaviour is, the greater the possibility that a more exact separation of anticompetitive and procompetitive behaviour (and therefore a reduction of both types of errors) might be possible. From this perspective, a rule of reason approach, which allows for any amount of differentiation in specific cases, seems superior to a rule-based approach such as per se rules.

However, this line of argument does not take into account the fact that such a rule of reason approach can lead to various additional costs:

1. The more differentiated the assessment is, especially if this includes the hearing of experts and/or making specific empirical studies on the effects of vertical agreements, the higher the costs for both the parties and the competition authorities – both in terms of direct monetary costs and in terms of lost time.

2. Another kind of cost, both for the parties and the economy, stems from the increased potential for rent-seeking activities. These are accompanied by the larger discretionary scope afforded both to competition authorities and to courts in the case of a rule of reason approach (as opposed to a strict legal rule-based approach). As far as these rent-seeking activities lead to distorted (and therefore wrong) decisions, the quality of the distinction between anticompetitive and procompetitive business behaviour or market structures is reduced, leading to welfare losses.

3. The third problem is that often the knowledge about the effects of these vertical agreements in the specific cases is very limited. This is partly a consequence of our limited general knowledge on the conditions under which certain vertical agreements lead to more positive than negative effects. In addition, often we also do not have enough precise information about the situation in the specific case to make correct assessments. The less knowledge and information we have, the less productive a more in-depth analysis of the competitive effects of vertical agreements is. As a consequence, the value of any additional differentiation depends critically on the amount of reliable knowledge and information available.

4. Another critical issue is the problem of legal certainty. In a rule of reason approach, the outcome of a decision is less predictable because it depends on an overall assessment of all the positive or negative effects in a specific case. The absence of legal certainty leads to additional costs for firms because there is a greater risk that they will prosecuted by competition authorities or sued by other firms.[6]

---

[6]   For a recent analysis of the consequences of the reform of the Merger Regulation for the predictability of merger decisions and therefore for legal certainty,

All of these kinds of costs and problems (increasing administrative costs, rent-seeking and knowledge problems, legal uncertainty) can be interpreted as typical examples of state failure. The importance of the latter costs is also emphasized by the claim of the EU Commission that, in addition to the aim underlying a more economics-based approach, the aims of legal certainty and enforcement efficiency are also important in the modernisation of European competition policy. The critical point is that all of these costs and problems are aggravated by using a rule of reason approach instead of a more rule-based approach. As is well known in the theory of economic policy, narrow rule-based approaches to economic policy have many advantages compared to approaches which rely on the discretionary behaviour of governmental agencies or courts because they cause fewer administrative costs and fewer rent-seeking problems, need less information and knowledge, and lead to higher legal certainty. As a consequence, we should economise on these costs by trying to use a more strictly legal rules-based approach. From this perspective, there is a trade-off between the potential advantages of additional differentiation, which might be achieved by a rule of reason approach, and the above-mentioned costs which can be presumed to be smaller by a more narrow rule-oriented approach.

What are the consequences for Waelbroeck's critique of the concept of hardcore restrictions? Whether *per se* prohibitions of particular vertical agreements are appropriate depends on an overall evaluation of the advantages and disadvantages of a more differentiated assessment. If in most cases of particular restraints it can be expected that the negative effects predominate and if the costs and problems of identifying the smaller number of cases, in which these agreements have no negative effects or even have positive net effects, are larger than the benefits of this additional differentiation, then a per se rule of prohibiting this particular vertical agreement can be the appropriate solution. The most important conclusion of these considerations is that it is not sufficient to show that there are cases, in which vertical agreements, as for example resale price maintenance, have no negative or even positive net effects, for rejecting a per se prohibition of these vertical agreements. Rather, it must be shown that a transition from a per se prohibition to a more differentiated approach has positive net benefits, that is that the positive effects of an additional assessment are larger than the ensuing additional costs and problems.

Waelbroeck is right in questioning whether resale price maintenance and territorial protection should be per se prohibited, because economics can show

---

see Voigt & Schmidt, 'Switching to Substantial Impediments of Competition (SIC) can have Substantial Costs – SIC!', *European Competition Law Review*, 2004, 580–86, and Christiansen, 'Die "Ökonomisierung" der EU-Fusionskontrolle: Mehr Kosten als Nutzen?', *Wirtschaft und Wettbewerb*, 2005, 285 et seq.

that these vertical agreements do not always have negative net effects on competition and welfare. However, it is also necessary to take into account the question of whether there are sufficient, clear and reliable criteria for distinguishing procompetitive from anticompetitive forms of resale price maintenance in a particular case, what the costs of any increased legal uncertainty are, and whether the additional administrative costs are smaller than the potential benefits. It cannot be discussed here whether and to what extent a more differentiated treatment of resale price maintenance might be worthwhile.[7] In some respect, a more differentiated approach does already exist, because some variants of resale price maintenance, as, for example, resale price recommendations or maximum prices (price ceilings) are not per se prohibited.[8]

4 THE ARCHITECTURE OF EUROPEAN COMPETITION RULES: SOME FUNDAMENTAL PROBLEMS

Finally, some fundamental questions with regard to the overall architecture of European competition policy, which in my opinion are raised by Waelbroeck's proposals, should be briefly discussed. From these proposals, the following overall picture emerges: (1) Vertical agreements, which so far are prohibited *per se*, should be subjected to a rule of reason test; (2) All other vertical agreements should be generally allowed without further assessment up to the level of market dominance; (3) Any competition problems with those vertical agreements should be solved by Article 82 EC, implying that anticompetitive vertical agreements are only illegal if they can be proved as being abusive behaviour of market dominant firms. This would be a far-reaching reduction of the control of vertical agreements which – as has already been shown – cannot be supported by economics.

Beyond this, accepting these proposals would raise additional fundamental questions about the future significance of Article 81 EC, because this can also

---

[7]   The assessment of territorial protection as the second hardcore restriction critically discussed by Waelbroeck is much more complex. On the one hand, other aims of European competition policy are also relevant here (in particular the aim of market integration, but beyond that also social and health policy considerations regarding, for example, pharmaceuticals). On the other, the economic assessment of price discrimination is very difficult because permitting price discriminations by territorial protection has complex distributional effects which cannot be ignored.

[8]   See for example, Mestmäcker & Schweitzer, *Europäisches Wettbewerbsrecht*, 2nd edn, 2004, p. 371; for the very differentiated development in the US Antitrust law, see Scherer/Ross, *supra* n. 2, at 548–58.

have severe consequences for the assessment of horizontal agreements. For example, the market share thresholds in regard to R&D cooperation and specialisation agreements can be questioned in a similar way. Here the question can also be raised why we do not allow these (presumably efficiency-enhancing) horizontal agreements up to the level of market dominance, and limit control to whether or not these horizontal agreements are abusive behaviour by dominant firms. Such a development, which seems to be driven by some plausible logic, would considerably endanger the position of Article 81 EC in the overall architecture of European competition policy. The decisive point is that it starts from the dichotomy (also used by Waelbroeck) that in markets there is either effective market competition or market dominance, and that real competition problems can only arise in the second case. This leads to the conclusion that Article 82 EC would become the most important instrument for controlling vertical (and perhaps in the end also horizontal) agreements.

This dichotomy, however, is not supported by modern industrial economics. If market power is defined as the price/cost margin, as it is in industrial economics, then in most markets we have a continuum of firms with more or less market power. Additionally, firms with moderate market shares can have market power, particularly in markets with heterogeneous products. From the perspective of industrial economics, 'perfect competition' and 'no competition' are only extreme cases in a wide continuum of more or less competition (and more or less market power). From a purely economic point of view, there is no clear-cut criterion where unproblematic market power ends and problematic market dominance begins.[9] The question is, at which level of impediments to competition or market power should competition be protected by competition policy? This question clearly also has an important normative dimension. Two conclusions can be drawn. Firstly we should be very cautious in making market dominance the fulcrum of competition policy because it is both theoretically and normatively a much less clear concept than it looks at first sight. Secondly, market power and, in turn, impediments to competition also exist below the level of market dominance. Therefore, from an economic point of view, there are well-founded arguments that competition policy should not only protect competition in cases of already existing dominant firms, but also below this level of market dominance. From my point of view this has always been seen as the main task of Article 81 EC. The 'effects-based' approach in the reform process of European competition policy does not call this role of Article 81 EC into

---

[9] See also Azevedo & Walker, 'Market Dominance: Measurement Problems and Mistakes', *Eur. Comp. L. Rev.* 24, 2003, pp. 640–43.

question because considerable anticompetitive effects can also emerge below the level of market dominance.[10]

5 CONCLUSION

Although my remarks on the proposals of Waelbroeck seem to be rather critical, I sympathise greatly with the general approach of Denis Waelbroeck of seeking to frame more appropriate (and as far as possible also less restrictive) rules for assessing vertical restraints with a view to their economic effects. Since his proposals are very clear and represent one consistent possibility on how to develop the policy in regard to vertical restraints, they enrich the discussion and help to clarify the basic options for the future development of European competition policy.

---

[10]   It would be interesting to link this discussion to the reform of the European Merger Regulation 139/2004. With the introduction of the SIEC-test the ultimate criterion for assessing mergers now is whether the merger leads to a 'significant impediment to effective competition', and the emergence or strengthening of market dominance is only one (but presumably also in future the most important) possibility. From that perspective it has been presumed that now mergers can also be prohibited below the level of market dominance; see, for example, Zimmer, 'Significant Impediment to Effective Competition. Das neue Untersagungskriterium der EU-Fusionskontrolle', *Zeitschrift für Wettbewerbsrecht*, 2004, pp. 250–67 (who – in regard to the architecture of European competition policy – also notes an increasing convergence between Article 81 EC and merger control in EU competition policy) and Díaz, 'The Reform of European Merger Control: Quid Novi Sub Sole?', *World Competition* 27, pp. 177–99.

Comment

Roger Zäch*

1 PRELIMINARY REMARKS

I would like to criticize a couple of the statements and considerations in Denis Waelbroeck's chapter. I also want to give some additional information which will put my criticism in the right perspective.

The chapter deals with the so-called 'more economic approach' versus the so-called 'formalistic regulatory approach'.

I practise competition law as a member of the Swiss Competition Commission. My experience is that in many cases economic considerations are a hindrance to a quick and clear decision. Since there are many controversies about vertical restraints and their effects among economists, one may always find reasons to justify behaviour that can be anticompetitive. Such behaviour is then called behaviour resulting from the competition process. Therefore I advocate a clear distinction between the law-making process and the law application process. In the law-making process economic considerations play an important role. By contrast, their role in the application process should be limited. When implementing Article 81 EC or Article 82 EC for example, economic considerations should come into consideration only in appraising whether an agreement leads to the elimination of competition (3(b)) or if the issue turns on whether a firm really has market dominance.

In experiencing and observing Swiss competition and restraints of competition, I realized that Switzerland is still a country where the willingness-to-pay is very high. Prices for almost all products are 50 per cent to 100 per cent higher than in neighbouring countries.[1]

This high price level strongly affects the competitiveness of Switzerland's industry in the global economy.

There is no doubt that this high price level is to a great extent due to vertical

* Prof. Dr. iur., University of Zürich, Vice-President of the Swiss Competition Commission. The author thanks Mrs. Sabrina Carron from the office of the Swiss Competition Commission for her help in formally drafting this text.

[1] For a comparison of prices see F. Prümmer, 'Preisunterschiede zwischen der Gemeinschaft und der Schweiz – Erklärungsansätze', *WuW* 2003, 248.

market foreclosure,[2] a distribution policy that makes resale price maintenance unnecessary by assigning dealers in Switzerland absolute territorial protection.

The revision of the Swiss Act on Cartels in 2003 introduced a new provision in order to fight vertical resale price maintenance and vertical market segmentation. I hope that the Swiss Competition Commission will strongly enforce this provision in the near future.

2 MAIN CRITICISM

In Waelbroeck's chapter, the Block Exemption Regulation is mainly assessed under economic aspects such as welfare.[3] To me an even more important aspect is the commercial freedom of the firms on the market. There cannot be any effective competition in markets in which firms do not have the freedom to set their own prices and choose whom to deal with.[4]

The presented chapter gives great credit to efficiency justifications.[5]

I doubt whether we should rely so much on economic considerations in the application process. Efficiency considerations are typical of a centrally planned economy since they need a lot of 'unknown' information. Such considerations make it inevitable to judge results that are based on theoretical calculations. Competition law should not assess these results; it should rather outlaw certain practices which are proven to have negative effects. Vertical agreements on minimum resale prices and vertical agreements that grant absolute territorial protection do have negative effects.[6] This is what long experience, economic theory and US and EC competition laws show us. Such vertical agreements should therefore be outlawed in principle.

Let me add another consideration. It is well understood that each case is different.[7] In my opinion, this does not mean that rules of per se illegality are

---

    2   Y. Flückiger, 'La politique de la concurrence d'un petit état sous l'angle économique', in: W. A. Stoffel, R. Zäch, *Die Kartellgesetzrevision 2003 – Neuerungen und Folgen*, Zürich/Basel/Genf 2004, 327 f.
    3   Waelbroeck, *supra* sub II, III.
    4   E. Hoppmann, *Wirtschaftsordnung und Wettbewerb*, Baden-Baden 1988, 259 ff.; I. Schmidt, *Wettbewerbspolitik und Kartellrecht*, 7. A., Stuttgart 2001, p. 14; H. Schröter, 'Vorbemerkungen zu Artikel 81 bis 89 EG', in H. von der Groeben, J. Schwarze, *Vertrag über die Europäische Union und Vertrag zur Gründung der Europäischen Gemeinschaft*, Baden-Baden 2003, mn. 13.
    5   Waelbroek, *supra* sub II.
    6   For an example of negative effects see: Recht und Politik des Wettbewerbs, Publikationsorgan der schweizerischen Wettbewerbsbehörden, 2000/4, 588 ff., Wettbewerbskommission, Markt für Strassenbelege.
    7   Waelbroek, *supra* sub III.

never accurate. In other words, if we do not accept that horizontal or vertical hard core restrictions must be declared illegal in principle, every case might go to court. This would cause competition law to become inefficient and ineffective.

3 ADDITIONAL CRITICISMS

I will now come to some specific points:

i.   The market share threshold. The chapter proposes the removal of that threshold, because many firms 'could not behave anti-competitively even if they tried to'.[8]

I would agree to this under the conditions that the notion of market dominance of Article 82 EC is understood:
   * in the sense of the German law which also covers vertical dependencies; and
   * in the sense that enterprises with strong brands are also covered.

ii. The chapter seems to make the assumption that in most cases vertical restraints are imposed by a manufacturer.[9] This assumption is flawed: vertical restrictions mainly restrain competition among dealers.[10] Therefore, dealers have strong incentives to initiate such restrictions themselves. In principle, a manufacturer has no reason to impose for example minimum resale prices since price competition at the dealer level allows him to maximize his sales. Therefore vertical agreements of minimum resale prices or absolute territorial protection can be almost as bad as horizontal agreements of that kind.

iii. The argument is made that price-fixing may be justified as it prevents 'free riding';[11] this means that 'free riding' is bad.

I am not so sure about that. 'Free riding' is in principle part of the competition process, like imitation. Imitation is only unlawful when intellectual property rights or unfair competition are at stake. But, for instance, in cases where so-called presale service is provided but not really needed, complaints about free riding are not founded.

---

   8   Waelbroek, *supra* sub III.
   9   Waelbroek, *supra* sub II, referring in footnote 4 to S. Bishop, D. Ridyard, 'E.C. Vertical Restraints Guidelines: Effects-Based or Per Se Policy', [2002] *ECLR* 1, p. 35.
   10 Vertical restrictions can also be called 'vertically imposed horizontal restraints', U. Immenga, *Die Marke im Wettbewerb – Wettbewerb innerhalb der Marke*, [sic!] 2002, p. 375.
   11 Waelbroek, *supra* sub III.1.

Even if 'free riding' is considered 'bad', it remains questionable whether the prevention of 'free riding' by resale price maintenance justifies the complete elimination of price competition among dealers or retailers. There are instruments such as promotional allowances or service requirements which can circumvent 'free riding' without the anti-competitive side effect of eliminating price competition among dealers and retailers.

iv.   The argument has been made that vertical territorial market segmentation is undesirable because it hinders market integration within the European Union.[12]

Some forty years ago, when 'Consten-Grundig'[13] was decided this was certainly an important point. But market segmentation has always been and will continue to be an important point of competition: market segmentation can create a monopoly situation which allows the monopolist to set abusive prices.

The EU and the USA are the biggest players in the global economy. Since the USA does everything to prevent monopolies from evolving in their domestic markets, the EU must do the same or it will create inefficient firms which will lose in competition against more efficient US firms.[14]

v.   The Chicago School advocates treating vertical agreements on prices and market segmentation softly.[15] This policy may be accurate within the USA where it would be unthinkable to prevent a car dealer in Michigan from selling to a customer in Ohio. The situation is very different in Europe.[16] Due to still existing political borderlines, language, cultural, legal and other barriers it is often possible to effectively prevent dealers from serving customers in other territories which are often other countries.

Many US scholars do not take into account that it is a fact that the situation in other parts of the world differs from the one in their own country. That Swiss scholars do not realize the existing differences in my opinion is not acceptable. I do not criticize EU scholars, for in the EU

---

12   Waelbroek, *supra* sub III.2.
13   Vgl. EuGH, Rs. 56/64 und 58/64, Slg. 1966, 320, Consten und Grundig/Kommission.
14   H. G. Koppensteiner, *Österreichisches und europäisches Wettbewerbsrecht*, 3. A., Wien 1997, §1 annot. 20; or in other words: 'Firms that do not have to compete at home rarely succeed abroad', M. E. Porter, *The Competitive Advantage of Nations*, New York, The Free Press, 1990, p. 662.
15   Waelbroek, *supra* sub III.2.
16   V. Emmerich, Art. 85 Abs. 1, in U. Immenga, E. J. Mestmäcker, *EG-Wettbewerbsrecht*, München 1997, annot. 91.

the factual situation resembles more and more that in the USA. The single market already exists to a large extent. But authorities should not ease up and give companies the opportunity to use vertical restraints to divide that market again.

vi.   We all heard that the LSE study reveals that in the case of parallel trade in pharmaceuticals the vast majority of benefits accrue directly to parallel importers and not to health insurances or patients.[17] As I take commercial freedom into consideration more than results, I advocate the possibility of parallel imports. From the Swiss point of view, I may add that parallel importers are mostly located in Switzerland. Therefore the benefits are at least partly transferred to Switzerland and do not remain abroad.

vii.   A final and well documented argument for market segmentation is the necessity to introduce new products or penetrate new markets. This is clearly no problem for new products from relatively unknown manufacturers. But it is a problem if market segmentation is used by well-known brand manufacturers to introduce variations of existing products and/or segment markets along borders or income per capita in order to discriminate in their pricing policies.

---

[17]   cf. Waelbroek, *supra* sub III.2., at n. 73.

6. Cooperative networking: bridging the cooperation–concentration gap

Maria Manuel Leitão Marques and Ana Abrunhosa*

I INTRODUCTION

Cooperation between firms is now a powerful tool in the orchestration of markets in a world economy. In some sectors, such as airlines, cooperation has been losing its contractual nature and is becoming much more institutional, closer to a concentration. In others, like the electronics or automobile industries, the contractual element is still there and cooperation is far more precarious and flexible. But even in these sectors, cooperation has become a structural necessity to ensure competitiveness rather than being a cyclical instrument for resolving a short-term problem.

Are these changes so important and widespread as to change the basic paradigm that has inspired competition law and policy during the 20th century? In a new emergent paradigm, should networks (far more than firms) become the units to be considered by competition law? In that case, should competition law be chiefly concerned with cooperation between networks and rather less with the formation of networks themselves, except when these totally eliminate competition? Ought competition law to confine itself to securing conditions which guarantee that other competitors (new entrants) have access to the relevant market? Should it devalue the restrictions that arise, for the partners themselves, from such an alliance or network? Or should competition law consider both internal and external competition restrictions?

These are some of the questions that we are going to discuss in this study. First, we will describe three cases of inter-firm horizontal cooperation (airline

* M. M. Leitão Marques is Professor of Law, Ana Abrunhosa assistant at the Faculty of Economics, University of Coimbra. We would like to thank Aerosoles (especially Artur Duarte and Ana Duro) and AutoEuropa (especially Sofia Dinis and Miriam Santos) for their collaboration when we visited the factories, and for all the information provided. We are also grateful to J. Baganha, from Instituto Nacional de Aviação Civil – Lisbon, for supplying us with information on airlines.

alliances, Ford-Volkswagen and Aerosoles) which will subsequently be used as references. Then we will demonstrate the consequences of changes in global markets for firms' organisation. We will also briefly examine the network concept and its typology as well as discuss the implications for competition. In this context, particular emphasis will be laid on the concept of *co-opetition*. Finally, we shall see to what extent this new competition model, especially when it involves horizontal cooperation, is reflected in European competition law, *in theory* (the way it is formulated) and *in practice* (the way it is applied).

1 Flying, Driving or Walking?

We can get to Florence from Lisbon in 3 hours, 3 days or 30 days. Planes and tickets from two companies, a safe car or some comfortable shoes are services and/or products that are essential to be able to make this journey. What shall we choose?

a. TAP or Alitalia, which means the Star or Skyteam alliance? Why not OneWorld? It is possible to buy an indirect flight, profiting from Iberia's control of the hub-and-spoke system of Barajas-Madrid. They offer the best price. But Skyteam has the shortest flight and for this journey we are very *time-sensitive travellers*. No, neither OneWorld nor Skyteam. We are Star frequent flyers. We choose to fly to Bologna with TAP, profiting from its code sharing agreement with Portugalia. We will have to finish our journey by train, but we will increase our air-miles. We choose the network instead of the company.

b. Should we drive a Volkswagen Sharan/Ford Galaxy or a Renault Espace? Probably a Sharan. The model and many of its spare parts are produced in Portugal. Servicing may be cheaper. We know that servicing and spare parts production are markets where there are significant restrictions on competition, despite the best efforts of the European Commission to reduce them.

c. And for walking? Aerosoles or Timberland shoes? Aerosoles, surely. They are of similar quality, good design and a reasonable price, instead of paying a lot of money for the Timberland brand name. As Aerosoles' distribution network is spread across the city, it will be easy to buy the shoes. We have no time for a long shopping day.

We are looking for a result, compared to what is on offer. Even if this result is reduced to one word (an acronym, a brand or a company name, like those just mentioned), there will be more than just a single firm behind it. There will be several, linked by cooperation agreements, alliances, vertical or horizontal networks that are, in fact, all interconnected. Some networks are more stable and resemble a concentration; others are more flexible, being the exchange of partners inherent to the network itself; and others yet combine great stability with a high degree of flexibility, a model that could well become dominant in the future.

2   Illustrative Models of Cooperation

Case 1 – The Airline Alliances: cooperation very close to a merger

An *airline alliance* is an agreement between two or more airline companies to cooperate for the foreseeable future on a substantial level. The agreement allows the integration of the airline services and networks which operate as a 'single entity but without the implied irreversibility of a merger. The airlines retain their corporate identities'.[1] The first large alliance was founded in 1989 when Northwest Airlines and KLM Royal joined forces. Air transport deregulation has accelerated the process of alliances formation and has multiplied cooperation ties within them.[2] According to Mason:

> Airline Business Alliance Survey of 2000 reports that there are 579 alliance agreements in place, up from 280 agreements (more than double) in 1994 when the survey was first conducted. Five major alliances (Star, OneWorld, Qualiflyer, Sky Team, and Wings) account for some 60 per cent of all air travel.[3]

Nowadays, the number of major airline alliances has been reduced to three: Star, OneWorld and Skyteam which cover 755, 571 and 500 destinations respectively.

According to Goel there are different types of airline alliances:

> *Strategic alliances*, when the partners co-mingle their assets in order to pursue a single or joint set of business objectives. These co-mingled assets may be terminal facilities, maintenance bases, aircraft, staff, traffic rights or capital resources. The fact that they share a common objective of leveraging the alliance to increase their profits makes the alliance strategic. And *marketing (commercial) alliances*, when the partners stay independent of each other and each partner pursues their own objectives. Thus, many code-sharing agreements, joint frequent flyer programmes and some block space arrangements are essentially marketing alliances.[4]

---

[1]   ECA, European Competition Authorities, Report of the ECA Air Traffic Working Group – Merger and Alliances in Civil Aviation, 2002. Available at http://europa.eu.int/comm/competition/publications/eca/report_air_traffic.pdf.

[2]   Many airline alliances were a way of overcoming the regulatory restrictions on mergers and acquisitions.

[3]   K.J. Mason, 'Future Trends in Business Travel Decision Making', *Journal of Air Transportation*, Vol. 7, No. 1, 2002, pp. 47–68.

[4]   A. Goel, *Strategic Alliances in the Global Airline Industry*, 2003. Available at http://www.iimahd.ernet.in/publications/data/2003-01-02AbhishekGoel.pdf.

In spite of the different degrees of cooperation between alliances, the tendency is to share more and more services between the partners involved in the alliance. In fact, an extended and optimised network is one of the main objectives of an alliance. For instance, it is not possible to provide a good frequent flyer service without sharing the ticketing system, so nowadays airline alliances tend to be more strategic.

The activities and operations that are shared in these alliances cover activities upstream of the main operation (for example joint purchasing initiatives), the main operation itself (for example common network planning, code sharing, co-ordination of pricing), and ancillary operations (for example common approach towards cargo activities), as well as activities downstream of it, that is, relations with customers (for example co-ordination of sales and marketing, joint contracting with travel agencies). The extension of shared operations is thus bound to affect competition in the relevant markets in which the companies belonging to the agreement operate.

We can look at the example of the agreement between British Airways/Iberia/GB Airways as an example of this.[5] The three companies belong to the OneWorld alliance.

The parties intend to co-operate 'to the maximum extent that is commercially feasible and permitted by applicable law', including:
(1) extension of *code-sharing* services (that is placing the code of one carrier on certain of the others' service);
(2) co-ordination of *pricing* and commission policy, with respect to those services they deem relevant;
(3) *common network planning*, in order to better adapt capacity to customer demand;
(4) common approach towards *cargo activities*, including co-operation in planning, pricing, capacity management, sales and handling activities;
(5) revenue and *profit sharing* (passenger and cargo);
(6) *customer service*; the parties intend to provide each other with data relating to customer service performance and customer satisfaction;
(7) inventory and yield management;
(8) other joint activities to be agreed between the parties.
In addition BA and Iberia plan to co-operate in the following areas:
(1) development of *Frequent Flyer Programmes* ('FFPs'); (. . .)
(2) co-ordination of *sales and marketing*; the parties intend to converge their sales, e.g. through the combination of retail outlets, joint advertising, but the *parties will maintain their individual brands*;
(3) *ground-handling*; the parties intend to use common handling agents and consider opportunities of shared facilities;
(4) *joint contracting with travel agencies*, distributors, general sales agents and other organisations and individuals;

---

[5] See Case COMP/D2/38.479 – British Airways/Iberia/GB Airways, 14.01.2004.

(5) harmonisation of service and product standards in order to provide a *seamless product* to passengers travelling on code share flights;
(6) *joint purchasing* initiatives;
(7) information technology.[6]

Code sharing agreements are a fundamental tool to construct airline alliances as they allow the expansion of supply without the acquisition of new aeroplanes.[7] Buying tickets becomes easier and check-in procedures are simplified. For example, in the case of flights which use the services of more than one company, passengers can buy just one ticket and get all their boarding passes at the departure airport.

Code sharing has become simpler by the development of the *hub-and-spoke system*, a system of air transportation in which local airports offer flights to a central airport where long-distance flights are available. Frankfurt, Charles-de-Gaulle and Singapore are examples of central airports. This is a system that is likely to change competition conditions, expanding the relevant markets.

Joint development of a network obviously permits globalisation and speeds up the rate of expansion of the supply of services.

Although many of the operations may be shared, alliances between companies continue to be, for the time being, distinct from a merger.[8] The regulation of the air transport sector and the fact that most of the partners are flag carriers, that is companies that have been national emblems for many years (most of them state owned), partly justifies continuing with their individual brand image.

---

6   Ibid., n. 8–9.
7   'Code sharing is a business term used in the airline industry for a procedure whereby one airline operates a service using its own flight number, e.g. XX123, and one or more other airlines, in agreement with airline XX, apply their own "code share" flight number to this operation. Under a code sharing agreement participating airlines can present a common flight number for: connecting flights (. . .); and flights from both airlines that fly the same route. (. . .). There are also code sharing agreements between airlines and rail lines (for instance, SNCF French Rail out of Charles de Gaulle International Airport near Roissy, France). They involve some integration of both types of transport (. . .).' in http://encyclopedia.thefreedictionary.com/business.
8   According to Lu, A. Cheng-Jui, *International Airline Alliances: EC Competition Law/US Antitrust Law and International Air Transport*, Aspen Pub, 2003, p. 57, there are three models of integration and cooperation among airlines: the merger/acquisition model; the investor model, when one airline invests in another; and strategic alliance, which involves a very wide range of cooperation.

Case 2 – Ford and Volkswagen: a restrictive horizontal cooperation agreement

Ford and Volkswagen set up a joint venture for joint production, taking advantage of the Community funds then available for Portugal. This agreement led to the creation of the AutoEuropa plant, in Palmela, in the south of Lisbon.[9] This factory began to produce VW Sharan and Ford Galaxy models. The two companies intended to challenge Japanese competition with the joint construction of a so-called multipurpose vehicle. The project incorporated the very latest production technologies in the automotive sector (JIT/Kaban, Kaizan, lean production, and so on). The Portuguese government's strong financial and political involvement in the venture was negotiated as a counterpart of the local inclusion of components in the new vehicle. In this way, the vertical network of suppliers is local, national and international but some of the national suppliers are themselves joint ventures with foreign firms and do not only supply the Portuguese plant.

The joint venture agreement that preceded AutoEuropa was notified to the European Commission, giving rise to one of the Ford-Volkswagen cases.[10]

In 1999, Ford sold its stake in AutoEuropa to Volkswagen but AutoEuropa continues to produce the Ford Galaxy through a contract with Ford. Today, AutoEuropa is the second most efficient plant of the VW group. In spite of this, its permanence in Portugal is not guaranteed and there is always the possibility of delocalisation.

Case 3 – Aerosoles: Cooperation not harmful to competition

The Investvar/Aerosoles group was founded in 1985. In 1992, the group negotiated a licence for the exclusive commercialisation rights of the American Aerosoles brand in Europe, Africa and the Middle East.

Aerosoles' products are created in Italy, in a fashion design office in Florence, IN-IT, which is controlled by Aerosoles. This office, placed in a nerve centre of footwear fashion, captures trends in terms of design, components, materials and colours. The technical product development of Aerosoles shoes produced in Europe is carried out by KA&KA, which is a firm owned by a German partner of the Aerosoles group.[11] The same product development

---

[9] For more details on AutoEuropa network see M. Vale, 'Sistema Auto-Europa: inovação numa rede polarizada por uma empresa transnacional', in C. Antonelli, J. Ferrão (eds), *Comunicação, Conhecimento Colectivo e Inovação*, Lisboa, 2001, pp. 121–52.

[10] See reference *infra* n. 55; the other case is related to the State aids that Portugal granted for the project.

[11] KA&KA used to be responsible for Aerosoles product conception before Aerosoles had created its own office (IN-IT). Product development of Aerosoles shoes in China, Vietnam, India and Brazil is carried out separately in each of these countries due to differences in their labour environment.

office also works for other customers who are, in fact, competitors of Aerosoles, including the factories that work for the German partner. Aerosoles is thus indirectly cooperating with some of their potential competitors, especially in the technical development stage of the product.

Besides its own factories in Portugal and Romania, in the production phase Aerosoles subcontracts Portuguese firms and firms from India, Brazil, China and Vietnam.

Aerosoles also owns a soles firm that is an equity joint venture with an Italian soles firm, IlpItália. This JV, IlpeIbérica, sells soles to the Aerosoles group and to other footwear firms which compete with Aerosoles.

In 1996, Marks & Spencer (M&S) signed an agreement with the group for the exclusive production of the FootGlove brand for the English chain. This agreement was a cornerstone in the group life. The cooperation relationship between the Aerosoles group and M&S has compelled the group to rethink its way of looking at the market and its own position in the industry. The change in behaviour and procedures, inside and outside the group, was also influenced by the partnership with M&S. From the beginning of the relationship, M&S imposed its 'Ethical Code' on the Aerosoles group and their subcontractors. Thus, the influence of M&S is felt in the production process, in the management and integration of information systems and in the relations within its network. One example of this influence and even control is the fact that the factories under the Aerosoles 'umbrella' – both its owned and subcontracted ones – are the target of frequent audits by M&S.

The Aerosoles network extends downstream of production too. In retail, Aerosoles has a firm, Aeroshoes, which is particularly important. Created in 1998, this firm runs the Aerosoles chain of stores. The retail chain consists of 75 own stores or franchisees, 18 of which are in Portugal. Aerosoles also has a partnership with other Portuguese footwear firms in a company, Frontshoes. This company owns a chain of stores in France. Besides the Portuguese brands, this company sells its own brands.

In the area of wholesale, the group has another firm, What's What Portugal, which sells to the group's distributors. Most of them are also affiliated firms, like Seven Seasons, which distributes the brand in Germany, Austria and Switzerland.

Today, Aerosoles is considered one of the most successful groups in the Portuguese footwear sector.

II   HOW TO SURVIVE IN A FAST-CHANGING GLOBAL MARKET

During the 1980s and the 1990s, a number of changes in the economic and political environment had important effects on the mode of competition. In the section that follows, we provide a brief description of the most important ones, that is, those that help to explain cooperative networking development and also to understand and contextualise our cases. We then go on to discuss the reactions of firms to those challenges and opportunities, trying to demonstrate that cooperative networks are crucial for firms' survival in this new environment.

1 The Changes in the Global Market

a) The globalisation of competition

The growing globalisation and regionalisation (EU, North America, and so on) of markets since the mid-1980s, with the steady reduction of barriers to trade and capital movements, has encouraged firms to expand the geographical base of their operations. Today, almost all firms face competition from around the world.

These changes have been accompanied by considerable economic turbulence and uncertainty in world markets. In these circumstances, alliances may provide some security and buffering against external threats to survival.

b) The rapid pace of technological change

Furthermore, advances in information and communication technologies have played a considerable part in making innovation a fluid and permanent process which affects not only products and processes but also the way firms and markets are organised. Technological innovation is no longer a discrete phenomenon arising from a succession of breakthroughs. Therefore, a new feature of modern competition in a global world is that competition is based on a *permanent innovation process*.

2 The Reaction of the Firms

These two inter-related changes lead firms to develop dynamic comparative advantages that will allow them to gain and maintain a sustainable level of competitiveness. This is reflected in two ways: first, by making a stronger effort to improve the efficiency with which they produce their existing products; and second, by successfully innovating new products and upgrading the resources and competencies throughout their value chains.

To achieve these objectives firms need to change the way they organise themselves and the way they relate to each other.

a) Concentration on critical competencies and resources

There is a general movement by firms to '*de-internalise*' activities both along and between value chains, and towards specialisation in those activities where they have a competitive advantage.[12] At the same time, and because of the interdependence of technical advances, firms need to assure access to those products or assets whose control they have abandoned. As a result, this deconstruction of the value chain is frequently replaced, not by arm's length transactions, but by inter-firm cooperative networks.

b)   Permanent creation of new products

A combination of fast-changing technologies and the growth of fashion demand in many sectors, such as the footwear industry, have resulted in a constant shortening of product life cycles, leading to growing demand for investment in new technology and development of new products. Since few firms have the internal resources and competencies to meet these requirements, cooperation has been a way of coping with the needs of the new economic order. Faulkner[13] has studied a few such alliances and concluded that they are vehicles for sharing the risks and assets needed to cope with fast technological change and the shortening of product life cycles.

c)   From products to systems

New market opportunities force firms to offer systems and solutions rather than discrete products. This is the result of the increased interdependence between technologies that have to be used jointly to supply a product. For example, the latest generation of large commercial aircraft requires the combined skills of metallurgy, aeronautical engineering and aero-electronics. The same happens with cars. This makes an individual firm less likely to be the sole source of the skills and capabilities needed for exploiting new opportunities.

Alliances are now used both to co-produce single products and to increasingly develop complete systems and solutions that call for the resources and competencies of many partners.

d)   Market-positioning alliances

In a fast-changing global market, international cooperation among firms can be the answer to the need to improve access to markets and speed to market. Cultural differences can be a problem for firms wishing to enter unfamiliar markets. Cooperation with firms from those potential markets (China for example) can be a way to mitigate those differences. Market-seeking alliances

---

12   See J.H. Dunning, 'Reappraising the Eclectic Paradigm in an Age of Alliance Capitalism', *Journal of International Business Studies*, Vol. 26(3), 1995, pp. 461–91.

13   D. Faulkner, *International Strategic Alliances: Co-operation to Compete*, Maidenhead, 1995.

also serve for firms to widen the markets for their core products, so as to benefit fully from the economies of scale. This itself is a cost-reducing strategy.

In a fast-changing global market, firms need to reach the market quickly
with new solutions and new systems because first-mover advantages are
becoming paramount. An alliance is sometimes the only way to take advantage
of an opportunity in time.[14] Alliances and networks can be the fastest means of
achieving market presence to seize an opportunity. In increasing-returns industries, speed to market can make the difference between market dominance and
marginalisation, regardless of how superior one's technology may be.

To sum up, when today we want to assess the competitiveness of a firm, we
should not look solely at its resources and competencies, since in certain activities its performance depends to a large extent on partnerships and on sharing
activities with other firms, as well as on its ability to orchestrate those activities. The networks of relations that firms establish with one another are therefore increasingly regarded as the appropriate units of analysis. We shall next
characterise networks, describe their typology, and show that they themselves
are an evolutive concept.

III   COOPERATION AGREEMENTS

1   Cooperative Networks: between the Market and the Hierarchy

The production and distribution of goods and services to the consumer have
always resulted from the input of many different activities and firms. In order
to produce and sell a car like the VW Sharan, a huge number of operations
have to be performed, from designing the car, to designing the thousands of
spare parts, producing and delivering those parts, assembling, marketing and
distributing the car, after sales service, and so on. Whoever buys a shoe from
Aerosoles is buying a product to which several firms have contributed. The
shoe is composed of a number of parts and operations: the technical product
development comes from Italy, the sole from Portugal, the leather from Italy,
the uppers are made in India, the shoe is assembled in Portugal, and different
distributors and franchisees deliver the product to the final customer.

This system is therefore characterised by a high division of labour among
the firms, which means that they are interdependent. Consequently, it involves
important coordination activities which glue together design/conception,
procurement, manufacture and distribution operations.

---

[14]   J. Child, D. Faulkner, *Strategies of Co-operation, Managing Alliances,
Networks, and Joint Ventures*, Oxford, 1998.

There are two classic ways to coordinate economic activities.[15] The first is the *market* mechanism: the non-ownership of suppliers and the non-integration of the intermediate activities between the firm and the customer. The second is *hierarchy:* firms make most things in-house – most of the activities needed to deliver the final product or service are carried out within its boundaries. Vertical integration has long been the preferred organisational form in many industries dominated by large firms.

The changes which occurred in the last two decades and which have been described above resulted from the world economy's entering a new phase: 'alliance capitalism', as opposed to the previous one: 'hierarchical capitalism'.[16]

As a reaction to this new environment, firms are changing the way they organise their production and transactions. The integration of a large number of different activities in a hierarchy revealed some important disadvantages in a fast-changing global market: bureaucracy, rigidity, inefficiency and lack of innovation.[17]

These problems have prompted firms to de-integrate 'non core' activities in an effort to focus the firm on certain core activities and competencies. As we have shown, this means that many of the skills and resources essential to a firm's future prosperity lie outside the firm's boundaries and outside management's direct control. 'The capacity to collaborate' has become an important competence for firms.[18] Traditionally, cooperation was achieved through bilateral agreements. Today, cooperation normally involves multiple partners from several countries and even from different sectors of activity as well as different types of agreements. These agreements should be analysed as a set, like ties in a cooperative network.

A third coordination mechanism has thus appeared, one which is neither the firm (organisational hierarchy) nor the market (through the price mechanism). This hybrid mode of governance structure is formed by the interaction of relationships between firms in the networks they form. What characterises a network, relative to the hierarchical model of organisation or to pure market relations?

An intra or inter-organisation hierarchy is characterised by the existence of an external structure to the governance of the activity engaged in by separate units. This structure appears in a top-down command structure, with binding

---

15   See R. Coase, 'The Nature of the Firm', *Economica*, Vol. 4, 1937, pp. 386–405.

16   See Dunning, *supra* n. 12.

17   See J. Jarrillo, *Strategic Networks*, Oxford, 1993.

18   See M.G. Doz, G. Hamel, *Alliance Advantage, The Art of Creating Value through Partnering*, Boston, Massachusetts, 1998.

force. The result sought is pre-defined and coordination is *ex ante*. The market, on the other hand, is based on dispersed, decentralised decisions made by various independent economic agents, and is characterised by the fact that coordination is achieved by price mechanisms spontaneously resulting from them (*ex post*). In other words, there is no system of governance in the market as such.[19]

What distinguishes the network model from either the market or the hierarchical model is the combination of autonomy with interdependence and continuous interaction among the partners. According to Johanson and Mattsson,[20] a firm's network is characterised, in the first place, by the existence of a strategic pluralism: each firm pursues its own strategic goals independently, not bound or controlled by external centres, thus getting close to the market.[21,22]

Firms in networks share a specific language, through the reciprocal exchange of knowledge (tacit, codified, and so on). The more often such sharing takes

---

[19]   See G. Thompson, *Between Hierarchies & Markets – The Logic and the Limits of Network Forms of Organization*, Oxford 2003.

[20]   See J. Johanson, L.-G. Mattsson, 'Inter-organizational Relations in Industrial Systems: a Network Approach Compared with the Transaction-Cost Approach', *International Studies of Management & Organization*, 1987.

[21]   For more information on organisation networks, see, among others: A.-P. Man, *The Network Economy – Strategy, Structure and Management*, Cheltenham, 2004; M.M.L. Marques, 'Du commerce international aux échanges intra-groupes et entre membres d'associations de coopération. L'entreprise poly-locale et les réseaux', *Revue Internationale de Droit Economique*, No. 3–4, 2003, pp. 411–41; Thompson, *supra* n. 20; R. Achrol, 'Changes in the Theory of Inter-organizational Relations in Marketing: Toward a Network Paradigm', *Journal of Academy of Marketing Science*, Vol. 25, No. 1, 1997, pp. 56–71; M.M.L. Marques, *A Cooperação entre Empresas – Dos Acordos às Redes: Prospecções sobre Portugal*, Research Project Report, 1996; G. Grabher (ed.), *The Embedded Firm: on the Socioeconomics of Industrial Networks*, London, 1995; L. Araújo, G. Easton, *Networks in Socio-Economic Systems: a Critical Review*, 1995 (offprint); H. Håkansson, I. Snehota (eds), *Developing Relationships in Business Networks*, London, 1995; Forsgren et al., 'Firms in Networks – A New Perspective on Competitive Power', *Actas Universitatis Upsaliensis*, Uppsala, 1995; G. Lorenzoni, C. Baden-Fuller, *Creating a Strategic Centre to Manage a Web of Partners*, Working paper, 1993; M. Benassi, *Dalla Gerarchia alla Rete: Modelli ed Esperienze Organizzative*, Milano, 1993; N. Nohria, R.G. Eccles (eds), *Networks and Organizations, Structure, Form and Action*, Boston, Massachusetts, 1992; B. Axelsson, G. Easton (eds), *Industrial Networks: a New View of Reality*, London, 1992; G. Lorenzoni (ed.), *Accordi, Reti e Vantaggio Competitivo – le innovazioni nell'economia d'impresa e negli asseti organizzativi*, Milano, 1992; and A. Lomi, *Reti organizzative: teoria, tecnica e applicazione*, Bologna, Il Mulino/Ricerca, 1991.

[22]   'The multiplicity of decision-takers is a distinctive feature of network architectures relative to the quasi-hierarchical organizations' (Benassi, *supra* n. 21, pp. 22–23). But the relative autonomy of the firms that make up a network is not incompatible with the existence, in some of them, of a leading firm (focal or nodal organisation).

place in strategic areas, including customer relations, the more the network will tend to move towards a concentration process. This happens with airline alliances but not with the Aerosoles network. Furthermore, a kind of *reciprocal dependence* occurs in networks. Each firm relies on the resources controlled by the other firms.[23]

2   Types of Networks

There are different types of cooperative networks. Typologies may be based on the contractual relations between the partners involved, on their place in the value chain, on the network's goal or function, on the nature of the ties that relate the partners in the network, and so on.

A distinction is usually drawn between *internal* and *external* networks. The first concerns the way a single firm or organisation organises its own internal activities, giving more autonomy to the different departments. The second – external networks – concerns a set of relationships among different and independent firms or organisations. All our cases belong to this last type, and only external networks could create legal problems for competition.

Networks can be externally organised, such as when a firm intentionally acts to create and maintain the network (networks *pre-organised* by a leader). This is the case of the relationships between AutoEuropa and its suppliers. But they could also be *self-organised* when they arise spontaneously from successive interactions between the firms and organisations that compose them. Research networks at the universities are frequently an example of this kind.

When the network has a leader and the leader's autonomy is much greater than that of the units operating around it, then it is obvious that the network is capable of generating relations of *dependence* that are not necessarily reciprocal. Analysis of the level of dependence or interdependence within a network is particularly important for assessing some of its effects on competition.

There is likewise a distinction between *vertical* and *horizontal* networks. This distinction is based on the nature of the operations of the firms involved and on their place in the added value chain. If the network involves relations with companies that lie upstream or downstream, then we are looking at a *vertical network*. But if the firms involved are on the same level of activity, then we can talk about a *horizontal network*. The underlying characteristic is commonality of management with respect to certain resources or the performance of certain activities in common, such as in the airline alliances.[24]

---

23   See A. Marcati, A. Manaresi, 'Accordi fra Imprese e Strategie di Marketing', in G. Lorenzoni (ed.), *supra* n. 21, p. 98.

24   See B. Bosworth, St. Rosenfeld, *Significant Others: Exploring the Potential of Manufacturing Networks*, Aspen Institute, 1992, 19 and 20.

While they may be typically vertical or horizontal, firms' networks are increasingly combining the two formats and are capable of shifting from one to the other. This combination can clearly be seen in any of the three cases described above. For instance, in the automobile industry, the tendency since the 1990s is to pass from a 'dependence network' (in the relation between manufacturer and suppliers) to a 'permeable network' where interactions among suppliers themselves are also a feature of the network.[25]

Furthermore, networks are showing an increasing tendency to integrate production and distribution, linking them interactively and extending them to related businesses, especially in the financial domain. For instance, networks can associate credit brokers or firms supplying services for e-commerce. This is why certain authors prefer to use the term *business networks*, rather than vertical or horizontal networks.

In spite of considering these different types of networks, we will focus on horizontal networks when discussing networks and competition law problems in section V below.

3 Strategic Networks

Cooperation among firms tends more and more to be developed in *strategic areas* (new products, new systems or new technologies) on a continuous basis. For instance, in airline alliances we are moving from marketing alliances to strategic alliances. A *strategic alliance* is commonly identified with a long-term cooperative arrangement, normally between two or more independent firms who pool and share resources, competencies and know-how for mutual gain and control. Here, 'long-term' does not refer to any specific period of time but rather to the intention of the partners concerned that the arrangement is not going to be a temporary one. The long-lasting commitment, as opposed to a tactical decision, means that the alliance is strategic in nature.[26]

---

[25]   See F.J. Ritcher, *Strategic Networks – The Art of Japanese Inter-Firm Cooperation*, New York, 2000, p. 93.

[26]   On the concept of strategic alliance see N-H. Kang, K. Sakai, *International Strategic Alliances: their Role in Industrial Globalisation*, STI-Working Paper 2000/5, OECD, 2000; E.W.K. Tsang, 'A preliminary Typology of Learning in International Alliances', *Journal of World Business*, Vol. 34(3), 1999, pp. 211–29; R. Narula, J. Hagedoorn, 'Innovating through Strategic Alliances: Moving towards International Partnerships and Contractual Agreements', *Technovation*, 19, 1999, pp. 283–94; J. Hagedoorn, 'Understanding the Rationale of Strategic Technology Partnering: Inter-organizational Modes of Cooperation and Sectoral Differences', *Strategic Management Journal*, No. 14, 1993, pp. 3171–85; and J. Hagedoorn, 'Organisational Modes of Inter-firm Cooperation and Technology Transfer', *Technovation*, Vol. 10, No. 1, 1990, pp. 17–30.

The concept of strategic alliance was initially identified with that of joint venture, that is, a horizontal cooperation agreement between two firms. However, as agreements evolved from bilateral agreements to networks, the concept of strategic alliance also changed. Now, in the majority of cases, strategic alliances can be characterised as *strategic networks*.[27] They exhibit a growing tendency to seek to meld very different skills and capabilities from dissimilar partners of different sizes and countries, histories and management styles. This involves not only a simple complementation of resources but also a complex 'cospecialisation':[28] the value of each partner's contribution is enhanced when combined with the contribution of other partners.

Consequently, strategic networks 'are not about the statics of allocative choices but about the dynamics of innovation and competition'.[29] Dynamic efficiency is their main advantage.[30]

We can take the example of airline alliances, where the sharing of operations and spheres of competencies is highly diversified. In the case of Ford-Volkswagen, strategic cooperation is much more limited since it is confined to the development and production of a car model. In the case of Aerosoles, cooperation is an evolutive process, which permits the constant entry of new partners and the evolution of the group's objectives and business areas. Besides some delocalisation of production (to Brazil, China, India, Romania and Vietnam), there is strategic horizontal cooperation in technical product development (in Italy), in the joint production of soles and in distribution.

4   The Evolutionary Nature of Strategic Networks: more and more Flexibility

Cooperation agreements among firms and the networks they form are now no more stable than before. On the contrary, they tend to have an evolutionary nature. According to Doz and Hamel,[31] contemporary cooperation among firms is characterised by the following:

---

[27]   Doz, Hammel, *supra* n. 18, designate these networks of agreements in a single alliance as '*alliance networks*'.

[28]   See Doz, Hamel, *supra* n. 18, p. 5.

[29]   M. Delapierre, L.K. Mytelca, 'Blurring Boundaries: New Inter-firm Relationships and the Emergence of Networked, Knowledge-Based Oligopolies', in M.G. Colombo (ed.), *The Changing Boundaries of the Firm, Explaining Evolving Inter-firm Relations*, London and New York, 1998, p. 79.

[30]   See M. Motta, *Competition Policy*, Cambridge, Cambridge University Press, 2004, pp. 55–64. On the importance of dynamic efficiency for anti-trust policy see M.E. Porter, 'Competition and Anti-Trust: Productivity Based Approach', in C. Weller (ed.), *Unique Value: Competition Based on Innovation Creating Unique Value*, Cleveland-Ohio, 2004.

[31]   See Doz, Hamel, *supra* n. 18.

- Greater uncertainty and ambiguity; the ultimate consequences cannot be accurately anticipated;
- A partner relationship which evolves in ways that are hard to predict;
- More importance is given to managing the agreement or the network over time rather than to crafting the initial formal design; and
- The fact that today's ally may be tomorrow's rival – or may be a current rival in some other market or activity.

In these new patterns of cooperation, partners must be flexible in order to adapt to changes, instability and uncertainty. They must see an agreement as a relationship whose objectives are bound to evolve in ways that cannot be fully anticipated. Changes in the market, in technology, in competitors, partners and regulatory conditions may imply that stated objectives should be frequently reviewed. Therefore, the phases of 'search, negotiation, and integration' are step-by-step processes. This means that the search for partners does not stop when the agreement is signed. Nor should negotiation stop when the deal is signed; external conditions are constantly changing, and the contributions and benefits of the various partners must also change. Integration of activities between partners also takes place over time. As the benefits or costs of cooperation become more obvious, partners increase or decrease their commitments.

In a fast-changing global world, the need for commitment must be balanced with the desire of partners to keep their options open. Firms must be free to pursue better opportunities when they appear and the network must keep the door open for new partners who can increase the creation of value of a partnership.[32]

In our opinion, the resemblance to the evolutionary model is likely to make some cooperative networks less harmful to competition than others.

Aerosoles is the closest case to this approach. The management of cooperation, the constant search for new partners all over the world, as well as keeping control over the product conception and the brand are crucial to Aerosoles.

Global airline alliances tend to be much more stable and distant from the evolutionary model, even if some changes could occur in the alliance (for example newcomers). Thus stability and commitment are more important than

---

[32]   In a network, the '*exit*' strategy (which leads to dispensing or cutting commercial relations with whoever does not meet the requirements) coexists both with the '*voice*' strategy (which demands active collaboration of each partner to change conditions and adjust behaviours), and with '*loyalty*' strategy (which presupposes remaining in the network, even without an active voice). The greater the interdependence among the participants, the greater the possibility of having a '*voice*' strategy. If the level of dependence is high, '*loyalty*' will have more weight.

a constant changing of partners. These networks are therefore very close to a merger and potentially more harmful to competition.

Whether they are closer to or further from the evolutionary model, all our cases try to combine both cooperation and competition benefits. But is this actually possible without severe restraints on competition? This will be the focus of the following section, which discusses the hypothesis of a new model of competition.

IV   A NEW MODEL OF COMPETITION: HOW COMPETITION CAN BE COMPATIBLE WITH COOPERATION

In mainstream economics there has been a dichotomy between competition and cooperation. Until the 1980s, the dominant paradigm emphasised that individuals are selfish and independent. From this perspective, firms try to accomplish their individual objectives and interests when they briefly meet at the market to make transactions. Inter-firm interdependence is based on a zero-sum game. This means that when a firm wins, another loses. In this way, firms have divergent interests.

As Hardin and Joshua[33] argue in their book on cartels, economic theory suggests that competition is in some sense a natural condition. Therefore, the cessation of rivalry is an unexpected and problematic phenomenon. But empirical data show that there is a natural disposition towards either collaboration or rivalry, and that both should be considered. The competitor may wish not to compete.

In fact, as mentioned above, the last years of the 1980s witnessed the spread of cooperative agreements among firms. These inter-firm relations have become interactive, involving several partners and agreements and tend to have a long-term nature. The creation of economic value is a result of firms' relationships. Firms' interdependence is a plus-sum game. This means that the success of a partner could benefit the other partner. From this perspective, firms have convergent interests and derive mutual benefits.

These days, recent research demonstrates that most networks are simultaneously competitive and cooperative. Even in the same contractual relationship partners can cooperate in the production phase and compete when they discuss the value distribution. This means that 'trust' and 'opportunism' can co-exist.

---

[33]   C. Hardin, J. Joshua, *Regulating Cartels in Europe – A Study of Legal Control of Corporate Delinquency*, Oxford, 2003, pp. 17 ff.

Nalebuff and Branderburguer[34] created the concept 'co-opetition' to describe this type of relationship. Co-opetition is a new way to conceptualise inter-firm dynamic interdependence.[35]

In fact, it is possible to demonstrate that in each of our three cases (and indeed in many other similar cases) cooperation is possible between rival firms. In these cases, there is a continuous tension between cooperation and competition.[36] This tension also exists in vertical cooperation relationships but is more visible in the horizontal ones.

Bengtsson and Kock[37] show that rival firms tend to cooperate in activities that are further away from the customer while they compete in activities closer to the customer. These firms are not competitors or rivals in a traditional sense since they are also partners who cooperate. They are thus 'co-opetitors'.

According to Culpan,[38] patterns of cooperation and competition can be categorised into three groups, that is those that:

i.   Cooperate and then compete: when companies are not ready for competition in a particular area, they first cooperate with competitors for short-run objectives and, afterwards, the cooperating firms compete among themselves when they have built up their competences or achieved a common standard. This is seen in the case of Aerosoles. Here, cooperation was a way of overcoming bottlenecks in product conception and design. Now, Aerosoles is creating its own affiliated product conception and is planning to sell their creation services to other footwear firms. Should this happen, Aerosoles will be competing with its former partner.

ii. Cooperate while competing: companies may continue to compete while they cooperate in some business areas. Such cooperation is generally regarded as a reciprocal learning experience to strengthen weak areas. Ford and Volkswagen cooperated to develop a new model of multipurpose vehicle but they were rivals either in distribution or in the production of other vehicles.

---

34   B. Nalebuff, A. Branderburguer, *La Co-opétition*, Paris, 1996.
35   See G.B. Dagnino, G. Padula, *Coopetition Strategy: A New Kind of Inter-firm Dynamics for Value Creation.* Paper presented at EURAM – The European Academy of Management, Second Annual Conference, Stockholm, 9–11 May 2002, about the hybrid behaviour comprising competition and cooperation.
36   Man sustains that networks enhance competition and presents several examples to illustrate his argument that 'increased collaboration and increased competition go hand in hand'. See Man, *supra* n. 21, p. 131.
37   M. Bengtsson, S. Kock, 'Coopetition in Business Networks – to Cooperate and Compete Simultaneously', *Industrial Marketing Management,* No. 29, 2000, pp. 411–26.
38   R. Culpan, *Multinational Strategic Alliances*, New York, 1993.

iii.   Cooperate among themselves and compete with others: companies may cooperate to compete with third parties. This is the case of airline alliances.

In all these cases, we should consider the possibility of rival firms making some strategic collusion while still cooperating. This means that competitors that cooperate can implicitly agree when or where they are competing or not. As Ullrich states, this could be cartel behaviour where the 'functions of competition are divided and competitive roles attributed'.[39] It is therefore important to identify the risks of collusive cooperation because they can be harmful to competition instead of increasing it. This means that in each case there is the need to distinguish accurately between cartel behaviour and a mere cooperation relation.

Bengtsson and Kock[40] also argue that, depending on the degree of cooperation and competition, we can conceptualise three basic different forms of co-opetition: *cooperation-dominated relationship*, where we have more cooperation than competition; *equal relationship*, where cooperation and competition are equally distributed; and *competition-dominated relationship*, where we have more competition than cooperation.

As we have explained, our three cases fit this model (see Figure 6.1).

All these forms of co-opetition can pave the way for a new model of competition and, especially in the first and the second cases, bring new problems to competition policy and competition law.

V   COOPERATIVE NETWORKS AND COMPETITION LAW

1   A more Indulgent Approach to Undertakings' Cooperation Agreements

The more sympathetic and complacent way in which competition authorities, most notably the European Commission, tend to treat cooperation agreements reflects both new competition conditions in markets, which are ever more global, and an understanding of the readjustments that firms are being forced to make in order to cope with the challenges they face. It is also the outcome

---

[39]   H. Ullrich, 'Competitor Cooperation and Evolution of Competition Law: Issues for Research in a Perspective of Globalization', in J. Drexl (ed.), *The Future of Transnational Antitrust – From Comparative to Common Competition Law,* Hague, Kluwer, 2003, pp.159–223.
[40]   Bengtsson, Kock, *supra* n. 37.

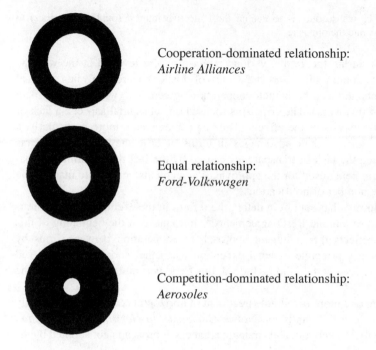

Cooperation-dominated relationship:
Airline Alliances

Equal relationship:
Ford-Volkswagen

Competition-dominated relationship:
Aerosoles

Source: Adapted from Bengtsson and Kock[41]

Figure 6.1   Forms of Co-opetition

of the importance placed on dynamic efficiency,[42] and on the theory of contestable markets[43] in relation to the classical models of competition theory. Finally, though in a somewhat less visible way, it also reflects the influence of transaction costs theory,[44] with a favourable presumption regarding cooperation and the inversion of the burden of proof.

> Firms involved in a merger or a cooperation agreement should not have to show the justice of their option in organisational terms (in the light of the criterion of efficiency), instead, it is up to those that might consider themselves harmed (other

[41]   Bengtsson and Kock, *supra* n. 37, p. 416.

[42]   See J. Schumpeter, *Capitalisme, Socialisme et Démocratie*, Paris, 1951.

[43]   See W.J. Baumol, J. Panzar, R. Willig, *Contestable Markets and the Theory of Industry Structure*, New York, 1982.

[44]   See O.E. Williamson (ed.), *Industrial Organization*, Cheltenham, 1990; O.E. Williamson, *The Economic Institutions of Capitalism*, New York, 1985; O.E. Williamson, *Markets and Hierarchies*, New York, 1975; and Coase, *supra* n. 15.

firms) or whose duty is to defend the collective interest (public authorities) to demonstrate the opposite.[45]

In fact during the 1990s, various criticisms were levelled at the way the European Commission (and the Court of Justice) were analysing vertical agreements and also horizontal cooperation agreements (which are the main subject of this work). The criticisms focused on substantial aspects: a lack of economic analysis of the effects of the agreements and, more particularly, a failure to look at their advantages in terms of efficiency. Other criticisms emphasised the lack of transparency caused by the fact that informal mechanisms were being used for the approval of agreements, in order to manage the excessive number of notifications.[46]

As Ullrich[47] has set out in detail, the reform in the exemption Regulations of Specialisation and R&D agreements,[48] introduced at the beginning of this century, reflects this indulgent approach to cooperation between firms by establishing a principle of legal exception when the market share involved does not exceed certain limits. Indeed, this trend was quite evident before the reform.

In spite of a more favourable treatment of horizontal cooperation especially expressed in the Commission Notice *Guidelines to Horizontal Cooperation Agreements*,[49] a network and strategic alliances approach is not adopted by the European Commission.

> More complex arrangements such as strategic alliances that combine a number of different areas and instruments of cooperation in varying ways are not covered by the guidelines. The assessment of each individual area of cooperation within an alliance may be carried out with the help of the corresponding chapter in the guidelines.[50]

---

[45]   A.R. Marques, *A política da Concorrência da EU aplicável às empresas*, 2004 (offprint).

[46]   See, especially, the study by the Centre for Economic Policy Research of D. Neven, P. Papandropoulos, P. Seabright, *Trawling for Minnows – European Competition Policy and Agreements between Firms*, London, 1998, on European competition policy and agreements between firms where the authors use empirical data to indicate several negative aspects of this policy.

[47]   Ullrich, *supra* n. 39.

[48]   See Commission Regulation (EC) No 2658/2000 of 29 November 2000 on the application of Article 81(3) EC to categories of specialisation agreements, Official Journal L 304, 05.12.2000, p. 3; and Commission Regulation (EC) No 2659/2000 of 29 November 2000 on the application of Article 81(3) of the Treaty to categories of research and development agreements, Official Journal L 304, 05.12.2000, p. 7.

[49]   Commission Notice – Guidelines on the Applicability of Article 81 to Horizontal Co-operation Agreements, OJEC C 3, 06.01.2001, p. 2.

[50]   See Guidelines, ibid., No. 12.

However, the Commission recognises the limits of this approach when it writes in the same notice that: 'complex arrangements must also be analyzed in their totality'.[51]

In general, strategic alliances are not considered as a form of concentration. In its Green Paper on the Review of Council Regulation (EEC) no. 4064/89, the Commission maintains that a strategic alliance which does not entail an acquisition of control falls outside the scope of the Merger Regulation. As a rule, the Commission currently examines such transactions especially under Article 81 EC. However, in its Green Paper on the Review of Council Regulation (EEC) no. 4064/89,[52] the Commission '[I]s conscious of the fact that such transactions may have a 'structural' impact on the markets involved. It is also conscious, however, of the difficulty in sufficiently defining the transactions in question for the purposes of mandatory ex-ante notification.'

Thus the concept of concentration covers only 'operations bringing about a lasting change in the structure of the undertakings concerned'. The Commission considers (at no. 113) that 'strategic alliances are normally not designed to bring about the structural change' and 'may not necessarily result in the creation of an autonomous economic entity'. Article 81, therefore, still appears to be the most appropriate legal instrument for assessing such transactions.

Nevertheless, our analysis of some airline strategic alliances, where a lot of activities are shared, questions some of the Commission's conclusions and shows an extremely clear economic similarity between some strategic alliances and concentrations. In the same document, even the Commission (at no. 111) maintains that 'strategic alliances are often concluded among actual competitors who are seeking to compete with other similar alliances' and 'provide a means to compete in markets integrating on a global scale'.

2 Inter-party and Third Party Restraints on Competition

Particularly when the assessment of strategic alliances is made under Article 81 EC (or the equivalent rule in national law), competition authorities should not ignore inter-party restraints on competition, besides the necessity of considering the third-party restraints by looking at the set of agreements as a unit.

In fact, authorities should be aware that cooperative networks not only afford gains in efficiency but they also help to *organise competition* through

---

[51] See Guidelines, ibid., No. 12

[52] See Green Paper on the Review of Council Regulation (EEC) n. 4064/89 (COM(2001) 745/6 final), Nos. 101, 111, 112 and 113.

the rules they establish for the markets in which they operate.[53] To this extent, they are private forms of market regulation, expressed in codes of conduct or in standard contracts. Like public regulation, private regulation can also replace competition. This happens when firms use agreements to share markets, fix prices or impose discriminatory access conditions to essential facilities. Furthermore, private regulation sometimes emerges in the wake of public deregulation, filling the gap that it leaves.

Looking at the network itself and the effects it has on competition between the partners composing it (inter-party competition) is an important task for competition authorities. The greater the number and importance of the operations shared, the more attention they will pay to the network. That is, the more the network is like the hierarchical model (that is closer to a concentration as in say airline alliances) and less like the market model (flexible competition such as in Aerosoles). This is why it is crucial for competition authorities to understand the internal structure of the network, its architecture, the operations that are shared, its flexibility and resemblance to the evolutionary model, the relative importance of the 'voice', 'exit' and 'loyalty' strategies, dependence relationships, whether it is opened or closed and so forth.[54]

However, some recent decisions by the European Commission have shown that in order to assess the effects of a network on the respective relevant market (with regard to third-party competition), using the network as the unit of analysis has become an unavoidable task.[55] Thus the exclusion from the market or from the chance to access it on the part of firms that do not belong to the network will be given much more attention.

---

[53]   As we have shown before, there are different types of networks that can coexist and interact in the same case (Aerosoles and Ford-Volkswagen are examples of this coexistence), but at this point, when discussing cooperative networks and competition law, we focus especially on horizontal networks.

[54]   'How networks affect competition in an industry depends on the type of network being formed and the type of competition in and around networks.' See Man, *supra* n. 21, p. 136.

[55]   In a recent book, Iansiti and Levien argue that networks should be understood as ecosystems which compete with other ecosystems and that antitrust policy should take into account this new reality. See M. Iansiti, R. Levien, *The Keystone Advantage: What the New Dynamics of Business Ecosystems Mean for Strategy, Innovation, and Sustainability*, Boston, 2004. But Foer, in a book review of Iansiti and Levien's work, draws our attention to the fact that we need to continue to pay attention to the conduct of the firms, which belong to the network, and especially to the conduct of the leader firm. Only this attention will allow us to distinguish between a 'dominator' firm, with predator behaviour, and a 'keystone' firm which contributes to the health of the ecosystem. See A. Foer, *Do the 'New Dynamics of Business Ecosystems' Spell the End of Antitrust?*, available at http://www.antitrustinstitute.org/recent2/356.pdf.

Let us return now to the three cooperation cases described above and analyse their relations with competition rules and policy.

3 Competition Problems in our Three Cases

a. The situation of *Aerosoles* is very close to the market model. The restrictive effects on competition arising from this cooperation are either non-existent or irrelevant from a competition law point of view. Aerosoles' subcontracting agreements in the EU for product development, for leather cut and stitch activities, and the joint-production agreement of components (like soles) have no sensitive effects on competition. The market share involved is not relevant and foreclosure problems do not occur. Even if some inputs like soles are important components of costs, the parties in the agreement do not have a strong position in the downstream market for the final product. Besides, the joint venture which produces soles sells this component to other firms.

b. The same cannot be said about *Ford-Volkswagen* joint venture.[56] These two companies are important competitors in the European and world automobile market. As was argued in the EC Decision, the agreement to jointly produce a multipurpose vehicle to be sold throughout the EU would have a considerable impact on trade between Member States. The financial, technical and research capacities would, in principle, permit each firm to produce its own vehicle. The development of new models used to be one of the key elements of competition in the automobile sector and a determining factor for a manufacturer's success. The obligation on the parent companies to buy fixed numbers of vehicles from the joint venture would encourage the former to lose any economic interest in individually pursuing any activity in this relevant market. Any agreement between the two competitors would therefore be likely to seriously restrict competition.

This is why the exemption granted by the Commission, under Article 81(3) EC, had to be fully justified and was contested by the principal competitor, Matra Hachette, SA, which assembled the Renault Espace, the market leader in the multipurpose vehicle sector. It was then considered that the new factory would use modern production technology and would develop a new concept for supplying components; this new concept aimed to become a new logistical 'just-in-time' system for components that would be the most efficient in the world; an industrial park would be

---

[56] Commission Decision of 23 December 1992 (93/49/EEC – Ford Volkswagen), OJEC L 020, 28/01/1993, pp. 14–22, confirmed by the Court of First Instance of 15 July 1994, Case T-17/93, Matra Hachette/Commission, Rep 1994 II 595.

created, allowing suppliers to set up facilities next to the factory with direct access to the production line; the technology developed would be environmentally friendly; the joint venture was considered to have positive effects in terms of infrastructures and employment in one of the poorest regions in Europe.[57]

Even with its favourable attitude to cooperation, the arguments deployed by the European Commission to approve this agreement were largely time-honoured ones. Nonetheless, it should be noted that considerable attention was given to dynamic efficiency gains, the creation of a network of suppliers and also to competition in the global market, namely by admitting that this agreement would help to promote competition with Japanese vehicles.

The remedies to limit the negative effects on competition were the separation of the distribution networks for the VW Sharan and the Ford Galaxy.

The equity joint venture disappeared when Ford left the project, as mentioned above. The plant is currently producing the Sharan, the Galaxy (through an agreement with Ford) and the Alhambra (Seat) models. Ten years after the EC Decision, it does not seem that the project has harmed competition, although more detailed information is needed to sustain this thesis.

c.	It is in *airline alliances* that we find closer proximity to the hierarchical model and clearer restrictive effects on competition (either inter-party or third-party competition). The process of creating networks or alliances has become faster, more formalised, and the cooperation has become more structural. This is the reason why we shall give special attention to them in this part of our work.

The deregulation and liberalisation of the air transport sector has fostered a favourable climate for the private reordering of the market. As explained above, this reordering is being achieved for the global market, not merely at the national or regional level. The global alliances resulting from these changes in market conditions have not only significantly reduced competition between the airline companies participating in them but they can also potentially raise new entry barriers and eradicate competition or make it difficult in the relevant markets. This impact is further favoured by the fact that air transport operations depend on the availability of slot conditions and access to essential facilities such as airports.

It should not come as a surprise, therefore, that several cases of

---

[57]	See Commission Decision of 23 December 1992, ibid., especially n. 23, 25, 26, 27 and 33.

alliances are under consideration by the European Commission. Several agreements in the air transport sector were notified to the European Commission or investigated by its services.[58] The cooperation involved is spread all over the airline functions. Some of them are ambitious strategic alliances such as Air France/Alitalia.[59] Others have a more limited objective: cooperation is restricted to some routes such as British Airways/SN Brussels Airlines[60] or cooperation to organise supporting air transport activities, like an Online Travel Portal.[61,62]

In addition to those cases already settled or under investigation, the attention given to the sector by competition authorities is also expressed in the report published by the European Competition Authorities network (ECA) and in a detailed study by the OECD.[63] The main guidelines of these studies and decisions and the extent to which they allow a new vision of networks and alliances will be discussed in the next section.

4   Entry Conditions as a core aspect for Competition Assessment of Airline Alliances

More efficiency can be obtained by sharing each company's tangible and intangible resources (like technology, reputation and corporate culture). This results in lower costs and greater differentiation. To achieve positive results, the companies involved in each airline alliance need at least to harmonise their schedules, ticketing and baggage handling services. Apart from improved efficiency, it is recognised that only by increasing cooperation and expanding the network will it be possible to compete in the world market. At this level, then, alliances encourage increased competition. Advantages in terms of customer satisfaction also accrue from the development of airline alliances. As well as code sharing, frequent-flyer programmes and online destinations are further

---

[58]   Available at http://europa.eu.int/comm/competition/antitrust/cases/index/by_nace_code_i.html#I_62.

[59]   See Case COMP/38.284/D2 – Société Air France/Alitalia Linee Aeree Italiane S.p.A., OJEC, C 297/10, 9.12.2003.

[60]   See Case COMP/A.38.477/D2 – British Airways/SN Brussels Airlines, OJEC 306/4, 10.12.2002.

[61]   See Case COMP/38.006 – OPODO (Online Travel Portal), OJEC C 323/6, 20.11.2001.

[62]   Besides cooperation, *concentration* has also occurred in this sector. Thirty cases were notified to the EC. Decisions are available at http://europa.eu.int/comm/competition/antitrust/cases/index/by_nace_code_i.html#I_62.

[63]   ECA, 2000, *supra* n. 1 and OECD, Airline Mergers and Alliances, DAFFE/CLP(2000)1, 2002. Available at http://www.oecd.org/dataoecd/1/15/2379233.pdf.

benefits. Moreover, passengers look for benefits in terms of prices and flight availability which demand competition.

However, it should not be forgotten that the need to reduce the level of competition in more and more deregulated and liberalized markets is also a strong motivation for the companies that are leading developing alliances. Thus, if the advantages to consumers or the gains of efficiency that may come from airline alliances are to continue in the long term, the reduction in competition must be controlled. If not, competition might vanish completely in each of the relevant markets with negative effects for consumer welfare.

As a consequence, it will be up to the competition authorities to perform their usual task of assessing competition in the market in question. Once an exemption is granted for an alliance to be set up, they will have to impose the necessary conditions to guarantee some competition in the relevant market. The novelty in this task, in air transport as well as other sectors, is that the authorities now have to take the network effect into account. Besides agreements between undertakings, the network is increasingly becoming the unit of analysis.

This has to be the case when the relevant market is defined. Traditionally, the relevant market is the route that links the point-of-origin to the point-of-destination (O&D). If there is more than one possibility of flying from one city to another (for example from Lisbon to Florence), then the lifestyles and travel objectives of the passengers have to be analysed too. The greater or lesser flexibility of the passengers with regard to schedules, in-flight comfort, non-stop or indirect routes, landing at a specific airport (for example Heathrow or Luton) will all serve to broaden or diminish the choice of routes and their substitutability, increasing the intensity of competition on a particular route. Time-sensitive travellers normally expect faster connections and better punctuality. These are the ones who have to be considered if we want to measure the effects of a merger or alliance on competition.

However, it is not enough to consider the convenience of flights for passengers and the respective degree of substitutability. The *network effect* can even modify the customers' preferences. In this case, the network effect means that the importance of the product or service supplied by a company is greater the more its consumers benefit from the complementary products and services provided by other companies belonging to the same network (namely, the number of 'hubs and spokes').[64] The network effect has implications for each company supply, and may actually force the consideration of alternatives to the OECD approach on the definition of the relevant market.[65] The conclusions of the OECD[66] report point in the same direction:

---

[64]   See R. Whish, *Competition Law*, London, 2003, p. 10.
[65]   See ECA, *supra* n. 1, p. 15.
[66]   OECD, *supra* n. 63, p. 8.

Travellers prefer 'seamless' connections and more frequent services. In the presence of loyalty schemes such as frequent-flyer programs, many travellers also prefer networks that serve a larger number of destinations. Larger airline networks organised in the 'hub and spoke' form can take advantage of cost economies and can offer more seamless connections, more frequent services and a greater range of destinations than can smaller airline networks, making their networks more attractive, especially to full-fare paying passengers. (...). Hub and spoke airlines tend to be dominant on spoke and hub–hub routes, and jointly dominant (with the corresponding rival networks) on routes to and from other networks' hubs.

Henceforth, guaranteeing access to airports (demand for take-off and landing slots and for gate facilities), especially the most sought-after ones, is becoming an essential question for fostering competition in the sector. Thus, an incumbent flag-carrier airline (and perhaps the network to which it belongs) must be prevented from benefiting in terms of pricing access to airport facilities.[67]

The network is once again the most suitable unit of analysis when it comes to controlling anticompetitive practices with respect to prices (including predatory prices) and especially loyalty clauses (frequent-flyer and other loyalty schemes) or access to essential facilities.

Therefore, when assessing an alliance for competition purposes, authorities need to consider structural factors (which are concerned with the technical operating conditions in the sector), regulatory factors (administrative restrictions or State aid) and strategic behaviour. In addition, they now have to take into account the effects of the network. A merger or alliance that eliminates a network, for instance, could be much more aggressive for competition than others that do not have this effect. This particular aspect was considered relevant in the merger between Air France and KLM because of the disappearance of Wings.[68]

The establishment of conditions and remedies to allow agreements, alliances or mergers also requires looking at networks. Divestment of slots, provisions ensuring access to computer reservation systems, open frequent flyer programmes, access to airport facilities, an obligation to inter-line and market share restraints on key routes are the more frequent conditions.[69]

The aforementioned agreement between British Airways/Iberia/GB Airways[70] is a good example of these concerns.[71] The Commission has held that 'given the scope of the cooperation there will clearly no longer be any

---

[67]   See the Case No. IV/35.703 – Portuguese authorities/ANA, OJEC L 69/31, 16.3.1999.

[68]   See the case COMP/M.3280 – Air France/KLM, 11.02.2004.

[69]   For a detailed analysis of the different remedies that have been used, see ECA, *supra* n. 1, pp. 31–7.

[70]   See *supra* n. 5.

[71]   To consider the conditions to grant an exemption to air transport agreements see Regulation (EEC) No. 3975/87 of 14 December 1987.

154 Controlling restrictions of competition

competition between the parties (inter-party competition). The question is then how many competitive constraints from third parties remain (third-party competition).'[72] Therefore, an Article 81(3) EC exemption was dependent on different commitments submitted by the parties with regard to point-to-point time-sensitive passengers on the routes London–Madrid, London–Bilbao, London–Valencia and London–Seville. All of them try to assure competition in the relevant markets and *allow new competitors to enter* the problematic routes. We can see some examples of these kinds of commitments:

– the Parties in the agreement shall provide to an airline independent of the Parties, wishing to commence or increase services on one or more of the Routes after the exemption becomes effective (the Competitor), slots as set out below (the Slot Conditions.)(. . .);
– the Parties shall not add frequencies on London Heathrow/Gatwick-Barcelona until the end of the 2004/2005 Winter season and on the Route(s) on which the Competitor uses slots obtained under the Slot Conditions (. . .);
– at the Competitor's request, the Parties shall conclude one interline agreement concerning the Route(s) operated by it if it does not have an existing interline agreement with the Parties;
– if the Competitor does not participate in one of the Parties' FFPs or does not have its own comparable FFP, the Parties shall allow it, on request, to participate in their joint FFP at market competitive rates for the Route(s) it operates.[73]

For these reasons, Nannes[74] asserts that: 'if you detect a common theme to these proceedings, you are not alone. In each of them – whether foreign or domestic, merger or non-merger, multiple firm or single firm – entry conditions are central to antitrust analysis.'

This statement neatly synthesises the common guidelines of the decisions and reports on air transport competition policy. Alliances can be allowed, benefiting from an exemption under Article 81(3) EC, if some competition is able to be maintained or introduced in the relevant market. Accordingly, the main question could not be to limit operations-sharing but ensuring slot conditions and equivalent access to the airports for companies that are not part of the alliance.[75]

---

72 Ibid. n. 51.
[73] Ibid., n. 74–94, where all the commitments of this Decision are referred.
[74] J. Nannes, *The Importance of Entry Conditions in Analyzing Airline Antitrust Issues*, 1999, available at http://www.usdoj.gov/atr/public/speeches/2574.htm. About the relevance of entry conditions for the evaluation of agreements among competitors in USA, see Antitrust Guidelines for Collaborations Among Competitors (point 3.35), available at http://www.ftc.gov/os/2000/04/ftcdojguidelines.pdf.
[75] In the same sense, Man holds that 'closed networks may have a bigger impact on competition, because they exclude companies from a source of competitive advantages.' See Man, *supra* n. 21, p. 137.

Thus, the assessment of an airline alliance is very similar to that of a concentration, not only because of the importance that authorities attribute to the efficiency gains but also because of the attention they give to the potential for competition as a condition for permitting the formation of such alliances.

To sum up, the decisions taken in the field of air transport indicate that there is a certain amount of regulation and market interference. Furthermore, administrative guarantees of access to essential facilities and entry conditions in general are needed if competition is to be maintained. *Ex ante,* sector-based regulation by specialised bodies could be replaced by *ex ante* or *ex post* transversal regulation by competition authorities but the sector should nonetheless remain under surveillance.

VI CONCLUSIONS

The dilemmas and questions raised by Ullrich[76] endure in competition policy, challenging the research agenda and researchers' imagination. The competition law research agenda will have to be more case-based, more complex and more micro, yet still pay heed to the macro effects of the changes that result from the re-organisation of firms in the global market. It has to be more case-based, to the extent that decisions and judgments are inspiring changes in competition law rather than the other way round. It has to be more complex, to the extent that it is acknowledged today that competition and cooperation can co-exist in the same alliance or network, and the concept of 'co-opetition' is an attempt to express this reality. It has to be more micro, since cooperative networks do not follow a single model nor do they have a static pattern.

The knowledge that we are gathering on their architecture is inductive and is the result of empirical studies we have carried out on the actual operations of different networks in various sectors and on the way they have been evolving. This knowledge is indispensable for assessing the impact of networks on competition (inter-party and third-party restrictions), and for finding the appropriate remedies to combat their less competition-desirable effects which will make the competition authorities' task more difficult and complex. As Man maintains: '[A]s the true effects of networks on competition are often hard to assess, it is more difficult to maintain an anti-trust policy in a network economy than in an economy dominated by competition between individual companies.'[77]

Our three case studies are examples of different forms of 'co-opetition'

---

[76] Ullrich, 2003, *supra* n. 39.
[77] See Man, *supra* n. 21, p. 142.

with dissimilar effects on respective relevant markets. Airline alliances actually bridge the cooperation–concentration gap, and is thus closer to a merger, while in the case of Aerosoles 'co-opetition' is closer to the market, promoting competition instead of restricting it. The Ford-Volkswagen case is in between these two cases.

In conclusion, cooperative networks are almost absent from the competition law theory. They are still interstitial in competition law in practice, with the exception of air transport. However, it seems clear that cooperative networks compel us to think differently about competition with unavoidable consequences for the way competition law is going to be applied in the near future.

Comment: Cooperative networks: a new challenge to competition law or old wine in new bottles?

Andreas Fuchs*

1 INTRODUCTION

In their comprehensive and profound analysis Maria Leitão Marques and Ana Abrunhosa have provided us with a detailed picture of the wide range and different forms of possible cooperation schemes in fast changing global markets. Interestingly, the carefully selected cases not only cover different types of cooperation but also different modes of moving – from walking to driving to flying. On our way to Florence many of us probably have used at least one of the products mentioned in the case studies. I took a Star Alliance flight from Osnabruck to Florence but I drove a car other than a Volkswagen Sharan or Ford Galaxy to get to the airport, and as a pedestrian here in Florence I do not wear Aerosole shoes. Since I have been in contact with only one of the products in question, and because of the tight time constraints, I am not going to comment on the case studies but shall constrain myself to some general remarks mainly on the *legal* implications of cooperative networks and strategic alliances.

The first question coming to my mind as a lawyer is whether these modern features of cooperation really present a new challenge to competition law or whether they are just old wine in new bottles. Traditional joint ventures have also covered a wide range of different types, some being merely cooperative, others being more or purely concentrative in nature. As a starting point, I am rather sceptical as to the assumption that we might need a new model of competition or a new set of competition rules in order to be able to cope with strategic alliances and cooperative networks. There has always been a wide variety of different types of collaboration, from rather loose cooperation in limited areas to establishing intense structural links or ties coming close to a concentration. On the other hand, significant changes have recently taken

* Prof. Dr. iur., LL.M. (University of Michigan, Ann Arbor), Director, Institute of Commercial and Business Law, University of Osnabrück.

place in European competition law that will probably influence the way of handling competition issues of cooperation in general and of cooperative networks and strategic alliances in particular. These changes include the implementation of a system of legal exception under Article 81 EC by Regulation No. 1/2003 and the introduction of a new substantive test – known as the SIEC-test (significant impediment to effective competition) – in merger control by Regulation No. 139/2004. While the merger control reform is primarily designed to cope better with the problem of uncoordinated effects in oligopoly situations,[1] the direct applicability of Article 81(3) EC immediately affects the legal framework for analysing cooperative networks. Whether the new system of legal exception will provide for an adequate set of rules for the competition law assessment of (new kinds of) cooperation also depends on the question how far the economic or factual changes really go.

2   FUNDAMENTAL ECONOMIC CHANGES

In their analysis, the authors have primarily identified two fundamental changes in the economic environment in which the firms have to act: the globalisation of competition and the rapid pace of technological development.[2] Both developments force firms to concentrate on their core activities and to ensure access to markets as well as technologies and other input factors by pursuing constant and reliable cooperation, often with many different firms. The need for cooperation is enhanced by shorter product life cycles and the trend to offer systems and solutions rather than discrete products.[3] Of course, one could argue that this is really a qualitative change rather than a mere quantitative increase in competitive pressure. In the end, however, I share the view of the authors that the building of cooperative networks in order to cope with the permanent innovation process and to ensure the firms' competitiveness has reached – at least in some instances – a new level or intensity of collaboration.

The question remains, however, whether 'cooperative networks' and 'strategic alliances' are just terminological short-cuts for describing an interesting (more or less new) factual phenomenon in the business world or whether they require a specific kind of competition law analysis and special legal treatment. Maria Leitão Marques and Ana Abrunhosa characterise networks as a hybrid mode of governance structure, a third kind of coordina-

---

[1]   Cf. D. Zimmer, 'Significant Impediment to Effective Competition – Das neue Untersagungskriterium der EU-Fusionskontrollverordnung', 2004 *Zeitschrift für Wettbewerbsrecht – Journal of Competition Law* (ZWeR) 250, 253 et seq.

[2]   See II.1. of the chapter.

[3]   See II.2. of the chapter.

tion mechanism that lies somewhere between the models of hierarchy and market.[4] In their view, the network model shows a combination of autonomy with interdependence and continuous interaction among the partners. Each firm pursues its own strategic goals independently but often a kind of reciprocal dependence arises because each firm relies on the resources controlled by the other firms and because of the steady, reciprocal exchange of knowledge. But this remains a rather general and vague qualification.

The same is true with regard to strategic alliances which are characterised in a very similar way as a 'long-term cooperative arrangement, normally between two or more independent firms, which pool and share resources, competencies and know-how for mutual gain and control'.[5] For me it is not really clear whether there is any meaningful distinction between these two notions. Both cooperative networks as well as strategic alliances (now also called strategic networks) contain a certain mixture of cooperation and competition which may be labelled as 'co-opetition'. This term may serve as a short form for indicating that there is something like a 'middle ground' between classic (merely) contractual cooperation in limited areas among independent firms on the one hand, and pure concentrations on the other. However, one must keep in mind that no definite conclusions or legal consequences may be derived from such a term which, by the way, could also be phrased the other way round as 'com-operation'.[6] Anyway, the legally relevant criteria defining this special phenomenon and distinguishing it from already quite common features involving a similar coordination mechanism between market and hierarchy are far from clear.

For example, could not franchising also be called a form of 'co-opetition', a vertical cooperative network? Economists have described franchising as occupying a middle ground in a continuum of distribution forms with *ad hoc* sales transactions at one end and full vertical integration at the other end. Franchising contracts usually involve a continuing and close vertical relation between franchisee and franchisor that is easily distinguished from an isolated sales transaction, but does not constitute true vertical integration either, since the franchisor has little or no ownership interest in the franchised outlets.[7] The franchisor's control over commercial decisions of the franchisee is a source of both competitive strength and anticompetitive risk in the franchise relationship. However, the question precisely is which restrictions on the competitive behaviour of the franchisee may be justified by the need to guarantee uniform quality standards and enhance good-will, and which must be seen as overly

---

[4] See III.1. of the chapter.
[5] See III.3. of the chapter.
[6] 'Co-opetition', admittedly, sounds better.
[7] Sullivan, Grimes, *The Law of Antitrust: An Integrated Handbook*, 2000, p. 452.

restrictive and causing competitive harm threatening injury, in particular, to the franchisee, to consumers, and/or to efficient outside suppliers of goods and services to the franchisee. This can only be decided after a careful case-by-case analysis. This has been done in the past, at least with regard to franchising, under the traditional concept of restraint of trade, and it must be done in the future even if the new legal regime under Regulation 1/2003 brings about a change in the concept of identifying competition concerns.

My point is that the description of the more or less new economic phenomenon of cooperative networks, strategic alliances or other forms of 'co-opetition', or 'com-operation', does not, in itself, demonstrate the need for a different legal approach. Rather, it is necessary to look to the specific facts of each type of cooperation, to identify the relevant criteria which may justify certain restrictions, and to weigh competitive risks against the benefits to be achieved by the particular cooperation.

This leads to the question of whether the legal framework is adequate to cope with the task of providing rules which, on the one hand, enable the undertakings to evaluate the competitive risks with a sufficient degree of legal certainty, and, on the other, are flexible enough to deal with the wide variety of different forms and resulting competitive risks of cooperative networks. I shall constrain my comments in this regard to the rules governing cooperation among competitors.[8]

3   THE LEGAL RULES GOVERNING HORIZONTAL COOPERATION – RECENT MODIFICATIONS AND POSSIBLE FUTURE DEVELOPMENTS

It is noteworthy that even before the fundamental change in the competition law administration introduced by Regulation No. 1/2003 came into force, the European Commission put forward a new concept of restraint of trade, especially in its Guidelines on horizontal cooperation[9] and in its new notice on agreements of minor importance.[10] The implementation of the system of legal exemption by Regulation No. 1/2003 will facilitate the obviously intended shift in antitrust analysis which, by the way, would bring European competition law

---

[8]   For an analysis of merger cases (under the old European merger regulation) see Nikolinakos, 'Mergers and Strategic Alliances in the Emerging Multi-Media Sector: The EU Competition Policy', 2004 *ECLR* 625 et seq.

[9]   European Commission, 'Guidelines on the applicability of Article 81 EC Treaty to agreements on horizontal cooperation', OJEC 2001, C 3, p. 2.

[10]   European Commission, 'Notice of 20 December 2001 on agreements of minor importance which do not appreciably restrict competition under Article 81(1) of the Treaty' (*de minimis* Notice), OJEC 2001, C 368, p. 13.

more into line with US antitrust law. My thesis is that the 'more economic approach' of the Commission is the attempt to introduce some sort of a 'rule-of-reason analysis' under European competition law.[11]

Let me briefly explain this. Under the traditional European concept of restraint of competition only a formal restriction of competitive activities between the parties is required, provided it has appreciable effects in the market place. Apart from certain inherently justified exceptions from Article 81(1), the positive effects of the agreement can only be considered within the framework of Article 81(3). Before the introduction of the system of legal exception this meant that the agreement was prohibited unless a specific exemption was granted by a separate legal act – either through a regulation or through an administrative decision by the Commission. Now a violation of Article 81(1) can only be determined if at the same time it is decided that the criteria for the (legal) exception under Article 81(3) are not fulfilled. This makes the distinction between Article 81(1) and (3) less important than in the past, but not superfluous, because it is still relevant for distributing the burden of proof (see Article 2 of Regulation No. 1/2003).

According to the new concept of the Commission, in its 'more economic approach' a relevant restriction of competition in violation of Article 81(1) is only assumed if an agreement is 'likely to affect competition to such an extent that negative market effects as to prices, output, innovation or the variety or quality of goods and services can be expected'.[12] Whether the agreement is able to cause such negative market effects 'depends on the economic context taking into account both the nature of the agreement and the parties' combined market power which determines – together with other structural factors – the capability of the cooperation to affect overall competition to such a significant extent'.[13] In my view, this kind of analysis comes quite close to a rule-of-reason analysis as is common in US antitrust law.

The effect of the Horizontal Guidelines if read together with the *de minimis* Notice, is to establish a much more structural test for cooperative strategies than before. Four levels may be distinguished:[14] Article 81(1) is not applicable

---

[11]   See A. Fuchs, 'Collaboration among Competitors and the Concept of Restraint of Competition: Comments on Hanns Ullrich', in J. Drexl (ed.), *The Future of Transnational Antitrust – From Comparative to Common Competition Law*, 2003, pp. 225, 229 et seq.

[12]   Horizontal Guidelines, *supra* n. 9, at para. 19.

[13]   Horizontal Guidelines, *supra* n. 9; at para. 20.

[14]   See the comprehensive and convincing analysis of H. Ullrich, 'Competitor Cooperation and the Evolution of Competition Law: Issues for Research in a Perspective of Globalization', in J. Drexl (ed.), *The Future of Transnational Antitrust – From Comparative to Common Competition Law*, 2003, pp. 159, 205 et seq. ('four level structure matrix').

at all to agreements among competitors involving market shares of less than 10 per cent, agreements with combined market shares from 10 per cent to 15 per cent remain virtually uncontrolled because of insufficient market power, and agreements with more than 15 per cent market share are subjected to a benefits/restraints balancing test. As far as block exemptions apply, the assumed 'area of no competitive concern' even extends to 25 per cent for R&D and 20 per cent for specialisation agreements. Above these thresholds there is still the possibility that the criteria of Article 81(3) are met due to the specific circumstances of the individual case.

In my view, the different market share thresholds are far from convincing. However, I shall abstain from a detailed critique and rather would only like to point to the fact that, so far, the Horizontal Cooperation Guidelines as well as the *de minimis* Notice of 2001 substantially deviate from, or at least do not find sufficient support in, European case law.[15] Apart from the change in the concept of restraint of competition, there are some other problematic aspects in the new approach of the Commission. Little value, for example, is attached to some forms of competition that do not directly affect prices and output. Thus, negative long-term effects such as the loss of potential alternative products or technologies due to joint research and development are neglected as well as the implications of restraints of competition on purchasing markets. Traditionally, each level of competition has been protected separately, whereas now the trend is to look at strengthening overall competition and competitiveness.

In this regard, it would be better if, as regards cooperative networks, the Commission focused its attention on preserving competition between different network centres and on ensuring market access for other comparable units rather than protecting some residual competition among the parties to the respective cooperative networks. However, this is only true with regard to vertical restraints. If more than 50 per cent of a relevant market is covered by networks of similar vertical restraints, the Commission may withdraw the broad exceptions granted under block exemption regulations by declaring the regulations to be inapplicable.[16] Even below this threshold the Commission may withdraw the benefit of a block exemption by decision in individual cases when it finds that an agreement, decision or concerted practice has certain effects which are incompatible with Article 81(3) EC.[17] Such a finding may

---

[15]   See A. Fuchs, *supra* n. 11, at p. 228 et seq.
[16]   See Article 1(a) Council Regulation 19/65/EEC, Article 8 Regulation 2790/1999 on Vertical Restraints, Article 7 Regulation 1400/2002 on Distribution in the Automobile Sector, Article 7 Regulation 772/2004 on Technology Transfer Agreements.
[17]   See generally Article 29(1) Regulation 1/2003.

particularly be made if access to the relevant market, or competition in it, is restrained, to a considerable extent, by the cumulative effects of parallel networks of comparable vertical restraints.[18]

By contrast, as regards horizontal cooperative networks, the Commission follows a rather reluctant or reserved approach. Thus, it expressly states in the Horizontal Cooperation Guidelines that

> more complex arrangements such as strategic alliances that combine a number of different areas and instruments of cooperation in varying ways are not covered by the guidelines. The assessment of each individual area of cooperation within an alliance may be carried out with the help of the corresponding chapter in the guidelines.[19]

The Guidelines only apply to six specific types of collaboration which, according to the Commission, have the potential for substantial efficiency gains.[20] Therefore, many networks encompassing one or more of the covered areas will benefit from the very benign approach of the Commission to these forms of competitor collaboration. However, it must be mentioned that the Commission has introduced a *caveat* by expressly stating that 'complex arrangements must also be analysed in their totality'.[21] Maria Marques and Ana Abrunhosa have also rightly stressed the point that cooperative networks and strategic alliances may be used as a means of private market regulation. This definitely has to be prevented by competition authorities.

Ultimately, the substantial facilitation of cooperation among competitors considerably reduces the differences in the standards of review for concentration strategies on the one hand and for cooperative strategies on the other. Of course, hard core cartel restrictions will remain *per se* violations. However, once a certain probability of beneficial effects, in particular for efficiencies, can be shown, a much more lenient standard of review seems to apply in the evaluation of the competitive effects of the cooperation. The greater the potential for benefits that is generally attributed to a certain form of cooperation, for example joint R&D, joint production or specialisation agreements, the more severe restrictions on competition are accepted. The limit ultimately is the same as in concentration cases: the establishment or reinforcement of a market-dominating position, or – according to the new SIEC-test – a significant impediment to effective competition. Apart from solving oligopoly problems, whether this

---

[18]   See in particular Article 7(1)(a) Regulation 2790/1999, Article 6(1)(a) Regulation 1400/2002, Article 6(1)(a), (b) Regulation 772/2004.

[19]   Horizontal Guidelines, *supra* n. 9, at para. 12.

[20]   These are: agreements on R&D, production, purchasing, commercialisation, standardisation, and environmental agreements.

[21]   Horizontal Guidelines, *supra* n. 9, at para. 12.

new merger control standard will generally result in a considerably lower threshold for prohibiting concentrations remains to be seen.

In any case we can observe a considerable approximation of the relevant standards of review for cooperation and concentration strategies. This appears to be justified to a certain degree, in particular with regard to joint ventures that lead to some integration of competitive resources. The same, I think, is true for many forms of cooperative networks as long as they involve a specific collaboration that mutually benefits the parties to the agreement by enabling them to achieve real synergies or efficiencies without causing direct competitive harm to third parties.

As to the question that the authors have raised on the first page of their paper: 'should networks (far more than firms) become the units to be considered by competition law?', I would, therefore, answer: 'yes' but not exclusively, and only if some qualifying criteria are met that distinguish the network from a pure cartel or private market regulation. A concentration type analysis is only justified if the network becomes itself a new actor in the market.

4   CONCLUSION

Whether the new concept underlying the competition policy of the Commission will find the approval of the European Courts remains to be seen. I think that under the new system of legal exception – if it is accepted by the European Court of Justice[22] – the chances are rather good that something approximate to a rule-of-reason type analysis will be established under an integrated application of Article 81(1) and (3) EC. However, the current shift in competition policy in some respects goes far beyond an adequate and necessary adjustment to economic developments as evidenced by the rise of cooperative networks. In my view, a more careful and cautious shift in the analysis of competitor cooperation including networks and strategic alliances would be desirable which, on the one hand, acknowledges the benefits of cooperation but does not, on the other, neglect the risks for competition. In the long run, I would call for the development of a kind of European-style 'structured rule of reason', where the structural aspects to be taken into account are to be developed in due time, preferably by case law and not only by individual decisions or guidelines of the Commission. Even though the Commission will still have

---

[22]   In Germany, some authors still express their doubts as to the legality of implementing such a fundamental change as the introduction of a system of legal exception under Article 81 EC by a mere regulation rather than by an amendment to the Treaty, cf. Mestmäcker, Schweitzer, *Europäisches Wettbewerbsrecht*, 2nd edn, 2004, p. 333 et seq.

considerable influence on the development of the legal framework for competition analysis, it will mainly be up to the European as well as the national courts whether, under the new system of direct applicability of Article 81(3) EC, adequate rules for dealing with cooperative networks will be developed.

Comment

Daniel Zimmer*

By using three cases as examples, Leitão Marques and Abrunhosa demonstrate that economic reality has brought about a wide range of cooperative arrangements between competitors as well as between non-competitors. Key statements in their chapter include:

- In the last two decades, the world economy has been 'entering into a new phase: "alliance capitalism", as opposed to the previous one: "hierarchical capitalism" ' (sub III.1.).
- Firms' networks are increasingly combining vertical and horizontal formats and 'are capable of shifting from one to the other' (sub III.2.).
- Alliances are increasingly global and plural (sub III.3.).
- 'Co-opetition', which means a mix of cooperation and competition between the same firms, might pave the way for a new model of competition and bring new problems to competition policy and law (sub IV.).
- The network, rather than the parties to it, is 'increasingly becoming the analysis unit' (sub V.2. at n. 54, also sub V.4.).
- Competition law thus will not so much be concerned about the loss of competition between the firms within the network but, far more, about the exclusion from the market or from the chance of accessing it of other firms (third-party-competition) (sub V.2.).
- So entry conditions are central to antitrust analysis (sub V.4.).
- After all, 'the assessment of an airline alliance is very similar to that of a concentration, not only because of the importance authorities attribute to the efficiency gains but also because of the attention they give to the potential for competition as a condition for permitting the formation of such alliances' (sub V.4.).

The theses of Leitão Marques and Abrunhosa touch upon central issues of competition policy: is it permissible to take into consideration no longer just the single firm, but also the network as such, thus substituting legal protection

---

*   Professor, LL.M., Rheinische Friedrich-Wilhelms Universität, Bonn.

of inter-party competition (competition within the network) with possibly reinforced competition towards other business units (third-party competition)? To this commentator, the three cases presented in the chapter do not suggest a fundamental change in competition policy. It even seems dubious whether they represent new forms of cooperation. The Aerosoles case, in which a shoe manufacturer used numerous contracts to ensure the supply of goods necessary to produce and distribute their goods, whilst complex, does not appear to be a new arrangement posing new questions to competition policy. The Volkswagen/Ford cooperation concerning the joint development of a car is, as Leitão Marques and Abrunhosa note, an example of a more traditional joint venture. The Star-Alliance case (sub I.2.a) appears to be the most interesting one: a number of airlines share – according to their needs – terminal facilities, maintenance bases, aircraft, staff, traffic rights or capital resources. 'Code sharing' is a core issue in these arrangements: participating airlines can apply their own flight numbers to an operation carried out by another member of the alliance. Even if we conceded that this case gives an impressive example of how competitors can work together to use scarce resources and at the same time improve services it appears dubious whether we face a new phenomenon. Centralised transaction systems in the banking industry are but one 'old' example of complex but successful cooperation among competitors.

In a paper presented at an earlier conference Hanns Ullrich described the Commission's change of attitude towards the legal assessment of cooperation:[1] whereas under traditional competition law cooperation among competitors is principally caught by the cartel provision as long as it has – at least – some appreciable effect on the market, the Commission's recent Guidelines on Horizontal Cooperation provide for much higher thresholds of market shares of 15 per cent (for joint commercialisation or purchasing), 20 per cent (for agreements on production, including specialisation agreements) and 25 per cent (for agreements on research and development).[2] To the commentator, it appears even more remarkable that the Commission, in order to assess the market effect of cooperation, relies on the Herfindahl–Hirschman Index, a measure for the degree of *concentration in a market* initially developed in the context of *merger control*.[3]

---

[1] Hanns Ullrich, 'Competitor Competition and the Evolution of Competition Law: Issues for Research in a Perspective of Globalization', in Josef Drexl (ed.), *The Future of Transnational Antitrust – From Comparative to Common Competition Law*, Berne et al 2003) pp. 159, 198 et seq.

[2] Guidelines on the applicability of Art. 81 EC Treaty to agreements on horizontal cooperation, OJEC 2001, C 3 p. 2 et seq., Nos 62, 93, 130 and 149.

[3] Guidelines on the applicability of Art. 81 EC Treaty to agreements on horizontal cooperation (*supra* n. 2) No. 29.

Interestingly, we can observe a tendency to 'bridge' the cooperation–concentration gap on the shore of merger control, as well. By introducing a 'significant impediment to effective competition' criterion which extends the reach of merger control to the area of 'non-coordinated effects' in oligopolies, the EC merger regulation of 2004 arguably lowers the threshold for a declaration of incompatibility with the Common Market.[4] More importantly, the new merger regulation expressly provides for the recognition of an efficiency defence in merger control. This instrument appears to be in important respects similar to Art. 81(3) of the EC Treaty, the exemption provision for agreements.[5]

If, according to the statements given earlier in this comment, the real world has not changed in a way which could induce us to revoke well-established measures such as the appreciability rules applied with respect to Article 81(1) of the EC Treaty, what then might have driven the Commission to change its policy? The tendency for convergence of criteria in the fields of cooperation and concentration control might be explained by the convincing force of argument: the former distinction between a high threshold of control in merger control and much lower thresholds for an application of Article 81(1) EC could appear inconsistent. Given that a merger creates a much more stable combination than cooperation does, concerns of competition law should be at least as strong here – with respect to mergers – as they are in the field of cooperation. It did not make sense to treat cooperative agreements in a much more severe way than transactions leading to a concentration. There is a well-known counter-argument to this reasoning: it is presumed that a stable combination, by eliminating the need to negotiate contractual terms between the parties for the future, will in itself bring certain efficiency gains. This argument in favour of a general privilege for concentrations seems to be invalidated under the EC Merger Regulation of 2004 since the Commission now has to take into consideration efficiency claims in all cases.

If we consider that competition policy pursues the same goals in the fields of cooperation control and concentration control it can appear inconsistent to treat cooperation agreements under a less favourable rule than concentrations. Instead of a general presumption that mergers generate efficiency gains we should take into consideration a presumption that business units will opt for the type of arrangement which serves their needs in the most favourable way – that includes the aspect of efficiency gains. After all, competition policy seems to be well advised if it does not privilege one or another *form* of combination. In fact, the history of competition policy in the

---

[4] D. Zimmer, 'Significant Impediment to Effective Competition: Das neue Untersagungskriterium der EU-Fusionskontrollverordnung', *Zeitschrift für Wettbewerbsrecht* 2 (2004), p. 250 (253 et seq.).

[5] Cf. Ullrich, *supra* n. 1, at p. 165; see also Zimmer, *supra* n. 4, at p. 263 et seq.

EU is among other things a history of an ever more favourable treatment of cooperation,[6] hereby shifting control standards in the area of Art. 81 EC more and more towards the structural criteria set for merger control in Germany by the 1973 revision of the 'Gesetz gegen Wettbewerbsbeschränkungen' and in Community law by the EC Merger Regulation of 1989. The obvious tension between the two control standards was set aside for the most critical types of cases, which are joint ventures, by the Commission's notice on cooperative joint ventures of 1993.[7] One might interpret the history of competition law in the sense that when introducing rules on merger control at a relatively late stage of antitrust legislation, rule makers at the national as well as the Community level chose a more reasonable standard for the legal treatment of distortions of competition than their predecessors did in the early days of German and Community competition legislation. In this view, the introduction of merger control led to the need for legislators and law-enforcers to adjust to the new standard in the field of cooperation as well. If it is right that cooperations and concentrations, due to the identity of competition policy objectives in both fields, have to be assessed under common substantive standards, their legal treatment will still differ in one important respect. With a view to the stability and largely irreversible nature of a merger, it appears necessary that the control of concentrations is subject to specific procedural rules, providing for a suspension period until the transaction has been cleared by the competent authority.

---

[6]   This has been analysed in the most detailed way by Ullrich, *supra* n. 1, p. 186 et seq.

[7]   OJEC 1993, No. C 43, p. 2 et seq.; see also the amendments of regulations 417/85 and 418/85 by regulation 151/93, OJEC 1993 No. L 21, p. 8 et seq.

7. Mergers in the media sector: business as usual?

Laurence Idot*

I INTRODUCTION

The subject at hand calls for two general and preliminary remarks.

Firstly, the very fact that the topic of mergers in the audiovisual sector was selected assumes that this domain constitutes a category especially suited to the issue chosen for this conference: 'The Evolution of European Competition Law. Whose Regulation, which Competition?'

In addition, the subtitle 'Business as usual' added by the organizer of this convention, Hanns Ullrich, is decidedly provocative. Does this indicate that in this particular domain business concerns take priority over more general considerations such as plurality of opinions or cultural diversity? It is still too soon to respond to this query, but consideration should be given to the European Parliament's report of 5 April 2004 concerning the violation of freedom of expression and information laws in the European Union, and most notably in Italy. We will not go further into this debate, as the afore-mentioned report is based on a study, carried out in eight member states by the European Institute for Consumer Affairs, to which the author did not have access. However, as regards the present topic, it should be pointed out that the level of concentration of ownership is already quite elevated in several countries (in particular the Netherlands, Sweden and Italy), is partic-ularly high in several of the new Member States, and that the Parliament has indicated its wish for a directive on the protection of pluralism in European media.[1]

To begin, how exactly should the term 'media' be defined? The word media is immediately evocative of audiovisual channels – television, radio – but such a definition would be oversimplified. Clearly, the role of the press should not

---

*   Professor at the Université Paris I-Panthéon/Sorbonne. Originally this contri-bution was presented in French (published as such in RIDE 2005, 5); the translation by Amber M. Larsen is gratefully acknowledged.
[1]   European Parliament 339.618 DEF, 5 April 2004.

be forgotten. The key difficulty in defining the media results from the increasing breakdown of traditional categories. We are currently living in a multimedia era and, as we have observed over the last months with the arrival of digital television and broadband web television, traditional classifications are no longer adapted to the reality of today's situation. We are witnessing a phenomenon of convergence which, although easily dealt with by consumers, proves more difficult to grasp on the legal level.[2]

On this day of reflection, why should the only presentation on mergers concern the media? The economic importance of the sector does not require demonstration. During a conference that took place a year ago,[3] Mr. Ungerer, Head of Division at the Directorate General for Competition in charge of 'Information, Communication and Multimedia', indicated that at the end of the 1990s the European Union media sector represented 145 billion euros, of which one third was accounted for by television, one third by radio, and the last third by magazines and newspapers.

Once again however, above and beyond the purely quantitative – business-based – data, the interest accorded to the media is easily explained. Information is not a consumer good like others and states cannot disregard the media operator's role in delivering information. Their activities are closely linked to the exercise of a fundamental public freedom, the liberty of expression.

Guaranteeing freedom of speech also implicates protecting pluralism, cultural diversity and citizen choice. Under French law, protecting pluralism of socio-cultural expression is in itself important enough to merit inclusion at the constitutional level.[4] Similar concerns have resulted in the development of specific legislation and intra-sector regulation in those European Member States that, in name of the public good, have attempted to limit mergers between market players.[5] That said, in 1986 the French Constitutional Council (*le Conseil constitutionnel français*) remarked that the provisions of the freedom of communications law (*loi relative à la liberté de communication*), intended to combat any abuse of a dominant market position, could not alone ensure compliance with the constitutional goal of pluralism.[6]

---

[2]   On this point, see also the approach used by economists and the comparative study of media mergers carried out by the Competition Committee of the Organization for Economic Co-operation and Development (OECD), 'Mergers in the Media' Volume 5, *OECD Journal of Competition Law and Policy* [2003], number 4, pp. 79–193.

[3]   H. Ungerer *Legal and Regulatory Aspects of Public Service Broadcasting*, 19–20 September 2003, Bucharest.

[4]   Constitutional Council, decision number 86-217, 18 September 1986.

[5]   It appears that France was a pioneer in this matter, at least insofar as audiovisual media are concerned.

[6]   Constitutional Council, decision number 86-217, *supra* n. 4.

The Community legal context is also narrower.[7] Nevertheless, fundamental liberties are included in the applicable body of law: in addition to the integration of Article 10 of the European Convention of Human Rights into the Community legal system, one must henceforth take into account Article 11 of the Charter of Fundamental Rights of the EU, which again affirms freedom of speech. However, regulation within the sector is limited: apart from the well known 'Television without Frontiers' directive[8] that is currently being revised,[9] it is essentially via the application of general rules on freedom of circulation and free market competition that these community institutions are involved.[10]

If we are then to restrict ourselves to the domain of competition law, it appears that for a lengthy period of time at least, the involvement of Community institutions was severely limited. Indeed, up until the arrival of newer cases involving sports event broadcasting agreements (which have recently increased in number),[11] the application of antitrust laws in this sector was the exception rather than the rule: one may cite the long-standing *Binon*[12] judgment in the press sector and the more recent *Bronner*[13] judgment in relation to home newspaper delivery. The situation has changed significantly over the last ten years.

In the audiovisual sector, the disappearance of state monopolies that occurred without any Community intervention,[14] allowed for the emergence

---

[7]   For an overview, see H. Ungerer *Legal framework to secure open Media Markets and the Independence of the Press – The Role of EU Competition Law*, Opole, 5 June 2004; *Application of EU Competition Rules to Broadcasting – The Transition from Analogue to Digital*, Naples, 20 September 2004.

[8]   Council Directive 89/552/EEC, first Council directive of 3 October 1989 on the coordination of certain provisions laid down by Law, Regulation or Administrative Action in Member States concerning the pursuit of television broadcasting activities, OJ 1989 L298, as amended, OJ 1997 L202.

[9]   H. Ungerer *Impact of Competition Law on Media – some comments on current developments*, Brussels, 10 December 2003. See European Commission document *The Future of European Regulatory Audiovisual Policy*, COM (2003) 784, 15 December 2003.

[10]   See study by I. Pingel, 'Audiovisuel', *J. Clas. Europe*, Fasc. 1220.

[11]   M. Pereira, 'Scope and Duration of media rights agreements: balancing contractual rights and competition law concerns', presentation made in Brussels, 10 October 2003.

[12]   Case 243/83, *SA Binon & Cie v SA Agence et messageries de la presse*, judgment of the Court of Justice of 3 July 1985, [1985] ECR 2015.

[13]   Case 7/97, *Oscar Bronner GmbH v Mediaprint*, judgment of the Court of Justice of 26 November 1998, [1998] ECR I-7817.

[14]   See, for instance, *CEDECE* (Commission for the Study of the European Union/*Commission pour l'étude des communautés européennes*), '*Service public et Communauté européenne: entre l'intérêt général et le marché*', Strasbourg, October

of new operators in the 1980s. Community merger control that came into effect in the 1990s naturally applied to this sector amongst others.

Nevertheless, over the last few years, these operators have been confronted with new challenges. The integration of new technologies, along with the diversification of media outlets, required increasingly high levels of investment (one need only read the TPS decision)[15] while at the same time the sector was facing financial difficulties due to a downturn in advertising proceeds. It is not surprising that the last two years have been characterized by a phase of consolidation,[16] during which operations have increasingly come under the public spotlight, eventually leading the European Parliament to express its concerns in respect of certain recent mergers and especially those in Italy.

This issue leads inevitably to the question: what is the most adequate tool to ensure merger control while guaranteeing both compliance with pluralism and free market competition? This question encapsulates the classic problem of the relationship between regulations applicable to a specific sector and competition law itself. It is an issue of sufficient importance as to have been the subject of an ICN working group. This relational problem concerns a much broader scope of issues than those covered by the media sector alone, but it is nevertheless of particular interest to the matter at hand.

More than in any other domain, there has always been a certain tension in the media sector, which was for example expressed in the 1997 report by the French High Council on Audiovisual Matters (*Conseil supérieur de l'audiovisuel* or *CSA*) concerning pay television in France:

> It is striking to note that the European Court of Justice, when applying an economic law, speaks of the 'consumer' and not the 'television viewer'. The very difference between the respect of pluralism and the exercise of free market competition lies in this semantic distinction. In addition to laws of an economic nature, audiovisual law brings with it certain distinctive characteristics linked either to cultural issues or to the protection of pluralism.[17]

1996, under the direction of R. Kovar and D. Simon, Paris, *La documentation française*, 1998; see, most particularly the workshop concerning the sector, *Communication, culture et formation*, G. Chatillon, M. Juhan, J.L. Piotraut, M.F. Christophe Tchakaloff, vol. I, p. 337 et seq.

[15] Commission Decision 1999/242/EC of 3 March, *TPS*, Case IV/36.237, OJ 1999 L90. Handed down prior to the reform implemented by Regulation 1310/97, this joint venture was examined pursuant to Regulation 17/62; the conclusions, and most particularly those in reference to markets, remain valid for merger control.

[16] H. Ungerer 'Competition policy and the issue of access in broadcasting markets: the Commission perspective', presentation made in Brussels, 14 January 2003.

[17] 'Il est frappant de constater que la Cour de Justice des Communautés européennes, lorsqu'elle applique un droit économique, parle de 'consommateur' et non de 'téléspectateur'. Toute la différence entre le respect du pluralisme et le libre jeu

In any event, under substantive law the facts are clear: we are faced with two different types of control. As a result of this duality, two different approaches are possible: a conflict-based, competition approach, entailing a power struggle, or a more complementary method. The subtitle proposed by Hanns Ullrich, 'Business as usual,' suggests that we fall into the first category and that competition law, concerned strictly with business matters, will prevail. This is not entirely false, but I personally believe that the principle of complementary coexistence is taking the upper hand. Indeed, this is the concept that I wish to pursue further here by considering the development of both its institutional (II) and substantive (III) nature.

II   THE INSTITUTIONAL APPROACH: MOVING TOWARDS A COEXISTENCE OF SOURCES

The dual nature of media control rules in at least half of the European Union Member States poses an initial problem:[18] how to reconcile the standard regime of law (*droit commun*) that governs merger control with regulation applicable to the specific sector (*régulation sectorielle*) (1)? In Europe, a second difficulty may be encountered in addition to the former due to the Community dimension and the problems resulting from attribution of competency amongst the Member States (2). However, it appears that following an initial period of reasoning based on choice and opposition, coexistence increasingly constitutes the underlying logic in this domain.

1   From the Alternative 'Specific Law or Standard Regime' to Coexistence of 'Sector-specific Law and Standard Regime'

I shall concentrate on the French example here, given the time available and

---

de la concurrence se résout dans cette différence sémantique. A un droit de nature économique (. . .) le droit de l'audiovisuel emporte des particularités liées soit à une problématique culturelle, soit à la sauvegarde du pluralisme.' Cited by the Competition Council in its notice (*avis*) 03-A-08 of 26 May 2003 in relation to a request for the additional notification of the French Minister of Culture and Communication (*ministre de la culture et de la communication*) and the French Deputy Minister of Industry (*ministre déléguée à l'industrie*) concerning a bill on electronic communications, Report to the Council (*rapport du Conseil*) for 2003, available on the internet, www.conseil-concurrence.fr.

[18]   On this point see also L. Vogel, 'Pluralisme culturel et contrôle des structures', presentation made at the competition workshop on 'Culture et concurrence', 10 October 2001, published in 124 *Revue Concurrence et Consommation* 26 (November–December 2001).

my better knowledge in this area, but it is highly probable that these conclusions also apply to other Member States.[19]

At first in France, sector-specific regulations took priority and competition law was essentially excluded (a), but later on merger control began to be applied to the sector and a form of coexistence with the existing regulations has developed (b).

a) The initial dominance of sector-based law

(i) Historically in France, it was in the press sector that the first provisions intended to ensure pluralism appeared. The 1944 ordinance, and later a law on the press dated 23 October 1984, put in place a Commission for transparency and pluralism (*Commission de la transparence et du pluralisme*). In June 1986, a new law was ratified under which Article 11 specifically prohibited the acquisition of daily periodicals above the threshold of 30 per cent of nationwide distribution. However, this provision was overturned by the Constitutional Council (*Conseil Constitutionnel*)[20] on the grounds that it did not sufficiently guarantee protection of pluralism.

Under the law adopted on 27 November 1986, which still applies today,[21] the direct or indirect acquisition of a daily publication is prohibited beyond the threshold of 30 per cent, with variants based on the single media or multimedia nature of the given operation. The penalty for violation of this law is twofold: civil sanctions render the operation null and void, and criminal penalties may be imposed. The CSA may also become involved in audiovisual aspects of multimedia operations.

In practice, for various institutional reasons, this form of control is not successful. The Minister of Justice (*Le Ministre de la justice*) is the only individual authorized to petition the Public Prosecutor (*Parquet*) in the event of the threshold being crossed, but he tends not to do so. A prime example was provided during the acquisition of *Dernières Nouvelles d'Alsace* by the

---

[19]   It shouldn't be overlooked that the 7th reform of the German competition act (*GWB*) made necessary by Regulation 1/2003 is currently delayed due to a heated debate on the regime that should be applied to mergers in the press sector. See V.U. Immenga, 'Pressemärkte in der Wettbewerbs und Medienpolitik' *ZWeR*, 2004/3, pp. 329–54.

[20]   Constitutional Council decision number 86-217 of 18 September 1986 in relation to the 'Freedom of Communications' (*liberté de communication*) law.

[21]   J-M. Cot, J.P. de la Laurencie, *Le contrôle français des concentrations*, Paris, LGDJ collection droit des affaires, 2nd edn, 2003, numbers 31–34; D. Brault, *Politique et pratique du droit de la concurrence en France*, Paris, LGDJ, collection droit des affaires, numbers 198–202; D. Ferrier, D. Ferré, Droit du contrôle national des concentrations', Paris, *Dalloz référence*, 2004, number 12, p. 36 et seq.

Hersant Group. Investigatory proceedings were opened following journalistic pressure, but the matter has yet to result in any legal action.[22]

(ii) The second specific regime is that providing for audiovisual matters.[23] This is a complex system implemented by the law of 30 September 1986,[24] amended at various times, most recently in July 2004.[25] No less than four rules must be respected. Through the use of thresholds, they attempt:

- to limit ownership of media by restricting the stake of companies authorized to exploit audiovisual services;[26] this threshold (40 or 50 per cent) varies in accordance with the broadcasting means involved (national television by radio wave, regional channels, satellite television); it was updated by the law of 17 July 2001 which added a threshold based on audience share (set at 2.5 per cent);
- to limit any given person's stake in several companies;[27]
- to limit cumulative permits for any one form of distribution;[28]
- to limit multimedia mergers (in this case the thresholds differ between analogue, digital, national, regional and local television).[29]

These texts are implemented by an independent government authority (hereinafter IGA), known as the High Council on Audiovisual Matters (*le Conseil supérieur de l'Audiovisuel* or *CSA*). This administrative body was founded in 1986, but it took over from a much older body called the High Authority (*Haute Autorité*). In 2000, a department for the development of media was also put in place under the authority of the Prime Minister (*Premier Ministre*), which was intended to 'participate in the implementation of procedures pertaining to competition law' (*participer à la mise en œuvre des procédures relevant du droit de la concurrence*).[30]

---

[22]   D. Brault, *supra* note 21, number 200.

[23]   For an overview of this regime, see D. Brault, *supra* note 21, number 203–214; J.M. Cot, J.P. de La Laurencie, *supra* note 21, number 26–30–1.

[24]   Law number 86-1067 of 30 September 1986 in respect of the freedom of communication; refer to the consolidated text, as amended, on the CSA (*Conseil Supérieur de l'Audiovisuel*) website.

[25]   Law number 2004-669 of 9 July 2004 relating to electronic and audiovisual communications services, Official Journal of the French Republic (*Journal Officiel de la République Française* or *JORF*), number 159, 10 July 2004.

[26]   Law number 86–1067, article 39–I.

[27]   Law number 86–1067, article 39–II and 39–III.

[28]   Law number 86–1067, article 41.

[29]   Law number 86–1067, article 41–1 and 41–2 for analogue television; article 41–1–1 and 41–2–1 for digital television.

[30]   D. Brault, *supra* n. 21, number 197.

All of these texts stress the need to protect pluralism, but the so-called 'competition' concerns also appear. Did they arise before the development of merger control? For the sake of clarity, it should be pointed out that whilst merger control was put in place in France in 1977, de facto it was not enforced until the beginning of the 1990s.

b) The gradual integration of merger control

From the 1990s on, the issue arose of possibly subjecting mergers in these sectors to the control procedures provided for under the 1977 law, and reiterated in the 1986 law. This breakthrough did not occur without obstacles, as initially the wrong question was being asked, namely, did the existence of specific rules exclude the enforcement of the standard regime?

(i) As far as the press sector was concerned, the former Competition Commission (*Commission de la concurrence*), which had a purely consultative role, issued a notice indicating that the existence of the special regime excluded the application of the law of 19 July 1977 on competition (which had established merger control).[31]

Later on, this decision went largely unquestioned, mainly because only those operations which did not fall within the scope of the specific provisions were examined.[32] In my personal opinion, it would have been logical to apply both regimes,[33] as is the case in other Member States.[34]

(ii) In any case, this is the solution that was eventually adopted in the audiovisual sector, but not without difficulties. The law of 30 September 1986 maintained the general validity of merger control. However, pursuant to the reforms implemented by the law of 17 January 1989,[35] the legislator chose to exclude the sector from Article V of the Ordinance of 1 December 1986, which at the time governed merger control.

Once control began to be effectively implemented, tensions immediately

---

[31]   Notice of the Competition Commission on 2 October 1986, selective price cuts in the daily local informational periodical sector, Commission report for 1986 (*Rapport de la Commission pour l'année 1986*), page 12.

[32]   Please refer to the case of *Pearson's* acquisition of *Les Echos* (the decision has not yet been published); the purchase of hunting and leisure periodicals by EMAP (letter dated 14 November 1994, magazine sector, Official Bulletin for Competition, Consumption, and Repression of Fraud (*Bulletin Officiel de la Concurrence, de la Consommation et de la Répression des Fraudes* or the *BOCCRF*), 9 December 1994); more recently, the acquisition of the Express-Expansion group by Socpresse (letter dated 31 December 2002, written press sector); for additional information on these matters refer to J.M. Cot, J.P. de la Laurencie, *supra* n. 21, number 32.

[33]   For an analysis of these arguments, D. Brault, *supra* n. 21, number 201.

[34]   H.P. Nehl, *Europäische Pressemärkte im Lichte des EG-Wettbewerbsrechts*, 1 February 2002, which cites German, Austrian and British decisions.

[35]   New article 41-4 of law number 86-1067.

appeared. The Minister of the Economy, who was competent in merger cases, had a very rigid view of the audiovisual matters subject to his jurisdiction.[36] As European Community control was also applicable where sizeable operations were concerned, an answer to the question rapidly became necessary.

The law of 1 August 2000,[37] as modified by the New Economic Regulation (NRE) law of 15 May 2001, solved this problem. Mergers in the audiovisual sector became subject to the standard regime, except where the operation fell under the second request phase (phase II), in which case the Competition Council (*Conseil de la Concurrence*), petitioned by the Minister of the Economy, must also consult the CSA.[38] Since then, at least two operations have been examined under the new regime.[39]

This said, the fact that mergers are subject to the standard regime in no way prevents the CSA's enforcement of specific rules intended to protect pluralism.[40] Such a situation has resulted in two levels of control, which appears entirely normal given that the issues covered by each form of control do not necessarily overlap. The competition authority carries out its mission; it is up to the authority charged with pluralism to carry out its own.

However, it is true that the situation is slightly complicated by the fact that a second dimension has been added to this first one.

---

[36]   Refer in particular to the acquisition of Fun Radio and M.40 by CLT (letter dated 19 December 1994, notice 94-A-26, radiophonic advertising sector, BOCCRF, 28 December 1994). For additional information on this era, see Vogel, *supra* n. 18, p. 27; L. Idot 'Les autorités de contrôle et de régulation', in *La concurrence dans la société de l'information*, PU Paris II, 2002, pp. 33–48, (37–38).

[37]   Law number 2000-719 of 1 August 2000, *amending* article 41-4 of the 1986 law. The law made it compulsory to notify the Competition Council, whereas in the case of French control only those operations posing competitive problems resulted in such filings. The Minister of the Economy, who retains the power of decision, also had a monopoly over the choice to send an operation to phase II.

[38]   Vogel, *supra* n. 18, page 27; L. Idot 'Les autorités de contrôle et de régulation', *supra* n. 36, pp. 37–8 and 'Le nouveau contrôle français des concentration', in *JCP* éd. E, supp. *Cah. Dr. Ent.*, 2001/5; J.M. Cot, J.P. de la Laurencie, *supra* n. 21, number 30-1.

[39]   NRJ/RMC case, letter dated 10 February 2001; M6/TF1/TPS+TPS gestion case, letter dated 12 September 2002.

[40]   Refer to the CSA's intervention, before any reform in merger control, in the case of CLT/Fun Radio/M.40, J.M. Cot, J.P. de la Laurencie, *supra* n. 21, number 30. In the NRJ/RMC case, the proposed operation obviously presented competitive threats as it was referred to phase II, and the Competition Council became involved as well as the CSA. The planned operation was later discontinued, apparently due to the negative intervention of the CSA, whose *avis* was never published (J.M. Cot, J.P. de la Laurencie, *supra* n. 21, numbers 30-1).

2 From the Alternative 'Community or National Control' to the Coexistence of Control at the Community and at National Levels

This distinction between standard regime versus sector-specific law overlaps with the other European Community/national distinction, which is no doubt of even greater importance. It is significant that the development of Community merger control has shed light on the difficulties inherent in combining sector-specific and community-based law. The system assigning competence does give first rank to Community control, to competition, to business, but it is nevertheless possible to reintegrate national rights.

a) The preeminence of Community control

The one stop shop system is such that all operations of a certain size are subject to Community control which, it should be noted, imposes mandatory notification.

This is particularly true of mergers in the media sector. While decisions concerning the press are indeed limited in number,[41] this is not the case in the audiovisual sector, and all the more so given that certain Member States (who previously did not have any form of merger control) have not hesitated to use the referral procedure provided for under Article 22(3) of Regulation 4064/89.[42]

According to a search by NACE code on the Commission's website, 60 operations have been notified since the introduction of control procedures, of which exactly 51 correspond to radio and television activities,[43] and eight concern cinema and video operations, to which should be added several isolated operations (a prime example of which was the *Vivendi/Canal+/Seagram*[44] transaction).

Even though limited in number, these matters always command attention, and all the more so given that under Community law the proportion of mergers

---

[41] Refer to Commission Decision of 20 April 1999, *Financial Times/Gruner + Jahr*, Case IV/M.1455, OJ 1999 C80/5 for a joint venture concerning the *Financial Times* in Germany; the aborted legal publishing merger between ReedElsevier and Wolters Kluwer (Commission Press Release IP/98/230 of 10 March 1998).

[42] In the Commission Decision 96/346/EC of 20 September 1995, *RTL/Veronica/Endemol*, Case IV/M.553, OJ 1996 L134/32, and on appeal, Case T-221/95, *Endemol Entertainment Holding BV v Commission*, judgment of the Court of First Instance of 28 April 1999, [1999] ECR II-1299.

[43] These figures should be regarded with caution: the M.469 *MSG Media Service* case, which resulted in the first decision blocking a merger in the sector, does not appear in this list.

[44] Commission Decision of 13 September 2000, *Vivendi/Canal+/Seagram*, Case COMP/M.2050.

blocked is exceptionally high: the audiovisual sector represents only about 60 cases out of approximately 3000 (2 per cent), but in terms of refusals to approve mergers it represents 5 out of 18[45] or 27 per cent!

During the first years of control and up until 1995, the audiovisual sector was particularly targeted: three out of the first four blocked mergers concerned the audiovisual sector.[46] The most 'recent' operations rejected were the *Bertelsmann/Kirch/Première*[47] and *Deutsche Telekom Beta Research*[48] transactions in 1998,[49] to which the *MCI/Worldcom/Sprint*[50] refusal may be added, although it was of more interest to the telecommunications sector.

Amongst those operations given the 'green light' in phase II, apart from the *Lagardère/Natexis/VUP*[51] case which does not clearly fall under the category of 'media', the *Newscorp/Telepiù* decision of 2 April 2003 should be noted.[52] This operation is worthy of interest for several reasons and not exclusively for its relevance to competition law. It may also be noted that as of today, in the case of operations referred to phase II, all approval decisions were coordinated upon commitments given by the merging parties.[53]

Such a system leaves little place for control at the national level.[54] Under

---

45   Six, if the Commission Decision of 28 June 2000, *MCI/Worldcom/Sprint*, Case COMP/M.1741 case is included.

46   Commission Decision 94/922/EC of 9 November 1994, *MSG Media Services*, Case IV/M.469, OJ 1994 L364/01; Commission Decision 96/177/EC of 19 July 1995, *Nordic Satellite Distribution*, Case IV/M.490, OJ 1996 L53/20; *RTL/Veronica/Endemol supra* note 42.

47   Commission Decision 99/153/EC of 27 May 1998, *Bertelsmann/Kirch/ Première*, Case IV/M.993, OJ 1999 L53/1.

48   Commission Decision 99/154/EC of 27 May 1998, *Deutsche Telekom/ BetaResearch*, Case COMP/M.1027, OJ 1999 L53/31.

49   For an overview of the policies now applicable, see J.P. Gunther, 'La politique communautaire de l'audiovisuel: état des lieux', *RTDeur.*, 1998.1.

50   Commission Decision 2003/790/EC of 28 June 2000, *MCI WorldCom/Sprint*, Case COMP/M.1741, OJ 2003 L300.

51   Commission Decision 2004/422/EC of 7 January 2004, *Lagardère/ Natexis/VUP*, Case COMP/M.2978, OJ 2004 L125/54.

52   Commission Decision 2004/311/EC of 2 April 2003, *Newscorp/Telepiù*, Case COMP/M.2876, OJ 2004 L110.

53   Also refer to the Commission Decision 1999/287/EC of 8 July 1998, *Worldcom/MCI*, Case IV/M.1069, OJ 1999 L116/1; Commission Decision 2001/718/EC of 11 October 2000, *AOL/Time Warner*, Case COMP/M.1845, OJ 2001 L268/28.

54   For a discussion of community law's pertinence to mergers in the press sector that were notified to Austrian authorities, see Case C-170/02 P, *Schlüsselverlag J.S. Moser and Others v Commission*, judgment of the Court of Justice of 25 September 2002, [2003] OJ C275/36, which denied an appeal against the TPICE on 11 March 2002, having manifestly determined that the appeal on grounds of the Commission's failure to act was without merit. More recently, in Italy, the initial version of the

French law, there exist fewer than twelve cases concerning the press and television, divided in an approximately equal manner between the old regime, where notification was voluntary,[55] and the new regime, dating from the NRE in effect since May 2002.[56]

As to sector-specific regulations, these are outside the realm of Community competency,[57] therefore resulting in diversified national legislation,[58] and leading to the possible issue of Community involvement in order to attempt a harmonization of such legislation. Such harmonization is regularly called for by the European Parliament, but the Member States remain reticent, to say the least.

The convention on the Constitution, if ratified, will not modify this state of affairs.

Nevertheless, even in the current system national rights could have a greater role to play than they do currently.

b) Reintegration of national control

Two methods may be used to increase national media merger control. Both are already provided for by merger control regulations.

(i) The first consists of increased reliance on a technique by which cases are referred to Member States. In the previous system under Regulation 4064/89,

---

Telepiù/Stream merger was filed with Italian authorities and blocked by l'Autorità Garante della Concorrenza e del Mercato in its decision of 13 May 2002 (www.agcm.it). It was filed again in a modified version and fell within community jurisdiction. See V.H. Ungerer, *supra* n. 16, 14–15.

[55] See, most notably, the Minister's letter of 4 August 1993, société générale occidentale – société d'exploitation de l'hebdomadaire Le Point, notice of the Competition Council, 93-A-13 (BOCCRF, 10 September 1993); Minister's letter of 30 November 1994, Emap International magazines-Editions mondiales–Editions périodiques (BOCCRF, 9 December 1994); Minister's letter of 2 September 1999, Pathé-Vivendi (BOCCRF, 14 October 1999).

[56] Refer in particular to the Minister's letter of 12 December 2002, TF1/M6/TPS (BOCCRF, 31 March 2003); Minister's letter of 31 December 2002 relating to a merger in the written press sector (BOCCRF, 30 September 2004); Minister's letter dated 26 April 2004 relating to a merger in the pay TV sector; Minister's letter of 27 October 2004 relating to a merger in the audiovisual sector (available on the website of the French Ministry of the Economy (*Ministère de l'économie*), www.minefi.gouv.fr). In the press sector, there exist other decisions, outside those concerning general newspapers, which are subject to a specific regime, refer to the letters of 29 April 2003, merger in free press sector (BOCCRF, 5 December 2003), and of 11 February 2004 (BOCCRF, 15 June 2004).

[57] For a review of this principle, refer for example to H. Ungerer '*Application of EU Competition Rules to Broadcasting – The Transition from Analogue to Digital*', presentation made in Naples, 20 September 2004.

[58] Green Paper, COM (92) 480, 23 December 1992.

the Commission originally appeared reticent.[59] More recently, it accepted just such a referral to the Spanish authorities in the matter of *Digital/Sogecable*,[60] because the operation threatened to reinforce the dominant position on Spanish markets that could be characterized as distinct, and most particularly on the pay TV market, the market for acquisition of soccer event broadcasting rights and markets for various other rights.

An action for invalidation of this referral decision was rejected by the Court in its 30 September 2003 judgment.[61] One of the arguments put forth to contest the referral was based on the fact that the Commission had examined the Italian *Newscorp/Telepiù*[62] operation, but this argument was not decisive given that Italian authorities had not requested a referral in that matter.

New Regulation 139/2004 should allow national controls to intensify as it multiplies the various referral mechanisms and accords them increased flexibility.[63] It is true that in any case, this form of control remains in the realm of competition law and not of media plurality.

(ii) The second technique, which was provided for from the outset of regulation, and which was retained in the new regulation, consists of allowing the Member State to intervene so as to protect its legitimate interests. However, maintaining the plurality of the media is expressly provided for by Article 21(4).

To our knowledge, at least in the audiovisual sector, it appears that to this day no Member State has used this opportunity in order to impose additional constraints on an operation that had already received the green light from the Commission.

It may be tempting to object that in the ruling of *Portugal v Commission* of

---

[59]   For example, the German authorities requested a referral in the decision to reject the MSG Média Service merger (Commission Decision 94/922/EC of 9 November 1994, *MSG Media Service*, Case IV/M.469, OJ 1994 L364/1), and this request was refused.

[60]   Commission Press Release IP/02/1216 of 16 August 2002. Commission Decision of 14 August 2002, *Sogecable/Canalsatélite/Via Digital*, Case COMP/M. 2845; on the final decision made by the Spanish authorities, decision of the Council of Ministers dated 29 November 2002 (N-280), www.mineco.es/dgdc/sdc.

[61]   Joined cases T-346/02 and T-347/02, *Cableuropa and Others v Commission*, judgment of the Court of First Instance of 30 September 2003, OJ 2003 C17, note L. Idot.

[62]   *Supra* note 54.

[63]   For French language comments, refer to 'Le nouveau règlement CE sur les concentrations', Europe, March, 2004; F. Brunet 'La double réforme du contrôle communautaire des concentrations', *RTDeur.*, 2004/1, pages 1–3; J.M. Cot 'Le nouveau contrôle des concentration: plus de transparence contre plus de pouvoirs pour la Commission', *Revue Lamy Droit des Affaires*, 2004, number 72.

22 June 2004,[64] the Court of Justice proceeded with a restrictive interpretation of Article 21(3) of Regulation 4064/89 that may have effects on the ability to block a media merger in the name of pluralism.

Such a fear does not appear founded, as it is based on an incorrect interpretation of the verdict. In the matter in question, Portugal was acting out of self-interest – the substance of which was later judged to be contrary to the principles of Community law as it had to do with the regime governing those actions permitted following a privatization operation, and it above all did not follow the Commission notification procedure that was called for by this text.

To conclude this first point, it appears that various instruments of control do exist. They are principally in the hands of the Member States, and this is in fact the crux of the problem. Indeed, competition authorities, and more particularly the Commission, were the only administrative bodies to attempt to limit media mergers. This said, they can only act in their specific context, which is not necessarily the best adapted for enforcing compliance with pluralism. Therefore, it becomes necessary to go beyond the institutional approach so as to examine more carefully the various mechanisms used.

III   THE SUBSTANTIVE APPROACH: TOWARDS COMPLEMENTARY INSTRUMENTS

There is no antagonism between the goals of competition law, and in particular merger control that attempts to prevent the creation of strong groups within markets, and those of sector regulation, which prohibit the accumulation of media to the benefit of a certain person. Indeed, the French Competition Council recently indicated that 'insofar as it is desirable, from a competition point of view, to guarantee that sufficient plurality of content is offered by independent agents at an economic level, the goals of competition and pluralism in the audiovisual sector may converge.'[65]

The two instruments are undeniably complementary and this holds true

---

[64]   Case C-42/01, *Portugal v Commission*, judgment of the Court of Justice of 22 June 2004, OJ 2004 201/01, note L. Idot, *Concurrences*, 2004/1, obs. S. Martin, pages 72–3.

[65]   Notice number 03-A-08 of 26 May 2003 concerning the supplementary request made by the Minister of Culture and Communication and that of the Deputy Minister of Industry concerning a proposed law pertaining to electronic communications, report of the Competition Council for 2003 (*rapport du Conseil pour l'année 2003*), available on the website, www.conseil-concurrence.fr. Also in the same line of thought, refer to the OECD report, *supra* note 2, and specifically part 6 'Fusions de médias et pluralisme', page 131 et seq.

based both at the level of the purpose of control (1), as well as at the level of the methods used (2).

1   Complementary Goals

Duality in control requires that the respective merits of instruments for dealing with media mergers be studied. A preliminary remark is necessary: it may be summed up by the following formula which, although oversimplified, is also quite evocative: legal/economic. At least in the French example, since merger control is part of the branch of competition law, it has an essentially economic approach that is not necessarily present in sector-specific regulation.

This conclusion may be drawn at two different levels: first at the level of the concepts applied (a), and secondly that of the purpose of control (b).

a)   Concepts

(i) Sector-specific regulation uses legal more often than economic categories.

The first key idea is that of the individual. The intent is to prevent the concentration of media in the hands of one person, whether he be Mr Hersant, Mr Berlusconi, or Mr Murdoch.

In other terms, this is based on a fundamental principle of civil law. The provisions of the French law of 1986 on audiovisual materials are enlightening in this regard: Article 38: 'any natural person or entity that comes to hold any fraction' (*toute personne physique ou morale qui vient à détenir toute fraction*); Article 39: 'any given natural person or entity acting alone or in connection with' (*une même personne physique ou moral agissant seul ou de concert*); Article 40: 'no foreign national' (*aucune personne de nationalité étrangère*); Article 41: 'any one individual or entity' (*une même personne physique ou morale*). This is the classic approach of corporate law, that we are also familiar with in other branches or law such as in the regulation of investments.

Of course, this legal approach is not without risk: one must not attempt to circumvent the rules. This explains the inclusion of phrases such as 'acting alone or in connection with' (Article 39), and even more so the alternative, 'direct or indirect holding'. It appears obvious then that the legislator was aware of the limits of the legal approach.

The second key principle of sector regulation is the holding of securities. Acquisition and reinforcement of shares in a company, and more importantly assumption of control of a given company, are all regulated. This is not founded on the economic principle of market share or power, but rather on the legal concepts of ownership and holdings.

A priori, this approach appears easier to deal with, but not all the related difficulties have been discussed. For example, in listed companies where the number of floating shares is sometimes quite significant, the calculation of the infamous threshold is difficult. Operators have always pleaded that floating shares be omitted from this calculation.[66]

(ii) The facts are different in the case of merger control, which depends primarily on economic concepts, even if such concepts also have legal significance.

The object of the rule in this case is not the individual, but rather the enterprise. Competition law deals with economic realities via the notion of the functional and plurivalent enterprise, which necessarily includes the concept of groups of companies.[67]

However, the greatest specificity of competition law resides in the fact that its underlying logic is based on the idea of the market. Although there have been a limited number of decisions in the press sector,[68] we now have access to quite a bit of case law in the audiovisual sector,[69] as well as studies on the subject regularly carried out at the Commission's request.[70]

In the television sector, case law has allowed for the identification of the principal product markets: this is based on a distinction amongst modes of content delivery – pay TV market versus the free television market,[71] theme-based stations included in pay TV services,[72] and cable network markets[73] –

---

[66] This issue was particularly relevant for the Vivendi group after the acquisition of Universal. The matter was put to the French Council of State (*Conseil d'état*).

[67] For a recent study see L. Idot, 'La notion d'entreprise révélateur de l'ordre concurrentiel', in *L'ordre concurrentiel, Mélanges en l'honneur d' A. Pirovano*, Paris: Frison-Roche, 2003, pp. 523–46.

[68] Nevertheless, refer to Case IV/M.1455 (*supra* note 41) for a joint venture involving the Financial Times in Germany; the planned merger of legal publishing services between ReedElsevier and Wolters Kluwer was aborted (Commission Press Release IP/98/230 of 10 March 1998).

[69] Aside from *sensu stricto* decisions in respect of mergers, a relatively complete analysis of markets appears in the ruling founded on Article 81 EC and relating to the TPS joint venture (OJ 1999 L90). For an overview of related legal doctrine, refer to J.B. Blaise 'L'accès aux marchés', in *La concurrence dans la société de l'information*, PU Paris II, 2002, pages 19–32; R. Saint-Esteben 'Les opérateurs du marché: rapprochements, concentrations', idem, pages 89–93. More recently, N.Th. Nikolinakos 'Mergers and Strategic Alliances in the Emerging Multi-Media Sector: The EU Competition Policy', [2004] *ECLR*, issue 10, pp. 625–37.

[70] '*Market definitions in the Media Sector*', europa.eu.int/comm/competition/publications. For the purposes of comparison, also refer to the OECD study 'Mergers in the media', *supra* n. 2.

[71] See for example the rulings on *MSG Media Services, Bertelsmann/Kirch/Première, TPS, supra* n. 47. For a review of French law in this field, refer to the Minister's letter dated 26 April 2004, *supra* n. 56.

[72] Refer in particular to the Minister's letter dated 26 April 2004, *supra* n. 56.

[73] Refer to the *MSG Media Service* decision, *supra* n. 59.

and the content itself, such as the market for production of programmes or markets for the acquisition of broadcast rights, whether this concerns cinematography works, or the right to broadcast sports events, and notably soccer matches . . .[74] There may also exist fundamentally related markets such as advertising,[75] services provided to operators, and decoder markets.

The principal difficulty here is of a technical nature: the phenomenon of media convergence is breaking down our traditional categories and requires a change in the delimitation of markets, with all of the risks that such a modification entails.[76] The inclusion of competition law methods within sector-specific regulation in the new regulatory bundle of 2002,[77] which has already been transposed into the law of Member States, should at least prevent differing approaches between competition law and sector regulation, such as is the case with telecommunications.

When the goal is efficiency in control, in reality the principal difficulties arise from the limits of geographical markets. We have already observed this phenomenon in the first audiovisual cases. Since geographic markets are very often national in scope for legal and linguistic reasons, the Commission chose to give the green light to a series of acquisitions carried out by Mr Bertelsmann, in countries other than Germany, on the grounds that there was no geographic overlap.[78]

b)   The subject of control
Supervision carried out to ensure plurality in the media is automatic in nature. Even if it is based on the principle of control as defined in corporate law, the goal is simple: it suffices to verify if one person controls the media.

Under competition law, this step is undeniably more complex. In the framework of Regulation 4064/89, the Commission had to play with the criteria for dominant market position so as to assess the risks generated by certain operations, and to deal with three types of problems: horizontal effects, vertical inte-

---

[74]   For a recent presentation of the various markets in France, refer to the Minister's letter of 27 October 2004, *supra* n. 56.

[75]   Refer to the *RTL/Veronica/Endemol* judgment *supra* n. 42; under French law, see the Minister's letter of 26 April 2004, *supra* n. 56.

[76]   Already in 2000, see 'Réglementation et concurrence dans le secteur audiovisuel dans une perspective de convergence', *OECD review droit et politique de la concurrence*, volume 2/number 3, page 7 et seq.

[77]   Directives 2002/21/EC and 2002/19/EC of the European Parliament and Council, (respectively 'Framework Directive' (*directive cadre*) and 'Access Directive' (*directive accès*)), respectively OJ 2002 L108/33 and OJ 2002 L108/7.

[78]   Commission Decision of 2 August 1994, *Kirch/Richemont/Telepiù*, Case IV/M.410, OJ 1994 C225/4; Commission Decision of 5 May 1995, *Kirch/Richemont/Multichoice/Telepiù*, Case IV/M.584, OJ 1995 C129/7; Commission Decision, *Bertelsmann/CLT*, Case IV/M.779, OJ 1996 C364/3.

gration, which is the most frequent in this sector, and a combination of horizontal and vertical effects, which is evidently the worst case scenario.[79] The Commission often did so in a rather audacious manner by developing the concept of 'gate keeper' and by attempting to preserve access to content as well as to the medium.

In respect of content, the transition to digital technology has accentuated existing difficulties, but the Commission hopes that the new regulatory context applicable to electronic communications will limit such problems. As to the market for related technical services, which notably includes the question of decoders, the Commission deems that the analyses set out in the cases of *MSG, Kirch/Bertelsmann*[80] and *BskyB/Kirch* remain valid.

Concerning content access, the line has been drawn most notably in the cases of *AOL/Time Warner* and *Vivendi/Seagram*,[81] and the same stance was taken by antitrust law in the case of *Champions League/UEFA*.[82]

The *Newscorp/Telepiù*[83] decision adopted in 2003, an Article 8 decision concerning commitments, is considered most representative of the Commission's current position. Indeed, a horizontal merger between two Italian pay TV entities, which for all practical purposes resulted in a monopoly, was approved. That said, the Commission simply acted within the boundaries of the instrument at its disposition.

Overall, it does not appear that competition authorities, least of all the Commission, have been lax in implementing media control, even if the rigor of the first few years seems to have tapered off slightly. This can no doubt be explained by the fact that the practice of commitments is generally better handled by the parties.[84]

---

[79]   For example, refer to the first decisions to block the operation, NDP (1995), HMG. For a presentation of the Commission's analysis, refer to H. Ungerer *supra* n. 3; H. Ungerer, *supra* n. 9.

[80]   Also in respect of this case refer to J.F. Pons 'La politique européenne de concurrence dans le secteur de l'audiovisuel', Brussels, 15 November 2001.

[81]   Decision COMP/M.2050, *supra* note 44. Also, J.F. Pons, *supra* n. 80.

[82]   Commission Decision of 23 July 2003, *Joint selling of the commercial rights of the UEFA Champions League*, Case COMP/C.2-37.398, OJ 2003 L291/25. And, for a presentation of these cases, M. Pereira 'Scope and Duration of media rights agreements: balancing contractual rights and competition law concerns', presentation made in Brussels, 10 October 2003.

[83]   Decision COMP/M.2876, *supra* n. 52.

[84]   Under French law, the use of undertakings has also enabled parties to obtain the 'green light'. Refer in particular to an approval granted in phase II in the press sector, in the Minister's letter of 29 April 2003, where the undertakings are both structural as well as behavioral in nature; more recently, for an approval in phase II in the audiovisual sector, refer to the Minister's letter of 27 October 2004, *supra* n. 56. Concerning the role of 'corrective measures' also see the OECD report, *supra* n. 2, part 7, pages 142–4.

One may hope that the new Regulation 139/2004, with its more flexible test based on threats to competition, should facilitate the identification of these vertical integrations. In no sense does it modify the methods of control that prove to be complementary.

2   Complementary Methods

Concerning means of control, competition law presents undeniable advantages over sector-specific regulation. These advantages exist in two respects.

a)   Ex ante or ex post control?

The first remark does not call for lengthy commentary. In the entirety of the laws of the European Union, with the exception of the United Kingdom, the control of mergers is done by means of *ex ante* control, that is to say control prior to the fact based on compulsory notification of an operation along with a mandatory waiting period. The advantages of such a system are obvious. They allow for a control of the operation that under the system of voluntary notification could be avoided in case the government agreed. This was well illustrated by the previous French system.

Sector-specific regulation is often more ambiguous in that it is a mix of *ex post* and *ex ante* control. Such is the case of French law, which is based both on prohibition, accompanied by penalties, that is *ex post* control, and on *ex ante* control as regards the attribution of permits and licenses.

b)   Prohibition or modification?

The penalties are linked to the nature of these controls. In respect of sector-specific regulation, the instruments put in place are not necessarily operational. These are either *a posteriori* penalties, which are not always applied, or automatic measures – such as the reduction of excessive ownership participation – which do not necessarily take into account the realities of the market.

Because of their flexibility, tools of competition law are much more operational.

Indeed, the authority exercising control may proceed to refuse approval of an operation, and, in the Community framework, the Commission has demonstrated several times that it was prepared do likewise.[85] That said, nothing prohibits operators from re-filing a proposed operation in an amended form so as to follow more closely the requirements of competition law, and consequently from obtaining approval, as was demonstrated in the case of *Endemol*.[86]

---

[85]   See Decisions *supra* nn. 44, 46.
[86]   See *supra* n. 42; a new form of the proposed transaction was filed and the operation was eventually approved.

Above all, by the practice of commitments, the supervisory authority may truly mold the operation to fit its requirements. This method has frequently been used in the audiovisual sector as can be seen by the large numbers of mergers obtaining a green light as early as phase I, due to the substantial undertakings agreed to by the parties – as, for example, in the case of *Vivendi/Canal+/Seagram*.[87] Even more interesting, in the case of operations referred to phase II, commitments have always been made by the enterprises. The same trend may be noted under French law.[88]

Moreover, it is in these domains that the Commission displayed great ingenuity. If, in the beginning, the Commission appeared quite rigid by deeming commitments insufficient or invalid because they were behavioral in nature, it has become much more flexible of late. The commitments are indeed numerous, but they are often of a behavioral nature in order to guarantee access both to the means of content delivery and to the content itself. These commitments may go as far as instituting arbitration procedures that delegate supervision of compliance with commitments to a third party.

The Commission's decision in the *Newscorp/Telepiù* case is a perfect example of this situation. The goal was to reduce as far as possible all barriers to entry, and to allow for entry into future markets, while at the same time protecting access to content and access to the means of content delivery. This occurred by way of a reduction in the number of exclusivity contracts for event broadcasting, and by a decrease in the scope of exclusivity of access to the means of content delivery through the use of mandatory licenses, and the introduction of possibilities for third party channel distribution.[89]

The most recent event in this domain is the judgment rendered by the Court of First Instance on 30 September 2003.[90] A competitor, operating in the same market as 'free' television, contested the decision under which the Commission had approved the *BskyB-Kirch Pay TV operation* at the end of phase I subject to certain undertakings by the parties. The many commitments, ten in all, attempted to guarantee third party access to the Kirch platform and to the d-box system, as well as ensuring that the systems could be interchanged. Whether what was at issue was the possibility of introducing substantial commitments as early as phase I, the content of such commitments,

---

[87]   Case COMP/M.2050, *supra* n. 44.

[88]   As an example, refer to the undertakings in the cases of France Antilles (Minister's letter dated 29 April 2003) and TF1/AB (Minister's letter dated 27 October 2004), *supra* n. 56.

[89]   For an insider commentary, refer to H. Ungerer, *supra* n. 7.

[90]   CFI of 30 September 2003, Case T-158/00, *ARD v Commission*, ECR 2003 II (not yet officially reported) see Europe 2003(12) 401, note L. Idot.

or the procedural methods used, the Court upheld the analysis of the Commission and rejected the appeal.

IV   CONCLUSION

In conclusion, application of the catch phrase 'business as usual' would appear harsh to say the least. With the tools made available to them, the competition authorities and more particularly the Commission have regulated media mergers to the best of their ability. The principal reason for the 'deficit' that has appeared resides, I believe,

- in the insufficient use that the Member States have made of their intra-sector regulation (this at least holds true in the French example);
- in the lack of use by Member States of Article 21(4) of the Merger Regulation, which would have allowed such states to impose additional conditions on proposed operations in the interests of the protection of pluralism;
- in the absence of political will by Member States to work together to consider a harmonization of legislation within the European Union which would guarantee media pluralism.

This is above all a question of political will.

November 2004

Comment

Peristera Kremmyda*

1 PRELIMINARY REMARKS

As Professor Idot, very rightly, makes clear in her chapter, one of the core issues that we are faced with when discussing 'media concentration' is the question of the balance between sector-specific regulation and competition law. However, before going ahead to discuss the issue, there are two preliminary questions that need to be answered. First, is competition law alone a sufficient tool to tackle concentration in the media? In other words, can we envisage getting rid of sector-specific regulation altogether? And, second, what kind of sector-specific regulation do we talk about in the context of the media? The two issues are clearly and closely inter-linked.

The first question can be answered very rapidly. No, competition law alone is not a sufficient or an adequate tool to tackle concentration in the media. The reason being that, if concentration in the media is considered a subject worth discussing in its own right, as opposed to concentration in the automobile or food industries, it is because the concerns raised are not solely of an economic nature. The media is, indeed, a multi-billion industry with important repercussions on growth and employment but, at the same time, the structure of ownership in the sector can have, and does have, even more important implications with regard to the functioning of a democratic society. It is this second function of the media, which is often discussed in terms of cultural and political pluralism in the media, which makes concentration of ownership in this sector a problem different in nature and in importance from that encountered in other sectors of the economy.

Competition law is economic law and it is aimed at maintaining a competitive structure in the various markets. Sector-specific regulation of media concentration, on the other hand, was not introduced with economic considerations in mind but with the aim of addressing issues that are linked to the function of the

---

* PhD. (European University Institute); the author is a case-handler with DG Competition of the European Commission. All opinions expressed are personal and do not represent the views of the Commission or DG Competition on any of the issues discussed.

media as a 'medium and factor in the process of free formation of opinion'[1]. These are two very different aims, which are of a very different nature, and this is why, if they are going to be met, both sets of legislation are necessary. Competition law is by its nature inadequate to cater for questions of a cultural and political order. This was clearly also recognised by the Community legislator through the introduction of Article 21(4) in the Merger Regulation.[2]

The second preliminary question refers to the nature of sector-specific regulation that we have in mind when discussing media concentration. The wider debate about 'regulation or competition' has been going on for quite some time and with regard to a number of sectors of the economy, especially those sectors that were recently liberalised and are trying to move from monopolistic conditions to competitive market structures. It is inevitable that the temptation is high to subsequently apply certain conclusions from this debate to the media concentration debate. However, this is a temptation that should be resisted. In the telecommunications or electricity fields, to use two examples, the distinction we are called to make is between *economic* regulation and competition law. In such fields regulation has been introduced in order to facilitate the introduction of fully-fledged competition in previously monopolistic markets and is essentially aimed at the same objectives as competition law. It constitutes a different tool with which to achieve the same aims. It is in this context that the balancing and choice between different tools is made and it is these conditions that have informed the 'regulation or competition' debate.

This is not, however, the case with sector-specific legislation concerning media concentration. Such legislation is not economic in nature, as it does not aim to introduce or maintain competition in the market but, rather, to ensure that a plurality of voices finds access to the media and, through the media, to public opinion. The utility and effectiveness of this kind of regulation cannot, therefore, be balanced against competition law using the same criteria as are applied to economic regulation in the telecommunications or electricity markets. It is an altogether different kind of regulation, with different aims and which should ideally have tools different from those of economic law. It is, therefore, one question whether we need economic regulation in addition to

---

[1]   BVerGE 57, 295.
[2]   Article 21(4) of the Merger Regulation reads: 'Notwithstanding paragraphs 2 and 3, Member States may take appropriate measures to protect legitimate interests other than those taken into consideration by this Regulation and compatible with the general principles and other provisions of Community Law. Public security, plurality of the media and prudential rules shall be regarded as legitimate interests within the meaning of the first paragraph.'

competition law to obtain or maintain competitive media markets, and a totally different question whether sector-specific legislation aimed at ensuring media pluralism is necessary or not.

The following discussion is, consequently, premised upon the assumption that: a) there are two different sets of aims that need to be met, economic ones and non-economic ones (defined for the sake of brevity as pluralism aims); and b) we need two sets of rules of a different nature to tackle the problems that arise: economic rules, which may be either regulatory rules or competition law, and non-economic, sector-specific, regulation.

2 EVOLVING ATTITUDES TO REGULATION

Professor Idot rightly distinguished between the tools of sector-specific legislation and the use of competition law in France, drawing some conclusions. Her analysis is perfectly valid for France, where, despite a significant number of amendments, the law, since it was initially adopted in 1986, has retained much of its original essence.[3] This is not, however, the case with the rest of Europe where changes have touched upon the very nature of sector-specific regulation.

In the mid-1990s, media-specific legislation for the protection of pluralism saw amendments in the criteria and means used that have altered the very nature of these laws leading to an increased 'economisation' of sector-specific laws. The most important among such modifications concerns the introduction of the notion of 'audience share' as the unique criterion for control.[4] In the context of the media (and especially television) 'audience share' is a criterion that is extremely similar to 'market share', given that audience share is the one most decisive factor in effectively achieving a certain market share. It is also significant that audience share thresholds have been generally placed at around 30 per cent. This threshold is very similar to the informal threshold below which, in general, a dominant position in a market is not to be

---

3   Law no 86-1067 of 30/09/1986 limits the number of media outlets each operator can control without imposing any limits on the growth of each individual outlet in terms of revenues, market share or audience share.

4   Audience share was introduced as the sole criterion for controlling concentration in the media in Germany by the fourth modification of the RStV in 1996, and in the UK by the 1996 Broadcasting Act. In Italy the so-called 'Legge Mammì' chose instead the criterion of share of the advertising market, a criterion even less related to pluralism concerns and rather resembling industry regulation in the traditional sense. For details see P. Kremmyda, *European Competitiveness and Pluralism: Concentration in the Broadcasting Industry in the EU*, PhD thesis, European University Institute 2004, 237 et seq.

presumed. It is also the same threshold provided for in the various block exemption regulations, below which agreements are held not to be caught by Article 81(1) of the EC Treaty.

By means of the use of the 'audience share' criterion and the 30 per cent thresholds, the logic of economic law has been introduced in media-specific legislation. It seems somehow to be presumed that if the minimum conditions of market competition are met (that is no dominant position), then pluralism concerns will equally be answered. In this light the question of the balance between sector-specific regulation and competition law is answered in a different context. Thus, if the safeguards imposed by sector-specific regulation amount to nothing more than can be achieved through application of competition law and if the tools used to measure the level of pluralism are to all effects equivalent to those used to identify the presence or lack of competition in a market, it is only a small step to concluding that sector-specific regulation is superfluous.

This step has, indeed, already been made by two European legislators. The UK has explicitly abolished all mono-media concentration controls, retaining only a couple of cross-media checks. In fact, the Communications Act clearly allows the same person to control all commercial television licences, subject only to the general competition rules. In Italy, the legislator has essentially abolished all kinds of controls, only this has not been done explicitly but through the introduction of the notion of the 'combined media sector' which includes everything from television and press, to advertisement, to books, to the internet and more.[5] This evolution means that the sector is now regulated by purely economic considerations. As a result, the protection of pluralism as such is only an incidental effect, to the extent that competitive market structures are likely to achieve that.

At this point it should be made clear that the application of competition law in the media sector is not likely to cause any harm to pluralism-related aims; quite the contrary. However, given its nature and inherent limitations, it is not, in itself, either an adequate or a sufficient tool to achieve such aims.

3   IS THERE AN ANSWER?

Professor Idot has very rightly pointed out that application of competition law,

---

[5]   The threshold of expansion has been set at 20% of this combined sector. It is clear that, given the vast number of resources involved, a single operator can completely monopolise a single sector (or more than one), say the press or television, without reaching the 20% threshold. Control of media concentration in any meaningful sense is then left to the general competition rules.

especially by the Commission, has been quite effective, and that the problem lies more with the perceived inadequacy of sector-specific regulation to deal effectively with concentration in the media. She attributed this inadequacy largely to the reluctance of Member States to deal with the issue. This reluctance is not accidental but can be attributed to the particular power which the media are able to exert upon political authorities. Unlike other sectors of the economy, the media are not only influential because of their importance in terms of turnover, growth potential and employment, but can directly influence electoral outcomes through their agenda-setting ability. This special power creates a vicious cycle, in which governments are wary of regulating, and hesitation to do so, in turn, increases the weight of the media's special power.

The reluctance of Member States to effectively tackle the problem of increasing concentration in the media inevitably brings forward the question whether legislation at the Community level should not, as a matter of subsidiarity, be adopted. Legislation at this level could arguably reduce the leverage power of media operators. The problem (leaving aside the questions of competence that have been convincingly raised in the past) is whether, at the present stage of development of the EU and under the current conditions, such legislation could be any more effective than what we already have at the national level.

In fact increasing 'economisation' has also characterised the approach of the Commission towards the issue of concentration in the media. The failed attempt to introduce a directive on the issue and the move within the proposal from 'pluralism and media concentration' to 'free movement of services' in broadcasting is a notorious example. A more recent example of Community level legislation that can illustrate the point is the fate of Directive 95/47, which regulated access issues in digital television. The Communications Review, despite maintaining the operative rules of this directive in force, changed the nature of these rules in two ways.

First, the content of the Directive was incorporated into the Access Directive,[6] which regulates access not only in television infrastructure but in all communications-related infrastructures. This choice removed the particular characteristics of television from the agenda and accepted the assimilation of broadcasting with other communications sectors. The second change comes from the fact that television was not excluded from the scope of Article 6 of the Directive, which provides that Member States can impose access obligations only on operators holding significant *market* power and this only after conducting a market analysis leading to the conclusion that such access is

---

[6]   Directive 2002/19/EC.

necessary.[7] This is so despite the fact that the Access Directive itself identifies as the reason for the adoption of Directive 95/47 the fact that: 'competition rules alone may not be sufficient to ensure cultural diversity and media pluralism in the area of digital television'.[8] In other words, despite nominally recognising that competition law alone is not sufficient to safeguard media pluralism, the Access Directive still bars Member States from imposing access obligations on operators on grounds other than that of a market analysis, conducted according to competition law methodology, which reveals an excessive *market* power.

It seems highly doubtful, therefore, that legislation at the community level could, under the current circumstances, be expected to deliver anything other than harmonisation at the minimum common denominator level. This is so because, on the one hand, if Member States are reluctant to introduce effective legislation at the national level there is no reason why they should be more daring when it comes to transferring regulatory power to the Community. On the other hand, even if Member States were ready to welcome Community level legislation, it is highly unlikely that this would take a form other than the audience share controls that Member States have opted for, given that the general orientation of the Community legislator with regard to media concentration does not seem to differ in anything from that of the various national ones. That is, at the Community as well as the national level, economic considerations dominate discussion of media concentration, with pluralism concerns gradually being removed from the foreground.

---

[7]   Recital 13 of the Access Directive provides, in addition, that such analysis should be based on the competition law methodology with the aim of reducing *ex ante* sector-specific rules.

[8]   Directive 2002/19/EC, Recital 10.

Comment: On the need and advantages of specific media regulation. Some critical remarks

Ulf Bernitz*

1   COMPETITION LAW V. MEDIA PLURALISM

As I understand the title of our theme, the main issue is whether or not concentration in the media sector of the economy should be subject to general competition law or to a specific regime, that is a specific kind of regulation. Such regulation can be either complementary to general competition law or replace such law. In the latter case, the media sector will be exempted from general competition law, either completely or partially depending on certain additional qualifying prerequisites.

As is well known, the EC Merger Regulation of 2004 (139/2004/EC) is of a general nature and normally applicable to concentrations in all fields of economic activity. However, according to Article 21(4) of the Regulation, Member States may take appropriate measures to protect legitimate interests other than those taken into consideration by the Regulation, provided these measures are compatible with Community law. The statutory text specifically points at 'plurality of the media' as such a legitimate interest. Along with public security and prudential rules, plurality of the media is recognized as a privileged type of legitimate interest. Contrary to other 'legitimate interests' they do not need to be communicated and recognised by the Commission.

No doubt, the explanation behind this specific exemption in the Merger Regulation for plurality of the media is to a large extent to be found in the well-established French legislation in the area, which France has not been willing to give up. The chapter by Professor Idot contains a clear and comprehensive description of the specific French media regulation designed to protect plurality of the media and its application. Professor Idot takes a distinctly positive

---

*   Professor Dr. iur. of European Law, Stockholm University; Director, Oxford/Stockholm Wallenberg Venture, Institute of European and Comparative Law, University of Oxford.

view on the need for and virtues of such regulation. In the opinion of Professor Idot, Member States have made insufficient use of the possibilities offered by the provision in Article 21(4) of the Merger Regulation. She deplores the absence of a political will on the part of the Member States to consider harmonising EU legislation intended to guarantee media pluralism. What she seems to have in mind is specific Community regulation on media concentrations.

The nature of special legislation designed to safeguard media pluralism is discussed further in the comments offered by Dr Peristera Kremmyda. She seems to be willing to go a good bit further than Professor Idot in stressing the difference between regulation safeguarding media pluralism and competition law. To her mind, specific legislation concerning media concentration is not economic in nature and should not be balanced against competition law. It is an 'altogether different kind of regulation', with different aims, and should ideally have different tools to those used under economic law.

I find myself in disagreement, particularly with Dr Kremmyda, but also with Professor Idot. In my view, general competition law should play a basic and principal role also within the media sector of the economy. As far as I know, other Member States have not followed the French example and most Member States seem not to have made any use at all of the media pluralism exemption from the general provisions of the Merger Regulation offered in Article 21(4).

Here, it is not possible to discuss the problems in depth, but let me briefly express the reasons behind my divergent views.

2   IS THERE ANY CONSISTENT MEDIA SECTOR?

My first line of criticism is related to the vague concept of the 'media sector'. In my view, there are fundamental differences between different types of media and their economic activities. Traditionally, concentration in the field of newspapers was particularly under scrutiny. Another traditional area is book publishing. A new, very important area is television stations and, to a somewhat lesser degree, radio stations. Another well-known area is film production and distribution, including the cinema sector. But the 'media sector' is comprised of much more, for example the production and distribution of music, primarily popular music ('the music industry').

In addition, we have the rapidly expanding telecoms, Internet and computer sectors. Do these enormously important areas belong to the media sector or not? More and more people use their Internet connection and computer screen as primary devices for reading newspapers, viewing films and TV programmes and listening to music. The rapid expansion of broadband is quickly changing people's consumption habits. In my opinion, it would be unrealistic and outdated to try to exclude these areas from the general concept of the media sector. Taking this view, mergers within the telecoms and software areas would come under the media sector. I am not sure Article 21(4) of the Merger Regulation was intended to be applicable within the telecoms and software sectors, but, arguably, it might be so.

As can be seen, the concept of the media sector covers much and includes sectors which are distinctly different. Some of these sectors have a strong relation to what we traditionally regard as culture-bearing media, particularly among academics, such as quality newspapers, qualified book publishing, theatre, exhibitions or ambitious film production. But it seems hopeless to try to delimit the scope of the concept of media sector along such lines. It must also include popular and simple production, for example in the areas of popular music and entertainment-oriented TV channels. Obviously from a public policy point of view, the importance of media plurality varies greatly between these different areas.

To conclude, there is in my opinion no specific media sector that can be singled out as an entity different from other types of economic activity. On the contrary, the differences between culture-bearing media promoting freedom of expression, formation of public opinion and education, on the one hand, and many of the popular but economically much more viable media mentioned above, is enormous. In addition, with the ongoing development of the Internet, the media sector is in a state of flux and integration is beginning along new lines.

Hence, it is not a convincing idea to launch media-specific legislation based on the notion of media plurality.

3   SPECIFIC NATIONAL MEDIA REGULATION IN ADDITION TO THE APPLICATION OF COMPETITION LAW?

In my opinion, there are many disadvantages of national media regulation of mergers as a complement (and, even more so, as an alternative) to merger control under competition law. As we all know, the latter is based on the one-stop-shop principle. In other words, if a merger, for example in the media sector, is cleared according to Community law the parties can go ahead with the acquisition. As for mergers below the Community thresholds, national competition law normally functions in the same way. If the merger is cleared by the relevant national Competition Authority, the parties can go ahead. But, if there is specific national media regulation in place, there would exist a second net of control. The merger would have to be cleared a second time, according to criteria framed differently.

Here, I will only point out one of the major problems with such a dual system, viz. the relation between the criteria applied. In my opinion, it is difficult to distinguish between the criteria used in competition law and the media plurality criterion. In any case, one cannot, as Dr Kremmyda suggests, claim that they are of a completely different kind.

Let me give you two examples. The first one concerns a pending case in Sweden. Here, the number of cinemas has been declining for a long time and today there exist only two nationwide chains of cinema theatres of any importance. The smaller of these is in economic difficulty and its larger competitor has launched a bid for acquisition. The Competition Authority is opposing the merger as it would create a monopoly in the film distribution sector in Sweden which would threaten plurality in the market. In a case like this, it is obvious that the competition and the media plurality criteria converge.

Take another case. Over the years, there has been a comprehensive dying off of newspapers and in many large European cities there is today only one quality daily morning newspaper of importance. In Scandinavia, Helsinki and Oslo might be mentioned as examples (Helsingin Sanomat and Aftenposten, respectively). However, in Copenhagen and Stockholm there are still two quality morning newspapers on the market. Suppose, hypothetically, that they wished to merge. In such a case, what would be the difference between the application of competition rules and the media plurality criteria? As in the cinema case, the criteria would largely converge.

Much more could be said, but to sum up, in my opinion the case for specific regulation on media mergers, handled separately from merger control under competition law, is not convincing. The way to secure media plurality is via the maintenance of competition (unless the State offers subsidies or similar public aid to a specific medium, or media outlet, considered to be particularly valuable – a different issue). When competition authorities are assessing whether or not concentration significantly impedes effective competition, the assessment will include the importance of maintaining media plurality.

Possibly, it can sometimes be argued that competition authorities do not give the media plurality argument enough weight within their overall assessment, but that would be a matter for discussion concerning the proper application of competition law, not for the establishment of a separate regulatory regime for the control of media regulation. That should be avoided.

8. Abuse of market power:[*] controlling dominance or protecting competition?

Laurence Boy[**]

I INTRODUCTION

One of the impressive objectives that ASCOLA has set itself is to explore the theoretical and doctrinal foundations of competition in the European Union and to do so from a comparative perspective (particularly American and national European laws). This choice of methodology is all the more vital given that for years the market has assumed an almost mythical status and governs the legal and political action of all nation-states.[1] The system of competition in place takes a different form depending on the stronger or

---

[*]   Questions of choice of vocabulary can never be neutral. Lately, purely technical matters linked to the difficulties of legal translation which come up in different systems from time to time have become controversies concerning the predominent use of this or that language. It is clear that common vocabulary and syntax allow for the exchange of ideas. They also allow, in a somewhat more insidious manner, for the export of mental structures which then condition all forms of reasoning, especially in law. We know this only too well. However, this is not to declare war on English. I would only wish that British and American lawyers would turn their attention towards Romano-Germanic concepts (Europe but also Latin America) in competition law in order to understand that beyond problems of legal translation, there are cultures and social choices which ought to be debated. Linked to the question of linguistic pluralism, I would assert the 'right' to write in my own language in the hope that my foreign readers understand me as much as I understand them and that they try to read and translate into their own languages certain texts written in other European languages. Concerning cultural pluralism, I remain convinced that such a move cannot but enrich our scientific community and lead to a mutual learning of the concepts that we use. What follows should demonstrate the importance of language upon our mental structures.

[**]   Professor, Université Nice Sophia Antipolis, Director of CREDECO. The author gratefully acknowledges the translation from the French original (published in RIDE 2005, 27) by Paul Gerard Harvey, researcher, European University Institute.

[1]   A. Pirovano, 'L'expansion de l'ordre concurrentiel dans les pays de l'Union européenne', in R. Charvin and A. Guesmi (eds), *L'Algérie en mutation: les instruments juridiques du passage à l'économie de marché*, l'Harmattan, 2001, p. 129.

weaker influence of various economic theories of competition law[2] and the way they are received within different legal systems.

National and Community jurisprudence, illuminated by doctrine,[3] contribute to the elaboration of a European competition system where the synthesis between the two is ever more subtle such that competition law has become a patchwork quilt.[4] In this area of law, replete as it is with case-made law, one of the functions of doctrine is to humbly try to co-ordinate legal rules, to bring out general themes.[5]

Our basic hypothesis is that these days there is an evolution, which began in the United States, that could be characterised in European law by a shift from traditional control of restrictions on competition[6] towards an approach based on regulation of competition.[7] The latter of these should be put in perspective by various traditional political, economic and theoretical conceptions of competition. The eventual appearance of a European conception of the competition system may prove useful in the comparative law perspective.[8] This European legal order, influenced no doubt by American law, is under constant construction. It is extremely rich and is testimony to the diversity of national law approaches, from which general (or generalisable) solutions may emerge which respond to concerns for the coherence of that community legal order.[9] Oscillating between generalisation of principles and 'concretisation' of solutions, between different competition laws, between the politics and economics of competition,[10] there is without doubt merit in carrying out

---

[2]　The European lawyer is often surprised by economic literature that seems to be the only constant point of reference but which generally dates from many years ago.

[3]　H. Ullrich, 'L'ordre concurrentiel: rapport de synthèse', in L. Boy (ed.), *L'ordre concurrentiel, Mélanges en l'honneur d'A. Pirovano*, ouvrage collectif, Paris, 2003, p. 677.

[4]　A. Pirovano, *supra* n. 1 at p. 130 et seq.

[5]　C. Lucas de Leyssac, G. Parleani, *Droit du marché*, PUF, Thémis, Droit privé, 2002, p. 565.

[6]　In the sense of the Anglo-Saxon term 'restrictive agreements, abuse of monopolistic market power and mergers' and not in the French sense of 'pratiques restrictives de concurrence'.

[7]　See the call for papers by H. Ullrich: 'The evolution has been characterized by a shift in practical importance from the traditional antitrust control over restrictions of competition to a regulatory approach of establishing competition'; L. Boy, *Le droit de la concurrence: régulation et/ou contrôle des restrictions à la concurrence*, EUI working paper, No. law 2004:09; JCP (G) 2004, I, p. 166.

[8]　'Internormativité et réseaux d'autorités: l'ordre communautaire et les nouvelles formes de relation entre les ordres juridiques', in L. Idot, S. Poillot-Peruzzetto (eds), *Les Petites Affiches*, special issue Oct. 2004, No. 199 and 200.

[9]　M. Bazex, 'La libre concurrence, nouvelle source de l'action administrative', *GP*, 25–26 July 2001, p. 1155.

[10]　A. Pirovano, *supra* n. 1, at p. 130 et seq.

deeper and conflicting analyses in order to juxtapose these solutions with economic theories, public policies and social choices. Finally, with respect to the issue of how competition law and competition policy are interrelated, it poses the question of the theoretical and conceptual autonomy of European competition law from American anti-trust law.[11]

When it comes to competition, if we leave aside the theories of the ultra-liberal Chicago school (of whom Hayek is the most prominent representative),[12] all economic and political actors are agreed on the need for competition law, even if their conceptions of free competition and thus competition law are extremely diverse. In effect, it seems as though freedom requires the existence of constraint or at least an external regulation of competition.[13] Schematically, there are roughly two opposing conceptions of competition that correspond to two different economic approaches. We find these two approaches intermingled (albeit to different degrees) in various competition laws that lie somewhere between the two extremes. In the United States, under the influence of the 'Law and Economics' school,[14] a wholly abstract and purely competitive conception predominates. Europe for its part has opted from the outset for a concept within competition law which takes account of policies of competition,[15] and thus of diverse interests.

Competition can be seen as an ideal which would be beneficial in itself.[16] It leads to the 'highest public good' by the operation of the 'invisible hand of the market' that guides everyone, pursuing his or her selfish interest, to discover the public good. This conception of liberalism ought to permit the success of the most competitive who can ensure satisfaction of consumers (which, in the economic sense of the term, includes companies) and, in the end, the general interest.

Another conception of competition is to see it as no more than a means of

---

[11]   From the outset, we can see the role language plays in structuring our discourse. Anti-trust law also eliminates as irrelevant the concept of economic dependence.

[12]   F. A. von Hayek, *Droit, législation et liberté*, PUF, 1980–1983, 3 volumes.

[13]   F. Riem, 'Droits de la concurrence et ordre concurrentiel', in L. Boy (ed.), *supra* n. 3, p. 635; Colloque DGCCRF, 25 March 1998, 'La régulation, monisme ou pluralisme', *Petites affiches*, July 1998, No. 82; M. A. Frison-Roche, 'Le droit de la regulation', *Dalloz affaires*, 2001, p. 610; L. Boy, 'Réflexions sur le droit de la regulation', *Dalloz affaires*, 2001, p. 3031.

[14]   For an overview of Law and Economics see Th. Kirat, *Economie du droit*, *Repères*, Paris, La Découverte, 1999.

[15]   It may be recalled that it was the post-war reconstruction efforts that led to the adoption of the first treaties on the Coal and Steel Community. They were part of the logic of a European economic policy under construction.

[16]   A. Smith, *Enquête sur la Nature et la cause de la richesses des Nations*, Paris, PUF, 1998.

attaining other objectives: to maximise the general welfare, to ensure the best allocation of resources.[17] Innovation and scientific progress should permit the most innovative company to come out on top. There is therefore a necessary discrepancy between innovation and affirmation of the superiority of the enterprising company. It is even necessary sometimes to protect it against its competitors, even though, at that moment, it may be in a dominant position with respect to these other companies. Competition law is a necessary constraint on competition, without becoming a brake on innovation. This particular conception is often mobilised in the field of abuse of a dominant position by the dominant company in question.

To sum up, we might say that in the first conception, competition is an aim; in the second, a means. Nevertheless, the dominant position in and of itself is not condemned by either conception. The entrepreneur can, theoreticially, see its position threatened at any moment.[18] We can discern here a special treatment for the dominant position in competition law because it finds itself straddled between control of behaviour and control of structures. Certain proposals of economists, though different, can also lead to a lax appreciation of economic domination.

In a structuralist conception of competition, which is quite close to the idea of pure and perfect competition, the emphasis is on the causal relation between the structure of the market and the level of the economic well-being. Business arrangements which are monopolistic or oligopolistic are thus considered *a priori* as barely compatible with collective efficiency. The atomised structure of the market would, on the contrary, allow for the decentralisation of the decision making by economic actors and the dispersion of power. In this analysis, indicators of market concentration would allow us to assume anticompetitive behaviour. As a result of the assumptions that underpin this analysis, the legal consequence would, of course, be a strict and automatic control of the means of market concentration themselves as well as of abuse of dominant position.

The concept of competition as a process has been developed most recently in economics. This focuses more on the behaviour of economic actors than on market structures. It has become the basis of much current thinking which denies the existence of an automatic relationship, at least a significant one, between concentration and market power. A certain number of adherents of the Chicago school have thus developed the theory of contestable markets. According to the theory, if companies have a dominant position, this is nothing more than the temporary result of a process of redefining competition

---

[17] J. Schumpeter, *Théorie de l'évolution économique*, Paris, Dalloz, 1999.

[18] E. Chamberlain, *The theory of monopolistic competition*, New York, 1933; J. Robinson, *The economics of imperfect competition*, London, 1933.

which will eventually result in a more efficient organisation of the system of production. This mode of thinking advocates a minimalist competition law in which the role of the state would be limited to preventing entry barriers (legal barriers of a normative type which are prejudicial to entry to the market, non-tariff barriers in WTO jargon or measures of equivalent effect in EU jargon). Competition can temporarily create dominant positions: though such an asymmetry of positions is not in itself problematic, rather it is the abuse of a dominant position which we would condemn.[19]

Whatever the virtues of these analyses, we have to recognise that they fall within a logic of competition that we simply do not find in EU law. In EU law we see a greater mix of this desire for competition with other considerations (the interests of competitors, social interests, protection of the enivironment and so on). This explains the advent of a distinctive European competition law.

National law, European Community and American competition law are subject to various degrees to the appeal of these various schools of thought. Among the different models which influence competition law, the emphasis is sometimes on public regulation, sometimes on the economic efficiency which comes from 'natural' regulation of the market. It is submitted that competition law, while resting fundamentally on economic analyses, cannot be reduced to these analyses. Law never thinks only in terms of the optimal allocation of resources[20] but also of the distribution of these resources and of social choices.[21] Nonetheless, the originality of European competition law is being called into question not only from the outside but from the inside too by new followers of a certain conception of Law and Economics. This movement should be taken seriously. It may lead to a questioning of the European social model for which law is not simply the servant of economics but instead balances a number of different interests.[22]

For the last ten years, European competition law has been characterised by modernisation and decentralisation which seeks only to sanction those unfair

---

[19] ECJ C-333/94, *Tetra Pack International v. Commission*, 14 November 1996, *Rec.* p. 5951; D. Mainguy, 'L'abus de droit dans les contrats soumis au droit de la concurrence', *JCP, E.*, 1998, suppl. No. 6, p. 23; obs. L. Idot, Europe 2001, No. 62.

[20] Unlike a certain school of Law and Economics influenced by the neo-classical tradition. This also explains that 'competition among thieves will mean that the occasional thief (the small-time crook with no particular talent) will hardly earn more, given the occupationals hazards involved, than if he pursued an honest trade'. (P. Lemieux, L'analyse économique du droit, http://www.pierrelemieux.org/artecondroit.html.)

[21] H. Ullrich, *supra* n. 3, at p. 677.

[22] M. Saquemin, 'Le droit serviteur de l'économie?', *RTDCom.* 1972, p. 292; D. Danet, 'La science juridique, servante ou maîtresse de la science économique?', *RIDE* 1993, No. 1, p. 5.

trading practices that are most damaging to economic efficiency, and it does so by combining *a priori* and *a posteriori* forms of control. It is clear that control of anticompetitive behaviour and structures focuses on those unfair trading practices which are most damaging to competition.[23] This, though, seems influenced by those economic theories developed by the American school of Law and Economics,[24] and thus by the solutions offered by American case law.[25] This movement is particularly visible in the ambit of control of market concentration and abuse of dominant position. Nonetheless, a more discerning study of the decisions of national and European authorities leads us to qualify this first approach, whether with regard to control of concentrations or of cartels, or more specifically of abuse of a dominant position,[26] which we will focus on in subsequent sections.

Control of domination of a company in the market can give rise to two types of control, the boundaries of which are not altogether clear: *a priori* control of concentration and *a posteriori* control of abuse of dominant position. It is this aspect which concerns us here. Moreover, there are numerous decisions which affirm, at least in part, the existence of both an abuse interfering in the normal functioning of the market and of a concerted practice.[27] In these situations, we would also favour the abuse of dominant position approach.

Confining ourselves to the question of the dominant position, it is worth stating from the outset that competition law is characterised by an ambiguity. The principle is that every enterprise should determine its own competitive strategy which explains the traditional prohibition on cartels and control, however belatedly, of merger activities. This freedom of management can, in contradictory fashion, lead a dominant enterprise to elevate itself beyond the market and to impose its own conditions unilaterally. Between the freedom of management necessary for proper competition and the possibility that a company may isolate itself from the market completely, the determination of the existence of a dominant position always proves to be difficult in national

---

[23] The proliferation of barriers.
[24] R. A. Posner, *Antitrust Law*, second edition of *Antitrust Law: An Economic Perspective*, University of Chicago Press, 2001; D. D. Friedman, *Law's Order. What Economics has to do with the Law and why it matters*, Princeton University Press, 2000; E. Mackay, *L'analyse économique du droit*, Montréal et Bruxelles, éd. Thèmis and Bruylant, 2000.
[25] See references in R. A. Posner, *supra* n. 24, p. 194; E. M. Fox, 'What is harm to competition? Exclusionary practices and anti-competitive effect', 70 *Antitrust LJ*, p. 371; C. Prieto, 'Comparaisons transatlantiques dans les affaires Microsoft', *RDLC (Revue Des Droits de la Concurrence)*, No. 1, December 2004, p. 57.
[26] M. Malaurie-Vignal, *L'abus de position dominante*, Paris (Coll. Systèmes. Droit, LGDJ), 2002.
[27] See the numerous references in Lamy, *Droit économique*, Paris, 2004.

law, Community law as well as in American law and requires new tools for competition law.[28]

Orienting the assessment in accordance with a 'bilan concurrentiel' leads to an ever weaker competition law and legitimates many dominant positions. In Europe questions about establishing liability for abuse of economic dependence and more widely, about taking account of the interests affected by this approach (consumers, competitors and vertical relations) elicit radically different doctrinal responses. The traditional European conception, as incorporated in the national laws of various European countries, does not really put 'grand' and 'petit' competition law in contrast.[29] Abuse can allow for control of vertical relations between economic actors, which French law places in the category of practices which restrict competition, but which can also be prevented from the position of anticompetitive practices. Some, however, argue for a return to a more 'orthodox and objective' conception[30] which aims to deal with the abuse in question within the framework of a 'grand' competition law only. It raises a number of concerns even if it is advisable to remain prudent.

Actual developments and the wishes of a certain school of thought necessitate a re-thinking of the normative assumptions that currently prevail in competition law. Should it take an approach grounded exclusively in the idea of competition or should it also take into account other considerations: contractual power, consumer considerations, environmental considerations, social cohesion and so on? Such reflections are outside the scope of this study. In order to confine ourselves to examining abuse of dominant positions, we shall attempt to do so with regard to both the protection of competition and in a larger context of abuse of dominant positions.[31]

II ABUSE OF A DOMINANT POSITION AND THE PROTECTION OF COMPETITION

Protection of competition is the much vaunted aim of national and, above all,

---

[28]   As far as terminology is concerned, 'abuse of domination' seems far wider than 'dominant position' and might include abuse of economic dependence as is the case in European law.

[29]   The law concerning block exemptions in relation to cartels is also testimony to the double dimension of European competition law: protecting competition but also protecting competitors and parties to contracts.

[30]   D. Sinclair, 'Abuse of dominance at a crossroads – Potential effect, object and appreciability under article 82 EC', *ECLR*, 2004 (8), p. 491; B. Sher, 'The last of the steam-powered trains: modernising article 82', *ELCR*, 2004 (5), p. 243.

[31]   Again, we can only highlight the difficulties of translation related to the meaning of these concepts.

Community competition law, which ignores *sensu stricto* the concept of practices restrictive of competition developed in French and German law, even if there it is caught indirectly by the prevention of anticompetitive practices.[32] Competition law has been able to present itself as substantive constitutional law of the European Community.[33] In a 'pure – if not immaculate – conception'[34] of competition law the right of free competition is the 'highest' right, the only true right of competition which hounds anticompetitive practices and has no aim other than to maintain competition within the proper limits, notably that it is pursued in a reasonable, moderate and fair way. Other rules relating to unfair competition or to practices restrictive of competition would be unfamiliar to the economic aims of competition law.

Article 3(1) of the EC Treaty effectively refers to this objective as repeatedly explained by the ECJ. According to the latter, real competition: 'implies the existence on the market of workable competition, that is to say the degree of competition necessary to ensure the observance of the basic requirements and the attainment of the objectives of the Treaty'.

There are uncertainties and hesitation in European doctrine[35] in relation to abuse of a dominant position. Under the influence of certain American schools of thought, there is a tendency to advocate a certain benevolence towards dominant positions. We should reaffirm the difference between a dominant position and abuse of that position, and should do so using a normative assessment rather than 'empirical' bases, which have been extrapolated into seemingly objective models.[36]

The unilateral power of an enterprise can appear 'suspect' in a competitive economy. Nonetheless, it must be emphasised that nowadays a dominant position can be acquired thanks to the success of a product and of an organisation

---

[32]   D. Briand-Meledo, *Droit de la concurrence, droit constitutionnel substantiel de la communauté européenne*, Working paper, Institut Max Planck, Heidelberg, February 2003; L. Azoulay, 'La constitution et l'intégration', *RFDA* 2003, p. 859; A. Pirovano, *supra* n. 1, p. 4.

[33]   A. Pirovano, *Ibid*.

[34]   F. Riem, *supra* n. 13, p. 638.

[35]   D. Sinclair, *supra* n. 30, p. 491; B. Sher, *supra* n. 30, p. 243.

[36]   A deep problem exists in economics between model and objectivity. Modelling would be the surety of scientific objectivity. The model however has nothing scientific about it if it does not incorporate (or incorporates only rarely) certain subjective elements of a particular situation. The concept of the relevant market illustrates this confusion. For economists, the market is defined principally by demand that can be modelled (motorised land vehicles for example). For lawyers subjective preferences of consumers lead us to see that 'real scientific objectivity' means breaking markets down (for example, heavy goods vehicles, family cars, and, within this segment of the market, we might also reasonably distinguish between top of the range cars and small runaround cars).

and not by anticompetitive strategies. That is to say a dominant position is not to be condemned *per se*; merely its abuse.

This essential conception of competition law in the founding texts of the EU is still dominant today. It has been enriched in recent years under the influence notably (but not exclusively) of those Community directives opening up telecommunications industries to the demands of competition in terms of access to markets. The protection of 'competition', entrusted to horizontal authorities intervening *a posteriori* in a market which has already been created, has been complemented by a policy of opening up markets and the creation of competition in markets where there had previously been monopolies which were generally (but not necessarily) public. The combined efforts of general and sectoral competition authorities have, because of this, led to the blurring of the distinction between *ex post* control of anticompetitive practices and the *a priori* regulation of competition.[37]

1 Protection of Competition in an Existing Market

Paradoxically, the balance of competition leads sometimes to strictness and sometimes to laxity as far as abuse of domination is concerned or at least a benevolent attitude towards businesses, even if these movements are not always linear.

One of the principal means at the disposal of competition authorities to measure their action in this matter is in the definition of the relevant market. Abuse can only be sanctioned in a relevant market. Its definition therefore is the essential preliminary step for competition authorities[38] which gives them wide room for manoeuvre. To this effect they generally use two complementary analyses.

First an economic analysis. French and Community case law consider that the market is defined as the place where the supply and demand of products or services which are considered exchangeable between themselves (but not exchangeable with other goods or services offered) meet. This definition is therefore relatively fluid since goods are rarely perfectly exchangeable and the behaviour of buyers must be borne in mind. In practice, certain goods cannot be exchanged for others even though in theory they ought to be. This therefore must lead to a second analysis which proceeds from the perspective of demand rather than that of supply, which tends to be preferred by economists. It is

---

[37]   M. A. Frison-Roche, *supra* n. 13, p. 610; contra: L. Boy, 'Réflexions sur le droit de la regulation', *supra* n. 13, p. 3055; *supra* n. 7.

[38]   *Rev. JP de droit des affaires,* Nov. 1993, 83; Boutard-Labarde and D. Bureau, *RJDA,* 1993/11, p. 743; Vogel, *JCP* 1994, I, 3737; Campana de Barratin, G.P. 1, doct. 243.

immediately obvious that this demand is difficult to conceptualise by way of 'modellising', but it is the decisive test.[39]

That the Commission and then the French Competition Authority have based their doctrine on this test is essential. If we take a wide definition of the market, abuse is rarely found simply because the business is not considered as having a dominant position. On the other hand, if we take a restrictive definition, it is easier to condemn abuse because it is easier to find a dominant position, as a prerequisite before turning to the question of analysis of the abuse. One of the most famous cases in France which illustrates the difficulties of the definition of the relevant market is the case of *France Loisirs*. The Competition Council had defined the relevant market as the sale of books by book clubs and by mail order, narrower therefore than that of the book trade in general. For the same product supplied (a book), the idea is that there was a definition of the market which was made by reference to the clientele in question.

The Paris Cour d'Appel upheld the analysis of the Council in condemning France Loisirs. This decision was quashed by the Cour de Cassation which held that there were insufficient elements to establish the specific nature of the market of selling books by clubs. According to the Cour de Cassation, the relevant market was that of books in general.[40] As can be seen, this discretionary power leaves competition authorities a great deal of room for manoeuvre. According to certain authors, by virtue of this decision the Cour de Cassation would have put a stop to a conception of the market that was too fragmented and thus too strict toward abuse of a dominant position. However, the Paris Cour d'Appel persisted in its analysis in holding that the marketing methods in question allowed it to isolate the market of book club sales from the book market in general. This definition of the relevant market, which focuses principally on demand, has since been confirmed both in national and Community law, notably in the field of control of market concentration.

In the sense of severity, not only is the dominant position which has the 'aim but also that which has the propensity to affect the market' condemned. Consequently, the notion of abuse (objectively assessed) is in principle detached from all manner of moral connotations and based exclusively on the market effect. This is assessed *in concreto* on the basis of an analysis which is above all economic. The idea of abuse thus does not imply an intention to

---

[39]   This is how the Cour de Cassation affirmed that in order to determine the existence of a relevant market in treatment of waste in waste dumps and the substitutability of existing processes, it was necessary to take into account the behaviour of *users*: Com. 22 May 2001, C.C.C.2001, No. 135, obs. Malaurie-Vignal.

[40]   10 March 1992 D. 92, 355, Petites affiches, 22 January 1993.

cause harm[41] be it in Community[42] or French law.[43] Article 82 of the Treaty forbids, in effect, the abuse of a dominant position while in France Article L. 420-2(1) of the Commercial Code (former Article 8 of the 1986 Ordinance) prohibits the abusive exploitation of a dominant position 'in the internal market or a substantial part of it'. In both texts, reference to subjective criteria is in reality replaced by an objective analysis of market impairment which can appear, *a priori*, to be a severe approach.

However, if abuse is an objective concept, its assessment oscillates between analyses based on structure and behaviour,[44] the latter reintroducing a measure of leniency. Community case law had originally exacerbated the 'structural' conception in holding that the creation or strengthening of a dominant position was in itself abusive.[45] Impediments to the proper functioning of the market can, in certain circumstances, notably with regard to structure, result merely from the domination of the business even when no other illegal act has been committed.[46] This means that certain practices coming from businesses which are less powerful in the market could be permitted by competition authorities who would condemn, on the other hand, the same practices coming from businesses occupying a dominant position. There would then be more cumbersome obligations placed upon the most powerful operators. This analysis can lead to the condemning of a business on the basis of a structural assessment of parts of the market.[47] In this light, the characterisation of abuse is done in terms of the situation in the market and in those parts of the market where the company operates, and not in terms of the behaviour adopted by the company. In addition, as concerns the burden of proof, Community case law considers that proving the appropriate (and thus proportionate) nature of the impediment

---

[41]   Here abuse is separated from traditional criteria of abuse in law, or at least abuse in property law: the intention to cause harm or culpable negligence. Reference to abuse has been hotly contested: J. Azema, *Le droit français de la concurrence*, Paris, PUF, 1989, No. 508.

[42]   CFI T-128/98, *Aéroports de Paris v. Commission*, 12 Dec 2000, *Europe* 2001, no. 62, obs. L. Idot.

[43]   CA Paris, 15 May 2001, INC, BOCC 24 June 2002, p. 382.

[44]   R. Joliet, *Monopolisation et abus de position dominante*, RTD Europ 1969, p. 645.

[45]   *ECJ*, C-6/72, *Continental Can*, 21 February 1973, *Rec.* 215.

[46]   There would be many specific duties upon certain operators by virtue of their position: D. Sinclair, *supra* n. 30.

[47]   Report of the French Competition Commission, 1978: 'Certain commercial practices, which are largely tolerated and perfectly acceptable from the point of view of competition when they come from companies which have only a small market share and when they are exposed to effective competition, could be considered anticompetitive when they are carried out by companies in dominant positions.'

(which would then absolve the company of any wrong-doing) falls, in this analysis, on the dominant company.[48]

In the face of criticism of this position,[49] the European Commission has reintroduced, notably with the Hoffmann-La Roche case, a condition linked to the behaviour of the company in the definition of the abuse.[50] The behaviour of the latter, in order to be censured, should have the effect of creating an obstacle to the maintenance or development of competition principally by 'recourse to methods different from those which condition normal competition in products or services'. This behavioural analysis has since been adopted by national and Community competition authorities.[51] Numerous practices of a very diverse nature by businesses in a dominant position are also condemned: delaying tactics, pressure exerted,[52] threats made.[53] Some typologies of abuse have been proposed in the literature.[54] Among the abuses picked up on by French and European authorities, we might mention abusive pricing policies (too high prices or, on the other hand, predatory pricing, discriminatory pricing, rebates, imposed prices) as well as practices designed to allow the company in the dominant position to enjoy an undeserved advantage from this position. However, the boundaries between analyses in terms of structures and analyses in terms of behaviour remain vague. The different forms of domination, particularly collective domination,[55] further blur this distinction and cast doubt on the necessity of demonstrating abusive behaviour.[56] Thus, certain structural ties between businesses (joint capital ventures, family ties and so on) can be enough to establish a

---

[48]   CFI T-139/98, *Administrazione Autonoma dei monopoli di Stato, (AMMS)*, 22 November 2001, C.C.C. 2002, No. 30, obs. S. Poillot-Peruzzetto.

[49]   Ripert, Roblot, *Droit commercial*, LGDJ, 18e L. Vogel (ed.), No. 864; M. C. Boutard-Labarde, G. Canivet, *Droit français de la concurrence*, Paris, LGDJ, 1994, No. 97 et seq.; Stoffel-Munck, *Essai sur une théorie de l'abus*, LGDJ, Paris 2000, No. 620 et seq.

[50]   ECJ Case 85/76, *Hoffman-La Roche v. Commission*, 13 February 1979, *Rec.*, p. 1190; see also CFI T-228/97, *Irish Sugar v. Commission*, 7 October 1999, C.C.C. 2000, Comm. 28, obs. S. Poillot-Peruzzetto.

[51]   CFI T-374/94, *European Night Services and others v. Commission*, 15 September 1998, *Europe*, November 1998, No. 377, obs. L. Idot.

[52]   C. Conc. 18 November 1992, Sté Biwater, CA Paris, 7 May 1997 and CA 18 May 1999, BOCCRF 26 September 1999, p. 528.

[53]   CA Paris, 21 November 2001, BOCCRF, 31 January 2002, p. 98.

[54]   M. Malaurie-Vignal, *supra* n. 26, No. 148 and D. Sinclair, *supra* n. 30.

[55]   S. Cristin-Belmont, *Essai sur la position dominante collective en droit communautaire*, Thèse Lyon 3, PUS, 1999; DGCCRF, *Ateliers de la concurrence*, Rev. Conc. Consom. N. 126, March–April 2002.

[56]   For a behavioural analysis: CA Paris, 30 October 2001, FIFA and CFO, C.C.C. 2001, No. 173, obs. M. Malaurie-Vignal.

collective dominant position, meaning that its assessment is but the objective ascertainment of economic reality.[57]

'The links between market structures, market concentration, degree of competition, innovation and finally economic growth are extremely complex and numerous.'[58] It also seems that a return to structural analysis in Europe does not come by accident. This should be put in perspective of an increasing control of abuse in terms of access to markets, a control developed for many years by different competition authorities whether they be horizontal or sectoral. This reinforces the already blurred distinction between control *a priori* and *a posteriori* of restrictions on competition.

2 The Construction of Markets and the Essential Facilities Doctrine

Developed by the American authorities, the essential facilities doctrine was adopted by the European Commission and French competition authorities in the 1990s. This doctrine is cited more and more by market authorities, particularly sectoral authorities like ART and CRE. It seems almost as if they used it too often. It sometimes even seems that they are mobilised to excess.[59]

The principle is that a new entrant to a market can claim the right to use the resources held by another operator if they are essential for the exercise of its activity. The refusal of the operator to open its facilities to the competitor will constitute an abuse of a dominant position if three conditions are met: the holder of an essential facilities is in a dominant market position; the non-disposal of the essential facilities would impede the arrival of new entrants to the market; and the holder of the essential facilities, as a rule, intervenes in the derived market[60] where it is in competition with the other businesses.

It must be understood that this doctrine has a particularly important role to play in the European framework of the opening of public services to competition even though it has the potential to go beyond the latter. In effect, in the case of the demonopolisation of public services, the traditional operators generally have at their disposal the infrastructure indispensable for access to the market by competitors because the duplication of installations by competitors will either be impossible owing to the high costs which then constitute a

---

[57] See *Irish Sugar supra* n. 50, C.C.C. 2000, comm. 28, obs. S. Poillot-Peruzzetto; with slight differences CFI T-342/99, *Airtours v. Commission*, 6 June 2002, *JCP éd.* E 2002, 1209; C.C.C. 2003, No. 28, obs. Poillot–Peruzzetto.

[58] A. Perrot, 'Politiques de la concurrence, régulation et croissance: les choix de l'Europe et des Etats-Unis', *Le cercle des économistes*, Cahiers, No. 3, 2003, p. 78.

[59] S. Poillot-Peruzzetto, note under CFI, 17 June 2003, case T-52/00, C.C.C. November 2003, p. 31.

[60] Often indirectly through subsidiaries.

barrier to entry, or impossible for reasons of town and country planning (railway lines, electricity lines).

In certain markets there are therefore facilties which are so scarce, if not unique, that they are prerequisites for access to the clientele and thus also for competition.[61] This monopolistic situation creates for the owner of this infrastructure particular obligations vis-à-vis the other operators which want to join the market. The higher interest of competition imposes restrictions on the right to property and on contractual freedom.

The criteria for the concept of essential facilities are therefore the existence of a dominant position in the market and the absence of substitutability.[62] Obviously the notion of relevant market is essential here and gives rise to quite critical analyses. Thus, in France the Telecommunications Regulation Authority has on many occasions condemned France Télécom (the traditional operator) for abuse of its dominant position. On 1 September 1998 it held that it was a clearly illicit breach that the traditional operator was using its list of telephone subscribers to distribute an advertising brochure which promoted a new mobile phone product because competing companies did not have access to this essential facility which was the maintenance of a list of subscribers to the public telephone service.

Many decisions, both Community and national, testify to the importance of this doctrine in terms of access to markets. In a communication concerning agreements on access to telecommunications,[63] the European Commission has taken a general position. It considered that access to an infrastructure can be imposed on the holder of this facility if it is essential for a company to compete in the related market.[64]

---

61   F. Weingarten, 'La théorie des infrastructures essentielles et l'accès des tiers aux réseaux en droit communautaire', *CJCE* 1998, p. 461; M. Bazex, 'Entre concurrence et régulation, la théorie des facilités essentielles', *Rev. Conc. Consom.* January–February 2001, p. 37, L. Idot, 'Dans quelle mesure le droit de la concurrence (déloyale) impose-t-il de donner à d'autres opérateurs économiques l'accès à des infrastructures, services ou informations que l'on détient?', *Rev. Int. Conc.* 1998, No. 186-2, p. 30.

62   European Commission Decision, Port de Rødby, 21 December 1993, OJEC 1994 L 55, p. 52; European Commission decision, id. FAG airport, Frankfurt, 14 January 1998, OJEC 1998 L72, p. 30; C.C. 3 Sept. 1996, Héli-port, Rec. Lamy No. 401, V. Sélinsky; ECJ, *European Night Services, supra* n. 51; D. Aff. 2000, No. 44; Paris 1 September 1999, D. Aff. October 1999, 1559.

63   Commission Decision No. 98/190, 14 January 1998, OJEC 11 March 1998, L 72, p. 30.

64   One of the most debated questions today is whether or not the affected market should be a distinct market or not. Some decisions have, in effect, cited this theory in the case of constant abuse in the same market: Comm. 3 July, RD Prop. intellect, April 2002, p. 117; ECJ C-418/01 *IMS Health*, 29 April 2004, Rec. 2004, p. I-5039; B. Blaise, 'L'arrêt Macgill: une illustration de la théorie des installations essentielles', D.

Certain authors are highly critical of this case law.[65] They see in it a wide conception of the idea of essential facilities that is restrictive of the right to property and contractual freedom and is based on a doctrine which is very vague. It is however supported by the majority of the literature.[66]

The opening of telecommunications industries to competition will without doubt require the use of the essential facilities doctrine even more[67] particularly in terms of intellectual property. According to certain decisions, the owner of a copyright, the purpose of which is to protect an essential facility, commits an abuse of a dominant position in the sense of Article 82 of the Treaty if he refuses to give a third party a licence. This application of intellectual property is fiercely contested by many who see it as a denial, pure and simple, of the right to enjoy this property.[68] Here we find the classic arguments: attack on contractual freedom and the right to property. It seems, in reality, that one needs to be much more nuanced. In effect in these situations, the recognition of a right to property is itself highly contested. Moreover, we might agree with Caron that this case law, appealing to the right of competition, is a reaction to the constant denaturation of the right of copyright, because it can be imperative, particularly as regards likely abuses of a dominant position, to regulate the exercise of an exclusivity which would never have been granted by a judge. We awaited with impatience the decision of the European Court of Justice in the case of IMS Health & Co. OHG.[69] This is ambiguous: the Court held that, in principle, the use of an intellectual property right can constitute an abuse of a dominant position but only under certain conditions which it did not define. It places great emphasis, however, on the strict links between control of competition and access to competition.

Contested in its application in competition law, abuse of dominant position is even more the subject of controversies where it is used in a broader view of what might be an abuse of domination.

Aff. 1996, p. 859, Cass. Com. 18 April 2000, France télécom/numericable, Bull. civ, IV, No. 75. The company in the derived market was a wholly owned subsidiary of France Telecom.

[65] L. Richer, 'Le droit à la paresse? "Essential facilities" ', French Version, D. 1999. Chr. 523; D. Mainguy and F. Berthault, 'Concurrence et télécommunications', *Cah. Dt. Ent.* 2001, p.1.

[66] M. Malaurie-Vignal, *supra* n. 26, numerous references therein.

[67] C. A. Paris, 9 September 1999, EDF. This theory has been invoked recently in national law: Com. 4 December 2001, Propriété. ind. 2002, No. 11, C.C.C. 2002, No. 46.

[68] P. Y Gauthier, 'Le cédant malgré lui: étude du contrat forcé dans les propriétés intellectuelles', D. *Affaires* 1995, Chr. 123; Ch. Caron, note under TPCI, ord, 26 October 2001, JCP E 20 June 2002, p. 1050.

[69] ECJ 29 April 2004, C-418/01 *IMS Health*, Rec. 2004, p. I-5039.

III   CONTROL OF DOMINATION

The idea of dominant position reflects that of the market and leads *a priori* to an analysis in terms of the market, that is to say, of horizontal relations only taking account of the relations between competitors. At least this is what seems to happen in European competition law with its specific concern for a system of undistorted competition.[70] There are many questions about a concept of abuse of domination which goes beyond that of abuse of a dominant position. The control of domination nowadays represents a challenge for doctrine, and there is much debate on what the content of the concept of abuse of domination should be.

Generally, it seems that we can identify in the doctrine two types of preoccupations. One, in the European tradition, focuses on the eventual microeconomic objective of competition law. This also centres on the condemnation of abuse of economic dependence, taking account of contractual inequalities in vertical relations in so far as they are likely to distort *in fine* competition in horizontal relations. The other more abstract one tends to define, in terms of economic analysis, the only value that competition law ought to pursue – that of efficiency. This is reinforced by many streams of thought that converge: competition law is only the 'grand' law of competition; contract law has not to concern itself with contract inequalities save for, eventually, in terms of consumer law in the strict sense of the term.

1   Recognition or Refusal to Recognise Abuse of Economic Dependence

This concerns a recurring problem in Community law and which fundamentally poses the question of controlling vertical relations by way of competition law. Certain national laws (notably German and French) in an autonomous manner sanction abuse of economic dependence in order to try to limit abuse of domination in vertical relations. This approach would be heretical for the supporters of a liberal competition law. It seems useful to present these different solutions before tackling the question of an eventual 'immaculate conception' of competition law.

According to Article L 420-2 (2) of the French Commercial Code (ex-article 8 of the Ordinance): 'The abuse . . . of the state of economic dependence in which a client or supplier undertaking finds itself in respect of the above shall also be prohibited.' Article 8 went on to require that 'no alternative solution was available'. The actual text is a little different and adds 'abuses may in

---

[70]   L. Boy, *L'ordre concurrentiel, supra* n. 3, in particular L. Azoulay, 'L'ordre concurrentiel et le droit communautaire', p. 277; D. Briand-Meledo, *supra* n. 32, p. 6.

particular consist of refusals to sell, linked sales or the discriminatory practices referred to in Article L.442-6'. The text refers to refusal to sell, linked sales, discriminatory conditions of sale and the severing of established commercial relations when the sole reason is that the trading partner refuses to submit to unjustified commercial conditions.

This idea of abuse of economic dependence set out in the 1986 Ordinance was a major innovation in competition law, a revolutionary idea according to Mestre. It is a text which shattered academic stupor because it took place in an extremely liberal context but it set out to rebalance contractual relations. The ordinance seemed to signify a break, a qualitative leap in competition law. Article 50 of the 1945 Ordinance only applied to absolute abuses of domination. Article 8 of the 1986 Ordinance extended the concept of abusive exploitation as an anticompetitive practice to the simple fact of having another company under one's control. The case law of the French Competition Commission had prepared the ground. Different decisions had stigmatised the behaviour of certain distributors through their policy of de-linking. This qualification of abusive exploitation had been conceived of principally but not exclusively to put an end to purchasing power.

Two opposing conceptions have immediately been developed. The first, even if one must regret it from the point of view of contractual relations, was quite logical: given the place of this incrimination in Title III of the Ordinance, and thus of 'grand' competition law, it defends a pure logic of competition. It also tends to gain acceptance and is based upon the case law of the Competition Council, the Paris Cour d'Appel and the Cour de Cassation. The idea is that competition policy does not constitute social policy. This school of thought warns against too corporatist a vision which favours the weak. It has been applied to two types of situations of dependence: dependence towards the supplier and dependence towards the distributor.

In the case of the first, the Competition Council wanted to demonstrate from the outset a strict approach in a number of decisions. Nonetheless, in different cases, it enumerated a number of criteria which would indicate abuse of economic dependence. It was necessary not only to prove dependence but also abuse. In 1987, four criteria were proposed to identify a situation of economic dependence: the reputation of the brand in question; the supplier's share of the market; the proportion which these products represented in the sales of the distributor; and the possibility for the distributor to find other suppliers of equivalent products on identical terms. In only one decision was abuse found,[71] all other decisions held that there was neither abuse nor economic dependence.[72]

---

[71] 23 March 1987 Magnétoscopes JVC.
[72] 2 May 1989, 12 July 1990. On appeal, the Court of Cassation held on 2 June 1992 there was no abuse of economic dependence.

The second type of case concerned the dependence of suppliers towards buyers because of the abuse of purchasing power by the latter. The abuse of large retailers and wholesale retailers were the reasons for the 1986 reforms. Suppliers were at the mercy of buyers because of the threat of abusive de-linking. Doctrine has shown itself to be essentially sensitive to the state in which suppliers found themselves. Certain abuses have been revealed. Unfortunately in this type of case as well, the Competition Authority did not sanction these practices on the ground that there was no significant anticompetitive effect on the market in question. These practices did not limit competition.[73] The idea is that abuse of economic dependence does not seek to preserve the balance of economic relations but to ensure the proper functioning of the market. This practice should be sanctioned under the heading of restrictive practices (refusal to sell), but not under competition law. These examples, therefore, tend to show that the distinction between contract law and competition law is as subtle as that between 'grand' and 'petit' competition law.[74]

In spite of many cases of abuse in different sectors (the French advertising industry, the cable television market) the results of the 1986 Ordinance have been disappointing for victims of dominant abuse as far as, given its regulation in Title III, the abuse could only be condemned if it had a macro-economic anticompetitive effect. This, in turn, automatically discredits that part of the doctrine which aimed to ensure that the Ordinance also protect economic actors.

Distributors have mainly put the idea in perspective with Article 10 of the Ordinance (now Article 420-4 of the Commercial Code) aiming expressly at the macro-economic effect. This illustrates the difficulty of finding a reasonable balance between the two recognised aims of abuse of domination: the safeguarding of competition and/or the protection of weaker contractors against the actions of overly powerful partners.

The French law on New Economic Regulations of May 2001 has been innovative in introducing into competition law a more 'social' conception of abuse in that it now approaches abuse of economic dependence both from the angle of anticompetitive practices and of practices restricting competition. Article 420-2(2) states that: 'The abuse by an undertaking or group of undertakings of the state of economic dependence in which a client or supplier undertaking finds itself in respect of the above shall also be prohibited when it is likely to affect the operation or structure of competition.' This first text confirms the solutions which prevailed previously according to which the anticompetitive practice should have a macro-economic effect on the market.

---

[73]   C.C. 8 June 1993 D.93, IR, 192, L. Vogel, C.C.C. September 93.
[74]   Riem, *Transparence et droit de la concurrence*, Paris 2003.

However, the abuse of dependence is also from now on officially sanctioned under the rubric of practices restrictive of competition. Article 442-6(2)(b) read with 442-(6)-I states that

> The following acts committed by any producer, trader, manufacturer or person listed in the trade register render the perpetrator liable and entail the obligation to redress the prejudice caused: ... Taking unfair advantage of a trading partner's dependence on him or of his own purchasing power or selling capacity by subjecting him to unjustified trading conditions or obligations.

This comes within the competence of the courts of general jurisdiction and the law of personal liability. It is therefore part of 'petit' competition law. This approach from the angle of practices which restrict competition, practices which envisage behaviour that few legal systems formally recognise, forces us to reconsider the distinction between 'grand' and 'petit' competition law. The question seems to merit particular attention in a time when the dominant school of thought tends to privilege a purely competitive approach to competition law to the detriment of other positions which seem to be equally justified from the point of view of social choices. According to this school of thought, competition law in the strict sense of the word seeks only to protect the market; the other rules, particularly those concerning abuse of domination, are considered to be corrupted by objectives which may be commendable but are completely alien to the real concerns of competition law.

It seems more scientific to highlight the complementarity of the two ideas of competition law which are largely overlapping, each rule contributing to a subtle balance between sedative and incentive effects[75] thus instilling in the market a 'good dose' of competition. 'Different competition laws permit not only the application of the principle of free competition but also its adaptation to the particularities of each situation.'[76] The system of competition is global and thus it matters, contrary to certain ethereal remarks of economists or of Law and Economics, to show the strong connections between 'grand' and 'petit' competition law, that is between contract law and economic law.

2 Competitive Balance on Taking Account of Diverse Interests

Competition law intervenes essentially from a macro-economic perspective. It does not concern itself *a priori* with contractual relations but with the market

---

[75] F. Riem, *supra* n. 13, p. 641; A. Pirovano, 'Justice étatique, support de l'activité économique', *Justices*, 1995/1, p. 18.
[76] F. Riem, *supra* n. 13, p. 638.

situation. This concept goes back to the liberal theory of contract according to which it is for each person to defend him or herself.[77] This has been reappraised in professional/consumer relations,[78] particularly in France with the introduction of the Scrivener law on abusive clauses.[79] It remained however, the creed for relations between professionals until the introduction of various provisions, often fragmented but all linked to the idea of abuse of economic dependence.[80]

The recognition of abuse of economic dependence shows that competition law consists partly of rules that do not appear to be rules that are relevant to competition law but that do contribute, however, to its effectiveness.[81] The approach to vertical relations by competition law, both in national and Community law even if the idea is not the same, is testament to the desire to reconcile the global approach and the micro-economic approach of contractual relations. This seems to be more objective even though today it is perhaps not 'modelisable'. On this controversial question, it has been demonstrated quite clearly that the problems raised by restrictive practices also concern competition law.[82] The underlying but fundamental idea is that if the intensity of competition should only be measured on a horizontal level between companies acting at the same level in the relevant market, it is often in vertical relations that competition is restricted. These vertical relations effectively determine the competition game which can exist on the horizontal level. European competition authorites have progressively taken cognisance of the fact that the logic of competition cannot be 'cut off from the requirements of contractual equality because the market is based on the legal instrument of the contract'.[83]

Vertical relations which would introduce 'impure' elements into competition law have been examined quite early in Community law which, if it

---

[77]   'It is only in extreme cases that civil law defends the weakest, for example in case of defective or absent consent', M. Malaurie-Vignal, *supra* n. 26, p. 183.

[78]   This explains the appearance of consumer law in certain legal systems (J. Calais-Auloy) and control of abuse through abuse clauses. D. Mazeaud, 'Le nouvel ordre contractuel, ruptures et permanence dans le droit des contrats', *Rev. des contrats*, 2003, p. 295; Virassamy, 'La moralisation des contrats de distribution par la loi Doubin', *JCP. E.* 1990, No. 15809.

[79]   Riem, *supra* n. 74.

[80]   Article 1 of the Doubin Law of 31 December 1989 imposing a pre-contractual obligation to inform in favour of the would-be candidate for entry into a exclusive or quasi-exclusive distribution network.

[81]   M-C. Boutard-Labarde, *supra* n. 49, p. 3.

[82]   Ibid.

[83]   A. Pirovano, 'Logique concurrentielle et logique contractuelle: à propos du règlement européen relatif à la distribution des véhicules automobiles', in *Les transformations de la régulation juridique*, LGDJ, Paris 1998, p. 296.

ignores the concept of restrictive practices *per se*, has always sanctioned abuses by virtue of the general law of competition. From very early on, the law on cartels has used the concept of cumulative effect[84] to capture 'networks'[85] of distribution, vertical relations and their overall effect on competition. The theory of abuse of a dominant position has also been used in order to sanction certain activities originating in vertical relations.

This prompts us to wonder about the American movement which would seek to give a greater 'objectivity' to competition law, refocusing it on those practices which are considered to be the most serious and in so doing over-shadowing the numerous interests which Community authorities would seem to take into account by way of an economic rather than only a 'competitive' balance. Here as well, however, the paths of evolution are not entirely clear.

IV CONCLUSION

In recent years there has been an attempt to recentre competition law upon a hard core: the protection of the interests of consumers, those which are never, though, really canvassed.[86] An evolution has taken shape which makes the consumer a principal actor in competition law.[87] Abusive behaviour is thus prohibited from the moment that the interests of a consumer are damaged, whether or not a competing company has suffered a change in the conditions of competition.[88] The purpose of competition law would be the protection of competition and not the protection of competitors. A study of European decisions does not permit us to close this debate. There is the feeling that, faced with a rise in abstract solutions taken from Law and Economics, the Community responses continue to take account of not just the interest of the market and, *in fine*, of the consumer but of many different interests.

Competition law is enriched in Europe for taking account of interests that were previously foreign to it but which today fuel a new conception of the competitive order, especially in a global environment where the question of

---

[84]   ECJ, *Delimitis*, case C-234/89, 28 February 1991, Clunet 1991, p. 485, note M. A. Hernt; D. Ferrier, 'Les effets cumulatifs de réseaux au regard des restrictions verticales de concurrence', *Cah. Dr. Ent.* 1999, No. 5, p. 7.

[85]   On networks: G. Teubner, *Droit et réflexivité*, Diegem, Kluwer Éditions Juridiques Belgique, 1994.

[86]   M. Malaurie-Vignal, *supra* n. 26, No. 76; B. Sher, 'The last of the steam-powered trains: modernising article 82', *ECLR* Issue 5, 2004, p. 243; D. Sinclair, *supra* n. 30, p. 491.

[87]   It is rare that competition authorities would be seized of the matter.

[88]   Commission decision of 25 July 2001, *Deutsche Post AG*, case COMP/C-1/36.915, OJEC L 331, 15 December 2001, p. 40, C.C.C. 2002, No. 49, obs. S. Poillot-Peruzzetto.

sustainable development becomes primordial. In opposition to this enlarged conception of competition law[89] (integrating the environment, social questions, equality in contractual relations) there is a fundamentalist vision of competition law which comes from the United States. The latter is based upon the desire for a realignment of the positions of European authorities with those of a certain school of thought of an American university which, it must be recalled, date from many years ago. It would be in good taste to think today that it is the only one to carry the 'truth about competition'[90] which ought to inspire Europe both in terms of university doctrine and the work of competition authorities.[91] We might permit ourselves here a fit of bad temper.

In this light,[92] law ought to envisage, *according to the needs of the economy*, the problems of law. Competition law is seen not as a branch of law but as a simple technique for interpreting the teachings of economics. This Law and Economics approach has enjoyed a considerable following in the United States, especially in competition law aiming to promote economic efficiency, that is to say the best allocation of resources without worrying about their distribution. The structure of the legal system should be able to be deduced from liberal economic theory.

The transposition in Europe of this school does not happen automatically and ought to take account of the specificities of Romano-Germanic legal systems. The simplistic assimilation made between legal subject and rational economic agent by neo-classical economic theory[93] can lead to practising economics, not law, by denying the existence of the legal substratum.[94] The 'substantive legal dimension' is in effect not taken into account by the majority of these movements. The connections between substantive law and procedural law in competition law should be deepened in order to show the substratum of legal rules, which, even though we may not entirely subscribe to the theory of autopoïetic systems,[95] are different according to common law

---

[89]   See the contributions in L. Boy (ed.), *supra* n. 3.

[90]   R. A. Posner, see also his recent work: *Law, pragmatism and democracy*, Harvard University Press, 2003.

[91]   B. Sher, *supra* n. 86, p. 243; D. Sinclair, *supra* n. 30, p. 491.

[92]   Cl. Champaud, 'Contribution à la définition du droit économique', D. 1967, chr., p. 215.

[93]   G. Calabresi, 'Thoughts on the future of economics in Legal Education', *Journal of Legal Education*, 1983, No. 33, p. 553; R. A. Posner, 'What do judges maximize', *Supreme court economic review*, 1993, No. 3, 1.

[94]   Th. Kirat, 'Action juridique et calcul économique. Regards d'économie du droit', in Th. Kirat, E. Severin (eds), *Le droit dans l'action économique*, CNRS éditions, Paris, 2000.

[95]   N. Luhmann, G. Teubner. There is no sense reciting what everyone already knows. We would only point out the differences that exist between the authors. While

systems, Romano-Germanic systems and still others. To wish to import Anglo-Saxon law at whatever cost seems to us to be a mistake because this approach ignores societal choices which may be in operation.

One should be suspicious of a certain current of Law and Economics when 'it is not interested in either what law is or in the different processes of legal regulation which produce economic consequences'.[96] In its vocation for dictating its solutions 'in law', it oversteps its field of competence. It tends, *in fine*, to treat law in an instrumental manner, that is to say in the service of economics questions.[97] This is particularly true as regards competition law.

It seems to us to be essential to reject from the outset the 'natural' links between this current of thought and competition law. The economic analysis of law focuses on the allocation of resources and rights in society. In addition to its normative aim – to define the conditions of elaboration and selection of those rules which conform to the principle of efficiency – it would have the added effect of substituting itself unduly for the democratic and political processes that prevail in most of our societies for making societal choices. In sum, it instrumentalises law to an economic model that seems unacceptable for some lawyers for whom the values involved might be more than just economic efficiency.

In Europe, Law and Economics is less radical. It admits that economic analysis of law can account for a certain state of law, can explain the rules and functioning of it. But it rejects the idea, according to which, it would be the only relevant analysis for appreciating the rules of law or for constructing them. 'The economic analysis of law is not indissolubly linked to any given value such as the maximisation of resources. It can function at the service of a whole range of different values among which are solidarity and liberty.'[98]

A purely instrumentalist vision of law does not correspond to European competition law which is enriched by preoccupations as diverse as, among others, the entry of development and sustainable consumption among its fundamental references.[99]

Luhmann sees law as a completely autopoïetic system, where lawyers do not have to rule on social problems, G. Teubner has always claimed that lawyers take it upon themselves to consider social issues 'in law'.

[96]   Th. Kirat, *Economie du droit*, Coll. Repères, La découverte, 1999.

[97]   Th. Kirat, E. Severin, *supra* n. 94, 15.

[98]   T. Daintith, 'Problèmes et chances de l'analyse économique du droit en Europe', *RIDE* 1991, No. 3, p. 313.

[99]   In the 1970s the idea of 'integration' appeared in international and European law, this being the desire to bring coherence to sectoral policies. This approach attempts to consider economic and social effects (and more recently political and social effects) together in a more joined up fashion. M. Delmas-Marty, *Critique de l'intégration normative*, Les voies du droit, PUF, 2004.

Comment: Controlling dominance or protecting competition: from individual abuses to responsibility for competition

Peter Behrens*

1   INTRODUCTION

The author has submitted a very rich paper touching upon many of the fundamental problems of competition law in general and of the rules applicable to dominant firms in particular. The chapter takes a comparative approach to European and American antitrust law. It also infuses some typical French conceptions which should be welcomed in the hope that they further stimulate discussion. For reasons of concision, this comment will be limited to a critical reflection on some of the most fundamental issues raised in the chapter. The main objective is to put the chapter into the perspective of the general topic of Part III of this volume.

2   OBJECTIVES OF COMPETITION LAW

A first fundamental point raised in the chapter relates to the question whether competition is an objective in itself or an instrument for the achievement of certain objectives which may not exclusively be related to competition. In this context, the author presents a juxtaposition of the contemporary American school of antitrust which is said to be based on the Law and Economics movement, on the one hand, and, on the other, the European school of competition law which is said to go far beyond the pure logic of competition by including other objectives, such as the protection of competitors, consumers, social interests, environmental interests and so on.

First of all, I am not convinced that the protection of competitors or consumers are objectives beyond the proper scope of competition law; it is, however, precisely this question which is the central target of the controversy

---

*   Prof. Dr. iur., M. C. J. (N.Y. Univ.), Universität Hamburg.

between European and American antitrust lawyers. Secondly, it is also highly debatable whether it is correct to associate the European school of competition law with the inclusion of objectives unrelated to competition or even conflicting with competition, namely specific political objectives such as environmental policy, social policy or industrial policy. Since Art. 3(1)(g) of the EC Treaty provides for the establishment of a 'system ensuring that competition is not distorted', it is, I think, still safe to say that in Europe competition is also regarded as an objective in itself. Even the Community's authority to implement an industrial policy in order to ensure 'the conditions necessary for the competitiveness of the Community's industry' is explicitly limited so as to avoid 'any measure which could lead to a distortion of competition' (Art. 157 EC-Treaty). On the other hand, even Europeans – just like Americans – associate competition with certain positive effects. Hence, even in Europe competition may be regarded as a means to an end. The problem simply is to what end? To some extent, Europeans and Americans disagree on the answer to this question. And it is precisely this difference that has an important bearing on the subject we are discussing.

3   ECONOMIC ANALYSIS OF (COMPETITION) LAW

Before going into the author's contribution to our subject in more detail, some remarks are necessary with regard to the scepticism with which the chapter considers the influence of the American Law and Economics movement on the conceptualisation of competition law. The chapter supports a charge which is very commonly made in Europe, namely that economic analysis turns the law away from its own values and reshapes it exclusively in the name of economic efficiency. The chapter insists that we should instead continue to defend the substantially legal dimension of our Romano-Germanic legal traditions which, according to the author, are built on social values and political choices that are different from economic efficiency and that cannot be grasped by a purely economic analysis. Economic analysis, so the chapter goes on to say, dictates a kind of instrumentalisation of the law that is considered to be un-European.

There are some misunderstandings implicit in this sceptical position towards an economic analysis of law. First of all, we should recognise that human action is at the same time the subject matter of legal regulation and of economic analysis. So, we have very good reasons to believe that lawyers and economists are dealing with the same phenomena. Secondly, micro-economic theory (that is price theory) is an established analytical tool that has produced an impressive body of insights into human behaviour without claiming that it is the only possible approach to understanding human action. Thirdly, by modelling human action in terms of choices between alternative uses of scarce resources based on an evaluation of opportunity costs and benefits (that is on relative prices) and by looking at the legal environment in terms of incentives and disincentives that are shaping these choices, economic theory has been able to predict – at least statistically – with a remarkable degree of precision how market players react to different sets of legal institutions or institutional arrangements generally. This is why economic theory is able to provide us with some fundamental insights into the consequences that legal action may provoke.

We should therefore not easily dismiss what economic theory has to tell us with regard to the shaping of our legal system, especially if we want to establish an 'open market economy with free competition'. All this means is that if we believe we should sacrifice the welfare gains derived from a system of free competition in favour of other values, we are free to do so by taking appropriate democratic decisions. Economic theory does not prevent us from doing so. It simply tells us what price we will have to pay. However, since the political decision making process can easily be captured by special interest groups, there is always the risk that these 'other values' merely benefit some special interest groups, whereas the system of undistorted competition, if properly protected, is much more likely to operate in the interest of society at large. Certainly, markets are not always without their deficiencies in this respect. What matters in our context, however, are the lessons taught by economic theory which tell us that we should first organise the market system so as to stimulate market players to enhance efficiency and the welfare of the public at large. We have very good reasons therefore to shape our competition laws so as to bring them into line with the requirements of the proper functioning of an open market with free competition without expecting that the result will always be in line with our social values and justice. Any deficiencies of the market in this respect may be corrected afterwards. However, they should not be corrected by legal measures distorting the competitive system as such, but rather by specific regulatory measures that are more directly targeted and effective to the achievement of these other goals. Such measures that are designed in one way or another to correct the economic results of the competitive process must, however, never go as far as to undermine the workability of the competitive system altogether. A legal and economic system that disregards efficiency concerns completely is not only inefficient but at the same time is fundamentally unjust.

4   THE US/EU DIVIDE: CONTROLLING WHAT?

Returning to the specific subject of this session, what then are the truly relevant divergences and points of disagreements between the American school of antitrust and the European school of competition law? The first point to be made relates to the different approaches to market power.

There is consensus in so far as both schools agree that dominant positions should not be deemed to be illegal *per se*, because they may be the result of the competitive process even though they necessarily imply to a certain degree a concentration of the market structure. As Judge Learned Hand stated in Alcoa,[1] '[T]he successful competitor, having been urged to compete, must not be turned upon if he wins.' Beyond this common ground, however, remarkable differences have emerged. The conceptualisation of competition underlying Judge Learned Hand's statement is based on the notion of a *Schumpeterian* rivalry between competitors who are continuously striving for the largest possible market share, that is for market power. Modern American antitrust law as informed by economic analysis has turned away from this concept and has defined dominance in terms of a firm's power to set prices above marginal costs and/or reduce output below the demand that would prevail if prices were set at marginal costs. According to the American approach, the essence of market dominance is a relatively steeply downward sloping demand curve with which an individual firm is confronted, whereas the European approach still relies on the notion of weakened control of the dominant firm by its rival competitors. The European Court of Justice's definition of market power in terms of the power of a firm 'to behave to an appreciable extent independently of its competitors, customers and ultimately of consumers',[2] still holds. It would not be impossible to narrow the conceptual gap considerably between the US and Europe by infusing a little more economic analysis into the European approach, although the gap cannot be bridged altogether as long as Europeans insist that competition is based on rivalry between competitors whose access to the market is not restricted and whose market transactions are not dictated by a dominant player in the market.

However, as Boy's chapter amply demonstrates, defining market power in terms of independence from competitors is not the whole European story by far. The chapter quite correctly expands at some length on the concept of 'dependency' which is not only part of French and German competition law. It is also creeping into European competition law. Including 'dependency' in the definition of market power means looking at a dominant firm not only from the supply side but from the demand side as well. Hence the notion that dominance may also exist if a customer is dependent upon an individual supplier because there are no alternative sources of supply available to him. Implicit in this approach is the notion that competition not only means rivalry between suppliers but also freedom of choice on the part of the customers.

---

[1]   *US v. Aluminum Co. of America*, 148 F. 2d 416 (2nd Cir., 1945).
[2]   ECJ Case 27/76, *United Brands Co and United Brands Continental BV v. Commission* [1978] ECR 207, para. 65; Case 85/76, *Hoffmann-La Roche & Co AG v. Commission* [1979] ECR 461, para. 38.

When there is no room left for choice, competition is absent. It is this aspect of the European approach which has led Americans to blame Europeans for protecting competitors instead of competition. The response is easy: how can there be competition without competitors? It is precisely in the context of market dominance that the line between a restraint of competition (in terms of rivalry) and a restriction of competitors' freedom of action on the market becomes impossible to draw.

The chapter, however, demonstrates that the concept of dominance is sometimes expanded even further. French law is a case in point. French competition law has always been characterised by a conceptual dichotomy between 'anticompetitive practices' (*pratiques anticoncurrentielles*) and 'restrictive practices' (*pratiques restrictives*). The first concept which used to be associated with the notion of 'collective' restraints and which is characterised in the chapter as 'grand' competition law (*grand droit de la concurrence*) covers cartels as well as abuses of dominant positions or the exploitation of a state of dependence where dependence is still linked to firms' position on the market. So far French law is largely in line with German and European competition law on this point. However, the second concept, which used to be associated with the notion of 'individual' restraints and which is characterised in the chapter as 'petit' competition law (*petit droit de la concurrence*) relates to the concept of uneven bargaining power between contracting parties that may lead to unfair contractual terms imposed by the 'dominant' party upon the 'weaker' party. Quite a number of 'restrictive practices' are prohibited by French law without any requirement of anticompetitive effects on the relevant market. The main concern of the law is rather protection of the weaker party. It is from this perspective that the exploitation of a state of dependence becomes relevant in the context of 'restrictive practices'.

Here competition law is on slippery ground. Even though competition law does imply the protection of customers and consumers (after all, its objective is not producers' profits but consumer welfare), it cannot be said to be within the proper scope of competition law to protect them against any risk arising from the uneven bargaining power between contracting parties. This kind of policing of contractual relations is always based on notions of fairness and equity, not on competition. Certainly, judicial review of contractual terms based on notions of fairness and equity may be totally legitimate as a matter of contract law. However, if framed as a problem of competition law, it implies an *a posteriori* control of market transactions which leads to a control of dominance rather than to the protection of competition.

It must be admitted, however, that Community Law itself expressly authorises Member States to do just that. Article 3(2) of Regulation 1/2003 provides that Member States shall not be precluded 'from adopting and applying in their territory stricter national laws which prohibit or sanction unilateral conduct engaged in by undertakings'. This is further explained in Recital 8 of the Preamble to the Regulation to mean that 'stricter national laws may include provisions which prohibit or impose sanctions on abusive behaviour toward economically dependent undertakings'. It is therefore Community Law itself that legitimises the French approach and opens the door to controlling dominance beyond the proper scope of protecting competition.

5 THE CONCEPT OF ABUSE

Two further comments need to be made with regard to the diverging concepts of abuse. A first point relates to the divergence of the American and the European approaches to what may be regarded as the necessary and unavoidable consequences of dominance, namely the power to raise prices and to restrict output. Since dominance is not illegal *per se*, it appears unjustified and meaningless to control dominant firms' ordinary output restrictions or pricing behaviour. Instead of controlling dominance, we should protect competition by focusing exclusively on exclusionary conduct that clearly interferes with competitors' rivalry in the market. American antitrust law appears to limit itself quite logically to precisely this aspect of market dominance, whereas European competition law is in principle still concerned with exploitative conduct like excessive prices or unfair contractual terms. Even though these practices are explicitly mentioned in Article 82 EC, their logic is less than compelling. Characterising dominant firms' conduct as exploitative or unfair and then prohibiting it on that basis clearly leads to controlling dominance and to regulating rather than protecting competition.

A second point relates to the problem of determining which exclusionary conduct should be prohibited as an abuse of dominance. The core problem, of course, is this: how do we know whether observable market behaviour is a restriction of competition rather than an expression of it? If competition law draws the line according to unfounded distinctions, the result may again be that competition is regulated instead of being protected. The chapter quite correctly emphasises that an abuse cannot be determined either on a structural basis or according to the nature of the conduct alone. The two elements have always to be taken jointly into account. This means that market behaviour which would be totally legal under competitive circumstances may turn into a prohibited abuse if pursued by a dominant firm. According to what has been said before, however, only conduct that clearly goes beyond the restrictive effects of the less than fully competitive market structure should be caught. This means that the most important criterion for an evaluation of a dominant firm's market behaviour concerns the repercussions that its conduct may have upon the structure of the market. This is the idea which the European Court of

Justice has explicitly spelled out in *Hoffmann-La Roche*.[3] A dominant firm must refrain from doing anything that would hinder 'the maintenance of the degree of competition still existing in the market'. Consequently, the Court established in *Michelin*[4] a 'special responsibility' of the dominant firm 'not to allow its conduct to impair genuine undistorted competition in the common market'. This approach to competition is again based on the notion of rivalry between competitors. Consequently, Americans may in this context again argue that Europeans protect competitors. This cannot and does not imply, however, that we do not protect competition. The contrary is true as explained above.

Nevertheless, the concept of 'responsibility for competition' risks being construed so as to turn competition law into market regulation even though this risk may not yet have materialised. This can be demonstrated with regard to the 'essential facilities doctrine' to which the chapter quite correctly pays a lot of attention. As far as this doctrine is concerned, the American and the European schools of competition law appear to agree in principle that a dominant firm that exclusively controls an essential facility may be obliged to co-operate with firms whose market entry depends on the facility by granting them access to it. However, the ramifications of this doctrine have still not been fully clarified on both sides of the Atlantic. The main difficulty arises from the fact that even dominant firms' property rights and freedoms are in principle legally protected, which means that the exclusion of a competitor from using the resource owned by a dominant firm or a refusal by the dominant firm to deal are totally legitimate under the rules of private law and require no justification. 'Responsibility for competition' begins precisely where the right to exclude or to refuse ends. And this is at the point where the restriction of output by the dominant firm goes beyond what is implicit in its dominant position anyway. Where exactly the line should be drawn is generally determined by a weighing of the interests of the parties involved. That has been the approach followed by the American Supreme Court in its leading cases *Terminal Railroad*[5] and *Aspen Skiing*[6] as well as by the European Court

---

3   ECJ Case 85/76, *Hoffmann-La Roche v Commission* [1979] ECR 46, para. 91: 'The concept of an abuse is an objective concept relating to the behaviour of an under-taking in a dominant position which is such as to influence the structure of a market where, as a result of the very presence of the undertaking in question, the degree of competition is weakened and which, through recourse to methods different from those which condition normal competition in products or services on the basis of the trans-actions of commercial operators, has the effect of hindering the maintenance of the degree of competition still existing in the market or the growth of that competition.'
4   ECJ Case 322/81, *NV Nederlandsche Banden-Industrie Michelin v Commission* [1983] ECR 3461, para. 57.
5   224 US 383 (1912).
6   472 US 585 (1985).

of Justice in its leading cases *Magill*[7] and *European Night Services*.[8] Americans are nevertheless much more sceptical about the essential facilities concept than Europeans are.

In Europe, the concept of dependence becomes relevant in this context as well. In *IMS Health*,[9] the ECJ has recently restated that the resource owned by a dominant firm is a facility essential for the access of another firm to a downstream market only if there are no alternative sources of supply available for the other firm and if it would not be efficient for the other firm to develop its own competing device for accessing the downstream market. On the other hand, the Court requires that the firm asking for access to the essential facility intends to offer, on the downstream market, a new product for which there exists potential demand by consumers which cannot be satisfied unless this other firm has access to the facility in question. In other words, the Court protects competition in downstream markets by protecting potential market players, not in their own interest but in the interest of consumers who would be damaged if the dominant firm were allowed to prevent the establishment of a new downstream market. On the other hand, a dominant firm is not obliged to support its smaller competitors in its own market. 'Responsibility for competition' in the context of the essential facilities doctrine therefore does not imply that the dominant firm who has won the race in its own market is punished by an obligation to help the losers. Instead it implies that the dominant firm's responsibility for competition extends to other potential markets in which the dominant firm may not even intend to be active itself. However, the establishment of these other markets is controlled by the dominant firm.

What has been said so far with regard to the control of unilaterally restrictive market behaviour and of denials of access to essential facilities appears to keep within the limits of prohibiting individual abuses for the protection of competition. However, wherever access to an essential facility becomes a mass phenomenon, a case by case solution would be inadequate. This is the case with access to networks and this is where protection of competition may require open access regulation enforced by regulatory agencies instead of mere implementation of the rules of the game. The European Community has therefore used regulatory means to solve access problems especially in areas where there used to be monopolies over essential facilities such as network infrastructures for telecommunication and energy. For more details on these phenomena, this comment may refer back to Boy's chapter.

---

7   ECJ Cases C-241 and 242/91, *RTE and ITP v. Commission* [1995] ECR I-743.
8   ECJ Case C-7/97, *European Night Services v. Commission* [1998] ECR I-7791.
9   ECJ Case C-418/01, *IMS Health GmbH & Co. OHG v. NDC Health GmbH & Co. KG*, not yet officially reported.

6   CONCLUSION

To conclude, it can be said that Boy's chapter highlights fundamental points that are most important for a comparative account of the American and the European antitrust cultures. However, the differences are not always where they are said to exist and some of the differences are based on conceptions that require thorough reconsideration – on both sides of the Atlantic.

Comment: Abuse of a dominant position: the Americanization of European competition law? The critical role of perspective

Eleanor M. Fox*

1 INTRODUCTION

Professor Boy has raised central issues of competition law. She is deeply skeptical of the American influence on European competition law, especially the influence of the US law-and-economics movement. She fears that the US influence will turn competition law into a formula solely for efficiency at the expense of all other values.

I agree with Professor Behrens that economics is already embedded in European competition law, that insights from economics are critical to the mission of preserving competition for the good of consumers (and, I would add, for the good of enterprising entrepreneurs and the competitiveness of the economy). I agree with Professor Behrens that non-competition values can best be served by measures other than antitrust, such as environmental regulation.

I focus this chapter on one area: when is exclusionary conduct by a dominant firm an offense? The response to this question reveals one of the fault lines between US and EU law. Moreover, I address this question assuming that neither the United States nor the EU admits industrial policy or other non-competition considerations into the analysis, that neither system intends to protect inefficient competitors from competition itself, and that both seek to sustain hardy, efficient competition. Thus, I put to one side many of Professor Boy's central concerns and her thesis that a humane, sensitive antitrust would include non-competition values. Even given these assumptions, I argue, there is something important left of Professor Boy's concerns regarding the Americanization of EU competition law. US antitrust law of the 21st century has a narrow focus and as a

* Walter J. Derenberg Professor, New York University School of Law.

result has a limited scope for antitrust on matters other than cartels. Courts ask not whether a defendant monopolist is using and abusing its power,[1] but whether challenged conduct increases market power, lowering output and raising price. This is very hard to prove, and most plaintiffs lose. EU law, on the other hand, is by definition concerned with *abuse* of power. It focuses on preserving the competitive dynamic of the market and incentives to keep it competitive; thus, on free and open competition. The gap between Article 82 of the Treaty of Rome (abuse of dominance) and Section 2 of the Sherman Act (monopolization) is growing by reason of recent US case law that further increases the burdens of Section 2 plaintiffs in three sensitive areas – low pricing, innovation, and refusals to deal. The two jurisdictions' different baselines for analysis yield different results, particularly in foreclosure and refusal to deal cases.

The US starting point for analysis today is the recent Supreme Court case, *Verizon Communications Inc. v. Law Offices of Curtis V. Trinko* ('Trinko').[2] This chapter will discuss *Trinko* and its implications, and then turn to the European *Microsoft* case. The chapter concludes that, even under *economic* antitrust analysis on both sides of the Atlantic, the law (abuse of dominance/monopolization) turns on whether the starting presumption is European: trust the competitive structure of the market, or American: trust firms, even dominant firms. Economics does not identify these starting premises. The premises are drawn not from economics but from public policy choices. Thus, although this author takes a different perspective from Professor Boy on the capacity of antitrust to deal with non-economic goals and the wisdom of incorporating them into antitrust analysis, this essay endorses her statement, 'Competition law is clearly dependent on public policy choices'.

2   THE UNITED STATES: *TRINKO*

In *Trinko*, Verizon (formerly Bell Atlantic) was the incumbent in the local telephone service market and was preparing to enter the long distance market. It was the local monopolist at a time when the local market was a natural monopoly. As such, Verizon controlled the local loop, access to which is necessary to provide local service. Over time, technological advances allowed the local markets to become competitive, and Congress passed the 1996 Telecommunications Act to facilitate competition in those markets. The Act requires, among other things, that the incumbent make available the local loop or its elements to its down-

---

[1]   Section 2 is not an abuse of dominance statute. See 3 Areeda, Hovenkamp, *Antitrust Law*, ¶652, at 89.
[2]   540 US 398 (2004).

stream rivals to the same extent and quality that it makes these available to itself. Verizon degraded its rivals' access to the local loop, allegedly in order to keep its customers from switching to the new local service providers and thus to maintain its local service monopoly. The rivals complained to the Federal Communications Commission, which found that Verizon, in violation of the Act, provided an inferior service to its rivals compared to the service it gave to itself. The question in the antitrust case that followed was whether that violation was also and independently a violation of Section 2 of the Sherman Act, and particularly whether Section 2 prohibits a firm with monopoly control over a necessary input from degrading that input to its rivals. The Supreme Court held in the negative, at least in the context of an overlapping regulatory command.

Since the Telecoms Act expressly did not preempt the antitrust law, the Court examined, and restated, the jurisprudence of Section 2 of the Sherman Act. In an opinion by Justice Scalia, the Court stated first principles. The first principle is, said the Court, the freedom of a firm, even a monopoly firm, to choose to deal or to refuse to deal. This is a first principle because, said the Court, unilateral acts of private firms, in contrast with competitors' collaborations, are presumptively procompetitive or neutral; maximizing firms' freedom to act and freedom to use their property as they choose is procompetitive because it induces investment and innovation. Courts, on the other hand, are limited in knowledge and capacity; when they intervene and prohibit single firm acts they are likely to err and damage the market place (false positives).

Regarding the dangers of court-ordered duties to deal, the Court said:

> Firms may acquire monopoly power by establishing an infrastructure that renders them uniquely suited to serve their customers. Compelling such firms to share the source of their advantage is in some tension with the underlying purpose of antitrust law, since it may lessen the incentive . . . to invest in those economically beneficial facilities. Enforced sharing also requires antitrust courts to act as central planners.[3]

Moreover, the Court reflected, antitrust law is modest. It is not intended to eliminate monopolies but merely to prevent unlawful acts. It does not require 'a monopolist [to] alter its way of doing business whenever some other approach might yield greater competition'.[4]

3. THE EUROPEAN UNION: *MICROSOFT*

In Europe, the starting premise for analysis of dominant firm conduct is 180

---

[3] Ibid. at 407.
[4] Ibid. at 415–16.

degrees removed. The starting premise is that the dominant firm has a special responsibility not to distort competition. It has the duty not to tip the playing field its way by use of its power and leverage, appropriating advantages for itself.[5] Central to the European first principle is regard for open markets. This entails the right of firms to contest a market on their merits.

This perspective informs the European case against Microsoft, which controls more than 94 per cent of the operating system market for personal computers. Microsoft bundled its media player with its operating system and it refused to give full operating system interface information to rival workgroup server providers.[6] The European Commission brought proceedings against Microsoft for abuse of a dominant position in violation of Article 82 of the Treaty of Rome.

As to workgroup servers, the Commission found that interoperability with Microsoft's operating system is indispensable to effective competition; that Microsoft had disclosed the necessary interface information to server software providers while it was developing its own server; and that when its own server was satisfactorily developed, it 'disrupted' its previous level of disclosure. As a result, and as a result of Microsoft's changing designs, rivals' servers could not call up all of the functions of Windows, and sometimes operated more slowly. Microsoft's refusal to supply the technical information necessary for rivals' products to work seamlessly with Windows (the Commission found) deprived consumers of alternative products and undermined rivals' incentives to innovate, and constituted an abuse of dominance in violation of Article 82. The Commission required Microsoft to provide the interface information necessary for interoperability.

Also, the Commission found that Microsoft tied its Windows Media Player (WMP) to its operating system, forcing users to take WMP to get the operating system. The tie 'ensur[ed] that WMP is as ubiquitous on PCs worldwide as Windows is'. While consumers might prefer a bundled system 'that can be plugged in and run with minimum effort', the Commission said, the 'bundling of WMP is not a prerequisite for that benefit'.[7] It found that the tying violated Article 82. The Commission required Microsoft either not to bundle or to offer an unbundled version so that PC manufacturers would have a choice of whose media player to include with the operating system.

Regarding the interoperability issue, the Commission said:

---

5   E.g., CFI of 30 September 2003, T-203/01, *Manufacture Française des Pneumatiques Michelin v. Commission*, [2003] ECR II-407, para. 97.
6   Workgroup servers connect all desktop computers within an enterprise so that fellow workers can share applications, data, files and other functions.
7   Microsoft, Case Comp/C-3/37.792, Commission decision of 24.03.2004, appeal pending, stay of relief pending appeal denied, para. 848.

Microsoft's refusal puts Microsoft's competitors at a strong competitive disadvantage in the work group server operating system market, to an extent where there is a risk of elimination of competition.[8]

If Microsoft's competitors had access to the interoperability information . . . they could use [it] to make the advanced features of their own products available.[9]

The Commission's decision strongly reflects Europe's principle of special responsibility of the dominant firm and the prohibition against using leverage and power to obtain advantages over rivals. These principles overshadow any freedom of the dominant firm to choose with whom and how to deal.

4. CONCLUDING COMMENTS

In dominant firms cases, as a starting premise, US law trusts the dominant firm. EU law trusts openness and the competitive structure of the market. Thus, US law might err on the side of protecting firms with power. EU law might err on the side of protecting firms without power. These choices are public policy choices, exogenous to antitrust. In the words of Professor Boy, 'Competition law is clearly dependent on public choices'.

---

[8]   Para. 589.
[9]   Para. 694.

PART IV

Approaching competition by regulation

9. Regulating towards what? The concepts of competition in sector-specific regulation, the likelihood of their realisation and of their sustainability, and their relationship to rendering public infrastructure services

Christian Kirchner*

I INTRODUCTION

1 Why Sector-Specific Regulation?

Sector-specific regulation has long been regarded as a welfare enhancing device in cases of market failure.[1] One example of market failure is the so-called natural monopoly, defined as sub-additivity of the cost function over the relevant range of output.[2] In these cases, so the argument goes, the efficiency

---

* Professor, Dr. Iur., Dr. rer. pol., LL.M. (Harv.), Humbolt Universität, Berlin.

[1] S. F. Breyer, *Regulation and Its Reform*, Cambridge, Mass, 1982, p. 15; D. W. Carlton, J. M. Perloff, *Modern industrial organization*, 3rd edn, Reading, Mass, 2000, p. 783; A. E. Kahn, *The Economics of Regulations: Principles and Institutions*, Vol. 1, Economic Principles, New York et al, 1970, p. 11; D. L. Kaserman, J. W. Mayo, *Government and business. The economics of antitrust and regulation*, Orlando, 1995, pp. 9, 12; R. Richter, E. G. Furubotn, *Neue Institutionenökonomik*, 3. Aufl., Tübingen, 2004, p. 373; J. G. Sidak, D. F. Spulber, *Deregulatory Takings and the Regulatory Contract – The Competitive Transformation of Network Industries in the United States*, Cambridge, England, 1998, p. 20.

[2] S. V. Berg, J. Tschirhart, *Natural Monopoly Regulation – Principles and Practice*, Cambridge, England, 1988, p. 51; W. Kerber, 'Wettbewerbspolitik', in Bender et al., *Vahlens Kompendium der Wirtschaftstheorie und Wirtschaftspolitik*, Vol. 2, 8th edn, München, 2003, pp. 297–361, at p. 349; G. Knieps, *Wettbewerbsökonomie Regulierungstheorie, Industrieökonomie, Wettbewerbspolitik*, Berlin and Heidelberg, 2001, pp. 23–8; I. Schmidt, *Wettbewerbspolitik und Kartellrecht*, 7th edn, Stuttgart 2001, pp. 36, 37.

goal will be missed if two or more enterprises are competing.[3] Costs will be lower if only a single supplier serves the market.[4] Such a cost situation is typical in the case of so-called network sectors or network industries, characterised by economies of scale and scope, irreversibility of costs and network externalities.[5]

The old concept of sector-specific regulation has been a static one: regulating the prices of a private monopoly or substituting a state monopoly for the private monopoly. Competition had to be outlawed by law so that no private competitor could engage in cherry picking. The national monopolist was required to provide so-called universal services at political prices. Pressure to modernise the network or to develop innovative products was low, because a monopolist faces no competition. Thus investment in the infrastructure and technological innovation of products were determined by political forces. This more or less static regulatory approach served as a protectionist device as well, because no other competitor – national or foreign – was allowed to enter the market because of expected inefficiencies.

The existence of so-called natural monopolies, in many cases in network sectors, and their national regulation turned out to be an impediment to market integration in Europe. A new approach to handle the competition problems of network sectors had to be developed in order to break up closed national markets and to establish an Internal European Market in those sectors of the economy, which in the past had traditionally been reserved for national monopolies.

Such a move towards opening up regulated national markets was in line with a world-wide deregulation movement which began in the United States,[6] was then introduced in the United Kingdom,[7] and from there spread to the

---

3   A. E. Kahn, *supra* n. 1; S. V. Berg, J. Tschirhart, *supra* n. 2, at p. 21.

4   A. E. Kahn, *supra* n. 1; J. G. Sidak, D. F. Spulber, *supra* n. 1, at p. 20.

5   G. Knieps, *supra* n. 2, at pp. 21–23.

6   J. Scherer, *Telekommunikationsrecht und Telekommunikationspolitik*, Baden-Baden 1985, pp. 205–29; Ch. Koenig, J. Kuehling, 'Europäische Regulierungssysteme: Das Vereinigte Königreich als Vorreiter', in Koenig, Kuehling, Scheld (eds), *Liberalisierung der Telekommunikationsordnungen. Ein Rechtsvergleich*, Heidelberg 2000, pp. 21–48.

7   Matthias Bock, *Die Regulierung der britischen Telekommunikationsmärkte*, Baden-Baden 1995; Ch. Koenig, J. Kuehling, 'Aussereuropäische Regulierungssysteme: Die Vereinigten Staaten als Vorreiter', in Koenig, Kuehling, Scheld (eds), *Liberalisierung der Telekommunikationsordnunagen. Ein Rechtsvergleich*, Heidelberg 2000, pp. 100–139; J. Scherer, *supra* n. 6, pp. 230–42; Mark Thatcher, 'Liberalisation in Britain: From monopoly to regulation of competition', in Eliassen, Sjovaag (eds), *European Telecommunications Liberalisation*, London, New York 1999, pp. 93–109.

European Continent.[8] This deregulation movement represented a radical change with regard to old regulation concepts based on progress in the field of regulation theory.[9]

At the European level, deregulation in national markets was combined with a re-regulation move towards European sector-specific regulation of former national monopolies (in the fields of telecommunications, energy, postal services, railway transport, and so on).[10]

The basic regulatory concept was simple: access regulation, in order to allow competitors of the former monopoly (incumbent) the possibility of engaging in competition on downstream markets (for example markets for telecommunications services).[11] The success of such a concept, aimed at creating competition in some markets whilst regulating the monopoly infrastructure, depends on several factors. The market power of the incumbent must be controlled either by sector-specific regulation or by competition law. A minimum level of universal services should be offered. In cases where the market does not automatically provide such services, regulation might be the adequate instrument in order to determine which enterprise should deliver these services and under what conditions. Furthermore, it is necessary to find out whether competition within the given infrastructure (intra-network competition) can be supplemented by competition between networks (infrastructure competition).

---

[8] M. Geppert, E.-O. Ruhle, F. Schuster, *Handbuch Recht und Praxis der Telekommunikation*, Baden-Baden 1998, pp. 65–74; B. Holznagel, Ch. Enaux, Ch. Nienhans, *Grundzüge des Telekommunikationsrechts*, München 2001, pp. 214–30; J.-D. Braun, R. Capito, 'The Emergence of EC-Telecommunications Law as a New Self-Standing Field within Community Law', in Koenig, Bartosch, Braun (eds), *EC-Competition and Telecommunications Law*, The Hague, London, New York 2002, pp. 51–69; Ch. Kirchner, 'Europäische Regulierung der Telekommunikationsmärkte', in U. Immenga, Ch. Kirchner, G. Knieps, J. Kruse, *Telekommunikation im Wettbewerb*, München 2001, pp. 130–35.

[9] H. Demsetz, 'Why regulate utilities?', 11 *Journal of Law and Economics* (1968), p. 55; S. Peltzman, 'Towards a More General Theory of Regulation', 19 *Journal of Law and Economics* (1976), pp. 211–40; R. A. Posner, 'Theories of Economic Regulation', 5 *Bell Journal of Economics* (1974), pp. 335–58; J. Scherer, *supra* n. 6, pp. 185–204; G. J. Stigler, 'The Theory of Economic Regulation', 2 *Bell Journal of Economics* (1971), pp. 3–21; C. Ch. Weizsaecker, 'Staatliche Regulierung – positive und normative Theorie', 3 *Schweizerische Zeitschrift für Volkswirtschaft und Statistik* (1982), pp. 325–43.

[10] K. A. Eliassen, T. Mason, M. Sjovaag, 'European telecommunications policies – deregulation, re-regulation or real liberalisation?', in K. A. Eliassen, M. Sjovaag (eds), *European Telecommunications Liberalisation*, London, New York 1999, pp. 21–37.

[11] Immenga, Kirchner, Knieps, Kruse, *supra* n. 8, pp. 18–37.

2   Goal, Scope, and Organisation of the Chapter

The goal of the chapter is to find answers to the questions mentioned above. Different concepts of sector-specific regulation have been analysed in order to find out how they are supposed to function. The central issues are the relationship between sector-specific regulation and competition law, the relationship between intra-network and infrastructure competition and the compatibility between creating competition and guaranteeing universal services. These are relevant issues for all network sectors. But it would be beyond the scope of this chapter to discuss the problems of sector-specific regulation in all network sectors. Thus the chapter will concentrate on sector-specific regulation of the telecommunications market.

In order to understand the functioning of sector-specific regulation in the European context, it is necessary to analyse (1) concepts of competition in the markets to be regulated, (2) alternative (or complementary) regulatory approaches, (3) the interrelation between sector-specific regulation and the application of competition law and (4) the relation between sector-specific regulation and the rendering of universal services.

Because the methodological approach chosen may have a decisive impact on the findings, the first step of the analysis will be to decide which approach appears most adequate for the analysis.

II   METHODOLOGICAL APPROACH AND ITS APPLICATION TO COMPETITION POLICY AND REGULATION

1   New Institutional Economics Approach

In order to analyse concepts of competition and sector-specific regulation, different methodological approaches may be chosen. One may either focus on the welfare implications of competition policy and regulation and apply a welfare economics approach[12] or one may turn to a new institutional economics approach. Whereas the welfare economics approach has to introduce certain strict assumptions, tends to be static in style and does not fully take into account the institutional framework of the markets to be analysed, the new institutional economics approach relaxes certain assumptions (bounded rationality rather than full rationality; imperfect information rather than perfect

---

[12]   J. Eichberger, *Grundzüge der Mikroökonomik*, Tübingen 2004, pp. 163–79.

information) and concentrates on the positive analysis of alternative institutional settings.[13]

In dealing with issues of competition law and sector-specific regulation within the European context, new institutional economics appears to be an adequate approach. Decisions on the design of a regulatory approach and/or application of competition law are to be taken in a given institutional context. A positive analysis of alternative institutional designs of sector-specific regulation and application of competition law should be the foundation on which normative findings are based. Abstract welfare goals which neglect relevant factors in the institutional design supposedly do not offer good guidance as to more practical decisions, such as how to mould the institutional framework of markets. Thus the methodological approach chosen for this paper is that of new institutional economics.

2 Competition Policy in a New Institutional Economics Perspective

In a new institutional economics perspective *competition policy* may be understood as the design of an *institutional framework (competition law)* together with the *enforcement of such legal rules*.[14]

---

[13]   R. H. Coase, *The Firm, the Market and the Law*, Chicago 1988; R. H. Coase, 'The New Institutional Economics', 88 *American Economic Review* 72 (1998); H. Feldmann, *Eine institutionalistische Revolution? Zur dogmenhistorischen Bedeutung der modernen Institutionenökonomik*, Berlin et al. 1995, pp. 23–6; E. G. Furubotn, R. Richter, *Institutions and Economic Theory: The Contribution of the New Institutional Economics*, Ann Arbor 1997; K. Homann, 'Die Legitimation von Institutionen', in Korff et al. (eds), *Handbuch der Wirtschaftsethik*, Vol. 2, Gütersloh 1999, pp. 50–95; D. C. North, *Institutions, Institutional Change and Economic Performance*, Cambridge, Mass. 1990; D. C. North, 'Institutions', 1 *The Journal of Economic Perspectives* (Winter 1991), pp. 97–112; D. North, 'Understanding Institutions', in Ménard (ed.), *Institutions, Contracts and Organizations: Perspectives from Institutional Economics*, Cheltenham 2000, pp. 7–10; I. Pies, *Normative Institutionenökonomik. Zur Rationalisierung des politischen Liberalismus*, Tübingen 1993; I. Pies, *Institutionenökonomik als Ordnungstheorie*, Tübingen 2000; R. Richter, E. G. Furubotn, *supra* n. 1; V. J. Vanberg, 'Die Akzeptanz von Institutionen', in Korff et al. (eds), *Handbuch der Wirtschaftsethik*, Vol. 2, Guetersloh 1999, pp. 38–50; S. Voigt, *Institutionenökonomik*, München 2002; O. E. Williamson, *The Economic Institutions of Capitalism: Firms, Markets, Relational Contracting*, New York 1985; O. E. Williamson, 'The New Institutional Economics: Taking Stock, Looking Ahead', 38 *Journal of Economic Literature* (2000), pp. 595–613; a detailed discussion of the institutional economics approach in the field of regulation and competition law is provided by Ch. Kirchner, 'Competition policy vs. Regulation: administration vs. judiciary', in Neumann, Weigand (eds), *The International Handbook of Competition*, 306–20, Cheltenham, UK, Northampton, MA 2004, pp. 310–13.

[14]   Ch. Kirchner, *supra* n. 13, p. 310–12.

Competition law in a new institutional economics perspective provides generally applicable rules which function as constraints on competitors when they take strategic decisions on how to maintain or improve their position in a particular market.

Competition policy in this new institutional economics perspective may be understood as a game between lawmakers, administrators, law courts and private actors. All actors in this game are understood to pursue their own interest; they act in a world of incomplete information and positive transaction costs. Their rationality is bounded.

According to the institutional economics approach there is no pre-defined public interest.[15] Neither administrative authorities nor law courts are assumed to pursue *the* public interest. Rather individual actors on all levels are presumed to pursue their own objectives.

A new institutional economics approach necessarily makes a clear-cut distinction between a *positive* and a *normative* approach. Whereas the former analyses the given effect of alternative institutional arrangements and/or the creation and evolution of such institutional arrangements, the latter produces arguments for choosing between competing institutional solutions.[16]

This institutional economics approach may be applied to regulation as well. Most elements of the institutional approach are the same whether applied to competition policy or regulation. But there are some specific features of an institutional economics approach to regulation which have to be discussed below.

3   Regulation in a New Institutional Economics Perspective

Applying the new institutional economics approach to regulation means first of all clearly distinguishing between a *positive theory of regulation* – which explains why and how existing regulatory structures have been developed[17] and how the existing regulatory instruments work in practice[18] – and a *normative theory of regulation* which discusses the justification of regulation[19] and/or the merits of competing regulatory regimes and/or the rationale of a choice between regulation and the application of competition law.[20]

---

[15]   Ch. Kirchner, 'Gemeinwohl aus institutionenökonomischer Perspektive', in Schuppert, Neidhardt (eds), *Gemeinwohl – Auf der Suche nach Substanz, WZB-Jahrbuch 2002*, Berlin 2002, pp. 157–77.

[16]   I. Pies, (1993), *supra* n. 13; I. Pies, (2000), *supra* n. 13; K. Homann, 'Die Legitimation von Institutionen', in Korff et al. (eds), *Handbuch der Wirtschaftsethik*, Vol. 2, Guetersloh 1999), pp. 50–95.

[17]   S. Voigt, *Institutionenökonomik*, München 2002, pp. 179–243.

[18]   S. Voigt, *supra* n. 17, pp. 61–177.

[19]   I. Pies, (1993), *supra* n. 13; S. Voigt, *supra* n. 17, pp. 245–99.

[20]   Ch. Kirchner, *supra* n. 13.

As argued above, the assumption of self-interested (bounded) rational behaviour is combined with that of systematically incomplete information and positive transaction costs. As in competition policy there is no pre-defined public interest in a new institutional economics approach.

Regulation in an institutional economics perspective might be seen as an activity in which lawmakers, administrators and – to a certain degree – judges are engaged in *public control of business activities*. Market forces are totally or at least partially replaced by an administrative decision process.

Lawmakers, administrators and judges – as agents – have to justify their (costly) activities vis-à-vis the citizens, that is the principals, in the light of a positive balance between social benefits and social costs. Such a calculation has to take into account the cost of regulation as well. If regulation is justified by appeal to existing 'market failures', the problem arises that one cannot compare the existing market imperfections with perfect markets. These perfect markets would be a good benchmark, but they do not exist. Such a comparison would thus lead to a nirvana approach. And it has to take into account that there are imperfections in state activities as well which may produce high – often invisible – costs. A cost–benefit analysis of the pros and cons of regulation in a specific market has to weigh costs and benefits not just in a static model, but it has to take into account the impact of regulation on innovation as a driving force of future benefits as well. It must be remembered that all the relevant decisions – at the level of lawmaking, administration, and application of law by the law courts – take place in a world of systematically incomplete information.

Such an institutional economics approach to regulation is a far cry from the conventional welfare economics approaches to regulation which focus on the efficiency implications of regulation and sometimes confuse the positive and normative approaches. On the other hand, an institutional economics approach cannot be reduced to a simple positive analysis of the relevant factors of existing regulatory structures. A normative analysis of alternative institutional devices is necessary in which regulation and competition policy are analysed in a comparative setting. This type of normative comparative institutional approach then may serve as a basis for choosing between competition policy and regulation in given market situations.

III SECTOR-SPECIFIC REGULATION

1 The Economic Rationale of Sector-specific Regulation: an Overview

As has been mentioned, sector-specific regulation has a long history. It has been considered to be an alternative to state monopolies in fields in which competition appears not to be feasible. The case of 'natural monopolies' and the conventional wisdom to regulate them rather than to try to introduce competition has been discussed above. Network sectors – like telecommunication markets – are a special case. Here, so the argument goes, access to the infrastructure has to be regulated in order to enable competition on the downstream service markets.[21] Thus the underlying rationale of sector-specific regulation of network industries today focuses on *access regulation*. Regulatory devices have to be developed to make sure that competitors on downstream markets have non-discriminatory access to parts of the infrastructure which cannot be duplicated and which are essential to be able to stay in business on downstream markets.

The rationale of sector-specific regulation may thus be defined as *enabling competition in downstream markets* which hitherto were monopolies because of vertical integration between monopolistic networks and connected downstream markets. Sector-specific regulation in this modern sense is peculiar in so far as competition is created by means of regulation. Whereas regulation according to traditional concepts of so-called regulated industries had the task of curing existing market failures with the goal of enhancing overall welfare, the modern approach to sector-specific regulation is focused on regulating access to certain monopolistic bottlenecks in order to create competition at another level in the market.[22]

2   Sector-specific Regulation: a Closer Look

a)   Starting point: a simple concept of competition in network sectors

The simple version of a concept of competition in network sectors just distinguishes between the network, considered to be a 'natural monopoly' in the traditional sense, and downstream markets open to the introduction of effective competition if non-discriminatory access is granted to all competitors, the vertically-integrated owner of the network and the competitors which enjoy regulated access to this network. As an alternative solution, the common carrier approach is discussed. Here the network is completely separated from market activities on downstream markets. Vertically integrated enterprises have to be disintegrated. All operators on downstream markets enjoy (regulated) access to the network.

---

[21]   G. Knieps, 'Regulierungsökonomische Grundlagen. Der disaggregierte Regulierungsansatz der Netzökonomie', in Knieps, Brunekreeft (eds), *Zwischen Regulierung und Wettbewerbs, Netzsektoren in Deutschland*, 2nd edn, Heidelberg 2000, pp. 90–124; G. Knieps, *supra* n. 2; J. Kruse, 'Regulierungsbedarf in der deutschen Telekommunikation?', in Immenga, Kirchner, Knieps, Kruse (eds), *Telekommunikation im Wettbewerb*, München 2001, pp. 73–87; J. G. Sidak, D. F. Spulber, *supra* n. 1.

[22]   G. Knieps, 'Netzspezifische Marktmacht: Lokalisierung monopolistischer Bottlenecks', in Immenga et al., *supra* n. 21, pp. 89–99.

The deficiencies of this simple concept are twofold: (1) The concept is static and does not take into account the development of downstream markets and technological innovation. (2) The natural monopoly character of the network is taken as given.

Modifications of the simple competition concept will be necessary if it has to serve as a basis for policy advice.

b) Modification of the simple concept: dynamic regulation and bottle-neck approach

(i) From natural monopolies to competition in downstream markets A closer look into the economics of network industries shows that the character-istic feature of natural monopolies – so-called sub-additivity – can be traced back to the existence of *monopolistic bottlenecks*. Parts of the infrastructure which cannot be duplicated but which must be used in order to compete in other markets – in most cases downstream markets – form such monopolistic bottlenecks.[23] In the case of integrated business enterprises which control such bottlenecks and who are monopolists on downstream markets – owing to the fact that they have the power to exclude potential competitors from such markets – it was assumed under traditional economic approaches that both markets, the upstream and the downstream market, together formed a natural monopoly. In terms of property rights analysis one might argue that, owing to property rights in such bottlenecks, the owners of infrastructure carried on their monopolistic power from one market level to another.

If the problem is solved instead by tackling the issue of property rights, one may separate ownership of such parts of infrastructure which constitute bottle-necks, from ownership of assets being applied in downstream markets and creating a so-called common carrier. The common carrier is then controlling the network, that is the infrastructure which constitutes the bottlenecks. In such a scenario, it is easy to understand that regulation of non-discriminatory access by enterprises who want to compete on downstream markets leaves intact the natural monopoly of the common carrier whilst enabling competi-tion on downstream markets. Thus the core message of modern network economics is the application of a combination of ownership separation and access regulation in order to reduce natural monopolies to their core, that is monopolistic bottlenecks.

The simple message of combining separation and access regulation has its flaws when separation either is not legally feasible (for example because of constitutional protection of property rights) or would cause massive costs by

---

[23] G. Knieps, *supra* n. 22, pp. 89–99.

destroying existing synergies between the network and activities on down-stream markets. These costs caused by lost synergies may be avoided if ownership separation is substituted by organisational separation. In this case, the owner of the network – in most cases the former state monopoly (incumbent) – must internally distinguish clearly between its ownership position and its activities in downstream markets in order to avoid cross-subsidisation from one sector to another. Accounting separation is an instrument widely used in order to reach this goal. Access regulation, in scenarios without complete ownership separation, means establishing a regulatory framework which contains the precise obligations of the network owner to grant non-discriminatory access to competitors on downstream markets. Here, the sensitive issue is *non-discriminatory* access to existing bottlenecks. If the additional costs of accomplishing this goal are below the costs of lost synergies, this regulatory scenario is superior to the common carrier approach.

(ii)   Intra-network competition and inter-network competition   The new approach to natural monopolies in cases of network industries appears to be simple: whilst focusing on competition in downstream markets, access regulation has to optimise entry into such markets. The philosophy then is to set access prices at a level which invites many potential competitors who compete on downstream markets and who are sufficiently numerous to pay for the existing network on a cost base.

Such a one-eyed approach may neglect the potential impact of access regulation on the infrastructure as such. It is a static approach, which does not take into account changes in technology in the field of infrastructure. The old theory of natural monopolies suggests that technologies are constant so that cost-based access regulation just has to take into account necessary reinvestment in existing infrastructure under the assumption of static technologies. But if innovative technologies create potential for network competition, such – traditional – assumptions no longer hold. In the case of telecommunications networks, new technologies are threatening the monopoly of fixed-line networks, especially in countries of Central and Eastern Europe (in Estonia mobile phone networks, in Slovenia cable networks).

Conventional wisdom purports that sub-additivity of networks does not allow for competition of networks because of its static character. In a dynamic approach these assumptions must be given up.[24] Thus access regulation has to be critically evaluated as far as it has an impact on potential infrastructure

---

[24]   Ch. Kirchner, *Gemeinschaftsrechtliche Vorgaben für ein Konzept der dynamischen Regulierung der Telekommunikationsmärkte*, Telekommunikations- und Medienrecht (TKMR) Tagungsband zur Veranstaltung 'Das neue TKG', 5 December 2002, Humboldt-Universität zu Berlin (2003), pp. 38–51.

competition. Whereas low access prices may be favourable in terms of inviting more competitors to downstream markets, such prices may prevent or lower investment into the development of new technologies on the infrastructure level. There is a regulatory trade-off between competition on downstream markets (intra-network competition) and competition at the level of infrastructure (inter-network competition). With a dynamic concept of regulation such insight leads to the conclusion that after the first phase of sector-specific regulation – creating competition on downstream markets – the focus has to shift to potential inter-network competition. Regulatory devices of sector-specific regulation and a potential phase-out of such regulation and of competition law have to be analysed under the perspective of their potentially beneficial effect on inter-network competition.

(iii) Concept of significant market power and effective competition The turning point between sector-specific regulation and the application of competition law may be defined by the existence of significant market power in a given market. Whereas under the original concept of sector-specific regulation of network industries in the European Union, 'significant market power' was defined in a rough and mechanistic way, the 'New Regulatory Framework' has brought into line the definition of significant market power (SMP) with the concept of dominant position as used in Article 82 EC and elaborated upon by the European Court of Justice.[25] The SMP-concept then means that, in the absence of SMP, sector-specific regulation should be substituted by the application of competition law. According to a formula used in the 'New Regulatory Framework', 'effective competition' is defined as the absence of SMP. But that does not mean that in a market where SMP exists and which by definition is not in a state of effective competition, one may automatically draw the conclusion that such a market should be subject to sector-specific regulation. Rather, it must be evaluated on a case by case basis whether – even in a situation of existing SMP – the application of competition law is sufficient to deal with the existing competition problems. This position takes into account the fact that even in cases where one company or a group of companies has significant market power, there might nevertheless be enough competition from other competitors that the situation would be better handled by applying competition law than by sector-specific regulation.

---

[25]   Immenga, Kirchner, Knieps, Kruse, *supra* n. 21, pp. 25–37; U. Immenga, Ch. Kirchner, 'Zur Neugestaltung des Telekommunikationsrechts – Die Umsetzung des "Neuen Rechtsrahmens" für elektronische Kommunikationsnetze und -dienste der Europäischen Union in deutsches Recht', 54 *TeleKommunikations & Medienrecht* 340, (2002), pp. 348–53.

3   Harmonisation vs. Regulatory Competition

a)   Sector-specific regulation as an instrument for achieving the goal of market integration

As has been mentioned, sector-specific regulation may be regarded as an instrument for achieving the goal of market integration. The core concept of sector-specific regulation is a focus on *ex ante* access regulation, which is a powerful tool to allow competitors from other Member States to penetrate a national market which has been closed whilst dominated by national monopolies. If this concept is true, it seems it is necessary to harmonise sector-specific regulation in all Member States in order to attain this goal. Every national market should then be opened up to a regulatory approach which is not identical in all Member States, but which is to a high degree harmonised.

b)   Problems of a unitary regulation concept in the European Union

Applying a unitary regulation concept in the European Union may serve the purpose of better integrating formerly closed national markets. But such a unitary approach may (1) conflict with country-specific features of the markets of network sectors and (2) foreclose opportunities to learn from experience with different regulatory approaches.

If in Central and Eastern European Member States of the European Union, competition between mobile phone telecommunications and fixed line networks is substantially different from competition in the old Member States of the European Union, the introduction of a unitary regulatory approach, focused on regulating fixed line operators, may be counterproductive. A unitary approach over all Member States of the European Union may thus lead to totally different results, whether they be beneficial in some Member States or detrimental in others. In order to open up markets in all Member States and introduce competition in such markets where this appears to be feasible, it is necessary to allow for some kind of regulatory competition between Member States.

If one unitary regulatory approach is chosen across the European Union, there is no chance of learning from the experience of Member States that apply different approaches. The sources of information for such a learning process thus would be confined to the regulatory approach of sector-specific regulation of network industries in countries like Japan and the United States.

In order to define the minimum level of harmonisation of sector-specific regulation of network sectors across the European Union one should bear in mind the specific European goal of this type of regulation: opening up formerly closed national monopolies. Thus the minimum requirement of different national regulatory approaches should be effective bottleneck regulation.

4 Effectiveness and Sustainability of Sector-specific Regulation

Evaluating the effectiveness and sustainability of sector-specific regulation of network industries requires a combination of a useful theoretical approach and profound empirical research. The practical use of such studies should be to collect information on the comparative value of competing regulatory approaches in order to take decisions on regulatory approaches in the future.

In the field of telecommunications markets, the impact of regulation in national markets has been of interest in order to define the necessary adjustments of the regulatory framework to market developments.[26]

An example of an empirical investigation of the relative degree of openness of a network sector after the introduction of access regulation – other than the telecommunications sector – is the 'Rail Liberalization Index'.[27] The approach taken by this study is simple: what are the problems a new market entrant faces when trying to do business in railway markets on the basis of access regulation? The study clearly demonstrates that 'access' may have different meanings in different national contexts.

Whereas in the railway sector inter-network competition plays a relatively minor role so that analysis of emerging competition can concentrate on downstream markets, in other sectors – like telecommunications – the problem is more complex. If access regulation has created effective competition in downstream markets (for example in the market for long-distance phone calls in Germany) this does not automatically mean 'effective and sustainable sector-specific regulation'. If inter-network competition is feasible, it would be counterproductive to focus solely on the impact of access regulation on competition in downstream markets. Infrastructure-based competition is more viable in the long term, because it may lead to a point where access regulation will be no longer necessary. The sustainability of sector-specific regulation is a matter of degree: in the case of persistent bottlenecks, sector-specific regulation may be regarded as sustainable if, under the conditions of continuing access regulation, competition on downstream markets is effective. In cases of feasible inter-network competition – for example due to the introduction of new and innovative technologies – the question whether or not sector-specific regulation is sustainable has to be answered separately for each market level: competition at the network level (inter-network competition) and competition on downstream markets.

---

[26]   For Germany see: U. Immenga, Ch. Kirchner, G. Knieps, J. Kruse, *supra* n. 21, pp. 5–18; for a comparative analysis see: Ch. Koenig, J. Kuehling, *supra* n. 7, pp. 100–139.

[27]   IBM Business Consultations/Christian Kirchner, Rail Liberalization Index 2002, Berlin (2002); IBM Business Consultations/Christian Kirchner, Rail Liberalization Index 2004, Berlin (2004).

5 Universal Services

If a concept of dynamic regulation of sector-specific regulation is realised in network sectors within the European Union, competition in downstream markets will lead to the following results: according to the cost situation of providing services to different classes of customers, market prices will differ. Effective market competition will automatically lead to a situation where cost differentials will be reflected in price differentials. This may in turn lead to a situation where certain groups of customers, who previously benefited from 'political' price-setting by old state monopolies, are confronted with prices they consider to be 'unbearable'.

It is a political decision to subsidise 'universal services' in order to attain two goals: (1) provision of services at 'bearable' prices for certain groups of customers, and (2) provision of services in regions which under market conditions would not necessarily be served.

Subsidising 'universal services' does not fit neatly into a concept which tries to introduce competition into formerly monopolistic sectors. Nobody would argue that with the abolition of the state cigarette monopoly (for example in Austria), certain groups of consumers should enjoy subsidised cigarette prices. Where network sectors are concerned, the case may be different in so far as services provided in these sectors (rail transport, telecommunications, electricity) are essential for everyone. But the same is true for bread (which for a long time was subsidised in France). If a political decision is taken to subsidise services provided by network sectors, the full political price should be taken into consideration. If, for instance, certain services are defined as 'universal services' and have to be offered at identical prices regardless of the incurred cost, this will automatically provide incentives to settle in regions with low prices for land and housing without having to carry the burden of higher costs of services in these regions. There might be good political reasons to take such decisions. What is necessary is that all economic and political implications of subsidising 'universal services' are fully taken into account, including the fact that often, in such cases, not all tax payers will pay the subsidies, but only groups of customers who have to pay higher prices because of the burden of subsidisation. The latter problem can be avoided if provision of 'universal services' is auctioned by the state, which then pays the necessary subsidies. Such models are being used in the public transport sector and in the telecommunications sector in Switzerland.

IV CONCLUSION

In the years to come the discussion on sector-specific regulation of network sectors in the European Union will continue. In the light of experience in various network sectors and in different Member States, the traditional approaches will have to be re-evaluated. If Europe is interested in strengthening its position in these sectors on international markets, the quality of the institutional framework of these markets will be a decisive factor, because incentives for investment in technological innovations will be highly dependent on institutional factors. It would be dangerous to focus on static approaches to regulation stressing intra-network competition even in cases where inter network competition is – or becomes – technologically feasible. Issues of consumer protection – in the guise of providing 'universal services' – should not cloud the clear objectives of sector-specific regulation and competition law: to attain the goal of open and competitive markets in network sectors.

Comment

Kurt Stockmann*

1 INTRODUCTION

I agree with most of what Professor Kirchner has said on the subject. It is true, amongst other things, with regard to his view that sector-specific regulation in the European Union is meant not only to raise the level of general welfare and to protect consumers, but also to open up national markets and thereby fulfill an integrative function. As an instrument for achieving market integration, regulation focuses on *ex ante* access rules, allowing competitors from other Member States to penetrate a national market which has been controlled by national monopolies. In this sense, it may appear desirable, as Professor Kirchner states, to harmonize sector-specific regulation in Member States in such a way that national markets are opened up by a regulatory approach which need not be identical in all Member States, but highly harmonized. Although uniform regulation in the European Union could have an even stronger integrative effect, such a concept would, I think, once again in agreement with Professor Kirchner, probably conflict with country-specific features and foreclose opportunities to learn from experience with different regulatory approaches.

In analyzing the issues involved in sector-specific regulation, I share Professor Kirchner's preference for a dynamic approach. One of his conclusions, which I find particularly important and to which I fully subscribe, is that the basis for a first choice between sector-specific regulation and the application of general competition law should be the existence of significant market power in a given market. In the absence of such power, sector-specific regulation is not desirable and, where it exists, it should be substituted as far and as fast as possible by general competition law. Even where significant market power exists, there may be situations where general competition law suffices to deal with competition problems in the market so effectively that no sector-specific regulation is needed. It may well be, for instance, as Professor Kirchner states, that in a case in which one company or a group of companies

---

*   Dr. iur., former Vice-President Bundeskartellamt.

has significant market power, competition from other competitors is still so effective that the situation is better dealt with under general competition law.

According to Professor Kirchner's approach, with which I sympathize, competition policy in general and regulation policies in particular may be understood as a game between lawmakers, administrators, courts and private business, where all actors pursue their own interests. In my following brief remarks I shall concentrate on one of these categories of actors in the game, namely the administrators. Success and failure of the implementation of competition policies in general and sector-specific regulation in particular depend, in my experience, to a large extent on the type and functioning of enforcement agencies, their political environment and their relationships with each other.

2 THE ROLES OF REGULATORY AND COMPETITION AGENCIES

The factual position of agencies implementing general or sector-specific competition law depends on a number of factors. Amongst these are the rules regulating their establishment and powers, on the one hand, and the rules they are charged to apply, on the other. Their position depends also, however, to a large extent on the general political climate of a country and the degree to which competition issues are taken into account in the context of other governmental policies. Furthermore, it matters a great deal whether and to what extent a competition agency defends its scope of action or, on the contrary, how far it accepts the reduction of its scope of action by political pressure.

In Germany, we appear to be living in a phase of declining respect for the rules of the game. This decline in respect for the basic principles of the market economy, especially the need to protect effective competition between enterprises, affects not only 'administrators' in the sense of competition agencies as part of the executive branch of government, but also the judiciary, especially the courts charged with reviewing decisions of competition agencies, and finally, the legislator. An example of this is provided by the *E.ON* case.[1] In this case, at one point, a number of appeals were pending with the Düsseldorf Court of Appeal against a decision taken by the Minister of Economics and Labor, allowing a merger prohibited by the Federal Cartel Office (Bundeskartellamt). At the time, it appeared highly likely that the Court would decide against the Minister. In the media it was reported,[2] without any contestation from the government, that when all but one of the appeals had been

---

[1]   See for a summary of the history of the case Bundeskartellamt, Tactigkeitsbericht 2001/2002, Bundestagsdrucksache 15/1226, p. 170 et seq.

[2]   See 'Standpunkte', *Frankfurter Allgemeine Zeitung*, 16 April 2003.

withdrawn after the parties to the merger had offered certain compensations to the appellants, the Chancellor and the Minister of Foreign Affairs had contacted the Finnish government with the purpose and the effect that the last – Finnish – appellant also withdraw his appeal. Accordingly, the Minister's decision became final. To my mind, such conduct is not only incompatible with the respective roles of the Federal Cartel Office and of the Minister as established by law, it also shows a lack of respect from the executive branch vis-à-vis the judiciary and its role established by law. And finally, it shows a lack of respect vis-à-vis the carefully balanced merger control procedure, with clearly defined roles for competition agencies, courts and the Minister established by law; that is, vis-à-vis the legislator.

The role and functioning of general or sector-specific competition agencies, their degree of independence and their scope of action, is further defined by the existence of other agencies fulfilling functions in the same field. In the European Union, it is of course the Commission and the development of European competition law which has in the end reduced and redefined the role of national competition agencies. I shall not comment on the failures and successes encountered in this area. I prefer to make some remarks about the co-existence of competition agencies at the federal level in Germany. At this level, we have now, on the one hand, the Federal Cartel Office (Bundeskartellamt) as the agency charged with implementing general competition law; on the other, there are two agencies implementing, amongst other things, sector-specific competition law, that is the Regulation Agency for Telecommunication and Postal Services (Regulierungsbehörde für Telekommunikation und Post = RegTP), and the Federal Railways Office (Eisenbahnbundesamt). This co-existence of competition agencies implies not only the risk of inconsistent interpretation and application of the law, but also a decline in the authority of the agency enforcing general competition law thereby jeopardizing an important precondition for the effective implementation of such law. Both risks are aggravated by a trend towards 'regulatory capture' frequently observed after the establishment of sector-specific regulation and specialized enforcement agencies. Even in the sectors concerned, the impression of being dealt with by an independent and objective agency tends to disappear within a relatively short period.

The risk of inconsistent application of competition law is to some extent reduced, but not eliminated, by certain rules on mutual information and by certain consensus requirements in cases falling under the competence of more than one agency. Such rules are contained, for example, in § 82 TKG (Telekommunikationsgesetz = Telecommunication Act) as regards the relationship between the Federal Cartel Office and the RegTP, and in § 14(3)a (3ff) AEG (Allgemeines Eisenbahngesetz = General Railway Act) as regards the relationship between the Federal Cartel Office and the Federal Railways Office. The effectiveness of such rules is furthermore considerably reduced by practical problems. In the case of the RegTP, for instance, the relevant information is provided to the Federal Cartel Office frequently at such short notice that the time available to analyze the case and form an opinion is often – even in important cases – far too short. Obviously, this situation is hardly compatible with the legislator's intentions to safeguard consistent application of the law.

The risks involved in the sectionalization of competition law and the functions of agencies protecting competition in Germany have been frequently underlined, amongst others by the Chairman of the German Monopolies Commission.[3] An impression particularly difficult to avoid is that such sector-specific agencies tend to be more exposed to political pressure than agencies implementing general competition law. In the case of the RegTP, there is in fact some basis for this impression. The then Minister of Economics and Technology had issued in spring 2001 legally admissible 'general instructions' concerning postage rates, which was in fact an instruction concerning an individual case not provided for in the law.[4] Also, recommendations by the then Minister of Economics directing the Deutsche Telekom AG to withdraw an application to authorize certain fees for the provision of certain telephone lines (Teilnehmeranschlußleitungen) was widely regarded as a direct intervention affecting the functional independence in decision making of the competent regulatory agency.[5]

3 MAINTAINING INDEPENDENCE

Irrespective of the abovementioned changes in the overall political climate, the 'independence' of a competition agency implementing general or sector-specific competition law continues to be an important precondition for an

---

[3] See *Die Zeit*, 22 November 2001.

[4] See 'Monopolkommission, Wettbewerbspolitik in Netzstrukturen, Hauptgutachten' 1998/199, Tz. 63 ff. See also *Süddeutsche Zeitung*, 6 July 2001, and *Financial Times Deutschland*, 7 July 2001.

[5] For a more detailed analysis of the issue see Oertel, *Die Unabhängigkeit der Regulierungsbehörde nach §§ 66 ff TKG*, 2000, p. 409. In their Special Report 'Telekommunikation und Post 2003: Wettbewerbsintensivierung der Telekommunikation – Zementierung des Postmonopols', Tz. 112, the Monopolies Commission criticized very explicitly such political interventions because they 'put into doubt the independence of the agency'. For the same reason and just as explicitly, the Monopolies Commission rejected the introduction into law of the powers of the Minister of Economics and Labor to issue instructions in individual cases in § 115 of the Bill to Amend the TKG, Special Report of February 2004 'Zur Reform des Telekommunikationsgesetzes', Tz. 45 ff.

effective system to protect competition in the market economy. The Federal Cartel Office is widely regarded as such an independent competition agency, and, not long ago, a former German government had explicitly advocated a comparably independent 'European Competition Agency' at the European level. Again and again, Federal Ministers of Economics have emphasized the fact that none of them had ever tried to give an individual instruction to the Federal Cartel Office since its establishment on 1 January 1958. Competition among enterprises is the centerpiece of a market economy and the Federal Cartel Office can best fulfill its functions if it is kept free of political influences. Although the notion of 'independence' may not be sharply defined in all respects under German law, one of its constituent elements is widely accepted, namely, the freedom from case-specific instructions. According to the law[6] and in conformity with the practice of the Minister of Economics in the past, the Minister may issue general instructions under § 52 GWB (Act against Restraints on Competition),[7] but not instructions in individual cases. This independence does not mean, of course, that there should be no exchange of views between the Minister and the Office. Any intelligent view that can help in a difficult case is welcome, irrespective of its origin.

In Germany, the TKG[8] (Telekommunikationsgesetz = Telecommunication Act) and the PostG[9] (Postgesetz = Post Act) have led to a certain sectionalization of competition law and of its implementation. The agency charged with the sector-specific control under both Acts is, as already mentioned, the newly established RegTP. The RegTP, like the Federal Cartel Office, has its seat in Bonn. The RegTP makes its decisions, like the Federal Cartel Office, by means of panels which are involved in deciding individual cases 'independently' as the panels of the Federal Cartel Office.[10] Legislative documents supporting the TKG Bill emphasize explicitly the 'quasi-judicial nature' of the procedure to be applied by the panels of the RegTP.[11] In using a wording identical to the wording used in the GWB, the legislator confirmed the Federal

---

[6] See in particular Möschel, 'Die Unabhängigkeit des Bundeskartellamtes', in *ORDO*, Vol. 48 (1997), p. 241 ff, Langen/Schultz, GWB, 9th edn, 2000, § 51 Rdnr. 5. Disagreeing: Nägele in *Frankfurter Kommentar*, GWB, 2000, Rdnr. 5 ff; Bechtold, GWB, 3rd edn, 2002, § 52 Rdnr. 1 f. Distinguishing: Klaue in Immenga/Mestmäcker, GWB, 3rd edn, 2001, § 51 Rdnr. 11, Werner in Wiedemann, *Handbuch des Kartellrechts*, 1999, § 53 Rdnr. 2.

[7] So far only five such 'general directions' have been issued since 1958; see Klaue, *supra* n. 5, § 52 Rdnr. 3.

[8] Telekommunikationsgesetz of 25 July 1996, BGBl. I p. 1120.

[9] Postgesetz of 22 December 1997, BGBl. I p. 3294.

[10] See Kerkhoff, 'Kommentar zum Telekommunikationsgesetz' – TKG, 2nd edn, 2000, § 73 Rdnr. 17, 33.

[11] BT-Drucks. 13/3609, p. 51.

Cartel Office's independence in deciding individual cases. The RegTP has five such panels, of which the first one is chaired, according to § 73(3) TKG, by the President of the RegTP, deciding cases in areas both of Telecommunications and Postal Services. Of the other tribunals established according to § 73(2) TKG, panels 2 to 4 decide cases only in the field of telecommunications (TKG), and panel 5 cases only in the area of postal services (PostG).

Whether the 'independence' of the RegTP panels is as real as the independence of the panels of the Federal Cartel Office is not yet certain. Doubts have arisen not only as to the context of some of the ministerial interventions mentioned earlier, but also 'internally', as a consequence of some public comments made by the Presidency of the RegTP with regard to some of the decisions of RegTP panels. In the interests of effective and efficient protection of competition, such doubts are not helpful, irrespective of whether general competition law or sector-specific competition law is concerned. It should be remembered, in this context, that at the time of the adoption of the TKG and the PostG, both business circles concerned and the Minister of Economics unequivocally expressed the view that the 'independence' of the panels was 'indispensable'. Recent statements of the RegTP President, especially as it became more and more likely that the agency take on the new task of supervising the transition of the energy sector towards a more competitive environment, underlined the necessity of such independence. In this interview,[12] the President of the RegTP stated that 'an unjustified influence' (*sachlich nicht gerechtfertigte Einflußnahme*) had, in his time, not been exercised. With regard to the new functions in the energy sector, the RegTP would be 'totally independent of the energy sector' and directions of the Minister would have to be published. These remarks, however, do not touch upon the relationships between the RegTP and the Minister and between the presidency of the RegTP and its panels.

Not a competition agency, the 'Commission to Survey the Concentration in Private TV' ('*Kommission zur Ermittlung der Konzentration im privaten Fernsehen*' = KEK) was established under §§ 25 ff of the Third Treaty on Radio and Television between the Länder (*3. Rundfunkstaatsvertrag*). According to this Treaty, the KEK has as its aim to prevent further undue concentration. The purpose of this control is not to protect competition, but the freedom of information and of expression, both guaranteed under Article 5 Basic Law. In the absence of sufficiently concrete media-specific control criteria, the Treaty reverts to criteria used in general competition law. In the end this is not objectionable given the fact that insufficiently controlled economic

---

[12] *Frankfurter Allgemeine Zeitung*, 5 September 2003.

power in media markets implies at the same time insufficiently controlled media power. Still, the functions of the KEK remain such that they fall outside competition law and thus do not raise the same problems as sector-specific competition law created in the fields of telecommunications, postal services and the energy sector.

Sector-specific competition control is exercised, by contrast, to a limited extent, by the Federal Rail Office. This Office decides, according to § 14(1) AEG (*Allgemeines Eisenbahngesetz* = General Rail Act) in cases of legal conflict on the right of suppliers of rail services to obtain non-discriminatory access to rail infrastructure. The functions and jurisdiction of the general competition agencies, especially the Federal Cartel Office, remain unaffected under § 14 (3a–2) and (5–4) AEG. An 'independent' position comparable to the one of the Federal Cartel Office is not provided for by the Act. It remains to be noted that even in this case it was initially envisaged that these functions (of the Federal Rail Office) would be exercised by the Federal Cartel Office.[13]

---

[13]   See Ausschußbericht, BT-Drucks. 12/6269, p. 139 at § 12. See also Oertel, *supra* n. 4, p. 418 Fn. 1275.

Comment: The concepts of competition in electricity regulation in Italy

Fabiana Di Porto*

1   INTRODUCTION

In his brilliant chapter, Professor Kirchner compares competition and regulatory policies in the field of network industries, using the lens of new institutional economics. He posits, *inter alia*, that from a new institutional economics
perspective, 'no pre-defined public interest' can be said to exist in either regulation or competition policy; and that normative implications can only be
derived by means of a cost–benefit analysis that takes into account some positive analysis, inclusive of institutional factors. I share Professor Kirchner's
view on this point and therefore would like to add some empirical evidence to
bolster his positive analysis of alternative institutional designs, by offering
some insights with regard to the liberalization of the Italian electricity sector.

a)   Background: the Liberalization of the Italian Electricity Industry in a Nutshell

Besides minor changes in the early 1990s, the liberalization of the electricity
industry in Italy started in 1999 with the adoption of Legislative Decree n.
79/99[1] (the so-called Bersani Decree). Its main goal, as in most Member
States, was to introduce competition in order to increase efficiency, reduce
prices and provide better services to consumers. The industry was then characterized by a vertically integrated State-owned company, Enel, responsible
(under the nationalization law of 1962)[2] for the provision of generation,

---

*   Observatory on Intellectual Property, Competition and Communications –
LUISS Guido Carli University, Rome; PhD in Law, University of Perugia; MSc in
Regulation, London School of Economics.
[1]   Legislative Decree n. 79, 16 March 1999, dealing with 'Implementation of
directive 96/92/CE concerning common rules for the internal market in electricity',
Italian Official Journal n. 75, 31 March 1999.
[2]   Law n. 1643, 6 December 1962, dealing with the 'Institution of the Ente
nazionale per l'energia elettrica – ENEL and transfer to it of undertakings exercising
electric industries', *Italian Official Journal* n. 316, 12 December 1962.

import, export, transmission, distribution (with the exception of some municipality-owned companies) and resale of electricity within the whole territory.
From an institutional standpoint, an independent regulator to oversee the
sector was established in 1995[3] as a pre-condition (see Article 1-bis, Law n.
474/94)[4] in view of the full privatization of Enel. The 'institutional design'
which policy makers had in mind at that time was one of a vertically-integrated regulated private monopoly. Thus, the Authority's functions were
designed so as to ensure control of the monopolist's behaviour towards
consumers and final users (so as to make it consistent with energy policy). The
Authority was not responsible for ensuring adequate opportunities for new
entry.

The scenario changed in 1999. With the implementation of EC Directive
96/92, generation, import, export and resale of electricity (in Italy) were liberalized. Transmission activities were reserved for the State and assigned to a
State-owned company, the GRTN,[5] via a concession. As for distribution, a
concession was granted to all existing operators (mostly Enel and some 200
municipality-owned companies that were excluded from the nationalization of
1962). With respect to the incumbent, Enel was transformed into a holding
controlling five companies, each responsible for a single activity within the
electricity industry: Enel Production and Enel Erga for generation; Enel Terna
for the exercise of ownership rights over the transmission network; Enel
Distribution for the operation of distribution networks and the resale of electricity to captive consumers; and Enel Trade for electricity resale to 'eligible'
(that is larger industrial) customers. The regulator's powers were reinforced
but were constrained by governmental decisions regarding general energy
policy, so that many regulatory decisions had to be taken in cooperation with
the Government or were subject to governmental assent.

---

³   See Law n. 481, 14 November 1995, relative to 'Norms for competition and
regulation of public utility services. Creation of Authorities for regulation of public
utility services', *Italian Official Journal* n. 270, 18 November 1995.
⁴   Law decree n. 332, 31 May 1994, conv. in Law n. 474, 30 July 1994, relative
to 'Norms for acceleration of the procedures for the dismissal of shares owned by the
State and [by other] public entitites in private companies', *Italian Official Journal* n.
177, 30 July. According to Art. 1-bis of Law 474/94: '*any divestment of shares owned
by the State and [by other] public entities in companies [active in the fields of public
utilities] are subject to the creation of independent organisms for the regulation of
tariffs and the control of the quality of services of relevant public interest*'.
⁵   *Gestore della Rete di Trasmissione Nazionale*: the transmission network operator.

b) Outline of Comments

Among the pro-competitive regulatory measures adopted to implement competition, I shall focus on two aspects of the liberalization, which are borderline in the sense that they are at the intersection between regulation and antitrust, and which reveal a peculiar orientation of the principles and scope of competition policy in this sector.

These two aspects of liberalization are:

1. capacity divestiture and an antitrust cap, such as measures implementing competition in electricity generation, and
2. unbundling and third party access rules, such as measures relating to transmission networks.

For both, I will first illustrate what the measures are; what their impact on existing laws is; the regulatory and market conditions in which they are to be implemented; who is in charge of enforcing them (drawing on the relationship between regulators and antitrust authorities); and what sort of competition they aim to achieve.

2   MEASURES IMPLEMENTING COMPETITION IN ELECTRICITY GENERATION: CAPACITY DIVESTITURE AND THE ANTITRUST CAP

The implementation of competition in electricity generation (one of the two sectors of the industry where competition is deemed feasible) was addressed first of all using 'capacity divestiture' and 'antitrust caps'. With regard to the first measure, Article 8 of the Bersani Decree obliged Enel to divest 15 000 MW of its capacity so as to increase competition;[6] as for the second measure, Article 8 imposed a cap of 50 per cent on the market share firms could hold in the production and import of electricity. The aim of such an administrative threshold is to maintain, in the long run, a generation market with a pluralistic structure. In other words, while the compulsory divestiture is a one-shot

---

6   Following this obligation, in 1999 Enel spun off three Generation Companies (Gencos): Eurogen s.p.a., Elettrogen s.p.a. and Interpower s.p.a. Between 1999 and 2001, the Gencos were sold, respectively, to: Edipower (a consortium between Edison, AEM Milano, AEM Torino, Atel, Fiat, EdF and other financial partners); Endesa (leader of a consortium among whose members were ASM Brescia and Banco Santander); Tirreno Power (a consortium between ACEA-Electrabel and Energia Italiana).

measure aimed at creating competition and related to the 'genesis' of a competitive market, the cap aims at avoiding the re-monopolization of the market by functionally preserving its pluralistic structure. Apart from the question of the likelihood that this cap will achieve and maintain effective competition in the market (considering that a market share of 50 per cent might still give rise to market power concerns),[7] two points need to be considered. First, its enforcement is assigned to the antitrust authority; second, the cap is not transitory. The attribution of responsibility to enforce the cap to the competition authority confirms – in my opinion – its antitrust nature: in the electricity generation market (that is, in a pre-defined relevant market), the antitrust authority has a double responsibility: to police against anti-competitive conduct (by applying traditional antitrust rules) and to maintain a competitive structure (by enforcing concentration rules and the antitrust cap). This progressive attribution to the antitrust authority of regulatory responsibilities is the main sign of a 'reinforced' antitrust policy in electricity generation, which considers competition (along both its dynamic and static dimensions) as a value in itself (diverging, in this respect, from the pluralistic goal in the media sector), to be achieved via a combination of both 'traditional' and 'atypical' antitrust measures. As for its duration, the non-transitory nature of the cap has been criticized by many, as it should not be a goal of competition laws to limit firms' expansion. And indeed, from a long-run perspective, hindering a firm's growth may result in an excessively severe limitation of efficiency gains.

Nonetheless, despite this criticism, the law is a reality and prohibits (potentially forever) a sole firm from dominating the market, no matter whether such growth is attained by merger or by 'spontaneous' growth.

We should not, however, over-emphasize this finding because the antitrust authority, at present, lacks structural powers. Therefore, if the threshold is exceeded, the Authority can only address injunctive orders and impose fines.

---

[7] It should be noted that in the electricity market, due to highly rigid demand and the presence of a centralized spot market based on the System Marginal Price mechanism, market shares tend to be irrelevant, provided that market power can be exercised by any producer that happens to be the marginal producer supplying in the spot market. The economic literature on this point is immense; among the many 'interpreters' of the California energy crisis, see: S. Borenstein 'The trouble with electricity markets: understanding California's restructuring disaster', in *J. of Ec. Perspective*, vol. 16, 1/2002, pp. 191–211; P. Joskow 'La crisi elettrica in California', in *Energia*, 2/2002, pp. 16–37; A. De Michelis and M. Granieri 'Deregolamentazione e crisi energetica. Appunti di viaggio sul caso californiano', in *Mercato Concorrenza Regole*, 1/2002, pp. 73–94; G. Marzi, 'Fallimenti del mercato e fallimenti della regolazione', in *L'industria*, 2/2001, pp. 313–38.

3 TRANSMISSION NETWORK REGULATION: STRUCTURAL UNBUNDLING AND REGULATED THIRD PARTY ACCESS

With respect to measures relating to the transmission network, Articles 3 and 13 of the Bersani Decree required Enel to divest its transmission and dispatching activities and to ascribe them to a newly created state-owned company, the GRTN. At present, Enel maintains the ownership of the grid (94 per cent of all national networks): property rights have been legally unbundled and transferred to a subsidiary of Enel, Terna (which was recently partially floated on the stock market). In addition, a regulated third party access rule[8] on a non-discriminatory and transparent basis has been set to allow competition among operators in upstream and downstream markets. Prices for access to the transmission network are set by the regulator, and a refusal to grant access to the network is only allowed for technical difficulties.

As most commentators have outlined, the third party access rule has antitrust origins:[9] provided that transmission grids are non-duplicable and that their use is an indispensable input for competitors in related markets, a duty to share (or to deal) should be imposed on the facility operator in order to allow competitors to enter the market and to reach final customers. In other words, the 'formalization' of the essential facility doctrine has become the cornerstone of the liberalization of electricity markets.

As Professor Kirchner rightly points out, there are two salient institutional models: the simple third party access model, which permits vertical integration; and the common carrier model, which requires the separation of network activities. A 'third way' model has been implemented in Italy: a subsidiary of

---

[8]   According to Arts 16–18 of EC Directive 96/92, transmission system operators are obliged to connect to the network any person (producers, distributors and 'eligible' customers) who requests access on a transparent, equitable and non-discriminatory basis. Member States can choose among three different models for access to transmission networks: (1) the negotiated third party access model (neg-TPA), whereby producers and 'eligible' customers stipulate prices and conditions for accessing the network with the system operator; (2) the regulated third party access model (reg-TPA), whereby prices and conditions are set by a regulator; and (3) the single buyer model, whereby all purchases and resellings of electricity within a given network are centralized and operated by a legal entity: the single buyer.

[9]   See, for instance, P. Cameron, *Competition in energy markets*, Oxford University Press, Oxford 2002, p. 233: 'the transmission . . . undertaking has an obligation to open the network to third parties and third parties have a right to obtain access to a network as a result of Article 82 EC. . . . The provisions on TPA [Third Party Access] in the Electricity and Gas Directives [96/92/CE and 98/30/CE] can therefore be seen as creating a new right of access, and more as defining and clarifying the extent of a right that already exists.'

Enel maintains – so far – ownership of the grid and is responsible for improvements and investments in it, while a fully publicly-owned company (GRTN) operates the grid, decides which investments to make and is subject to regulated access obligations.

Following Professor Kirchner's suggestion, this institutional structure, by neutralizing property rights, makes it possible to avoid anti-competitive behaviour on the part of the vertically integrated firm, as it is not allowed to exercise control over the bottleneck facility.

Criticisms of such a model have pointed to the increase in transaction costs arising from the separation of grid ownership from its operation.[10] Following such criticisms, the Italian government has re-considered the whole design,[11] paving the way for re-unification of network operation and ownership.[12] The problem is that, instead of transferring network property rights to the GRTN, thus implementing a pure common carrier model, policy makers, without any cost–benefit analysis, have decided to put the unified entity in the hands of Enel, thus allowing re-integration and moving towards the simple third party access model.

a) Some Legal Insights concerning the Duty to share in Liberalized Network Industries: a New Paradigm for Property and Economic Rights?

Decisions relating to what network access model should be adopted are not without consequences from a legal standpoint. Indeed, when imposed on a company that both owns and operates the grid, the third party access rule impacts on both property rights and economic liberty; when imposed on a company that operates the network without owning it (as is still the case in Italy), it interferes with economic liberty, limiting the company's freedom to decide whether to deal or not and its freedom to choose its contractual counterpart.

---

[10]   See M. Grillo, L. Scorciarini Coppola (1999) 'La concorrenza nell'industria dell'energia: riassetto strutturale e intervento antitrust', in *Il Mulino* 2/1999, pp. 343–57.

[11]   See the position paper of the Parliamentary (X Commission on Productive Activities) enquiry on: 'Situation and perspectives of the Italian energy sector', 18 April 2002; as well as the Governmental Document on Economic and Financiary Programming (DPEF) for years 2003–2006 of July 2002, esp. p. 110.

[12]   See Art. 1-*ter*, Law n. 290, 27 October 2003, converting the Law Decree n. 239, 29 August 2003 (so-called anti-blackout Law-Decree), dealing with 'Urgent dispositions for the security and development of the national electric system and for the recovery of electricity power capacity', *Italian Official Journal* n. 251, 28 October 2003.

Although it is true that the essential facility doctrine has had limited application due to its exceptionality, the duty to share rules has been known to the Italian legal system since Roman times.[13] Without having to go that far back, Article 2598 of the Italian civil code of 1948 imposes a 'duty to contract' on all legal monopolists and Article 1679 of the civil code extends such a duty to transport public utilities, by obliging them 'to provide their service upon request', thus partially modifying the object of the obligation.

The Italian Constitution (Articles 41, 42 and 43) expressly entrusts the legislator with the power to restrict both property rights and economic liberty when this is consistent with the achievement of a prevailing public interest ('social utility' in the text).[14] Examples of constitutionally legitimate limitations on both property rights and economic liberty exist, ranging from conditional use (for example 'beni a destinazione pubblica'[15] and legal programmes and controls on economic activities) to complete abolition (for example non-disposable publicly-owned goods; nationalization and legal 'reserves' binding private economic initiative), and have been interpreted as a 'functionalization' of such fundamental rights. In other words, legal restrictions are understood as a way of orienting property rights and economic activities toward the achievement of general welfare.

It seems to follow that, by imposing a duty to share on transmission network owners/operators, the Italian legislator has decided to sacrifice property and economic rights on the part of one party so as to maximize the public interest (or social utility) of having a competitive electricity market. By doing so, it has somehow 'functionalized' the network[16] to the superior interest of competition. The means by which it obtains this effect is the third party access rule which, at its very heart, requires the incumbent, especially when vertically integrated, to 'cooperate' with its rivals. This 'imposed cooperation' is probably the new

---

[13]   On servitudes in Roman times and their evolution in modern civil codes, see: G. Grosso, *Scritti storico-giuridici, Vol. II – Diritto privato. Cose e diritti reali*, Giappichelli, Turin 2001.

[14]   Social welfare in economic terms.

[15]   Or 'goods for public use': goods whose use is legally linked to a public mission, for example State-owned railway tracks which can only be used for the provision of the related railway public service (see Arts 822 and 824 of the Italian civil code). See G. Corso *I beni pubblici come strumento essenziale dei servizi di pubblica utilità*, oral proceedings of the Workshop 'Titolarità pubblica e regolazione dei beni', organized by the Italian Association of Professors of Administrative Law, 2–3 October 2003, Florence 2004. See also B. Francario, 'Privatizzazioni, dismissioni e destinaizone "naturale" dei beni pubblici', in *Diritto Amministrativo*, vol. I 2004, pp. 89–134.

[16]   This feature is even stronger in local public utilities laws, where networks are to be maintained in public ownership, where public ownership is understood to be the best way to grant network independence and impartial access.

frontier of competition policy in electricity (and in most utilities): a competitive market being the prevailing interest, cooperation among competitors must be imposed (and not just incentivized), no matter what the efficiency gains or losses in the short run might be (I am thinking of the known problems of investments in network capacity and possible chilling of innovation in technology). Following a suggestion that was made in the oral proceedings of this workshop, we could say that cooperation is being used to overcome a bottleneck problem.

A last caveat on this point relates to the role of sectoral regulation. According to the law (Law n. 481/95 and Leg. Dec. n. 79/99, cit.), the regulator is responsible for enforcing the third party access rule by fixing technical and economic conditions: that is, it is allowed to implement and to specify the rule in greater detail, but not to modify it. This would confirm a 'reinforced' competition policy approach in electricity.

b)   A Caveat: the 'Promotion' vs 'Protection' of Competition Debate

Before moving to some final remarks on the kind of competition the two sets of analysed measures aim to implement in the electricity sector, we should assess the outcome we have reached so far against the Italian constitutional requirements, provided that the Constitution is rigid and that a new relationship between 'promotion' and 'protection' of competition should be fixed.

Promotion vs protection of competition. The issue might appear a bit odd and outdated for all those who – I believe correctly – posit that antitrust authorities and sectoral regulators share the same basic goal of implementing competition (low and economically efficient prices, innovation and efficient methods of production) by using different means.

I would agree with this position if Italy did not have a rigid constitution and if doctrine had not produced entire libraries full of countless works discussing how to differentiate the 'protection' of competition, which is a task for the antitrust authority and the 'promotion' of competition, the responsibility of the regulator. In its very essence, such an artificial distinction originated from the different wording contained, respectively, in the regulator's statute and in competition law. In reality, it has been used to affirm a constitutional difference between regulatory authorities and other authorities, such as the antitrust one, on the basis that only the latter pursue constitutionally granted rights, such as economic freedom. Consequently, it is said, the attribute of 'independence' should only be affirmed with regard to those authorities.

However, if independence is a consequence of the constitutional nature of the public interest at stake, then it should also be affirmed for regulatory authorities. In fact, by 'promoting competition', that is: by implementing market conditions in a sector that has historically been monopolized, sectoral regulators directly protect the constitutional right of economic freedom, just as antitrust authorities do. The difference resides precisely in the tools the two are empowered by the law to use.[17]

Unfortunately, this dispute is far from being settled. On the contrary, it has lately found new impetus due to the recently amended text of the Italian Constitution.[18] New Article 117 para. 2.e) includes the 'protection of competition' among the subjects in which the State has exclusive legislative powers, thus preventing regions from adopting laws that refer to it. Most constitutionalists have interpreted this clause merely to be a means of allocating legislative jurisdiction.[19] However, some rather isolated voices have underlined the breakthrough nature of the clause, which, it is argued, has finally constitutionalized the 'competition value', thus filling a historical gap in our economic constitution.[20] Such an interpretation is particularly interesting as it would be more consistent with the idea of a generally procompetitive constitutional stance, which, in turn, would cover and justify pro-competitive measures such as 'antitrust caps' and 'duties to share' in electricity regulation.

The Constitutional Court has recently interpreted the Article 117 'competition clause' in a decision (n. 14/2004)[21] that is innovative, if a little 'creative'.[22] By positing that the 'protection of competition' is a multi-dimensional concept which embraces both static and dynamic competition, it affirms – for what concerns us – that the clause includes both antitrust and

---

[17] For a demonstration of the fallacy of the double equivalence: regulation – *ex ante* intervention and antitrust/competition – *ex post* intervention, see P.L.G. Nihoul's comment on J. Monéger, 'Competition, Regulation and System Coherence', this volume, Chapter 10.

[18] See Constitutional Law n. 3, 18 October 2001 modifying Title V of the Italian Constitution, Italian Official Journal n. 248, 24 October 2001.

[19] See R. Caranta, 'La tutela della concorrenza, le competenze legislative e la difficile applicazione del nuovo Titolo V della Costituzione', comment to Corte cost., n. 14/2004, in *Le Regioni*, 4/2004, pp. 990–1014; L. Buffoni 'La "tutela della concorrenza" dopo la riforma del titolo V: il fondamento costituzionale ed il riparto di competenze legislative', in *Le istituzioni del federalismo*, vol. 2, 2003, pp. 345–87.

[20] L. Ammannati, *Concorrenza e regolazione tra Stato e regioni*, working paper, edited by the Department of Law and Economics of the University of Siena, 2003; M. Giampieretti, 'Il principio di libera concorrenza: fondamenti, interpretazioni, applicazioni', in *Diritto e società*, 2004, pp. 439–519 and, partially, M. Lottini, 'La libertà d'impresa come diritto fondamentale', in *Foro Amm. – TAR*, 2004, pp. 541–53.

[21] Constitutional Court, decision n. 14 of 13 December 2003, Italian Official Journal, 21 January 2004.

[22] Recent comments on this decision can be found in L. Cassetti, 'La Corte e le scelte di politica economica: la discutibile dilatazione dell'intervento statale a tutela della concorrenza', in *Federalismi*, vol. 5, 2004, pp. 2–12; R. Caranta, *supra* n. 19.

regulation,[23] thus indirectly (because the Court does not give any definition of the two, nor does it explain why the two should be included) recognizing that these sets of rules aim at the same goal: the 'protection of competition'.[24]

4   CONCLUSION

To sum up, despite doctrinal positions suggesting the contrary, it may be argued that there no longer exists a difference between the 'promotion' and 'protection' of competition: regulation and antitrust, at least in the electricity market, aim at the same objective of implementing competition, using instruments which are complementary and which involve overlapping competencies.[25]

Coming finally to the asserted peculiar '*déclinaison*' of competition policy in the electricity market, we have some evidence that the application of antitrust rules in this sector is, at least so far, as pervasive as regulatory intervention.

---

[23]   According to the Constitutional Court (dec. 14/2004) 'The Art. 117, para. 2.e) clause entrusts the State with the power of directly intervening in the market and pursuing strategies aimed at industrial development'. The fact that the 'protection of competition' clause is intrinsically linked (in the wording of Art. 117, para. 2.e) to other economic subjects (such as monetary issues, financial markets, etc.), confirms – according to the Court – the *dynamic* character of the competition clause. In other words – in the Court's view – the 'protection of competition' is one of the most important tools at the State's disposal for the implementation of its economic policy, and includes two *dimensions*: a *static* one, consisting of *regulatory* and *antitrust* intervention; and a *dynamic* one, inclusive of public restorative measures, as well as 'measures aimed at creating the conditions for a sufficient development of the market or at building up competitive market features'. The Court's interpretation of the 'competition clause' probably went too far, offering an excessively broad – and therefore hardly useful – notion of the 'protection of competition' concept. However, what needs to be underlined here is that the Court takes for granted (unfortunately without further explanation) the fact that regulation and antitrust are just two aspects of the same 'protection of competition' concept.

[24]   In perspective, and reasoning theoretically, such an interpretation could imply that regions and other regulatory bodies should not be allowed to adopt regulations that might prove anti-competitive, being otherwise unconstitutional. Furthermore – and almost outrageously – this could consequently lead to the recognition for both the antitrust authority and the regulators of a right to challenge such measures before the Constitutional Court, a right which is so far entrusted only to the State, regions and judges (*a quo*).

[25]   For reasons of space I will not illustrate the advantages of having overlapping competencies: suffice it to say that, on the one hand, applying antitrust rules in a regulated environment may help reduce the risks of capture and of over-regulation, whilst, on the other hand, the presence of sectoral regulators helps reduce the information asymmetries faced by antitrust authorities.

An example of this attitude can be observed in a relatively recent decision by the antitrust authority, regarding the Enel/Infostrada merger of 2001. When assessing the concentration, the antitrust authority rejected the argument that a conglomerate merger would improve efficiency due to the provision of combined telecommunications and electricity services. On the contrary, the authority took the view that this would have allowed Enel to further increase its power in the liberalized electricity resale market. As a condition for clearing the merger, it required Enel, *inter alia*, to divest more (5500 MW) generating capacity. Such a divestiture was clearly aimed at fostering competition in the upstream market, as this was considered the best means to produce competition downstream. This example clearly shows that efficiency claims, which might eventually justify a light-touch antitrust intervention, have not yet gained hold in the electricity sector.

The reasons for this approach, which may be observed in both the regulation and antitrust spheres (and in a broader sense: in competition policy as a whole) should be considered in light of the peculiarities of the electricity market, and especially in light of its early phase of liberalization. Therefore, it cannot be ruled out that in the relatively near future, different considerations (such as efficiency) will come to hold greater weight and justify a light-touch attitude in both antitrust and regulation.

This leads us to the final consideration that the present 'reinforced' pro-competitive attitude seems to be intrinsically linked to the 'incumbency problem': the stronger the position of the incumbent over the market, the stricter the antitrust and regulatory responses will be, and conversely, the weaker the position, the more latitude will be given.

I would like to conclude with some theoretical propositions, which require further assessment:

1. Regulation is the protection of competition in the age of incumbency (dominant position), and for that reason it is theoretically a kind of sunset form of intervention;
2. Antitrust is the protection of competition in the age of competitive markets, and for that reason it is 'normal' and permanent;
3. Antitrust in the age of incumbency integrates regulation, serving the function of ensuring that pro-competitive measures (such as antitrust caps and network access) are not deprived of their efficacy by 'standard' anticompetitive practices (for example cartels which 'annul' the effect of caps and thus of new entry);
4. Antitrust is complemented by regulation when problems of incumbency arise again.

10. Competition, regulation and system coherence

Joël Monéger*

For as much as your most excellent Majesty, in your royal judgment, and your blessed disposition to the weal and quiet of your subjects, did in the year of our Lord God one thousand six hundred and ten publish in print to the whole realm and all posterity that all monopolies are contrary to your Majesty's Laws; and whereas nevertheless upon misinformation and untrue pretences of public good, many such grants have been unduly obtained, and unlawfully put in execution, for avoiding whereof, and preventing of the like in time to come, be it declared and enacted that:

I. All monopolies and all commissions, grants, licenses, charters and letters patents heretofore made and granted, or hereafter to be made or granted, to any person or persons, bodies politick or corporate whatsoever, of or for the sole buying, selling, making, working or using of any thing within this realm, or of any other monopolies, or of power to give license or toleration to do, use or exercise any thing against any Law ... are contrary to the Law of this realm, and so are and shall be utterly void.

From 'The Statute of Monopolies' 21 Jac. 1, c 3 (1623)[1]

Competition where possible, regulation when necessary

From Kay and Vickers, 'Regulatory Reform; an appraisal',
in G. Majone (ed.), Pinter Publishers, p. 223, 1990

---

* Professor, Université Paris-Dauphine.

[1] From L. B. Schwartz, J. J. Flynn, H. First, *Free Enterprise and Economic Organization: Antitrust*, 6th edn, University Casebook series, Foundation Press 1993, p.1. This Statute was enacted against Royal Monopolies according to the Court judgment in the case of Monopolies, *Darcy v Allein*, 11 Coke 84b, 77 Eng. Rep. 1260 (Kings Bench, 1602). It is worth noting that it seems to be the first statute that is mentioned in the field, containing such a rule and indicating that the injured party should be granted triple damages.

I INTRODUCTION

Monopolies should not be granted by the King, but in exceptional cases by Parliament where there is a special need in the interest of the citizens. Thus, from the very beginning, *competition* law and *regulation* were intertwined. In some industries, governmental *regulation* might be more effective than market *competition*. It is not without reason that this proposition is taken as a starting point in our discussion of whether a coherent system might be built in which *regulation and competition law comprise a single body of rules with similar aims or objectives even if the tools are different* or in considering how they might remain two independent systems co-existing, acting or interacting in coherence.[2]

In English, words are generally used in their pure and original meaning. *Regulation* means *prima facie* enactment by the State, or a public entity or designated body, of specific rules to regulate, that is imposing rules for commanding or prohibiting certain practices in the market or attitudes of monopolist enterprises in their relations with consumers and customers and enforcing those rules through authorizations, controls and sanctions. The idea is that industries in a specific sector should not be able to act without consideration of the public interest as valued by the democratic institutions. The old English saying '*so-called public or common callings (to) must render, without discrimination, reasonably adequate service at a reasonable price*'[3] expresses it well. Regulation seems to appear where the market is not working to offer an efficient allocation of resources and cannot by itself prevent abuses from dominant economic agents. Direct prescriptions and direct orders are necessary because of the absence of competition.[4]

Regulation, in British and American English, means, not only *regulation* as a legal system of rules, but *regulation* as an action, a procedure of control, either *ex ante* or *ex post*. This is quite clear for English speaking people.[5] One could say regulation is a polysemous word. It is an intriguing word, in which can be mixed politics, economics, philosophy and law.[6]

---

[2] For a discussion in the specific sector of telecommunications, see P. Nihoul, 'Convergence in European Telecommunications – A case study on the Relationship between Regulation and Competition (Law)', *International Journal of Communication Law and Policy*, Issue 2, Winter 1998/99.

[3] See: L. B. Schwartz, J. J. Flynn, H. First, *supra* n. 1, p. 31, §10.

[4] See: A. Kahn, *The Economics of Regulation; Principles and Institutions*, New York 1970, and P. Nihoul, *supra* n. 2.

[5] See: L. A. Sullivan, W. D. Grimes, *The Law of Antitrust: An Integrated Handbook*, Hornborn Series, West group, 2000; H. Hovenkamp, *Federal Antitrust Policy, The Law of Competition and its Practice*, 2nd edn, Hornbook Series, West Group, 1999.

[6] P. Nihoul (*supra* n. 2) mentions K. Meier who considers that 'Regulation is a

In contrast, in other Latin languages – Spanish, Italian or French – two words are used.[7] On one hand, *reglamentacìon* or *réglementation* are linked to the rule applying to the regulated industry; and on the other hand, *regulacìon* and *régulation* are used for describing the control exercised over an institution, an action or a behavior. This includes authorization to launch a business, respect of rules of production and distribution of certain products or services, as well as the power to sue and penalize persons or enterprises violating the rules. This definition is so broad that any rule or prescription could be considered regulation if it aims to interfere with the free action of persons and enterprises in the market. In this sense, it is true to say, with K. Meir, that 'Regulation is a political process involving political actors seeking political ends'.[8] The debate on the coherence of competition and regulation is sometimes envisaged in this way in France by some specialists, and especially among the 'Nice School'.[9] Regulation, even in French, is a polysemous word.[10]

Today, there are no completely unregulated or completely regulated industries. Everything is a question of degree and depends on the health of the econ-

---

political process involving political actors seeking political ends', K. Meier, *Regulation: Politics, Bureaucracy and Economics*, St Martins Press, New York 1985.

[7]   It is rare that English has fewer words than French. Therefore, it was tempting to mention the poverty of the richest language. But in comparing languages, modesty is recommended, as René David noted with regard to comparative law. Sometimes, it is because the obvious various meanings of a word are unknown that one might think better of his/her own language. French persons writing in English know how rich is the latter and how poor the former. Therefore, we shall consider here that the English word 'Regulation' is as clear as the two words in French or Spanish. For a distinction between *concurrence* and *competition* in French and in French Law, see C. Lucas De Leyssac, *Concurrence et compétition*, Dalloz 2004, pp. 1722–3.

[8]   K. Meier, *supra* n. 6.

[9]   See: M.-A. Frison-Roche, 'Les différentes définitions de la régulation', in *La régulation, monisme ou pluralisme? Equilibres dans le secteur des services publics* Petites Affiches, 10 July 1998, p. 5; M.-A. Frison-Roche, *Le droit de la régulation*, Dalloz, 2001, pp. 610–16 and L. Boy and the members of the CREDECO, *Réflexions sur 'le droit de la régulation' à propos du texte de M.-A. Frison-Roche*, Dalloz 2001, pp. 3031–8. For a view in French Law, see: *L'ordre concurrentiel, Mélanges en l'honneur d'Antoine PIROVANO*, Paris, 2003, in particular, see: H. Ullrich, 'L'ordre concurrentiel: rapport de synthèse ou "variations sur un thème de Nice" ', pp. 663–86; G. Martin (ed.) *Les nouvelles formes de la régulation*, coll. Droit et société, LGDJ, Paris, 1998.

[10]   See. J. Gallot, 'Qu'est-ce que la régulation? Contribution pour une définition', in Journée européenne de la concurrence, 17 October 2000, *Rev. Contrat, concurrence, consommation*, 2001, No. 119, p. 7; S. Liger, *L'entreprise de réseaux en droit communautaire de la concurrence*, Doctoral thesis Orléans, 2003, No. 569. In France, there is a statute called New Economic Regulations. This is very bizarre and was criticized by Cl. Champaud and D. Danet, in RTD com. 2002, p. 17, at No. 20.

omy and on the ideology favored by citizens in the different countries throughout the world.

In the USA, if 'regulation' began in State legislation before the First World
War, the very first federal regulatory agency ever created was the Interstate
Commerce Commission set up as early as 1887. It is worth noting that this
legislation was enacted to give the appropriate powers to a public body to rule
directly against the big railways corporations and the trusts' rates and agreements not to compete. As decided most recently by the US Supreme Court in
Verizon Communications Inc. v Trinko, LLP:[11] when the Congress has
imposed specific duties on some regulated industries such as telecommunications, it cannot be concluded 'that they can be enforced by means of an
antitrust claim'. 'Indeed,' says Justice Scalia for the Court, 'a detailed regulatory scheme such as that created by the 1996 (Telecommunications) Act ordi-
narily raises the question whether the regulated entities are not shielded from
antitrust scrutiny altogether by the doctrine of implied immunity.' Justice
Scalia added that it might 'avoid the real possibility of judgments conflicting
with the agency's regulatory scheme that might be voiced by courts exercising
jurisdiction under the antitrust laws'. But Congress precluded that interpretation. There is in the Telecommunications Act of 1996 an antitrust specific
saving clause (Section 601(b)(1)) providing that nothing in this Act or the
amendments made by this Act shall be construed to modify, impair, or supersede the applicability of any of the antitrust laws. At the same time, the US
Supreme Court indicates that the 1996 Act did not create new claims that go
beyond existing antitrust standards. Regulation is for regulating and the regulated firms have to cope with their precise obligations as set out by the regulatory agency. Antitrust or competition laws are for the protection of users,
consumers, but not for the protection of competitors.[12] Regulation therefore
can be next to competition.

Competition rules must be enacted to prevent abuse by large corporations
of their power in the market and to fight against conspiracies between
competitors harming the interests of consumers. The meaning of competition
is at the same time clear and unclear. It is clear in the sense that it means that
enterprises in a specific market try to attract consumers and convince them to

---

[11]   *Verizon Communications Inc v Law Offices of Curtis V. Trinko, LLP* No. 02-
682, decided 13 January 2004, 540 US 398, 124 S. Ct. 872, 157 L.Ed 2nd 823, 72,
USLW 4114, 2004-1 Trade Cases P74,241,4 Cal. Daily Op. Serv. 269 Daily Journal
D.A.R. 346, 31 Communications Reg. (P&F) 542, 17 Fla. L. Weekly Fed. S 91.

[12]   According to US Law, the right to refuse to deal or cooperate with other
competing firms is fundamental, and nothing in the Sherman Act could be read so as to
require such cooperation. See *Aspen Skiing Co. v Aspen Highlands Skiing Corp.*, 472
US, 585,601, 105 S.Ct. 2847,86 L. Ed. 2nd 467 (1985) quoted at length by Justice
Scalia in the Trinko Case, *supra* n. 11.

buy their products or services and not those of other manufacturers or sellers. Best products, best prices, best marketing and advertising make the difference. Competition is difficult to define because the interest it holds for law or economics comes mostly from a negative approach. It is only when practices are unfair or are contrary to the law that it is possible to know precisely what the word means. Pure competition exists only in books, in the curves representing demand and supply, prices and quantities. But leaving theory behind, it becomes difficult to know what exactly is anticompetitive. In other words, with regulation the approach is a positive one, whilst with competition it is negative. Regulation seems to be systematic because it aims at organizing, limiting competition in a specific economic sector to special cases or occasions. Regulation is mostly an *ex ante* mechanism, while competition assessments are traditionally made *ex post*. But this is not true in all cases. For example, should the control of concentrations, which is an *ex ante* control, be considered as a regulatory or a competition mechanism?[13]

When one looks at the aims of antitrust law in the USA or anywhere else, one sees a conflict between economic freedom, which is supposed to be in the best interests of consumers and/or citizens, and the best allocation of scarce resources and limitation or elimination of economic power which might hinder consumer welfare or, according to Jefferson, Hamilton or Sherman's views,[14] supersede democratic political power. Some American authors consider that this approach remains a very modern one. Schwartz, Flynn and First contend that in a country, where the 'electoral success of political candidates is heavily dependent on campaign fundraising, large corporations commanding substantial sums of discretionary income exert a growing influence on the political process'.[15] Therefore, there is a clear link between politics and the regulatory power vested in an independent agency in order to protect and promote competition in the public interest. It might be considered that even when the nomination is made on a political basis, the appointed regulator is more independent than the Government itself.[16]

From the outset, competition rules were only some of the tools of the regulatory system in force. At least, it seems that this was the case in the USA. So one of the questions to answer is whether or not the same is true of the EU

---

[13]   See on this distinction; P. Nihoul, *supra* n. 2.
[14]   See S. F. Ross, *Principles of Antitrust*, University Textbook Series, Foundation Press, 1993, p. 6.
[15]   *Supra* n. 1, p. 91, § (4).
[16]   This seems to be the case in the UK where independent regulators and directors general are appointed by ministers. The EU Commission is generally considered as a body independent from the Member States. But there is some debate as to the interest in creating an independent agency for assessing anticompetitive practices and mergers.

legal system. In other words, is competition part of regulation or not and vice versa, or should they be considered as separate areas within the legal system?

Conversely, if evidence is found that regulation has to be separated from competition, the question arises as to how clear the separation between them is. In fact, the role, powers and actions taken by some regulatory agencies at the EU level or within Member States appear, like in the USA, to be a combination of both.[17]

Finally, this chapter aims to show that regulation is not separate from competition, except in those cases where it seems to set up only general rules (*réglementation* in French) that must be followed by enterprises in their relations with clients. But even here, it might be considered that the division does not mean that they are not part of a general system of consumer protection, but that they pertain in some way to the '*ordre concurrentiel*'[18] (or 'competition order'), which commands that a choice be offered to clients and that no transfer of wealth be imposed on them by the monopolist, independent of whether it is a residual public monopoly with a future in the free market or a private monopolist which because of its past or present aptitude might abuse its market power.

To substantiate such a proposal, it would seem necessary to first consider *regulation* as a substitute for *competition* (section II). But, as will be seen, this position cannot be upheld in all cases. The separation between *regulation* and *competition* then appears mostly contingent. They are intertwined like flowers atop a pillar in a Grecian temple or embedded in the same marble. Both work towards the same ends: the service of consumers and citizens who are entitled to the best allocation of resources at the lowest cost (section III).

II REGULATION AS A SUBSTITUTE FOR COMPETITION LAW: A DOUBLE, BUT COHERENT, SET OF RULES OF LAW FOR THE PROTECTION OF CONSUMERS

Substitution of Regulation Law for Competition Law is the first coherent answer when looking at the system as proper and unique and researching coherence. At first, Regulation Law precedes Competition Law (section 1). Then, two diverse situations, with slight differences, will be considered. First, regulation as a substitute, but in an alternate sense. This is the situation when

---

[17] See L. Idot, 'Mergers in the media sector: business as usual?', this volume, Chapter 7. S. Liger, *supra* n. 10, pp. 243–373.

[18] See: *L'ordre concurrentiel, supra* n. 9, pp. 23–56.

States, within the European Union or the United States, are unwilling or unable to tackle competition problems directly, either because of a lack of power to regulate or because the State or the federation of States is not considered the appropriate regulator (section 2). Finally, regulation may still be considered a substitute for competition, where there is no competition in the market or where the level of competition is not sufficient to protect the public interest (section 3).

1   Regulation Precedes Competition Law

There exists of course a view which contends that competition is a product of nature. According to the dominant ideology then, it is a natural situation; while according to anthropologists, both the most intensive competition (as between warriors) and the sweetest cooperation (as between lovers) have always existed in the past, although with varying intensity depending on the region and the peoples involved. Therefore, regulation was historically required either to prevent the excess of competition, or to promote it.

In this case, regulation is to be taken in its broad English sense. It is a set of rules prescribed for conduct. This was the case in early common law and in continental civil law. It remains true of the present systems of law. Regulation is a tool designed to promote or protect competition where the market structure or the behavior of actors is not competition oriented.

Under common law,[19] and as early as 1415, the restraint of trade through covenants in a contract was strictly prohibited by judges.[20] Then, in 1711,[21] it was decided that the reason for restricting competition was not based on consumer protection but on the protection of the seller or the market place from the risk of oversupply by the multiplication of competitors in the same town. It was only in 1831 that an English Court held that a contract in restraint of trade should be evaluated primarily according to its interference 'with the interests of the public'.[22] This was in the sense that, if the restraint of competition by the seller enhanced the marketability of the business itself and so provided incentives to develop the sold business, it should be limited to an appropriate length of time and geographical area. In other words, the judge was required to weigh the limitation of competition against the benefits in terms of economic development. The concept of public utilities was developed in the UK centuries ago and remains as strong today as it was then. This is why

---

19   See W. L. Twin, 'The English Common Law Concerning Monopolies', 21 *U. Chi. L. Rev.* 355 (1954); S. Ross, *supra* n. 14, p. 12
20   *Dyer's Case*, Y. B.2 Hen.5, pl. 26 (1415).
21   *Mitchell v Reynolds*, 24 Eng. Rep. 347 (K. B. 1711).
22   *Horner v Graves*, 131 Eng. Rep. 284, 287 (C.P. 1831).

regulation is an old concept and body of law in the UK and the USA. To use the words of Sullivan and Grimes, 'Regulation, like antitrust, is part of a recurrent American political consensus.'[23] American citizens consider that the market is the best system as long as businesses do not act wrongly, or the market itself cannot exist because of a natural monopoly or because an essential facility is involved. In these limited cases, there is a need for regulation. In the US, the government may only regulate in the public interest, a principle validated as long ago as 1877 by the Supreme Court in *Munn v Illinois*, a case involving grain elevator rates.[24] Soon afterwards, the Interstate Commerce Commission was established.[25]

On the continent, similar developments took place before and after the enactment of the French civil code on the legal basis of enforcement of contractual obligations or tort liability.[26]

When the Sherman Act was adopted by the US Congress in 1890, it aimed to give to farmers and businessmen, victims of abuse by the railroad companies and judges, a much more efficient system of rules than the common law system allowed in the USA. Judges were able to prevent or put an end to such anticompetitive and abusive practices and to grant the victims substantial damages. But regulated sectors remained regulated as public utilities or enterprises affected by a public interest. At the very same time, regulation and competition were linked. The former gave to the latter new tools to fight

---

23   L. A. Sullivan, W. D. Grimes, *supra* n. 5, p. 699.
24   *Munn v Illinois*, 94 US (4 Otto) 113, 24 L.Ed. 77 (1877). S. Liger, *supra* n. 10, at pp. 250 and 251, No. 583.
25   *Supra*, section I.
26   French and Belgium Civil code, art. 1134 and 1384. See: O.-M. Boudou, *La liberté contractuelle au regard du droit de la concurrence (droit communautaire et droit français)*, thèse Paris II, 2001; M. Chagny, *Droit de la concurrence et droit commun des obligations*, Paris, Dalloz, 2004; F. Dreyfuss-Netter, *Droit de la concurrence et droit des obligations*, RTD civ. 1990, pp. 369–93; M.-A. Frison-Roche, 'Les principes originels du droit de la concurrence déloyale et du parasitisme économique', in Y. Serra (ed.), *La concurrence déloyale*, Dalloz, 2001, p. 27; M.-A. Frison-Roche, *Contrat, concurrence, regulation*, RTD com. 2004, pp. 451–69; M. Malaurie-Vignal, *Droit de la concurrence et droit des contrats*, Dalloz, 1995, Chron., pp.51–4; *Droit civil des contrats et droit de la concurrence à l'aube de l'an 2000*, Contrats, concurrence et consommation 2000, p. 1; M.-S. Payet, 'Code civil et concurrence', in *Le Code civil, un passé, un présent, un avenir*, Univ. Panthéon-Assas (Paris II), Dalloz, 2004, pp. 715–30 et *Droit de la concurrence et droit de la consommation*, thèse Paris IX, Dalloz, 2001; Y. Picod (ed.), *Droit du marché et droit commun des obligations*, RTD com. 1998, pp. 1–130, especially B. Fages, J. Mestre, 'L'emprise du droit de la concurrence sur le contrat', pp. 71–80; R. Poesy, *Le Conseil de la concurrence, juge du contrat*, Petites affiches, 20 October 2002, p. 4; L. Vogel, 'L'articulation entre le droit civil, le droit commercial et le droit de la concurrence', *Rev. Contrat, Concurrence, Consommation*, 2000, p. 7.

against monopolization and cartelization that directly hindered consumers' interests or indirectly imposed unfair conditions on businesses or other producers or distributors in upstream or downstream markets. A quotation from E. Thomas Sullivan and Jeffrey L. Harrison is worth sharing here. The authors write:

> There are many industries, however, where competition has been replaced with regulation. Federal and state agencies have been established to regulate some or all of the market behavior within a given industry. The regulated behavior might include market entry, price, output or exit. Thus regulation or government intervention can take many forms. It generally is considered, on a continuum, as the opposite of antitrust.[27]

The same authors continue, quoting Harrison, 'Not all formal regulation displaces competition. Regulation and competition sometimes co-exist. Some regulated industries face scrutiny under both agency review and traditional antitrust.'[28] Thus, there exists one and the same set of rules. Coherence is inherent in the aim of the law. Sometimes, however, the relationship between regulation and competition law is different. As J. Kay and J. Vickers confirm, one may find a distribution of action between the two: 'Competition where possible, regulation where necessary'.[29] Regulation becomes a substitute for competition.

2   Regulation, a Substitute for Competition: the State does not Tackle Competition Issues

This might be so because the government is not considered or does not consider itself, for technical or political reasons, the appropriate regulator.[30] That was long the case in the UK and in the US. Such is also the case in Europe, when the industries to be regulated are former State departments or when it seems more efficient to set up a special institution to organize, divide and control the actions of entities being privatized or entering the market as new private investors.[31] There are many institutions or agencies of this kind in

---

[27]   *Understanding Antitrust and its Economics Implications*, 3rd edn, Mathew Bender, 1993, p. 73, § 3.06.

[28]   Ibid., p. 75. § 3.06, Harrison et al. *Regulation and Deregulation* (1997).

[29]   J. Kay and J. Vickers, 'Regulatory Reform in Britain', 8 *Economic Policy* 285, 1998.

[30]   On this point, see: M.-A. Frison-Roche, *Le droit de la régulation, supra* n. 9, p. 612.

[31]   See *Concurrence et régulation des marchés*, in Cahiers français, La documentation française, 2003, various authors, esp. L. Cartelier, 'Les autorités de régulation économique; bilan d'étape', pp. 57–63.

the EU Member States: agencies for the telecommunications sector, for radio and TV broadcasting, for electricity[32] and gas, transport,[33] or financial institutions and insurance companies in some states, and so on. In some cases, they allow the State to remain behind the agency in the form of a 'ghost power', such as through appointees on the agencies' boards. The making of competition regulations remains indirectly in the 'invisible hand' of the State, not of the market as Adam Smith would have preferred. *Regulation*, then, takes a dual meaning: ruling on what should be *competition* is done by the State, government or Parliament in the statute creating the 'agency' or 'authority' and, by delegation of power, by that new legal entity.[34] This is true for any kind of agency even if, as in the case of EU law, only the Commission retains real power, while agencies are only in charge of deciding when and how to apply the regulations to enterprises or entities placed under their jurisdiction.

This is quite a significant change in who establishes the objectives and priorities for competition policies. Previously such delegation of power was vested in the State as a legislator (and, in Europe, owner, in many cases, of the regulated industries) and to Courts (if the legality of a decision was concerned). Now, the State is less apparent, the power to regulate is given to or taken by agencies or authorities subject to the supervision of courts. We have to say here 'given to or taken by agencies', because in some sectors the power to regulate is shared with the sector itself, which sets up its own regulator. The financial markets are a good example of how complex the division of the power to issue regulations can be when the government attempts to regulate and to create, maintain and control competition in the sector. One of the more striking delegations of power from the States to an independent regulator is the Euro system which implies independence of the National Central Banks from national governments as well as independence of the European Central Bank from the EU institutions.

In all these situations, 'regulation' implies regulation in all senses of the

---

[32] On the French regulation authorities and European law, see *Autorités de régulation et droit européen*, Journées d'études du 20 February 2004, Univ. Bordeaux IV Montesquieu, JCP E 2004, Cahiers de Droit de l'Entreprise, 2004, No. 2 and on the Energy Commission, see M. de Monsenbernard, *La commission de régulation de l'énergie: la transition vers le marché ouvert de l'électricité*, ibid., Issue No. 3, p. 12; G. Quiot, 'Ordre concurrentiel et service public', in *L'ordre concurrentiel, supra* n. 9, p. 73, Ch. Stoffaes, *Vers une régulation européenne des réseaux*, rapport, July 2003 on Internet and *Services publics. Question d'avenir*, Commissariat général au plan, Paris, France, 1995, on Internet.

[33] See F. Peraldi-Leneuf, *La mise en agence de l'administration de la sécurité des transports*, CEDECE, Congrès de Bordeaux, October 2004, to be published.

[34] It is open to discussion whether or not such a delegation of power is actually democratic.

word: power to enact rules or regulations, power to apply them within the delegated jurisdiction, power to impose and maintain competition. The main question is to know whether or not the legislature has 'specifically addressed the matter of competition in the regulatory statute'.[35] And, 'If so, how clearly related are issues it addressed to questions raised in the dispute?' . . . 'Has the legislature been more explicit on related issues in this or other regulatory statutes?'; 'Is the antitrust court or the regulatory agency better equipped to resolve these questions?' The catalog of questions proposed by Sullivan and Grimes is longer and should be considered in detail because, as they say, there is no specific theory or criterion appropriate to solve those questions on a more general basis. In the USA, the Supreme Court has discussed thoroughly in a number of cases the conflict between antitrust and regulation where regulated industries or firms are involved, and it appears it is still difficult to declare that solid and reliable principles have been clearly established.[36] Statutory exemptions are considered as having supremacy over antitrust rules. This is the case for insurance, agriculture, labor, electric power, transportation organized markets and State action. Sometimes, competitive principles are injected into structural and behavioral controls by regulators at the state level or by federal law. So the balance between antitrust or competition on one hand and regulation on the other is not so evident and an important array of case law has developed over the century[37] with much discussion of the question of implied repeal of regulation rules by antitrust rules and vice versa. The principle governing the distribution of the sets of rules is as follows: a sector is either regulated or not, and if it is, competition or antitrust rules are not welcomed, or at least they must not be applied as against that which has been fixed by regulation. It is for the legislature when establishing the regulatory system to decide whether, and to what extent, the competition approach should interfere with the regulated system. But today, it is uncertain whether such an approach still finds favor. The trend tends to be the reverse. Regulation is costly compared to competition and efficiency is better served by the latter than the former. For example, the seventh circuit Federal Court decided that the 'mere pervasiveness' of a regulatory system does not offer the firm immunity from antitrust rules when the wrongful attitude has been 'voluntarily initiated'.[38] The opposite conclu-

---

[35]   Sullivan, Grimes, *supra* n. 5, p. 738 et seq.
[36]   In an air transport control case, the agency referred to the antitrust court, and the latter referred back to the former: *Pan Am case* 409 US 363, 93 S. Ct. 647, 34 L.Ed.2d 577 (1973); See Sulllivan and Grimes, *supra* n. 5, pp. 746–7.
[37]   See Sulllivan and Grimes, *supra* n. 5, pp. 697–769; Hovenkamp, *supra* n. 5, pp. 699–754.
[38]   *MCI Communication Corp. v AT&T*, 708 F.2nd 1081 (7th Circ.1983) quoted in Hovenkamp, *supra* n. 5, p. 704.

sion was reached concerning the New York Stock Exchange's Authority in 1975.[39]

In the USA, citizens and Congress have always been as wary of the power of large corporate entities, the 'trusts',[40] as they are of the intervention of federal power in the economy. The same analysis could be made at the level of each State. For an American citizen, competition laws must offer to consumers and competitors in the market, State attorneys, the Federal Department of Justice or special agencies, the means and procedures to obtain from courts the appropriate relief in cases of breach of market discipline. But as soon as the competitive balance is restored, there is no need for maintaining any government oversight over the market. This explains why, from the beginning, the takeover of companies or private assets by the government has been resisted. Finally, in the USA, even when the legislature grants power to federal regulatory agencies to deal with mergers and other antitrust matters, it is still unclear how the power should be divided between the regulatory body and the antitrust courts or authorities. Today, some commentators argue that 'many instances of regulation are the result of legislative or agency "capture" by special interest groups'.[41]

In Europe, the same phenomenon is sometimes observed, but the principle is reversed. Competition is a general system in which special rules are provided for the regulated sectors under Article 86.[42] Especially when privatizing enterprises in the public sector, governments have created special entities to regulate specific economic sectors because it appeared that this was a good way to avoid political responsibility, while taking great care to appoint

---

[39] *Gordon v New York Stock Exchange*, 422 US 659, 95 S. Ct. 2598 (1975) quoted in Hovenkamp, *supra* n. 5, p. 704. For a view on antitrust and State regulation, see: K. N. Hylton, *Antitrust Law, Economic Theory, and Common Law Evolution*, Cambridge University Press, 2003, chapter 17, p. 352 and R. Bork, *The Antitrust Paradox: A Policy at War with itself*, 1978, p. 347.

[40] At the time of the enactment of the Sherman Act in 1890, large corporations were organized under the form of a trust and so were known as such.

[41] Hovenkamp, *supra* n. 5, p. 701 and D. Farber, P. Frickey, *Law and Public Choice: a Critical Introduction*, Chicago, Univ. of Chicago Press, 1991.

[42] See: *Les entreprises publiques dans l'Union européenne: entre concurrence et intérêt général*, ed. A. Pedone, Paris, by various authors; P. Bauby, 'Les entreprises publiques face à la liberalisation', in *Concurrence et régulation des marchés, supra* n. 31, pp. 42–50; J. Monéger, 'Public Undertakings and "Private" Competition – A Few Remarks on Public Interest and Competition Regarding Public Undertakings', in H. Ullrich (ed.), *Comparative Competition Law: Approaching an International System of Antitrust Law, Proceedings of the workshop*, Bruges, College of Europe, 3–5 July 1997, Nomos Verlagsgesellschaft, Baden-Baden, pp. 151–74 and especially, p. 164 and pp. 171 to 174 on public undertakings and public regulation of enterprises entrusted with the public interest.

friends as heads of the new regulatory institutions. Often, however, the agency or the authority becomes quite fiercely independent. The history of the Conseil d'État is interesting in this respect. Although they are civil servants, the *conseillers d'État* are the harshest judges of the state and public bodies' actions. It may work the same way for persons appointed to an independent authority or agency.[43]

It is important here to bear in mind that the division between regulation and competition remains a difficult one. This is seen on both sides of the Atlantic,[44] even when completely different sets of rules or regulations for the purpose of regulating firms and preventing, correcting and punishing anti-competitive behavior are involved. In my opinion, it is possible to consider that a clear division might not be grounded in statute law. As it will be seen later, a division can only exist in the application of the rules. The distribution of jurisdictional power between regulatory bodies and competition authorities or courts is, in many cases, more the result of political constraint or sociological situation than that of a deliberated choice by the legislature. At this point, it appears that regulation in its double meaning may be the only system when there is no competition or where the market is recently privatized and open to competitors.

3   Regulation, a Substitute for Competition in Markets without Competitors

This is the case in the west and east of the EU, because of the twentieth century trend towards nationalization of large corporations, either because of bankruptcy or for ideological reasons. The new trend, which started as early as the Treaty of Paris in 1950, and gained in importance with the Treaty of Rome, is privatization. But there is a long way to go from ministry departments or State-owned enterprises to competition under free market conditions. Old habits, old beliefs in the need for governmental control of the economy or at least the main sectors (energy, transportation, telecommunications . . .), old traditions (at least in France) of offering good, well paid jobs to gifted and reliable civil servants by the end of their career, alongside privileged work conditions and social protection for employees, all make difficult the transition to a market oriented attitude.

But EU and world markets have been opening up more and more to the stiff

---

[43]   As it is sometimes said to a ministry by the president of such body: 'We do understand your position, but . . .'.

[44]   See for a very recent book: M.-A. Frison-Roche (ed.), *Règles et pouvoirs dans les systèmes de régulation*, coll. Droit et économie de la régulation, 2 vol., Dalloz/Presses de Sciences politiques, Paris 2004.

breezes of external competition. It has become quite intolerable to competitors that these monopolies block their national market and, at the same time, backed by their government, may act aggressively on others' geographical markets. Privatization, as a word, is easy to pronounce. But it is a complicated system to put in force when the privatized enterprise finds itself in a monopoly position. The legislature has to regulate the transitional period and the same will remain true as long as in the market the level of competition is insufficient for direct application of competition rules or regulations to the firms concerned.[45]

Herein lies the misunderstanding between the French and the English and American meanings of 'regulation'. For the leading French author in this area, *Marie-Anne Frison-Roche*,[46] one must distinguish between '*régulation*' and '*concurrence*'.[47] According to her they are different in nature. It is difficult not to agree. But should we consider that it follows from her analysis that regulation and competition cannot be in coherence? Clarification is now needed on this point.

III   REGULATION AND COMPETITION: INTERTWINED AND COHERENT SYSTEMS OR ELEMENTS OF A SOLE SYSTEM OF LAW AT THE SERVICE OF CONSUMERS

Whether competition is dominant or secondary as compared to *regulation* in law depends on the degree of competition in the regulated market. Either the general competition authority or the special regulatory agency applies competition rules or regulations. Therefore, it is tempting to consider that there are two different but intertwined and coherent systems (section 1). Once one accepts the differences between both policies, both sets of rules, both procedural and jurisdictional rules, the question is to decide whether they might nonetheless exist as elements of a single system in which regulation implies competition, or where competition is not contrary to regulation (section 2).

1   Regulation and Competition: Intertwined and Coherent Systems

The best cause is none the worse for needing help. Some years ago, Marie-Anne

---

[45]   S. Liger, *supra* n. 10, p. 256, No. 598.
[46]   See M.-A. Frison-Roche, *supra*, n. 30.
[47]   *Supra*, section I.

Frison-Roche[48] founded in France 'Le droit de la régulation' (Law of regulation). In her leading article, she set out the place of regulation within the
French system of law, and it appears from her analysis that competition law
might be separated from regulation. But in insisting so much on the appearance of a special branch of French law, she left open the question of a clear
separation between regulation as a new branch and competition as a pre-
existing and residual set of rules.

Soon afterwards, Laurence Boy and the 'École de Nice' criticized the
founding article.[49] For Laurence Boy, there was no doubt that Marie-Anne
Frison-Roche was right in showing that a new system called 'droit de la régulation' had emerged in French law, but she considered that Marie-Anne Frison-
Roche wrongly limited the field of the new branch to the rules which organize
the transition from monopoly to competition[50] and that it was unclear whether
she was limiting the field of the 'Law of Regulation' to the privatized monopolies or if she also included the rules enacted to protect consumers from
conspiracies or agreements among competitors and monopoly powers.

To get straight to the point, Laurence Boy contended that Marie-Anne
Frison-Roche should have taken into account the role played by the competition authority and compared it to the action of 'Independent Administrative
Authorities', as regulatory agencies are called in France. For the Nice School,
Marie-Anne Frison-Roche implied in her paper that a division did exist
between competition law and regulation and that in the field of regulation,
competition need not be taken into consideration at least insofar as the deregulated sectors are concerned.[51] Between the Paris and Nice Schools, disagreement over marginal questions and over the questions raised by the original
article stems in the main from linguistic interpretation rather than conceptual-
ization. Both authors are convincing. A mediation between the 'Schools' is
possible. Marie-Anne Frison-Roche should be thanked for offering the French
a new and clearer approach to what regulation is and Laurence Boy should be
considered, with her 'School', as having discovered in the paper new elements
and relations between regulation and competition. But it cannot be said that
the former set aside competition. She only focused on her subject.

Therefore, there is no doubt that both sets of rules do play their specific role
according to what the legislature decides. If they stand in apparent contrast,
they do not create any opposition between themselves. The only purpose of

---

48   M.-A. Frison-Roche, *supra* n. 30, pp. 610–16. See also M.-A. Frison-Roche,
supra n. 26, pp. 451–69 and Frison-Roche (ed.), *Règles et pouvoirs dans les systèmes
de régulation, supra* n. 44.
49   M.-A. Frison-Roche, *supra* n. 30, pp. 3031–38.
50   Ibid., p. 3032, final paragraph and p. 3036 (A).
51   L. Boy, *supra* n. 18, p. 3037.

both sets of rules is to control anticompetitive attitudes. The need for regulation is a preliminary need when there is no market at all or when the development of real competition in the newly created market is still impossible for structural reasons. As soon as the sector becomes competitive, competition rules are sufficient and should take over. The evolution in the sector of radio broadcasting in France is an example where regulation has progressively been superseded by competition. Another example can be found in the case 'No.12'. The French Conseil d'Etat, on appeal from a decision of the ART, the agency regulating telecommunications, on 25 June 2004,[52] decided to apply the principle of 'effective and loyal competition' within the regulated telecommunications sector by prohibiting the permanent use, by the former state monopoly, of the number 12 to call for an unknown telephone number on the telephone list because other operators could have access only through a more complicated number. This means that even if considered different, both sets are entangled, intertwined or in line, and that the legislative power, at the EU level or at the national state level, is right to consider that government regulation in some economic sectors where concentration of economic strength is dangerous for consumers and the general welfare, is more effective with regulation and special authorities and that in other cases competition rules are sufficiently efficient to obtain the same result. In between, either the regulatory authority applies competition law in addition to its proper regulation, or a double check should remain possible. And so it is.

Finally then, there are two groups of rules that work together in a coherent way according to what is needed for the protection of consumers.

Could they be parts or elements of a single system?

2   Regulation and Competition: Complementary Elements of a Sole System

It seems clear that the idea which allows for the merging of both sets of rules in a single system lies in the object of the rules pertaining to regulation or competition. From the early common law to the present law, this object has remained unchanged and is easy to pinpoint. It is the protection of the consumers against the abuse of monopoly power and against agreements among competitors. In other words, the *'ordre concurrentiel'* does include both sets of rules at the service of consumers and citizens. All competitors, public as well as private firms, should find themselves in similar positions in the market in order to promote its clear functioning, and when the market does

---

52   Conseil d'État, sect. contentieux, 25 June 2004, No. 249300–249722, Soc. Scoot France and soc. Fonecta.

not exist or is unduly under the control of one or more dominant firms, competition is transmuted into regulation, because there is no other way for making sure that enterprises serve the consumers on an equal footing. Regulation exists to serve consumers, that is when competition becomes ineffective to attain that same goal.[53]

This leads us back to the 'new old' debate on the systematization of the relations between regulation as a specific body of rules for some regulated sectors, regulation for all enterprises and competition law.[54] Division appears greater in Europe than in the USA, as seen earlier,[55] mostly because state-owned enterprises were appreciated by consumers as offering a better service to all. In the USA, the shift has been made in favor of antitrust over regulation, but it remains unclear to what extent. In Europe, it is much more complex. Even if the citizens of the new Member States do tend to favor privatization and competition because they know what abuse of regulation really means, it is not easy to change overnight a society's system and culture. The same is true of the 'old Europe'; consumers and citizens know now, following privatization of some of the state monopolies, that they have been swindled over a period of decades. Thus they are having to take a pragmatic approach on these matters. Ideology, no matter whether for or against competition, is considered with great prudence. What they want is better service for a better price for as many consumers or citizens as possible. Competition and regulation are the tools at their service for better, not for worse. Finally, depending on philosophical choice, authors might decide to consider that the competition concept is flexible enough to adopt where it works better as a substitute for regulation[56] or to reverse the principle, competition being only a tool to regulate the economy. In Florence, we are not in Nice or in Paris, and Florentines have been used for a long time to being smart enough not to choose a system, but to prefer a result. According to EU law, the Commission applies both without difficulty and both sets of rules come together in one and the same system to regulate competition.[57]

---

[53]   See *Verizon Communications v Law Offices of Curtis V. Trinko*, *supra* n. 11.

[54]   F. Riem, 'Droit de la concurrence et Ordre concurrentiel', in *L'ordre concurrentiel*, *supra* n. 9, pp. 635–60, pp. 651–5.

[55]   *Supra*, section II.2.

[56]   For example, S. Liger, *supra* n. 10, p. 263, No. 614, writes that regulation is at the origin of the enlargement of the field of competition law.

[57]   See: Schapira, Le Tallec, Blais, Idot, *Droit communautaire*, Thémis 1999, p. 5; S. Liger, *supra* n. 10, pp. 349–73.

Comment

Jens Fejø*

1 INTRODUCTION

In Joël Monéger's interesting chapter 'Competition, regulation and system coherence' one of the central issues is 'systems coherence', in which connection the word 'regulation' is submitted to scrutiny. The article points to the differences in meaning of the word 'regulation' in English, on the one hand, and in French and other languages of the Latin tongue, on the other. Coming from the less formalistic legal tradition of a Scandinavian country, I think it worthwhile to focus on another aspect of the topic 'regulation' in order to answer the question put by Joël Monéger in his chapter, namely whether a coherent system might be built in which regulation absorbs competition or whether two independent systems can be in coherence.

In my view, 'regulation' cannot be isolated when discussing regulation and competition. Rather, it should always be viewed in its context. This means that normally, when speaking of 'regulation' (in the English sense or in the Latin meaning of the word), one has to be careful not to overlook the fact that regulation usually crops up when other important phenomena are present, namely 'liberalization' and 'privatization'. These concepts, however, are only very briefly mentioned in Joël Monéger's article. Therefore, I intend to present my own view of the importance of regulation and in doing so turn the discussion in the direction I find most fruitful for discussion of the concepts of regulation and competition.

2 LIBERALIZATION, PRIVATIZATION AND REGULATION

a) The Traditional Situation[1]

In many European countries (and I will limit myself to Europe), the exercise

---

*   Professor, Law Department, Copenhagen Business School.
1   For an example of this, see T. Jenkinson, C. Mayer 'The Privatization Process

of economic activities has for centuries not been free, but subject to public constraints of one kind or another. In some countries, all kinds of economic activity, whether selling or buying outside of the remit of the household, have been made conditional on some form of allowance from the government, municipality or the king. The same has been the case for producers. So the markets for the production of goods or services have not traditionally been entirely free. Examples of this kind of restriction, common to many, if not all, European countries, are royal allowances for exercising craftsmanship or handicraft as carpenters, smiths, shoemakers or glaziers, or the requirement of having a public allowance for selling vegetables, meat or other unprepared products from one's own shop, in markets or in the streets.[2]

At the same time, some forms of economic activity have traditionally only been undertaken by public entities of some kind, and private persons or companies have not been allowed to exercise these kinds of economic activities. To some observers this appeared to be a natural public activity not possessing the character of an 'economic activity'. Instead, it was seen as the execution of public power or public authority. Here one might recall examples of common European history during which a government has established a postal service and prohibited all other persons or enterprises from offering such services. Another example is the situation in the mid 19th century in many countries, if not all over Europe, when railroad transportation emerged and the European countries decided that it was reserved to the state as such or a state-owned and managed company to establish and run railroad services of various sorts (building and owning rails, transportation of goods or passengers, arranging train connections to foreign train companies, and so on).

Over the centuries, this picture has varied from country to country and from situation to situation. But one could concentrate on an analysis of the economic situation, on the way many national societies were centred round the king, count or other public institution, who were generally in charge of regulating the economic activities of the society under their rule. To a large extent, this meant that launching any form of economic activity was dependent on an allowance or 'patent' from the sovereign or a public institution. And what we today might call 'economic activities' were in many situations in reality monopolized by a state institution and exercised only by that institution and its entities.

---

in France and the UK', 32 *European Economic Review* (1988), pp. 482–90; and W. L. Megginson, J. M. Netter 'From State to Market: A Survey of Empirical Studies on Privatization' in *Journal of Economic Literature* Vol. XXXIX (2001), pp. 321–89.

    [2] See A. E. Goldstein: 'Privatization of the Economy', *International Encyclopedia of the Social & Behavioral Sciences*, 2001, 12072–5.

b) The Philosophy of Economic Freedom – Liberalization

The reaction against these constraints on free access to and exercise of economic activities by private persons and private companies is natural, easy to understand and widespread. One reason for this reaction may be the desire for private entrepreneurship to be active within areas traditionally reserved to public entities or public enterprises. Another reason for wishing to open up to third parties the possibility of taking up activities traditionally undertaken by public authorities may be the interest from the point of view of fiscal policy in having private companies serve the public if it can be done in a less costly way than by a public company. On the other hand, for political reasons, there may exist a strong feeling against letting the private sector into areas traditionally seen as the public sphere or not suited to competition.

In recent times, however, and specifically within the European Union, the requirements of efficiency have led to situations where areas traditionally reserved to public entities within the Member States have been opened up to competition thanks to EU legislation. But also within a single Member State, political will may lead to revision of the national system without external pressure. A modern example from EU history may be most pertinent and interesting here.

3 THE EU APPROACH TO LIBERALIZATION AND COMPETITION[3]

Over the years, the EU legislature, mainly the Council but also the European Commission, has produced numerous examples of 'liberalization'. Hence, the vast amount of legislation in the form of Directives liberalizing the telecommunications sector and the many Directives liberalizing the energy sectors. These may serve as illustrations of what is meant here.

The European *telecommunications sector* has thus undergone a fundamental change from the widespread situation in which the only company allowed was a national publicly owned and managed company towards a situation with almost full competition.[4] This competitive situation has gradually been developed through subsequent EU Directives. The first step mandated by the

---

[3] See, for example: J. Clifton, F. Comin, D. Diaz Fuentes, *Privatisation in the European Union: Public Enterprises and Integration*, Dordrecht, 2003.

[4] See Ch. Koenig, A. Bartosch, J.-D. Braun, *EC Competition and Telecommunications Law*, Dordrecht, 2002. See, for a short survey W. Maxwell 'EU Telecommunications Law: A Primer for IT Lawyers', Computer Association Law, World Congress Washington DC, 2001.

Directives was a requirement that Member States legislate such that only companies owned by the state in question or companies awarded a special right by the state could in fact exercise and offer telecommunications services. The aim was to open the market up so that other companies (including companies from other EU Member States) might offer such services on an objective, transparent and equal basis. Furthermore, it was required by the Directives that the ordinary competition rules of the EU should apply to the telecommunications sector. This meant, first of all, that the previously state-owned or state-controlled telecommunications company or companies were not to be allowed to keep their previous prerogatives unless they acted in a transparent, non-discriminatory, objective and fair manner. This was first of all a question of regulating factual market power.

Fundamental change does not come overnight, so the several phases in this evolution had to take place gradually. It was not expected that the final result would be seen early on.

Likewise in the *energy sectors* the forms of energy linked to pipelines and leads – mainly natural gas and electricity, but also to some extent oil – have been regulated through EU Directives.[5] But it is striking to see that the very first steps in legislating this aspect of economic life were not taken until the 1990s, and there is still a long way to go before a real competitive situation can be said to exist. Within the energy sector, the clear intention has also been to bring about a competitive situation through the issuing of Directives. Thus access to pipelines and electric leads by third parties is one important goal towards which the EU Directives have been directed. Furthermore, it can be noted that an opening up of access to sources has also been addressed by the Directives.[6] This means that a Member State may no longer merely award a contract to a company or consortium that has shown interest in exploring underground within a Member State, but is required to let this part of the process go through a tender procedure. A state wishing to find a company or consortium willing to undertake the risky business of making costly studies of the soil, for example, in order to be able to extract gas or oil, must therefore publish a description of what is being contracted and must follow a very strict but well described procedure in order to find the company or consortium to whom the contract shall be awarded. Furthermore, regulation of natural gas networks or electricity lines requires that the Member States, through their national legislation, make this possible on an objective basis and through equal treatment.

---

[5]   See, for references, D. Geradin, *The Liberalization of Electricity and Natural Gas in the European Union*, Dordrecht, 2001.

[6]   Directive 94/22/EC of the European Parliament and the Council of 30 May 1994 on the conditions for granting and using authorizations for the prospection, exploration and production of hydrocarbons, OJ 1994 L 164/3.

4 NATIONAL LIBERALIZATION

Purely national measures designed to liberalize have also been seen throughout Europe. Owing to the interests of the different states, an incentive for liberalizing more or less of the state activities will often be implemented. This is, however, a purely national decision occurring outside the requirements of EU Directives or other EU demands. In principle, though, there is no difference as regards the question of regulation (and de-regulation), whether it derives from EU liberalization or from liberalization taking place solely on the state's own initiative. At the same time, when the liberalization process does take place, it very often will lead to the 'de-regulation' of formerly strictly regulated economic areas.

5 PRIVATIZATION

Under a liberalized system, privatization will often be required or sought after, partly because of political philosophy and partly for other reasons.[7] Where a liberalized situation has been created through changes in legislation, the public authority holding a specific right or preferential position over a company or entity, through the legislation or because of its previous status as exclusive party on the market, may be looked upon with some scepticism from the political angle. Thus, the political interest in a free and unregulated market may weaken the position of that company. Also the state may think it appropriate to benefit from this preferential position and get rid of the company or entity holding a preferential position by selling it at a high price. If, for example, a state agency has previously been responsible for producing military and other uniforms for public personnel, the change of status of such an agency into a state-owned company may be swiftly followed by a selling off of the state-owned company. The government might wish to sell at a high price in order to obtain certain financial resources from the company. But this might only be possible if the company to be sold is in a uniquely competitive situation having many long-term contracts with the public authority or having special rights connected with its activities. Another approach may, however, be at issue if, instead, the state wishes to benefit from competition within the industry. It might then sell the company on a competitive market where the company will not benefit from any special privileges, the result being that the selling price for the company will be that of a company in competition on the

---

[7]   See on privatization, for example, R. Mudambi, *Privatization and Globalization – The Changing Role of the State in Business*, Cheltenham, 2003.

ordinary market. So sale of a (former) state-owned company may either take the form of a monopoly sale or the sale of a company in a monopolistic position, yielding a higher price for the company, or it will be handled as the sale of a company without special rights or privileges. In the latter situation, competition will lead to lower prices in the case of the company sold, but will likely enhance competition to the benefit of consumers and citizens.

It should be recalled that the EC Treaty does not require the selling off of public companies. On the contrary, the Treaty spells out in Article 295 that it shall in no way prejudice the Member States' system of property ownership. Further, the directives do not require anything to this effect. One might, however, point to the provision of Article 4(1) where it is stated that

> For the purposes set out in Article 2,[8] the activities of the Member States and the Community shall include, as provided in this Treaty and in accordance with the timetable set out therein, the adoption of an economic policy which is based on the close coordination of Member States' economic policies, on the internal market and on the definition of common objectives, and conducted in accordance with the principle of an open market economy with free competition.

So an *open market economy with free competition* is a vital part of the Union.

6   THE EU LEGISLATION ON PUBLIC UNDERTAKINGS AND UNDERTAKINGS TO WHICH A MEMBER STATE HAS GRANTED SPECIAL OR EXCLUSIVE RIGHTS

In the EU system, the two most important provisions dealing with liberalization and privatization might be said to be the provisions of Article 86(1) and Article 86(2) of the EC Treaty.

Article 86(1) is directed towards the Member States and imposes certain requirements on them when they want to grant special rights to companies or to run the economic system through public undertakings. It provides that in the

---

[8]   Article 2 of the EC Treaty provides: 'The Community shall have as its task, by establishing a common market and an economic and monetary union and by implementing common policies or activities referred to in Articles 3 and 4, to promote throughout the Community a harmonious, balanced and sustainable development of economic activities, a high level of employment and of social protection, equality between men and women, sustainable and non-inflationary growth, a high degree of competitiveness and convergence of economic performance, a high level of protection and improvement of the quality of the environment, the raising of the standard of living and quality of life, and economic and social cohesion and solidarity among Member States.'

case of public undertakings and undertakings to which Member States grant special or exclusive rights, Member States shall neither enact nor maintain in force any measure contrary to the rules contained in the EC Treaty, in particular contrary to those rules provided for in Article 12 (the prohibition against discrimination on grounds of nationality) and in Articles 81 to 89 (the competition rules applying to undertakings and the state aid rules). Since the provision thus explicitly refers to the competition rules in Articles 81 et seq., it is clear from the very wording of the provision that it cannot be accepted in a national system within the Union to have legislation or administrative or judicial practices that are anti-competitive within the meaning of the Treaty.

Article 86(2), on the other hand, is directed towards the behaviour of the specific undertaking which has received a special position through the national legislative or administrative system or by being a public undertaking. Such undertakings must adhere to the competition system of the EU. Thus Article 86(2) provides that undertakings entrusted with the operation of services of general economic interest 'shall be subject to the rules contained in the EC Treaty, in particular to the rules on competition, insofar as the application of such rules does not obstruct the performance, in law or in fact, of the particular tasks assigned to them'. The development of trade must not be affected to the extent that it would be contrary to the interests of the Community.

It is interesting to see that the provisions in Article 86(2), on the one hand, require that the companies involved respect the Treaty rules on competition, but at the same time are open to some deviation from the strict rule. If these companies have been assigned particular tasks, a deviation from competition can be accepted 'insofar as' the application of such rules (meaning primarily the competition rules) do not obstruct the performance, in law or in fact, of the particular tasks assigned to them. The Article, however, only accepts such deviation to the extent expressed by the requirement that the 'development of trade must not be affected to such an extent as would be contrary to the interests of the Community'.

It is hard to tell exactly to what degree the possibility of deviating from the normal requirements of competition can be utilized. One thing is that the companies concerned must be assigned particular tasks. But it is not clear from the provision itself what kinds of tasks will be accepted by the European Court of Justice. Some judgments have been handed down in this respect, but they are far too few to give a clear description of the field of operation of the competition rules for these kinds of activities. It is clear from the wording that a Community trade off has been created with this piece of legislation in the Treaty and the clear political wording of the text is also of great interest.

7   REGULATION

When the directives mandate that Member States open up their markets to competition and that previously state-owned companies or state institutions undergo a process of privatization, sometimes through de-regulation, a new situation may arise. Very often there has been no need for regulating a sector or business activity undertaken by the state as such or by an undertaking owned by the state. This is because the tasks undertaken by that state entity or state-owned enterprise may have been clearly defined in the traditional administrative framework or administrative traditions or may be regulated through ownership by the state/government.

When, however, liberalization has been introduced and privatization of former state-managed or state-owned enterprises or entities has taken place, the future 'regulator' will be the market or markets. In this situation, the need for further regulation might be felt. Thus, for example, if a commercial area is characterized by technical requirements of some kind and the market is not able to assess the output of the enterprises on that market, the market situation might develop into an unwanted situation unless the market is serviced by additional help to understand and use the technical requirements. In such a situation – and in many others – the state may wish to help its citizens by requiring additional information from market participants. This will lead to the issuing of new legislation/regulation in an otherwise deregulated market, a situation often denominated as '*re-regulation*'. Thus, for instance, in the telecommunications sector a very clear need for additional regulation will normally be seen in the Member States.

8   SOME CONCLUSIONS

In my view the initial question in Joël Monéger's article has to be answered through the statement that there is no need for solving the question whether regulation absorbs competition or whether there are two independent systems that can be in coherence. Competition and regulation work without labelling the different phenomena with names that very easily would lead to a 'Begriffsjurisprudenz' otherwise left behind by modern legal thinking. The question is better served by confirming that around the development in society of new instruments to effect change in the market situation, there are different legal settings that might work in each direction and with different consequences, but they work without 'absorbing' one another.

As I see the situation, 'regulation' is not a substitute for competition but may easily exist at the same time. Regulation in this case may be necessary in order to pursue goals other than those pursued by competition and may well go hand in hand with competition. A very good and illustrative example of this is the trade-off built into Article 86(2) of the EC Treaty.

Another point to note is that where a regulatory measure has been taken, but does not cover the actual situation, competition law will apply.[9]

Thus, even within the regulated sectors, competition law is applicable and only restricted by the principles of Article 86(2).

---

[9]   See, for example, Joined cases C-264/01, C-306/01, C-354/01 and C-355/01, *AOK Bundesverband et al. v Ichthyol-Gesellschaft Cordes et al.,* judgment of the European Court of Justice of 16 March 2004, not yet officially reported, para. 58.

Comment: The opposition between competition and regulation – some nuances

Paul L. G. Nihoul*

1 BACK TO THE CLASSICS

Thank you very much, Joël, for your thoughtful presentation. As I was preparing the subject matter before the conference, I thought that I might start with a sentence of yours and try to build on it further. In this sentence, you make the point that it is often difficult to establish a clear distinction between regulation and competition law. In light of that sentence, I went back to the classics and examined what some important authors think about the relation existing between these two areas of the law. In carrying out this exercise, I concentrated on four authors: Viscusi, writing with Vernon and Harrington,[1] Breyer,[2] Kahn,[3] and Areeda.[4]

In the works published by these authors, I came across the idea that a distinction, and even an opposition,[5] must be made between competition and regulation. (a) In some instances, markets do not need to be regulated. In such cases, they perform their functions with businesses operating in conditions of competition, and the assistance of competition law where it is necessary to

---

*   Prof. Dr., Directeur, Centre de droit de la consummation, Université Catholique de Louvain, Belgium.
1   W. Viscusi, J. Vernon, J. Harrington, *Economics of Regulation and Antitrust*, Lexington (Mass.), Heath and Company, 1992.
2   S. Breyer, *Regulation and its Reform*, Cambridge, Harvard University Press, 1982.
3   A. Kahn, *The Economics of Regulation: Principles and Institutions*, New York, Wiley and Sons, 2 vols, 1971.
4   P. Areeda, D. Turner, *Antitrust Law: An Analysis of Antitrust Principles and Their Application*, Boston-Toronto, Little, Brown & Company, vol. 1, 1978.
5   See e.g. S. Breyer, *supra* n. 2, at 156: '[T]he antitrust laws differ from classical regulation both in their aims and their methods'; at 157: '[A]ntitrust is more accurately contrasted with, rather than viewed as another form of, government regulation'; at 158: '[R]egulation is an alternative to antitrust'.

control or avoid the excessive accumulation of market power.[6] (b) In other instances, markets must be regulated. This involves an additional step: the intervention of public authorities where competition, assisted by competition law, is insufficient to produce satisfactory outcomes.[7]

On the basis of this analysis, it is possible to envisage a progression in public intervention along the following lines of analysis proposed by these authors. Normally, markets operate freely, that is without any government intervention. Competition sometimes leads firms to acquire market power. The assistance of competition law may then be required to ensure that satisfactory outcomes are still obtained. That assistance may not be deemed sufficient in the last set of circumstances. A public intervention in the form of regulation must then take place.

2 LOOKING AT CRITERIA

I then looked further into the criteria generally used by these authors to describe the opposition. I found successively eight criteria: the time at which regulatory or competition law obligations are applied (*ex ante*, *ex post facto*); the form used to express the obligations; the effect they have on freedom in the markets; their degree of precision (vague vs. precise); the circumstances in which they are imposed; their object; their direct or indirect character; and the objectives that they pursue.

In the sections ahead, I propose to submit these criteria to a critical analysis. Examples are taken from European law – but I imagine that American scholars could provide a similar analysis based on US antitrust law. The examples concerning regulation are taken from the directives adopted by the Council and the European Parliament in the sector of electronic communications. The reason for this choice is twofold. Firstly, I have in that area a certain understanding of

---

[6] See Breyer, *supra* n. 2, at 156: 'The first alternative – antitrust – typically accompanies the *absence* of regulation'. See also W. Viscusi, J. Vernon, J. Harrington, *supra* n. 1, at 53: 'In this section of the book we shall be concerned with the unregulated sector of the economy. That is, we shall consider industries that are *not* subject to governmental controls on product standards, prices, profits, or entry and exit. In other words, these are the industries in which competition is the primary mechanism that society relies upon to produce good economic results'.

[7] Viscusi, Vernon, Harrington, *supra* n. 6, at 295–6: 'Economic regulation typically refers to government-imposed restrictions on firm decisions over price, quantity, and entry and exit . . . When an industry is regulated, industry performance in terms of allocative and productive efficiency is co-determined by market forces and administrative processes'. A similar approach may be found in A. Kahn, *supra* n. 3, vol. 2, point 4. See also P. Areeda, D. Turner, *supra* n. 4, vol. 1, 134s.

the goals pursued by authorities.[8] Secondly, the rules adopted in that sector form a regulatory body which is called 'sector-specific regulation' and which corresponds to what is generally called 'regulation' on both sides of the Atlantic.

This contribution is only a comment on the main paper on this topic presented by another participant. As a result, I have maintained in the written text the informal tone that prevailed during the oral conversation. Avid readers may consult more academic pieces, if they wish to obtain more analysis on the subject at hand.[9]

3   TIME OF APPLICATION

In the literature, competition law is generally presented as being applied *ex post facto* whereas regulation involves intervention *ex ante*. In this context, a typical example of a competition law-based intervention would be an enquiry launched by the Commission after the adoption of exclusionary practices by a dominant firm. These practices fall under the prohibition laid down in Article 82 EC, according to which abuses by dominant firms may not be accepted in the internal market. By contrast, the directives adopted by the EU Council and Parliament in the electronic communications sector would provide a good example of how regulation works. These directives allow national regulatory authorities to introduce access related obligations before abusive practices are adopted by incumbent operators. In the framework of regulation, there is thus no need to await the commission of an abuse, in order to have the authority to impose obligations.

To test the criterion, it is worth asking whether instances may be found where competition law is designed and/or applied *ex ante* – and not *ex post facto* as suggested by the criterion. The answer is in the positive – yes, such instances do exist. For example, the European Merger Regulation provides that operations of concentration must be prohibited where they significantly impede effective competition in the internal market. These operations are to be

---

8   See P. Nihoul, P. Rodford, *EU Electronic Communications Law – Regulation and Competition in the European Telecommunications Market*, Oxford University Press, 2004.

9   P. Nihoul, *Les télécommunications en Europe – Concurrence ou organisation de marché*, Presses universitaires de Louvain, Louvain-la-Neuve, 2004, p. 464; P. Nihoul, 'European Telecommunications: A Real Departure from Regulation?', in G. Haibach (ed.), *Services of General Interest in the EU: Reconciling Competition and Social Responsibility*, European Institute of Public Administration, Maastricht, 1999, pp. 127–66; P. Nihoul, 'Norme, régulation et réforme des telecommunications', *Annales de droit*, 1998, No. 4, pp. 389–423; P. Nihoul, 'Convergence in European telecommunications – A case study on the relationship between regulation and competition (law)', *International Journal of Communications Law and Policy*, Issue 2, Winter 1998/1999, pp. 1–33.

examined before they take place, thus *ex ante*. Another example is provided by the regulations adopted by the Council, and by the Commission, pursuant to Article 81(3) EC. Typically, these regulations establish the conditions to be satisfied for undertakings to benefit from an exemption from the Article 81(3) EC prohibition directed at anticompetitive agreements. As they explain what conditions have to be fulfilled by undertakings in their future agreements, these regulations introduce *ex ante* obligations and proscriptions.

Conversely, one may wonder whether regulation always takes the form of *ex ante* intervention. Is it not possible to find examples of regulation adopted *ex post facto*? The answer again seems clear-cut. Examples may be taken from the sector of electronic communications. In this sector, it is not uncommon for national regulatory authorities to adopt decisions aimed at stopping unsatisfactory practices assumed by dominant operators.[10] In these instances, the decision intervenes after the practice has been adopted, although it is considered part of the regulatory body.

These examples show that competition law is not always *ex post facto* and regulation not always *ex ante*. The absence of a clear distinction probably reflects the complex nature of rules. Most of the time, rules are adopted to solve issues raised by past practices. At the same time, they are aimed at ensuring that these practices do not occur again. As they combine these two aspects, it is natural that they have a clear link with both the past and the present.

4 FORMULATION OF OBLIGATIONS

Another frequently mentioned criterion is the form given to obligations introduced by regulation or competition law. In the latter case, obligations are said to have a negative form – firms are prohibited from acting in certain specific ways (concluding an anticompetitive agreement, abusing a dominant position, and so on). By contrast, regulatory obligations are said to have a positive formulation – for instance a decision by a national regulatory authority that the firms placed under its control must reach a certain level of output and commit to put the product on the market at a given price.

Again, this distinction does not appear to be convincing, as positive formulations may also be found in competition law. A typical example is the obligation imposed on dominant firms to share essential facilities where the conditions

---

10   For instance, the French 'Autorité de regulation des telecommunications' (French regulatory authority for telecommunications) announced, on 4 November 2004, an intention to force mobile operators to decrease call termination tariffs by 36%. This intention followed a survey, from which it appeared that the existing tariffs were not in line with those that could be expected on a competitive market.

imposed by case law are fulfilled.[11] Conversely, negative formulations may be found in regulation: in the EU Electronic Communications Framework Directive,[12] for instance, the Council and the Parliament prohibit firms with significant market power from applying discriminatory terms and conditions to their customers (Article 10).

The difficulty in distinguishing between competition and regulation shows, in my opinion, that, wherever possible, discussion of concepts should not be based on formulations, which are often interchangeable.[13]

5   EFFECT ON FREEDOM

Another criterion mentioned by authors is the effect that regulation or competition (and competition law) have on freedom within the market. According to these authors, competition law enhances freedom, whereas regulation restricts the freedom given to businesses. This criterion again appears no more convincing than the previous ones. On the one hand, it may not be said that freedom is enhanced in the case of all undertakings where competition law is applied. Look at the essential facility doctrine,[14] in so far as it is accepted in Europe. This doctrine imposes severe obligations on dominant firms. It thus severely limits the freedom of these firms. On the other hand, the freedom of firms appears in some instances enhanced, rather than restricted, by regulatory obligations. Think of the exclusive rights earlier granted to national monopolies: these prerogatives had a positive effect on the freedom of their beneficiaries, in that the latter were protected against potential competitors.

As these examples show, speaking of freedom in connection with rules is often dangerous. Rules necessarily have an impact on the persons or the businesses they intend to regulate. Depending on the content of these rules, some persons and businesses are protected while others are subject to obligations. Freedom thus depends on which side the person or business finds itself.

---

[11]   Court of Justice of 6 April 1995, Joined cases C-241/91 P and C-242/91 P, *Radio Telefis Eireann (RTE) and Independent Television Publications Ltd (ITP) v Commission*, [1995] ECR I-00743; Court of Justice of 26 November 1998, Case C-7/97, *Bronner v Mediaprint and others*, [1998] ECR I-7791; Court of Justice of 29 April 2004, Case C-418/01, *IMS Health*, not yet officially reported.

[12]   European Parliament and Council Directive (EC) 2002/21 on a common regulatory framework for electronic communications networks and services (Framework Directive), OJ 2002 L108/33.

[13]   It is often possible to obtain a similar result, by using a positive or a negative formulation. For instance, 'leave the door open' induces approximately the same result as 'do not close the door'.

[14]   See references *supra* n. 11.

6 PRECISION

Another regularly mentioned difference is that competition law is general and vague, whereas regulation is detailed and precise. This criterion has some obvious merit, in view of the general formulation of Articles 81 and 82 EC. But this is only a first step analysis. The idea of a general formulation for competition rules cannot be maintained if one looks at the regulations or guidelines adopted by the European or national authorities in this area. To cite just one example, one cannot say that the Horizontal Merger Guidelines[15] recently adopted by the European Commission, or the motor vehicle distribution regulation,[16] adopted by the Commission, are particularly general, or vague.

The same remark may be made with respect to regulation. Some detailed, precise and technical rules may be found in some documents. But others contain general provisions, which are as abstract as any general competition law principles. In this regard, one may consider the Framework Directive adopted by the Council and Parliament in the field of electronic communications. This Directive contains general principles which are further detailed and implemented by other instruments.

As these examples show, generality and precision are only one stage in the design and formulation of rules: rules can be summarized in general principles and applied in detailed provisions – be they part of competition law or regulation.

7 CIRCUMSTANCES WHERE AUTHORITIES INTERVENE

Another alleged difference is that competition law is limited to specific circumstances (agreements between firms, abuses of dominant position, concentrations) whereas regulation may be more systematic: depending on the power entrusted to them, regulatory authorities may have the power to regulate just about everything in a given sector without having to wait, in order to apply the regulation, for firms to enter into agreements or to abuse a dominant position.

This argument is relevant, in so far as competition law is indeed bound to

---

[15] Guidelines on the assessment of horizontal mergers under the Council Regulation on the control of concentrations between undertakings, OJ 2004 C31/5.

[16] Commission Regulation (EC) 1400/2002 of 31 July 2002 on the application of Article 81(3) of the Treaty to categories of vertical agreements and concerted practices in the motor vehicle sector, OJ 2002 L203/30.

the circumstances mentioned above.[17] One may, however, wonder about the implications for the allegedly non-systematic character of competition law-based interventions. Anticompetitive agreements, abuses of dominant positions and undesirable concentrations feature moments in the growth of a firm. Firms grow either internally – in which case they may acquire market power at some point and then be subject to competition law. Or they grow externally, through agreements or concentrations – competition law will be applied in this context as well. In this light, competition rules cannot be seen as deprived of any systematic character. On the contrary, it appears to be carefully directed at all the strategies employed by firms in order to grow.

Conversely, regulatory authorities are rarely entrusted with a general power to regulate an entire business sector. Their interventions are generally limited to one or several issues raising concerns. As a result, they cannot be said to be exhaustive or systematic. Thus, in the new electronic communications regulatory framework, the Council and the Parliament have entrusted the national regulatory authorities with two specific missions: to ensure access to essential networks; and to organize the provision of a universal service.[18]

8   OBJECTS OF INTERVENTION

Competition law has to do with market power whereas regulation entails the imposition of market parameters such as the number of undertakings admitted on a market, the prices and the output – this is a feature which, according to the abovementioned authors, distinguishes the two bodies of rules. A difficulty with this position is that some EU decisions clearly show that under EU law, in some circumstances, competition authorities have the right to set the price against which goods must be provided;[19] to set the quantity that must be sold;[20] and to determine how many competitors are admissible on a single

---

[17]   As regards competition rules applicable to undertakings: anticompetitive agreements, abuse of dominant position, concentration.

[18]   See European Parliament and Council Directive (EC) 2002/21 on a common regulatory framework for electronic communications networks and services (Framework Directive), OJ 2002 L108/33.

[19]   See Commission Decision of 15 October 1975, not published; the order of the president of the ECJ of 22 October 1975, Joined Cases 109 and 114/75, *National Carbonising Company v Commission*, [1977] ECR 381, 1193; and Commission Decision 76/185/ECSC of 29 October 1975 adopting interim measures concerning the National Coal Board, National Smokeless Fuels Limited and the National Carbonizing Company Limited, OJ 1976 L35/6 (no English version).

[20]   See ECJ of 3 March 1974, Joined Cases 6 and 7-73, *Istituto Chemioterapico Italiano S.p.A. and Commercial Solvents Corporation v Commission*, [1974] ECR 223.

market.[21] Conversely, regulation often deals with market power. Thus, the EC Access Directive[22] contains provisions aimed at ensuring that access to networks is provided, in the electronic communications sector, to competitors, by firms with significant market power.

9 DIRECT OR INDIRECT INTERVENTION

An additional difference, according to these authors, is that competition law has an indirect character, whereas regulation operates directly on the market. Under this argument, competition law is seen as an instrument designed to address issues arising in the context where firms operate, and aimed at ensuring that that context (the market) functions correctly. Competition law, however, refrains from addressing direct instructions to firms, instructing them how much they have to sell and at what price. So they would argue, this is rather the object of regulation, which does not address the context but instead directly addresses instructions to firms.

Part of this argument was addressed earlier. There, we saw that competition authorities sometimes address very specific instructions regarding prices or output to firms in a dominant position. Similarly, it is still a moot question whether regulation always acts in a direct fashion. In many cases, this is far from being so. A classical example concerns the measures that regulatory authorities may take to determine the level of network investment which they want to induce in the electronic communications sector. Suppose that an authority finds the level of investment too low at any given time in a given region. One way for that authority to enhance the level is to allow network operators to increase tariffs for access to the infrastructure. As access tariffs rise, entrants have an incentive to build their own infrastructure. At the same time, network operators find it lucrative to give access to their facilities and, hence, increase the quality of existing networks to attract clients.

10 OBJECTIVES

A last difference, according to the classics, is that competition law pursues economic objectives whereas regulation deals with other goals. This criterion

---

21 See ECJ of 23 May 2000, Case C-209/98, *Entreprenørforeningens Affalds/Miljøsektion (FFAD) v Københavns Kommune*, [2000] ECR I-03743.

22 European Parliament and Council Directive (EC) 2002/19 on access to, and interconnection of, electronic communications networks and associated facilities (Access Directive) OJ 2002 L108/7.

has gained acceptance over the last years, as literature has flourished to convince governments and authorities that they should only be concerned with efficiency when applying competition laws whilst other objectives should be attained using other bodies of law, including regulation. It is impossible to predict whether that call for a narrowing of the goals generally assigned to competition rules will meet with success. In contrast, it is possible to consider that competition rules have been applied, so far, in a substantial number of countries, to support a broad range of objectives, which are not limited to efficiency.

These objectives encompass: the avoidance of excessive power in the hands of any given undertaking; the equality of access to important facilities; the realization of a common or internal market in the European Union; loyalty in transactions, particularly where dominant firms are involved; industrial policy. These objectives are general in nature and may be found in several decisions. Other more specific objectives can be traced to particular decisions, or particular groups of decisions.

An example of such a specific decision is the *Ford/Volkswagen* case,[23] which is described at length in the chapter presented by our colleague Maria M. Leitão Marques.[24] In that decision, the European Commission decided that the joint venture created by the two motor vehicle companies deserved an exemption under Article 81(3) EC. The exemption was granted in view of, amongst other things, the positive impact that the new vehicle to be developed jointly would have on research into less polluting vehicles, and in view of the investments to be made in a region where unemployment was high.

An example of a group of decisions seeking to realize non-efficiency-based objectives may be taken from the 'Failing Firm Defence'.[25] Under this theory, antitrust authorities may declare compatible with competition rules a concentration which would otherwise be prohibited. Pursuant to the theory, the operation may be accepted, in substance, where: the failing firm would likely not be able to meet its financial obligations in the near future; it would not be able to reorganize successfully; in the absence of an acquisition, the assets and activities of the firm would be lost. An interesting question is whether the theory is based on efficiency-related arguments. Chances are that the new firm emerging from the concentration will operate at lower costs. However, it

---

[23]   Commission Decision 93/49/EEC of 23 December 1992 relating to a proceeding pursuant to Article 85 of the EEC Treaty, *Ford/Volkswagen*, Case IV/33.814, OJ 1992 L20/22.

[24]   'Cooperative Networking: bridging the cooperation–concentration gap', this volume, Chapter 6, with Ana Abrunhosa.

[25]   See para. 5 of the US Horizontal Merger Guidelines, quoted above. See para. 89 and following of the EU Horizontal Merger Guidelines, also quoted above.

should be stressed that no cost-based condition is attached to the application of the theory. Thus, it does not have to be demonstrated that the acquiring firm will be able to lower costs as a result of the acquisition. One may thus deem that other considerations explain, at least partly, the reasons why a normally anticompetitive operation is deemed justified under the application of the so-called theory despite the anticompetitive effects it has on the market. One reason, at least in the European Union, might be that accepting the operation will save assets, and jobs, which would otherwise be lost.

A last set of examples may be taken from instruments implementing the EC provisions which introduce exceptions, or derogations, within the realm of competition law. In all these cases, competition authorities weigh the prescriptions of competition against other objectives, of a different nature. We have already mentioned the Ford/Volkswagen joint venture, where an anticompetitive agreement was held acceptable under Article 81(3) EC in view of the positive impact the project would have on the environment and on jobs. Similarly, the European competition authorities accept that practices adopted by dominant firms may not be deemed abusive where they are based on objective justifications that are not related to efficiency – for instance the safety of users.[26] In the same vein, Article 86(2) allows public undertakings and undertakings entrusted with services of general interest to escape the application of competition rules in so far as that is necessary for them to realize their mission. In the application of that provision, other values come into play and the competition authorities sometimes accept that they must take precedence over efficiency-based orientations.[27]

11 CONCLUSION

The conclusion is that a clear distinction between competition and regulation is not easy to make (and perhaps is not possible), where the distinction is discussed in general, abstract terms. A suggestion might be to address the topic in a narrower context (for example EU or US law) and in a specific legal area (for example the electronic communications markets). The discussion can then be based on a concrete sample of rules and applications.

---

[26] See ECJ of 2 March 1994, Case C-53/92 P, *Hilti AG v Commission*, [1994] ECR I-667.

[27] For a general discussion on this subject matter, see P. Nihoul, P. Rodford, *supra* n. 8, chapter 5.

PART V

Conclusion: the new thinking

11. Efficiency claims in EC competition law and sector-specific regulation

Damien Geradin*

I INTRODUCTION

Many competition lawyers and economists argue that the primary objective of competition law regimes is to promote economic efficiency.[1] Yet few of these regimes define what should be understood by economic efficiency. For instance, although this concept is referred to in an increasingly large number of regulations, guidelines, and so on, EC competition law does not offer any precise definition of economic efficiency. The problem is made more serious by the fact that economists do not necessarily agree on the meaning of efficiency and that, in a given proceeding, the economic consultants of both parties will often disagree over the efficiency or inefficiency of a given practice or behaviour.

This issue has become of considerable importance as economic analysis is now at the core of competition law analysis.[2] Economic analysis not only plays a role in determining the types of agreements/mergers that create competition law concerns but also the types of justification that can be used to justify such agreements/mergers. When asked to examine a restrictive agreement or a merger, the test to be performed by competition authorities essentially amounts to determining whether the negative effects of the agreement/transaction on competition are more than compensated for by 'efficiencies' taking the form of the production of new and/or better products, the realization of

* Member of the Brussels bar. Professor of Law and Director of the Institute for European Legal Studies, University of Liège, Professor and Director of the Global Competition Law Centre, College of Europe, Bruges (d.geradin@ulg.ac.be). I would also like to thank Nicolas Petit and David Henry for excellent research assistance. This chapter benefited from financial support provided by the PAI P4/04 granted by the Belgian State, Prime Minister's Office, Science Policy Programming.

1 See E. Gellhorn, W. Kovacic, *Law in a Nutshell: Antitrust Law and Economics*, West, 1994, p. 42.
2 See generally S. Bishop, D. Walker, *The Economics of EC Competition Law – Concepts, Application and Measurement*, 2nd edn, Sweet & Maxwell, 2002.

economies of scale or scope, and so on. Such a balancing test will not necessarily be easy, as parties to a proceeding will generally try to inflate the 'negative' or 'positive' effects of the agreement/merger in question. It should thus not come as a surprise that, in some recent documents, the Commission has tried to clarify which type of efficiencies can be legitimately claimed by private parties.

Efficiency claims are also made in the context of the control of market dominance. First, there are circumstances in which dominant firms will try to justify conduct that would otherwise be abusive if judged solely by efficiency considerations. As will be seen below, it is clear that some practices such as rebates or tying can generate efficiencies, although such efficiencies will not necessarily be taken into account by the Commission and the European Courts, which tend to consider such practices *per se* to be contrary to Article 82 of the Treaty. Market-opening reforms in network industries are based on the idea that State monopolies were 'inefficient' and that a competitive market structure would deliver better results in terms of lower prices, better quality and greater consumer satisfaction.[3] Efficiency claims are also made with reference to the regulatory strategies that need to be designed in order to control the market power of incumbents. For instance, while incumbents will claim that a given pricing methodology (for example, the efficient component pricing rule, or 'ECPR') should be adopted to maintain their incentives to invest, new entrants will say that another pricing methodology (for example, long-run incremental cost, or 'LRIC') is preferable because it facilitates entry on the market.[4]

Against this background, this chapter seeks to clarify the meaning, scope and validity of 'efficiency claims' in EC competition law, as well as the importance of efficiency considerations in sector-specific regulation. This chapter is divided into six parts. Following this introduction, Part II discusses the 'notions' of efficiency. The term 'notions' is written in the plural form because, as we will see, economic efficiency has several components which are not necessarily consistent with each other. Part II also explains that, among the different welfare standards used by economists, it is the 'consumer welfare' standard that EC competition law seeks to promote. Part III observes, however, that one significant difference between EC competition law and other competition law regimes is that economic efficiency is not the only objective to be taken into account by enforcement authorities. Promoting market integration is another central objective of EC competition law. Part IV

---

[3]   See D. Geradin (ed.), *The Liberalization of State Monopolies in the European Union and Beyond*, Kluwer Law International, 2000.

[4]   See D. Geradin, M. Kerf, *Controlling Market Power in Telecommunications: Antitrust vs. Sector-specific Regulation*, Oxford University Press, 2003, pp. 34–45.

reviews efficiency claims in the assessment of restrictive agreements and merger control. In particular, it tries to identify the main principles that apply to the assessment of efficiencies in the context of the application of Article 81(3) of the Treaty to restrictive agreements as well as under the new Merger Regulation. Part V reviews efficiency claims in the context of the control of market dominance. It first analyses efficiency claims under Article 82 of the Treaty, which prohibits abuses of a dominant position. It then examines whether efficiency considerations play an important role in the context of the regulation of network industries, which have been progressively opened to competition over the last 15 years. Finally, Part VI contains a brief conclusion.

II THE NOTIONS OF 'EFFICIENCY'

Neither EC competition law nor sector-specific regulation defines what has to be understood by an agreement or a practice that is 'economically efficient'. Perhaps a good starting point is to say that economic efficiency has three components.[5] Allocative efficiency corresponds to a situation where goods and services are allocated between consumers according to the prices they are willing to pay, and prices never exceed the marginal cost of production. Allocative efficiency is achieved under a situation of perfect competition since, by reducing its output, a given producer cannot affect the market price and thus has no interest in doing so.[6] By contrast, allocative *inefficiency* occurs where firms holding market power are able to affect prices by reducing their output, with the result that prices exceed marginal costs. Agreements or mergers that allow firms to increase their market power will thus tend to contribute to allocative inefficiency. Productive efficiency means that goods and services will be produced at the lowest possible cost. Output is maximized by using the most effective combination of inputs, which means that as little of society's wealth as possible is used in the production of the good or service concerned.[7] Finally, dynamic efficiency is achieved when producers constantly innovate and develop new products as part of their battle to gain market shares by attracting new customers. Competition is said to promote economic efficiency by increasing both allocative and productive efficiency, and by encouraging innovation.

One problem, however, is that these three components of efficiency are not necessarily consistent with each other and, in the assessment of a given

---

5   See R. J. van den Bergh, P. D. Camesasca, *European Competition Law and Economics*, Intersentia, 2001, pp. 5–6.

6   See Bishop and Walker, *supra* n. 2, pp. 20–21.

7   See R. Whish, *Competition Law*, Butterworths, 4th edn, 2001, p. 3.

agreement or behaviour, some tension may appear between them. For instance, mergers may contribute to the realization of economies of scale and scope, thereby allowing greater productive efficiency.[8] On the other hand, the merged entity might have increased market power and thus a growing ability to impose supracompetitive prices, which runs counter to allocative efficiency. The question will then be whether the cost savings realized by the merger will be passed on to customers, thereby neutralizing the price effects of greater market concentration, or whether these cost savings will only translate into higher profits for the merging firms. Similarly, while forcing a dominant firm to give access to 'essential facilities' may stimulate competition in a downstream market and thus contribute to allocative efficiency, mandatory access may also negatively affect the dominant firm's incentives to invest with the consequence of impeding dynamic efficiency.[9] In some access cases, both access seekers and the holder of the facility will claim that the goal they seek to achieve is to stimulate innovation. For instance, in the *Microsoft* case, the plaintiff (Sun Microsystems) argued that Microsoft's refusal to give it access to interoperability information prevented it and other competitors of Microsoft on the work group server market to innovate. Microsoft claimed that forcing it to disclose such information, which is protected by intellectual property rights, would ruin years of research and development efforts and negatively affect its incentives to innovate in the future.[10] Thus, enforcement authorities will often have to engage in a complex balancing test to determine what are the net efficiency gains of a given agreement or behaviour.

In light of the above, a key issue is the relative importance given to these different efficiency components in EC competition law. This issue is directly related to the welfare standard that is promoted by EC competition law. While economists have traditionally focused on 'social welfare',[11] EC competition law seems primarily to focus on 'consumer welfare'.[12] For instance, Article 81(3) specifically requires that consumers receive a 'fair share' of efficiency benefits. From that standpoint, allocative efficiency should be the preferred form of efficiency. Indeed, it more directly benefits consumers since, in a situation of allocative efficiency, prices are equal to marginal costs. As pointed out by Bishop and Walker, this implies that 'mere producer surplus as a result of

---

[8]   See Van den Bergh and Camesasca, *supra* n. 5, p. 5.
[9]   See E. Elhauge, 'Defining Better Monopolization Standards', *Stanford Law Review* 253, 2003, p. 56.
[10]   See Commission Decision of 24 March 2004, Case COMP/C-3/37.792 *Microsoft*, at recital 709, not yet officially reported.
[11]   See Bishop and Walker, *supra* n. 2, p. 24.
[12]   Ibid.

increases in efficiency is not enough'.[13] However, the same authors rightly observe that productive efficiency may also generate benefits for consumers since, in the absence of market power, cost reductions will be passed on to the consumers in the form of lower prices.[14] Moreover, enforcement authorities should avoid focusing on short-term consumer welfare, as such an approach (which would treat any profits created by firms with suspicion), could damage the incentives of firms to invest.[15] Indeed, it is clear that firms invest and innovate in the expectation of earning profits by doing so.[16] Preventing such profits from being made could thus discourage firms from competing dynamically and consequently delay or even render impossible the development of new or improved products or services.

III TENSION BETWEEN EFFICIENCY AND OTHER OBJECTIVES OF EC COMPETITION LAW

As noted earlier, one significant difference between EC competition law and other competition law regimes is that economic efficiency is not the only objective to be taken into account by enforcement authorities.

First, it is widely admitted that another central objective of EC competition law is to promote economic integration between the different Member States.[17] The overarching goal of the EC Treaty is indeed the creation of a single European market where all national barriers to intra-Community trade are abolished.[18] However, this objective would be compromised if, for instance, undertakings were to conclude agreements designed to partition markets along national lines. As the Court of Justice pointed out in *Consten and Grundig*:

> an agreement between a producer and a distributor which might tend to restore the national divisions in trade between Member States might be such as to frustrate the most fundamental object of the Community. The Treaty, whose preamble and content aim at abolishing the barriers between States ... could not allow undertakings to reconstruct such barriers. Article [81(1)] is designed to pursue this aim, even in the case of agreements between undertakings placed at different levels in the economic process.[19]

---

13   Ibid.
14   Ibid. at p. 26.
15   Ibid.
16   See Elhauge, *supra* n. 9.
17   See, e.g., C. D. Ehlermann, 'The Contribution of EC Competition Policy to the Single Market', 29 *Common Market Law Review*, 1992, p. 257.
18   See Article 3(c) of the EC Treaty.
19   Court of Justice of 13 July 1966, Cases 56 & 58/64, *Consten and Grundig v Commission*, [1966] ECR 299.

In this regard, one of the largest fines ever imposed by the Commission on a single undertaking can be found in *Commission v. Volkswagen*, where Volkswagen was condemned to pay 102 million euros as a penalty for its attempt to prevent importation of its cars from Italy to Germany and Austria.[20] Although, as will be seen below, the objective of market integration may sometimes lead the Commission to prohibit restrictions that generate efficiencies, there is no real conflict between the promotion of economic efficiency and market integration. Indeed, the goal of market integration is also rooted in the idea of efficiency. First, the creation of an internal market stimulates competition between producers and thus contributes to allocative efficiency. Market integration also enlarges the size of the market and thus allows firms to expand their production and realize economies of scale, thereby promoting productive efficiency. Finally, the creation of an integrated market facilitates the dissemination of technologies across Member States and may thus stimulate innovation, thereby promoting dynamic efficiency.

In addition, EC competition law is on occasion influenced by other policy considerations, such as industrial policy, the protection of small and medium sized business, social cohesion, cultural diversity, and so on.[21] In this regard, it is interesting to note that the Commission Guidelines on the application of Article 81(3) of the Treaty, which are discussed below, specify that '[g]oals pursued by other Treaty provisions [that is, other than Article 81] can be taken into account to the extent that they can be subsumed under the four conditions of Article 81(3)'.[22] In addition, in the area of merger control, commentators have tried to explain some Commission decisions as being heavily influenced by industrial policy considerations.[23] Similarly, the protection of small and medium sized business and social cohesion can easily be perceived in the area of State aid where special instruments have been adopted to achieve such purposes.[24]

---

[20]   Commission Decision 2001/711/EC of 29 June 2001, *Volkswagen AG,* Case COMP/F-2/36.693, OJ 2001 L262/14.

[21]   See M. Motta, *Competition Policy – Theory and Practice*, Cambridge University Press, 2004, p. 15. Motta stresses that on various occasions, the Commission has been lenient with respect to crisis cartels and joint ventures that clearly had an anticompetitive effect. These agreements were nonetheless cleared by the Commission on the ground that they would lead to substantial creation of jobs or to a reduction in job losses.

[22]   See Commission, 'Guidelines on the application of Article 81(3) of the Treaty', OJ 2004 C101/97 at para. 42.

[23]   This is particularly significant in the *Mannesmann/Vallourec/Ilva* decision, where a concentration that had a real potential anticompetitive effect was cleared for reasons of this nature. See Commission Decision of 31 January 1994, *Mannesmann/Vallourec/Ilva*, Case IV/M.315, OJ 1994 L102/15.

[24]   See Commission Regulation 70/2001 of 12 January 2001 on the application

IV EFFICIENCY CLAIMS IN THE ASSESSMENT OF RESTRICTIVE AGREEMENTS AND MERGER CONTROL

In this part, I successively review the treatment of efficiency claims in restrictive agreements (section 1) and merger control (section 2). From a general standpoint, one can say that efficiencies are generally used by undertakings as a justification for the conclusion of an agreement that falls under Article 81(1) or a merger that has a Community dimension. The duty of the parties is thus to show that the negative effects of the agreement/merger on competition are more than compensated for by pro-competitive efficiencies.

1 Efficiency Claims in Restrictive Agreements

Reliance on efficiencies as a source of justification for restrictive agreements can implicitly be found in the first positive condition of Article 81(3) of the Treaty, which requires that the agreement in question contributes 'to improving the production or distribution of goods or to promoting technical or economic progress'. Thus, this provision requires parties seeking an exemption to demonstrate that the agreement in question will generate some productive or dynamic efficiencies. Over the years, the Commission, supported by the European Court of Justice (the ECJ), has accepted that an extremely wide range of benefits could be regarded as fulfilling this condition.[25]

Over the last few years, the Commission has, however, adopted several regulations and guidelines discussing, *inter alia*, how efficiency claims should be assessed in the context of Article 81(3) in a variety of categories of horizontal and vertical agreements. Although they tend to deal with rather distinct situations, these new instruments share at least two characteristics. The first is that Article 81 should only apply to agreements between firms holding some degree of market power. It is indeed obvious that an agreement between two firms holding a 5 per cent market share is much less likely to raise competition

---

of Articles 87 and 88 of the EC Treaty to State aid to small and medium-sized enterprises, OJ 2001 L10/33. See also Communication from the Commission, Community Guidelines on State Aid for Rescuing and Restructuring Firms in Difficulty, OJ 2004 C244/2 at para. 8: 'The provision of rescue or restructuring aid to firms in difficulty may only be regarded as legitimate subject to certain conditions. It may be justified, for instance, by social or regional policy considerations, by the need to take into account the beneficial role played by small and medium-sized enterprises (SMEs) in the economy or, exceptionally, by the desirability of maintaining a competitive market structure when the demise of firms could lead to a monopoly or to a tight oligopolistic situation.'

25   See J. Faull, A. Nikpay, *The EC Law of Competition*, Oxford University Press, 1999, pp. 303–10.

concerns than an agreement between two firms that hold a 40 per cent market share. To translate this observation into concrete tests, the new block exemption regulations automatically exempt agreements where the combined market share of the parties on the relevant market(s) is below a predetermined threshold. The second is that these instruments tend to attach much greater importance to economic analysis. This is, of course, illustrated by the weight given to the concept of market power, but also by the Commission's emphasis that alleged efficiencies must be clearly substantiated and must precisely show the benefits (for example, in terms of cost reductions) that will be generated, and so on. In other words, the burden of proof placed on parties invoking efficiencies is now quite high.

Hereafter, I provide an overview of these different instruments. For the sake of clarity, I draw a distinction between horizontal restrictions (subsection a) and vertical restrictions (subsection b) given that these two forms of restraints tend to raise different competition law concerns and rather distinct issues when it comes to assessing efficiencies.[26] Horizontal agreements involve restrictions between firms that operate at the same level in the production/distribution chain. Such agreements are able to create market power where none previously existed and thus generate serious risks of price increases.[27] Parties should, however, be able to justify such agreements by showing that they generate significant productive and dynamic efficiencies, such as the realization of economies of scale or the development of new products. Vertical agreements involve restrictions between firms involved at different levels in the production/distribution chain. Unlike horizontal agreements, such agreements do not create market power where none previously existed.[28] On the contrary, since each party benefits if the other party lowers its prices, vertical agreements tend to push towards price reductions. Vertical agreements will, however, often contain clauses which may have anticompetitive effects. As for horizontal restrictions, parties will generally be allowed to show that such anticompetitive effects are outweighed by the efficiencies generated by the agreement. However, unlike the case of horizontal agreements, such efficiencies will not generally consist in production cost savings or in the development of new products, but rather will take 'the form of better coordination of price reductions or the realization of mutually beneficial investments that boost consumer demand'.[29]

---

[26]   See D. Ridyard, 'The Commission's Notice on Article 81(3): An Economic Assessment of the Efficiency Defence', in Geradin (ed.), *Modernisation and Enlargement: Two Major Challenges for EC Competition Law*, Intersentia (forthcoming, 2005).

[27]   Ibid.

[28]   Ibid.

[29]   Ibid.

After this separate examination of horizontal and vertical restrictions (subsections a and b), I review the Commission Guidelines on the application of Article 81(3) of the EC Treaty (subsection c). I then briefly review the issue of efficiencies in the new Technology Transfer Block Exemption and its accompanying guidelines (subsection d). Finally, I identify a list of ten principles that will generally apply to the review of efficiencies invoked in the context of the assessment of a restrictive agreement under Article 81(3) (subsection e).

a) Horizontal restrictions

Horizontal agreements can be concluded with the object of restricting competition. This is, for instance, the case of price-fixing or market-sharing agreements. Such agreements are subject to a *per se* rule pursuant to which they will be declared incompatible with Article 81 without possible (yet unlikely) economic benefits being examined. The vast majority of horizontal agreements, however, do not have the object of restricting competition, but they may nevertheless have some anticompetitive effects. These agreements (often referred to as 'cooperation agreements') will be subject to a more detailed analysis whereby their pro-competitive effects will be weighed against the anticompetitive effects they may generate.

In order to avoid receiving notifications of too many standard and relatively harmless cooperation agreements, the Commission adopted two block exemption regulations: Regulation 417/85 on the application of Article 85(3) of the Treaty to categories of specialization agreements[30] and Regulation 418/85 on the application of Article 85(3) of the Treaty to categories of research and development agreements.[31] In November 2000, these two block exemption regulations were replaced by Commission Regulation 2658/2000 on the application of Article 81(3) of the Treaty to categories of specialization agreements and Regulation 2659/2000 on the application of Article 81(3) of the Treaty to categories of research and development agreements.[32] The preambles of these regulations explicitly refer to the efficiencies that can be generated by such agreements.

---

[30]   OJ 1985 L53/1.

[31]   OJ 1985 L53/5.

[32]   Commission Regulation 2658/2000 of 29 November 2000 on the application of Article 81(3) of the Treaty to categories of specialization agreements, OJ 2000 L304/3; Commission Regulation 2659/2000 of 29 November 2000 on the application of Article 81(3) of the Treaty to categories of research and development agreements OJ 2000 L304/7. See N. Jalabert-Doury, 'European and International Competition: the Reform of EC Rules on Horizontal Agreements', 2 *International Business Law Journal*, 2001, p. 203; F. Moreau, *Les accords de coopération en droit communautaire de la concurrence*, 19 Semaine Juridique – Entreprise et Affaires 6–11, 10 May 2001.

Recital 8 of Regulation 2658/2000 provides that:

> Agreements on specialisation in production generally contribute to improving the production or distribution of goods, because the undertakings concerned can concentrate on the manufacture of certain products and thus operate more efficiently and supply the products more cheaply. Agreements on specialisation in the provision of services can also be said to generally give rise to similar improvements. It is likely that, given effective competition, consumers will receive a fair share of the resulting benefit.

Similarly, Recital 10 of Regulation 2659/2000 provides that:

> Cooperation in research and development and in the exploitation of the results generally promotes technical and economic progress by increasing the dissemination of know-how between the parties and avoiding duplication of research and development work, by stimulating new advances through the exchange of complementary know-how, and by rationalising the manufacture of the products or application of the processes arising out of research and development.

These regulations were accompanied by the Commission Guidelines on the applicability of Article 81 of the EC Treaty to horizontal cooperation agreements.[33] This document discusses the various forms of efficiencies which will be admitted as proper justification for benefiting from the Article 81(3) exemption.

In its section entitled 'Basic Principles', the Commission states the general requirements that will apply to the assessment of efficiencies in the context of Article 81(3). In doing so, it goes through the four conditions imposed under that provision. As far as the first condition is concerned (that is, the requirement that the agreement must improve 'the production or distribution of goods or to promote technical or economic progress'), the Commission states that:

- The efficiencies to be taken into account include both 'static' and 'dynamic' efficiencies;
- Most efficiencies stem from the combination and integration of different skills or resources; and
- Efficiency claims must be substantiated; the Commission does not take into account cost savings that arise from output reduction, market sharing, or from the mere exercise of market power.[34]

In order for the other conditions of Article 81(3) to be fulfilled, the Guidelines

---

[33] Commission, Guidelines on the applicability of Article 81 to horizontal cooperation agreements, OJ 2001 C3/2 ('Horizontal Guidelines').

[34] Ibid. at para. 32.

also require that the efficiencies have to favour not only the parties to the agreements but also consumers (the principle of consumer 'pass-on'); the restrictions of competition must be necessary to achieve the economic benefits (in the sense that there should be no less restrictive means to achieve the same benefits); and the agreement in question must not eliminate competition.[35]

Regulation 2658/2000 and Regulation 2659/2000 respectively exempt production agreements and R&D agreements which fulfil certain conditions and do not contain hard core restrictions, provided that the combined market share of the parties in the affected market(s) does not exceed 25 per cent for R&D agreements and 20 per cent for production agreements.[36] There is no real explanation as to why these precise threshold percentages have been chosen. Unavoidably, there is some degree of arbitrariness in the selection of a precise percentage. In any event, agreements that exceed these thresholds will not necessarily be declared incompatible with Article 81. Simply, they will not be automatically exempted. The parties to the agreement have to demonstrate that the four conditions of Article 81(3) are met. The same is true for horizontal agreements which are not covered under the 'safe harbours' provided by Regulations 2658/2000 and 2659/2000, such as purchasing agreements, commercialization agreements, agreement on standards, and environmental agreements.

The developments that follow briefly summarize the main forms of efficiencies mentioned by the Commission in its Guidelines. For reasons of space, I focus on the four main forms of horizontal agreements, namely R&D agreements, production agreements, purchasing agreements, and commercialization agreements:

- R&D agreements: these agreements often bring about economic benefits by means of cost savings and cross-fertilization of ideas and experience, which result in improved or new products and technologies being placed on the market more rapidly than in the absence of the agreement.[37] The Guidelines specify that if considerable market power is created or strengthened by the cooperation (that is, when the 25 per cent threshold is (largely) exceeded), the parties have to show 'significant' benefits in carrying out joint R&D, a 'quicker' launch and other efficiencies.[38] In the case of innovation, the combination of the only two existing poles of

---

[35]   Ibid. at paras 34–36.
[36]   See Article 4 of Regulation 2659/2000, *supra* n. 32 and Article 4 of Regulation 2658/2000, *supra* n. 32.
[37]   See Horizontal Guidelines, *supra* n. 33, at para. 68.
[38]   Ibid. at para. 69.

research will not be exempted, as this risks eliminating competition in respect of the products or technologies concerned.[39]

• Production agreements: such agreements will generally generate efficiencies taking the form of economies of scale or scope or better production technologies. Where the 20 per cent market share threshold is exceeded, the agreement will not be automatically exempted. Efficiencies which only benefit the parties or cost savings that are caused by output reduction or market allocation will not be taken into account.[40] Agreements that give the parties considerable market power will only be justified when 'high' efficiency gains outweigh the negative effect on the market structure.[41] Agreements that lead to a high commonality of costs will be examined suspiciously.[42] Moreover, when the cooperation relates to an important intermediate product, account should also be taken of the spillover effects the agreement may have on the downstream market.[43]

• Purchasing agreements: the Guidelines state that such agreements can generate efficiencies, such as economies of scale in ordering or transportation, which may outweigh the restrictive effects they generate.[44] If the parties together hold significant buying or selling power, the question of efficiencies has to be examined very carefully.[45] When examining whether an agreement is likely to eliminate competition, the assessment must cover both buying and selling markets.[46] The combined market share of the parties will be examined in the light of mitigating factors, such as countervailing power of suppliers on the purchasing markets or potential entry on the selling markets.

• Commercialization agreements: the Guidelines explain that agreements leading to price fixing can generally not be justified, unless it is proved essential for the integration of other marketing functions and this integration will generate substantial efficiencies.[47] The size of the efficiencies will depend, *inter alia,* on the importance of the joint selling structure for the overall cost structure of the product concerned.[48] Claimed efficiencies must be demonstrated. They should not be savings

---

39 Ibid. at para. 71.
40 Ibid. at para. 103.
41 Ibid. at para. 107.
42 Ibid. at para. 111.
43 Ibid.
44 Ibid. at para. 132.
45 Ibid.
46 Ibid. at para. 134.
47 Ibid. at para. 151.
48 Ibid.

resulting from the elimination of costs that are normally part of the competitive process (for example, elimination of transport costs due to customer allocation), but rather must result from an integration of the parties' logistical systems.[49]

The above discussion helps us to identify some basic standards and principles that need to be taken into account when assessing efficiency claims in the context of horizontal agreements. First, it is clear that different types of cooperation will generate different types of efficiencies. Different types of efficiencies will thus be admitted by enforcement authorities depending on the nature and content of horizontal agreements. Second, in line with the economic approach pursued by the Commission, the Guidelines clearly suggest that the higher the degree of market power, the higher the need for the parties to demonstrate the presence of substantial efficiencies (this is often referred to as the 'sliding scale' approach). There is thus a clear connection between the degree of market power and the significance of the efficiencies that must be demonstrated by the parties. Third, the Guidelines make clear that the alleged efficiencies must 'outweigh' the restrictions imposed in horizontal agreements. This test seems to be stricter than the test applied by the ECJ in its case law, pursuant to which the objective advantages generated by an agreement must 'compensate' for the negative effects that the agreement imposes on the structure of competition.[50] Finally, the Commission makes clear that the efficiencies must be 'demonstrated'. Vague references to potential benefits of a given restriction will not be taken into account. In practice, this means that the parties will have to produce clear evidence of the efficiencies generated by the restrictions that stem from an agreement.

b) Vertical restrictions
During the 1980s and 1990s, much was written on the law and economics of vertical restrictions.[51] There was indeed a general feeling among commentators

---

49   Ibid. at para. 152.

50   See Case 56 & 58/64, *Consten and Grundig, supra* note 19.

51   See J. Baker, 'Recent Developments that Challenge Chicago School Views', 58 *Antitrust Law Journal* 645 (1989); P. Rey, J. Tirole, 'The Logic of Vertical Restraints', 76 *American Economic Review* 921 (1986); W. Comanor, 'Vertical Price Fixing, Vertical Market Restrictions and the New Antitrust Policy', 98 *Harvard Law Review* 983 (1985); R. L. Steiner, 'The Nature of Vertical Restraints', 30 *The Antitrust Bulletin* 143–97 (1985); R. Posner, 'The Next Step in Antitrust Treatment of Restricted Distribution: Per Se Legality', 48 *University of Chicago Law Review* 6 (1981); B. Klein, R. Crawford, A. Alchian, 'Vertical Integration, Appropriable Rents and the Competitive Contracting Process', 21 *Journal of Law and Economics* (1978), p. 297; R. Bork, *The Antitrust Paradox – A Policy at War with Itself*, Basic Books (1978), Chapter 13.

that the block exemption regulations adopted by the Commission were excessively rigid and formalistic and were thus poorly in line with economic
theory.[52] In fact, the economic literature tends to describe vertical restraints as
useful remedies to address a series of market failures. Economists thus see
such restraints as generally quite benign.

In an effort to rationalize and modernize its policy on vertical restrictions,
the Commission adopted Regulation 2790/1999 on the application of Article
81(3) to categories of vertical agreements and concerted practices,[53] which
replaced three previous exemptions.[54] This new regulation followed a new,
economically-oriented approach, which concentrates on two essential parameters, namely the nature of the vertical restrictions and the degree of market
power involved. The second element is particularly central.[55] It is indeed obvious that with respect to vertical restraints serious competition concerns only

---

[52]   See B. E. Hawk, 'System Failure, Vertical Restraints and EC Competition
Law', 32 *Common Market Law Review* 973 (1995); D. Deacon, *Vertical Restraints
under EU Competition Law: New Directions*, Fordham Corporate Law Institute (1995),
307; L. Gyselen, 'Vertical Restraints in the Distribution Process: Strength and
Weaknesses of the Free Rider Rationale under EEC Competition Law', 21 *Common
Market Law Review* (1984), p. 648.

[53]   See Commission Regulation 2790/1999 of 22 December 1999 on the application of Article 81(3) of the Treaty to categories of vertical agreements and concerted
practices, OJ 1999 L336/21. Generally, on Regulation 2790/1999, see S. Bishop, D.
Ridyard, L. Peeperkorn, 'EC vertical restraints guidelines: effects-based or per se
policy?', 23 *European Competition Law Review* (2002), p. 35; A. Schaub, *Vertical
restraints: key points and issues under the new EC block exemption regulation*, Annual
Proceedings of the Fordham Corporate Law Institute (2001), p. 201; M. Hughes, C.
Foss, K. Ross, 'The economic assessment of vertical restraints under UK and EC
competition law', 22 *European Competition Law Review* (2001), p. 424; S. C. Salop,
Analysis of foreclosure in the EC guidelines on vertical restraints, Annual Proceedings
of the Fordham Corporate Law Institute (2001), p. 17; R. Subiotto, F. Amato, 'The
Reform of the European Competition Policy Concerning Vertical Restraints', 69(1)
Antitrust Law Journal 147 (2001); R. Boscheck, 'The EU policy reform on vertical
restraints: an economic perspective', 23(4) *World Competition* 3 (2000); F. Bortolotti,
'The Revision of the Block Exemptions on Vertical Restraints: A Critique to the
Commission's Market Share Approach', 2 *International Business Law Journal* 207
(1999).

[54]   Commission Regulations 1983/83 (OJ 1983 L173/1), 1984/83 (OJ 1983
L173/5), and 4017/88 (OJ 1988 L359/46).

[55]   See recital 7 of Regulation 2790/1999, *supra* n. 53 ('The likelihood that such
efficiency-enhancing effects will outweigh any anti-competitive effects due to restrictions contained in vertical agreements depends on the degree of market power of the
undertakings concerned and, therefore, on the extent to which those undertakings face
competition from other suppliers of goods or services regarded by the buyer as interchangeable or substitutable for one another, by reason of the products' characteristics,
their prices and intended use').

arise when interbrand competition is restricted. Thus, the first question to be addressed when examining vertical restraints is whether there is significant market power at the production or retail levels, or both. As in the case of horizontal agreements, Regulation 2790/1999 introduces a presumption of legality of vertical agreements concluded by operators that do not hold more than 30 per cent of the relevant market(s) provided that such agreements do not contain a number of prohibited clauses (for example, resale price maintenance or absolute territorial protection).[56]

Recital 6 of Regulation 2790/1999 explicitly refers to the fact that vertical restrictions are able to generate efficiencies:

> Vertical agreements of the category defined in this Regulation can improve economic efficiency within a chain of production or distribution by facilitating better coordination between the participating undertakings; in particular, they can lead to a reduction in the transaction and distribution costs of the parties and to an optimization of their sales and investment levels.

The most relevant document when it comes to assessing efficiency claims in vertical agreements is the Commission Guidelines on vertical restraints.[57] Indeed, these Guidelines contain a detailed discussion of the positive effects that may be generated by vertical restrictions.[58] The main categories of efficiencies that can be generated by such restrictions include:

- Solving a 'free rider' problem: When several firms compete for the distribution of a given product or service, one distributor may free ride on the commercial efforts of another operator.[59] For instance, a distributor that makes a major newspaper marketing campaign for a given product will not only increase its sales of this product, but also the sales of its competitors. Instead of investing in their own marketing campaigns, some distributors may thus decide to free ride on the promotional efforts of other distributors. Similarly, a distributor that invests

---

56 See Article 3.

57 Commission notice – Guidelines on Vertical Restraints, OJ C 291 of 13 October 2000, pp. 1–44.

58 With respect to efficiencies, paragraph 115 of the Guidelines provides: 'It is important to recognise that vertical restraints often have positive effects by, in particular, promoting non-price competition and improved quality of services. When a company has no market power, it can only try to increase its profits by optimising its manufacturing or distribution processes. In a number of situations vertical restraints may be helpful in this respect since the usual arm's length dealings between the supplier and buyer, determining only price and quantity of a certain transaction, can lead to a sub-optimal level of investments'.

59 Ibid. at para. 116.

substantial sums in the creation of a showroom will attract customers who visit its showroom to obtain information about the products in question but who may then buy such products from the distributor offering the best price. In such situations, there is thus a clear market failure, as distributors are not able to appropriate all the benefits of their investments. This market failure will in turn reduce incentives to invest in demand-increasing pre-sales services. The Guidelines acknowledge that such problems may be solved through vertical restrictions taking the form of the granting of an exclusive right to distribute products in a given geographic area.[60]

- Solving the so-called 'hold-up' problem: In some circumstances, the buyer or the seller has to make some client-specific investments, such as for instance the building of certain facilities or the purchasing of certain equipment. Such investments may, however, be risky as they have the effect of rendering the investor dependent on the other contracting party.[61] This is particularly the case when the investment requires substantial sunk costs. Because of this hold-up problem,[62] the investor may thus not commit to the necessary investments unless the other party is prepared to enter into a vertical agreement, such as a long-term supply contract, which will guarantee that it will be able to amortize its investment over a sufficiently long period of time.[63]

The above examples illustrate that vertical restrictions will often be used to correct market failures which risk preventing certain categories of demand-increasing investments.[64] Thus, unlike efficiencies claimed in the context of horizontal agreements, efficiencies generated by vertical restrictions will not necessarily be linked with clearly identifiable benefits, such as cost reductions or increased output, but will contribute to the better functioning of distribution markets. However, as outlined in the Guidelines, vertical restrictions may also generate additional efficiencies that are perhaps more in line with the efficiencies found in horizontal agreements, such as the realization of economies of

---

[60] Ibid.
[61] Ibid.
[62] Ibid.
[63] Ibid.
[64] Interestingly, the same type of logic is often used to justify certain forms of State aid. For instance, aid to research and development will be justified by the fact that it is impossible for firms investing in research to capture all the benefits of that research. These firms will create externalities and thus have a negative incentive to invest in research activities. In order to correct this market failure, which could lead to under-investment in research and development activities, it is considered efficient for public authorities to subsidize such activities.

scale in distribution or the increased attractiveness of a product to the final consumer which may be created by a certain measure of uniformity and quality standardization observed by the distributors.[65]

Although the vertical restrictions regime brings significant improvements, it is, however, subject to question whether it is fully in line with economic theory. Van den Bergh and Camesasca, for instance, point to the fact that economic theory does not support a *per se* prohibition of resale price maintenance or of absolute territorial protection.[66] Economic theory teaches that different types of restraints tend to pursue the same goal and therefore may be used as substitutes. Both vertical price restraints and the allocation of exclusive territories can be used to deal with the free rider problem.[67] There is thus no reason to subject these restraints to a treatment that is different from that of other vertical restraints designed to respond to free riding. What matters in fact is not the form of a restriction, but its true impact on the conditions of competition. A true economics-based approach would thus focus on the existence of market power at one or both levels of the industry.[68] If no market power can be identified, it is unlikely that the above restrictions will create anticompetitive effects. The disconnect between the EC legal regime and economic analysis can probably be explained by the different objectives that influence EC competition law analysis.[69] Policy makers may, for instance, worry about the effects of minimum vertical price fixing on retail prices. Similarly, while it may be a source of efficiencies, absolute territorial protection goes against the objective of creating a single European market.

---

[65]   Guidelines on vertical restraints, at para. 116.

[66]   Van den Bergh, Camesasca, *supra* n. 5, pp. 241 et seq. See also Bishop, Walker, *supra* n. 2, p. 167 ('The concept of hard-core vertical restrictions has no corollary in economics: the competitive effects of vertical restraints need to be assessed on the facts of the particular case').

[67]   Van den Bergh, Camesasca, *supra* n. 5, p. 248.

[68]   Ibid. at 242. The Commission seems generally to agree with this fact. As it noted in its Green Paper on vertical restraints: 'The heated debate among economists concerning vertical restraints has calmed somewhat and a consensus is emerging. Vertical restraints are no longer regarded as per se suspicious or per se pro-competitive. Economists are less willing to make sweeping statements. Rather, they rely more on the analysis of the facts of the case in question. However, one element stands out: the importance of market structure in determining the impact of vertical restraints. The fiercer is inter-brand competition, the more likely are the pro-competitive and efficiency effects to outweigh any anti-competitive effects of vertical restraints. Anti-competitive effects are only likely where inter-brand competition is weak and there are barriers to entry at either producer or distributor level.' See Commission, Green Paper on Vertical Restraints in EC Competition Policy, 1997, available at http://europa.eu.int/comm/competition/antitrust/96721en_en.pdf.

[69]   Ibid. at 248.

Conclusion

c) The Commission Guidelines on the application of Article 81(3)

In addition to the various guidelines designed to clarify the content of block exemption regulations, the Commission in April 2004 released its Guidelines on the application of Article 81(3) of the Treaty.[70] These Guidelines are one of the set of guidelines issued by the Commission following the adoption of Regulation 1/2003 on the implementation of the competition rules laid down in Articles 81 and 82 of the Treaty.[71] As a result of the suppression of the notification system, firms will now have to self-assess their own agreements which may fall under Article 81 of the Treaty. In addition, national competition authorities and national courts will now be entitled to apply Article 81(3) of the Treaty.[72] The Commission thus felt it was important to clarify its interpretation of the conditions that need to be complied with to allow an agreement to benefit from the exception contained in Article 81(3).

These Guidelines on Article 81(3) represent a helpful codification of the current ECJ case law, although some commentators have argued that these Guidelines contain novel interpretations.[73] In this regard, the Commission itself acknowledges that the Guidelines go beyond a mere recording of the existing case law when it says that it 'intends to explain its policy with regard to issues that have not been dealt with in the case-law, or that are subject to interpretation'.[74]

Two general remarks should be made before examining the content of these Guidelines.

The first one is that these Guidelines examine both horizontal and vertical restrictions under the same roof. As pointed out by Ridyard, it is subject to

---

[70] Commission, Guidelines on the application of Article 81(3) of the Treaty, OJ 2004 C101/97. See also P. H. H. Lugard, L. Hancher, 'Honey, I Shrunk the Article! A Critical Assessment of the Commission's Notice on Article 81(3) of the EC Treaty', 25(7) *European Competition Law Review* (2004), p. 410; L. Kjølbye, 'The new Commission Guidelines on the application of Article 81(3): an economic approach to Article 81', 25(9) *European Competition Law Review* (2004), p. 566.

[71] See Commission Notice on cooperation within the Network of Competition Authorities, OJ 2004 C101/43; Commission Notice on the cooperation between the Commission and the courts of the EU Member States in the application of Articles 81 and 82 EC, OJ 2004 C101/54; Commission Notice on the handling of complaints by the Commission under Articles 81 and 82 of the EC Treaty, OJ 2004 C101/65 of 27; Commission Notice on informal guidance relating to novel questions concerning Articles 81 and 82 of the EC Treaty that arise in individual cases (guidance letters), OJ 2004 C101/78; Commission Notice – Guidelines on the effect on trade concept contained in Articles 81 and 82 of the Treaty, OJ 2004 C101/81.

[72] See Articles 5 and 6 of Council Regulation 1/2003, OJ 2003 L1/1.

[73] See F. Montag, T. Janssens, 'Article 81(3) in the Context of Modernisation – A Lawyer's View', in Geradin (ed.), *supra* n. 26.

[74] See Commission guidelines, *supra* n. 70, at para. 7.

question whether the Commission should have made a distinction between these two types of restrictions, which, as noted above, generate rather different types of efficiencies.[75] While horizontal agreements give rise to efficiencies that can generally be quantified through direct measurements (for example, cost reductions through the realization of economies), the vertical agreements' main form of efficiencies relate to the correcting of market failures which have a negative impact on demand-enhancing investments. While such forms of efficiencies are well-recognized in the economic literature, they may be much harder to quantify through direct measurements.

The second remark is that the Guidelines seem to impose a heavy burden of proof on parties wishing to benefit from the Article 81(3) exemption. It is not sufficient to simply allege the existence of efficiencies; these efficiencies must be substantiated. On the other hand, it seems that the Commission appears less inclined to see all or the vast majority of agreements as falling under Article 81(1).[76] Thus, the Commission seems willing to promote a narrower interpretation of Article 81(1) than the one that was *en vogue* these last decades.[77] While it remains the case that agreements whose object is to restrict competition will fall under Article 81(1) without the need for further analysis, agreements that are not restrictive of competition by object will be subject to a full economic evaluation. As pointed out in the Guidelines:

> In the case of restrictions of competition by effect there is no presumption of anti-competitive effects. For an agreement to be restrictive by effect it must affect actual or potential competition to such an extent that on the relevant market negative effects on prices, output, innovation or the variety or quality of goods and services can be expected within a reasonable degree of probability.[78]

One can thus perceive a form of re-balancing between Article 81(1) and Article 81(3) of the Treaty.

As far as the content of the Guidelines is concerned, one should say that these Guidelines reaffirm much of what was already said in the Guidelines on horizontal restrictions and on vertical restrictions examined above. They thus complement rather than replace these earlier guidelines. The Article 81(3) Guidelines explain why the Commission considers that efficiencies should be taken into account in the overall assessment of agreements:

> Agreements that restrict competition may at the same time have pro-competitive effects by way of efficiency gains. Efficiencies may create additional value by

---

75 See Ridyard, *supra* n. 26.
76 See Commission guidelines, *supra* n. 70, at paras 13–31.
77 See Montag and Janssens, *supra* n. 73.
78 See Commission guidelines, *supra* n. 70, at para. 24.

lowering the cost of producing an output, improving the quality of the product or creating a new product. When the pro-competitive effects of an agreement outweigh its anti-competitive effects the agreement is on balance pro-competitive and compatible with the objectives of the competition rules. The net effect of such agreements is to promote the very essence of the competitive process, namely to win customers by offering better products or better prices than those offered by rivals.[79]

In other words, the objective of the assessment process is to determine whether the net effect of an agreement that falls under Article 81(3) is pro-competitive, that is whether its anticompetitive effects are outweighed by pro-competitive effects taking the form of efficiencies. In this regard, the Guidelines establish some important principles regarding the assessment under Article 81(3) of the Treaty.

First, the Guidelines state that the assessment under Article 81(3) of the efficiencies flowing from restrictions is in principle made within the confines of each relevant market to which the agreement relates.[80] Thus, negative effects on consumers in one geographic or product market cannot be compensated for by benefits to consumers in another geographic or product market. However, efficiencies realized on separate but related markets can be taken into account provided that 'the group of consumers affected by the restriction and benefiting from the efficiency gains are substantially the same'.[81] As pointed out by some commentators, this 'market-specific' standard is excessively rigid and may result in forgoing large efficiencies on one or several markets for the sake of small potential consumer harm in the directly affected market(s).[82]

Second, the Guidelines state that the assessment under Article 81(3) is 'sensitive to material changes in the facts'.[83] This assessment of agreements is thus made in the actual context in which they occur and on the basis of the facts existing at a given point in time. The exception provided for under Article 81(3) should thus apply as long as the four conditions this provision contains are fulfilled, and cease to apply once these conditions are no longer met. Compared with the old regime where parties could obtain an exemption by notifying their agreement, the new system introduced by Regulation 1/2003 seems to increase the level of uncertainty. It also forces the parties to periodically reassess the validity of their agreement to verify whether its anticompetitive effects continue to be compensated for by sufficient efficien-

---

79 Ibid. at para. 33.
80 Ibid. at para. 43.
81 Ibid.
82 See Montag, Janssens, *supra* n. 73.
83 See Commission guidelines, *supra* n. 70, at para. 44.

cies.[84] Assessment under Article 81(3) should thus no longer be seen as a one-time event, but as a work in constant progress, although it is doubtful whether many firms will devote the resources necessary to an ongoing evaluation of their agreements.

The Guidelines then affirm (or in some cases reaffirm) the principles to be taken into account when assessing efficiency claims:

- Only objective benefits can be taken into account. This means that such efficiencies will not be assessed from the subjective viewpoint of the parties.[85]
- Cost savings that arise from the mere exercise of market power cannot be taken into account.[86]
- All efficiency claims must therefore be substantiated so that the following can be verified: (a) the nature of the claimed efficiencies; (b) the link between the agreement and the efficiencies; (c) the likelihood that each claimed efficiency will materialize and its magnitude; and (d) how and when each claimed efficiency would be achieved.[87]
- The causal link between the efficiencies and the agreement concerned must be direct, which means that indirect effects will not be taken into account.[88]

The Guidelines draw a distinction between two categories of efficiencies: cost efficiencies and efficiencies of a qualitative nature pursuant to which value is created in the form of new or improved products.[89] Sources of cost efficiencies include: the development of new production technologies and methods; synergies arising from the integration of existing assets; economies of scale, such as the reduction of transport costs through the combination of logistics operations; economies of scope, such as the distribution of similar

---

[84]   However, the guidelines note that the Article 81(3) assessment must take into account the initial sunk investment made by the parties and the time they need to recoup such an investment. See para. 44. Moreover, when the restrictive agreement is an irreversible event, such as for instance a specialization agreement whereby one or several parties decide to stop the production of a specific product or service, the assessment must be made exclusively on the facts relevant at the time of implementation. See para. 45.

[85]   Ibid. at para. 49.

[86]   Ibid.

[87]   Ibid. at para. 51.

[88]   Ibid. at para. 53.

[89]   Ibid. at para. 59. Note that the guidelines also state that both vertical and horizontal agreements can generate efficiencies by allowing the parties to produce a particular task at lower costs or with higher value added for consumers.

products together; and better planning of production.[90] Sources of qualitative efficiencies include: dynamic efficiencies, such as technical and technological advances; development of higher quality products or products with novel features; more rapid dissemination of technologies; and improvement of the distribution of the covered products or services.[91]

The document also stresses that, for an agreement generating efficiencies to be exempted under Article 81(3), the other conditions of that provision must also be fulfilled.

First, the agreement must not contain restrictions which are not 'necessary' for the realization of the claimed efficiencies.[92] This condition implies a two-fold test. First, there must be 'no other economically practicable and less restrictive means of achieving the efficiencies'.[93] This requires firms to prove a negative fact. However, the Guidelines admit that firms invoking the benefit of Article 81(3) are not required to examine hypothetical or theoretical alternatives.[94] Moreover, the Commission will not second guess the business judgement of the parties, but will only intervene when it is reasonably clear that there are realistic and attainable alternatives. Another aspect to take into account in the assessment is whether the parties could have achieved the efficiencies on their own.[95] Second, once it is found that the agreement in question is necessary to achieve the efficiencies, the indispensability of each restriction that flows from the agreement must be assessed.[96] A restriction is indispensable when in its absence the efficiencies would be eliminated or significantly reduced.[97]

Second, consumers must receive a 'fair share' of the efficiencies generated by a restrictive agreement.[98] This means the pass-on of benefits must at least compensate consumers for any actual or likely negative impact caused to them by the agreement. Thus, the net effect of the agreement must at least be neutral from the point of view of the consumers directly or likely to be affected by the agreement.[99] The Commission also notes that this condition of Article 81(3) contains a 'sliding scale': the greater the restrictions of competition found in the agreement in question, the greater must be the efficiencies and the pass-on

---

90   Ibid. at paras 64–68.
91   Ibid. at paras 70–72.
92   Ibid. at para. 73.
93   Ibid.
94   Ibid. at para. 75.
95   Ibid. at para. 76.
96   Ibid. at para. 78.
97   Ibid. at para. 78.
98   Ibid. at para. 73.
99   Ibid. at para. 85.

to consumers.[100] This implies that in situations where the efficiencies are great and the restrictions are limited, it is not necessary to enter into a detailed analysis of pass-on. Conversely, the presence of significant restrictions with only limited consumer benefits makes it unlikely that the condition that consumers must receive a fair share of the benefits will be fulfilled.[101] The most difficult situation arises where the agreement has both significant anti-competitive effects and pro-competitive effects, in which case a careful analysis is required.[102] The Guidelines acknowledge that in many cases it is difficult to accurately calculate the consumer pass-on rate and other types of consumer pass-on elements.[103] Thus, firms are only required to substantiate their claims by providing estimates and other data to the extent reasonably possible.

Finally, the agreement in question must not give the undertakings concerned the opportunity to eliminate competition in respect of a substantial part of the products concerned. According to the Commission, this condition

> recognises the fact that rivalry between undertakings is an essential driver of economic efficiency, including dynamic efficiencies in the shape of innovation. . . . When competition is eliminated the competitive process is brought to an end and short-term efficiency gains are outweighed by longer-term losses stemming *inter alia* from expenditures incurred by the incumbent to maintain its position (rent seeking), misallocation of resources, reduced innovation and higher prices.[104]

Some commentators have expressed concern that the second sentence in the above passage might lead to the creation of an 'efficiency offence' whereby the efficiency defence could be turned on its head when there is a 'threat to long term dynamic rivalry'.[105] Indeed, agreements leading to cost reductions, improvement in the quality of products, and so on may create an efficiency gap between the parties and their rivals, thereby leading to a less vibrant long-term rivalry on the market. The recognition of an efficiency offence could in turn induce competitors to challenge efficiency-enhancing agreements every time market power is involved, thereby reducing the chances of a successful efficiency defence for any dominant firm(s).[106] While it is not entirely clear that the language quoted above recognizes an efficiency offence, it is clear that the granting of an Article 81(3) exemption will be an uphill struggle when an agreement is concluded by parties that individually or collectively hold market power.

---

100   Ibid. at para. 90.
101   Ibid. at para. 91.
102   Ibid. at para. 92.
103   Ibid. at para. 94.
104   Ibid. at para. 105.
105   See Ridyard, *supra* n. 26.
106   Ibid.

The above discussion leads to the following remarks. First, the guidelines clearly promote an assessment methodology that is clearly based on economic analysis. In the future, both undertakings and the authorities in charge of enforcing competition rules (the Commission, NCAs, national courts, and in some cases NRAs) will have to be able to assess efficiencies and balance them against the restrictions of competition brought about by an agreement. Complex economic evaluations will represent a particular challenge for national courts and newly established competition authorities. Second, these economic evaluations will leave an important margin of discretion to the authorities in charge of performing them. Indeed, there is no magic formula for determining the net effect of a given agreement. Balancing anti-competitive effects with efficiencies is a bit like comparing apples and pears. While a given agreement may, for instance, present risks of price increases by decreasing the level of competition on a given market, it may also facilitate the development of new or improved products.

d)   Technology transfer agreements

On the same day the Commission adopted its Guidelines on the application of Article 81(3), it also adopted Commission Regulation 772/2004 on the application of Article 81(3) to categories of technology transfer agreements,[107] as well as its Guidelines on the application of Article 81(3) to technology transfer agreements.[108] As with the block exemption regulations on horizontal and vertical restraints, Regulation 772/2004 recognizes that technology transfer agreements may generate efficiencies:

> Technology transfer agreements concern the transfer of technology. Such agreements will usually improve economic efficiency and be pro-competitive as they can reduce duplication of research and development, strengthen the incentive for the initial research and development, spur incremental innovation, facilitate diffusion and generate product market competition.[109]

---

[107]   Commission Regulation 772/2004 of 27 April 2004 on the application of Article 81(3) of the Treaty to categories of technology transfer agreements, OJ 2004 L123/11; M. Hansen, O. Shah, 'The New EU Technology Transfer Regime – Out of the Straightjacket into the Safe Harbour?', 25(8) *European Competition Law Review* (2004), p. 465; M. Dolmans, A. Piilola, 'The new technology transfer block exemption: a welcome reform, after all', 27(3) *World Competition* 351 (2004); P. Treacy, T. Heide, 'The new EC technology transfer block exemption regulation', 26(9) *European Intellectual Property Review* (2004), p. 414; E. Vollebregt, 'The changes in the new technology transfer block exemption compared to the draft', 25(10) *European Competition Law Review* (2004), p. 660.

[108]   Commission, Guidelines on the application of Article 81 of the EC Treaty to technology transfer agreements ('technology transfer guidelines'), OJ 2004 C101/2.

[109]   Regulation 772/2004, *supra* n. 107, at recital 5.

Following the new Commission approach to assessments under Article 81(3), Regulation 772/2004 insists on the significance of the degree of market power of the firms concerned.[110] It also provides market share thresholds below which technology transfer agreements are presumed compatible with Article 81 (combined market shares of 20 per cent for agreements between competitors and individual market shares of 30 per cent for agreements between non-competitors).[111] Agreements exceeding these thresholds need to fulfil the four conditions imposed by Article 81(3) to benefit from the exception provided for by that provision.

The Guidelines on the application of Article 81(3) to technology transfer agreements lay out many of the principles that need to be followed in the assessment of efficiencies generated by the technology transfer agreements. These principles are largely similar to those found in the Commission guidelines on the application of Article 81(3).[112] The Guidelines also detail the various types of efficiencies, which can be taken into account when assessing technology transfer agreements under Article 81. Such efficiencies include:

- Licensing agreements may promote innovation by allowing the licensee to gain access to a technology which can be combined with its production assets, thereby allowing him to exploit new or improved products;[113]
- They may stimulate innovation when the combination of the licensee's technology with the licensor's technology gives rise to synergies. When the two technologies are combined, the licensee may be able to achieve a cost/output configuration that would not otherwise be possible;[114]

---

[110] Ibid. at recital 6 ('The likelihood that such efficiency-enhancing and pro-competitive effects will outweigh any anti-competitive effects due to restrictions contained in technology transfer agreements depends on the degree of market power of the undertakings concerned and, therefore, on the extent to which those undertakings face competition from undertakings owning substitute technologies or undertakings producing substitute products').

[111] Ibid. at Article 3.

[112] For example, the guidelines confirm that the assessment of restrictive agreements is made on the basis of the facts existing at a given point in time and is thus sensitive to material changes in the facts; the exception rule applies only as long as the four conditions provided in Article 81(3) are fulfilled and ceases to apply as soon as they are no longer fulfilled; with regard to the condition of indispensability, undertakings invoking the benefit of Article 81(3) are not required to consider hypothetical or theoretical alternatives, but to demonstrate why seemingly realistic and significantly less restrictive alternatives would be significantly less efficient; and with regard to the condition that consumers must receive a fair share of the benefits, efficiency gains must offset the likely negative impact on prices, output and other relevant factors caused by the agreement.

[113] See technology transfer guidelines, *supra* n. 108, at para. 148.

[114] Ibid.

- They may give rise to efficiencies at the distribution stage, similar to vertical agreements;
- Efficiency gains may also be generated where technology owners assemble a technology package for third parties. Such pooling arrangements may in particular reduce transaction costs;[115]
- Licensing agreements whereby firms agree not to assert their property rights against each other are generally pro-competitive, as they allow the parties to develop their respective technologies without fear of being subject to infringement claims.[116]

e) The 'Ten Commandments' applying to the assessment of efficiencies in the context of restrictive agreements

The analysis in the four preceding sections makes it possible to identify a list of ten principles that will generally apply to the review of efficiencies invoked in the context of the assessment of a restrictive agreement under Article 81(3). These principles are:

- *Efficiencies must be 'substantiated'.* Parties have to produce clear evidence of the efficiencies that are generated by the restriction(s) in question. Vague references to the potential benefits of the restriction(s) contained in the agreement in question will not be taken into account.
- *Efficiencies must be 'objective'.* They will not be assessed from the subjective points of view of the parties, but on the basis of unequivocal economic data.
- *The restrictions of competition must be 'necessary' to achieve the claimed efficiencies.* There must be no economically practicable and less restrictive means of realizing the efficiencies. The restrictions in question must thus be the only possible route to achieving the efficiencies that are claimed by the parties.
- *The claimed efficiencies must 'outweigh' the restrictions imposed in the agreement.* This suggests that the efficiencies must do more than compensate for the negative effects generated by the restrictions in the agreement. The net effect of an agreement must be positive.
- *Consumers must receive a 'fair share' of the efficiencies generated by the restriction(s) in question.* The pass-on of benefits must at least compensate consumers for any actual or likely impact caused to them by the restrictions contained in the agreement. The effect of the agreement must at least be neutral from the point of view of the consumers directly or likely to be affected by the agreement.

---

[115] Ibid.
[116] Ibid.

- *The greater the restrictions of competition, the greater must be the efficiencies and the pass-on to the consumers.* This is often referred to as a 'sliding scale' approach, whereby serious restrictions of competition will only be justified by substantial efficiencies.
- *No efficiencies will justify the complete elimination of competition.* The Commission recognizes that rivalry between firms is an essential driver of economic efficiency. Agreements that eliminate competition for a substantial part of the products in question may generate short-term efficiencies, but these short-term gains will be outweighed by longer term losses.
- *Efficiencies must be 'market-specific'.* The assessment under Article 81(3) of the efficiencies flowing from the restrictions in an agreement is in principle made within the confines of each of the relevant markets to which the agreement relates. Negative effects on consumers in one market cannot thus be compensated for by benefits to consumers in a separate market, unless these markets are related (and thus involve substantially the same group of consumers).
- *The assessment under Article 81(3) is 'sensitive to material changes in facts'.* The exception provided under Article 81(3) will thus apply only as long as the four conditions contained in this provision are complied with. The assessment of an agreement under Article 81(3) will thus not be a one-time event, but will have to be carried out again every time material changes occur.
- *The claimed efficiencies cannot result from the exercise of market power.* Cost savings generated by an agreement cannot simply be the result of the parties being in a position to exert greater market power.

2 Efficiency Claims in Merger Control

In addition to the modernization of the implementation of the competition rules, another major reform undertaken in the area of competition law relates to the adoption of a new merger control regulation.[117] Regulation 139/2004 on the control of concentrations between undertakings provides for a series of amendments to the old merger control regime, the most important of which

---

[117]   Council Regulation 139/2004 of 20 January 2004 on the control of concentrations between undertakings, OJ 2004 L24/1. F. E. González Díaz, 'The reform of European merger control: quid novi sub sole?', 27(2) *World Competition* 177 (2004); J. Peyre, I. Simic, 'Merger control overview of the Commission "Reform Package"', 4 *International Business Law Review* 519 (2004); F. Brunet, I. Girgenson, 'La double réforme du contrôle communautaire des concentrations', 40(1) *Revue Trimestrielle de Droit Européen* (2004), p. 1.

being the adoption of a new substantive test for the assessment of mergers. Article 2(3) of Regulation 139/2004 provides: 'A concentration which would significantly impede effective competition, in the common market or in a substantial part of it, in particular as a result of the creation or strengthening of a dominant position, shall be declared incompatible with the common market.'

Recital 29 of the regulation acknowledges the importance of taking efficiencies into account in the assessment of mergers:

> In order to determine the impact of a concentration on competition in the common market, it is appropriate to take account of any substantiated and likely efficiencies put forward by the undertakings concerned. It is possible that the efficiencies brought about by the concentration counteract the effects on competition, and in particular the potential harm to consumers, that it might otherwise have and that, as a consequence, the concentration would not significantly impede effective competition, in the common market or in a substantial part of it, in particular as a result of the creation or strengthening of a dominant position.

This represents an important development, as in the past the Commission has often shown reluctance towards efficiency-based justifications in merger control.[118] Implicit references could sometimes be found in certain merger decisions, but as a general matter the analysis of efficiencies was not formally part of the merger review process.[119] This new positive stance on efficiencies is to be welcomed, as from an economic standpoint there is an overwhelming case for taking efficiencies into account.[120] As will be seen below, most of the efficiency-based arguments made in the context of horizontal agreements are also relevant in the context of mergers.

But it is in the Guidelines on the assessment of horizontal mergers, which were published two weeks after the adoption of the new Merger Regulation, that a detailed discussion on efficiencies can be found.[121] Horizontal mergers are the type of mergers which generally raise the most serious competition law concerns, and it is thus in this area that efficiency-related issues will be most intensely discussed.

As in the case of restrictive agreements, the Commission considers that the efficiencies generated by a merger can counteract the negative effects it can

---

[118]   According to Faull and Nikpay, *supra* n. 25, at 250, the old Merger Regulation did 'not allow for an efficiency defence in the sense that the negative effects of a merger [would have been] weighed up against the positive effects of the merger'.

[119]   See van den Bergh, Camesasca, *supra* n. 5, pp. 345–9.

[120]   See Bishop, Walker, *supra* n. 2, at pp. 300–302.

[121]   Guidelines on the assessment of horizontal mergers under the Council Regulation on the control of concentrations between undertakings ('horizontal merger guidelines'), OJ 2004 C31/5. See also J. Venit, F. Depoortere, 'The new EC horizontal merger guidelines', *Global Competition Review* 29 (2004).

have on competition. Thus, in order to assess whether a merger would 'significantly impede effective competition' (the new substantive test), the Commission will perform an 'overall competitive appraisal of the merger'.[122] A merger will not be declared incompatible with the common market when the Commission

> is in a position to conclude on the basis of sufficient evidence that the efficiencies generated by the merger are likely to enhance the ability and incentive of the merged entity to act pro-competitively for the benefit of consumers, thereby countering the adverse effects on competition which the merger might otherwise have.[123]

The Guidelines provide that, in order for the Commission to take account of efficiency claims in its assessment of the merger and be in a position to clear the transaction as a consequence of efficiencies, these efficiencies must fulfil the following conditions.

First, the efficiencies have to benefit consumers. The relevant benchmark is thus that consumers should not be worse off as a result of the merger.[124] For that purpose, efficiencies should be 'substantial' and 'timely' and should, in principle, benefit consumers 'in those relevant markets where it is otherwise likely that competition concerns would occur'.[125] The Guidelines list various types of efficiencies that can lead to lower prices and benefit consumers:

- Efficiency gains that generate cost savings in production may give the merged entity the ability to charge lower prices. Efficiencies that lead to reductions in variable or marginal costs are more likely to be relevant in the assessment of a merger than efficiencies leading to a reduction of fixed costs. Moreover, cost reductions which result from anticompetitive reductions in output cannot be regarded as efficiencies beneficial to consumers;[126]
- Efficiency gains in the sphere of R&D and innovation may also generate consumer benefits, such as the development of new or improved products;[127]
- Efficiency gains may increase the merged entity's incentive to increase production and lower prices, thereby reducing its incentives to coordinate market behaviour with competitors. Efficiencies may thus lower the risks of coordinated effects in the relevant market.[128]

---

[122] Guidelines, *supra* n. 121, at para. 76.
[123] Ibid. at para. 77.
[124] Ibid. at para. 79.
[125] Ibid.
[126] Ibid. at para. 80.
[127] Ibid.
[128] Ibid. at para. 81.

The Guidelines also specify that, the later the efficiencies are expected to materialize in the future, the less weight the Commission can assign to them.[129] Moreover, the greater the possible negative effects on competition, the more the Commission has to be certain that the alleged efficiencies are substantial, likely to be realized, and likely to be passed on, to a sufficient degree, to consumers.[130] This is the so-called 'sliding scale' already discussed above.

Second, efficiencies must be merger-specific.[131] They must be the direct consequence of the notified merger and must be incapable of being realized to the same extent by less anticompetitive alternatives. It is for the merging parties to demonstrate that there are no less anticompetitive, realistic and achievable alternatives of a non-concentrative nature (for example, a licensing agreement) or of a concentrative nature (for example, a differently structured merger), other than the notified merger, which could achieve the claimed efficiencies.[132]

Third, efficiencies have to be verifiable.[133] This means that the Commission must be reasonably certain that the efficiencies are likely to materialize and be substantial enough to counteract the anticompetitive effects of the merger. When reasonably possible, the alleged efficiencies and the resulting benefits to consumers should be quantified. When the data are not available for a precise quantification, it must be possible to foresee a clearly identifiable impact on consumers, not a marginal one.[134]

The above discussion of the Guidelines invites the following remarks.

First, there is much similarity in the way the Commission proposes to analyse efficiencies generated by restrictive agreements under the Guidelines on the application of Article 81(3) and those generated by horizontal mergers under the Merger Regulation as interpreted by the Guidelines on horizontal mergers. There is some logic to this, since the Article 81(3) Guidelines essentially focus on horizontal agreements, and since horizontal agreements and horizontal mergers tend to create comparable competition concerns (that is, an increase of market power) and generate the same benefits (cost reductions, economies of scale and scope, and so on). Moreover, both sets of guidelines were adopted almost at the same time and reflect the new vision of the Commission when it comes to assessing efficiencies. First, there is the principle that the claimed efficiencies must benefit consumers (that is, consumer

---

129   Ibid. at para. 83.
130   Ibid. at para. 84.
131   Ibid. at para. 85.
132   Ibid
133   Ibid. at para. 86.
134   Ibid.

pass-on). As far as restrictive agreements are concerned, this principle is derived from the letter of Article 81(3), which, among its conditions, requires that consumers receive a 'fair share' of the benefits generated by the agreement. But the Merger Regulation also seems to embrace a consumer welfare standard. Second, there is the requirement of 'necessity' or 'specificity', pursuant to which the efficiencies could not have been achieved through a less restrictive type of agreement. The requirement of necessity is again found in Article 81(3), but, more generally, it can be regarded as a general principle of EC law. It is thus not surprising that it is also found in the Guidelines on horizontal mergers. Third, both instruments seem to follow a 'sliding scale' approach, pursuant to which the greater the possible negative effects of an agreement/merger on competition, the more the parties have to demonstrate that the claimed efficiencies will be substantial. Fourth, both instruments provide that the claimed efficiencies should be 'market-specific'. This means that the benefits generated by the efficiencies must be felt in the market(s) where the agreement/merger in question is likely to raise competition concerns.

Second, it is interesting to observe that most of the principles that are found in the Commission Guidelines of the assessment of horizontal mergers regarding the assessment of efficiencies can also be found in the US Horizontal Merger Guidelines.[135] Indeed, the US guidelines provide that:

- Mergers have the potential to 'generate significant efficiencies by permitting better utilization of existing assets, enabling the combined firm to achieve lower costs in producing a given quantity and quality than either firm could have achieved without the proposed transaction';
- The Agency will consider 'only those efficiencies likely to be accomplished with the proposed merger and unlikely to be accomplished in the absence of either the proposed merger or another means having comparable anticompetitive effects' (that is, the claimed efficiencies must be 'merger-specific');
- The merging firms must 'substantiate efficiency claims so that the

---

[135]   US Department of Justice, Horizontal Merger Guidelines, 2 April 1992 as revised in 1997, available at http://www.usdoj.gov/atr/public/guidelines/horiz_book/hmgl.html. See also W. J. Kolasky, A. R. Dick, 'The Merger Guidelines and the Integration of Efficiencies Into Antitrust Review of Horizontal Mergers', 71 *Antitrust Law Journal* 207 (2003); J. Baker, S. Salop, 'Should Concentration be Dropped from the Merger Guidelines?', 33 *UWLA Law Review* 3 (2001); M. Leddy, 'The 1992 US Horizontal Merger Guidelines and Some Comparisons with EC Enforcement Policy', 14(1) *European Competition Law Review* (1993), p. 15; R. P. McAfee, M. A. Williams, 'Horizontal Mergers and Antitrust Policy', 40(2) *Journal of Industrial Economics* (1992), p. 181.

Agency can verify by reasonable means the likelihood and magnitude of each asserted efficiency, how and when each would be achieved (and any costs of doing so), how each would enhance the merged firm's mobility and incentive to compete, and why each would be merger-specific' (that is, the claimed efficiencies must be substantiated);

- Cognizable efficiencies are merger-specific efficiencies 'that have been verified and do not arise from anticompetitive reductions in output or service' (that is, the benefits generated by claimed efficiencies cannot result from the exercise of market power);
- 'To make the requisite determination, the Agency considers whether cognizable efficiencies likely would be sufficient to reverse the merger's potential to harm consumers in the relevant market, e.g., by preventing price increases in that market' (that is, this seems to suggest that the claimed efficiency must be market-specific);
- 'The greater the potential adverse competitive effect of a merger [. . .], the greater must be cognizable efficiencies in order for the Agency to conclude that the merger will not have an anticompetitive effect in the relevant market' (that is, imposition of a 'sliding-scale' approach);
- 'Agencies almost never justify a merger to monopoly or near-monopoly' (that is, this translates the idea that no efficiency claim can justify a complete or near-complete elimination of competition in the relevant market(s)).

There thus seems to be a lot of convergence between the approach respectively followed by the Commission and the US antitrust authorities when it comes to the assessment of efficiencies. Clearly, the quasi-verbatim re-transcription of passages of the US Guidelines by the Commission in its Guidelines on the assessment of horizontal mergers suggests the Commission has been strongly influenced by the US Guidelines. More fundamentally, we have also seen above that the new Merger Regulation essentially relies on the same substantive test as the US test, that is, whether the proposed merger is likely 'to substantially lessen competition' in the relevant market(s).

In sum, there is an important degree of convergence in the way the Commission analyses efficiencies in restrictive agreements in the context of Article 81(3) of the EC Treaty and the way it analyses efficiencies in the framework of the Merger Regulation. This is particularly the case if one focuses on horizontal cooperation agreements and horizontal mergers. Moreover, one can see a significant degree of convergence in the principles put forward in the Commission Guidelines on horizontal mergers and those in the US horizontal merger guidelines with respect to the assessment of efficiencies. As recent practice indicates, however, it does not mean that merger control procedures will produce similar outcomes in the EC and the US, as the assessment of efficiencies is only one part of such procedures.[136] Moreover, the above-mentioned principles may be subject to different interpretations in the context of a given case.

V EFFICIENCY CLAIMS IN THE CONTEXT OF THE CONTROL OF MARKET DOMINANCE

As we have seen in Part IV, efficiency claims play a significant role in the assessment of restrictive agreements under Article 81(3) and of mergers under the Merger Regulation. In this part, we examine whether efficiency claims or efficiency considerations in general play an important role in the mechanisms that are designed to control the behaviour of dominant firms. Two such mechanisms can be identified. First, Article 82 of the Treaty prohibits dominant firms from abusing their market power at the expense of consumers (exploitative abuses) and competitors (exclusionary abuses). Second, in certain sectors characterized by the presence of monopolistic infrastructures (the so-called 'network industries'), sector-specific legislation seeks to maintain/enhance competition in the market by imposing regulatory requirements on certain categories of operators.

1 Efficiency Considerations under Article 82

Article 82 of the EC Treaty does not provide for an exception mechanism such as the one contained in Article 81(3). A dominant firm that has been found to commit an abuse thus cannot invoke efficiencies in order to benefit from an

---

[136] Commission Decision of 3 July 2001, *General Electric/Honeywell,* COMP/M.2220 OJ 2004 L48/1. See also D. Giotakos, L. Petit, G. Garnier, 'General Electric/Honeywell – An Insight into the Commission's Investigation and Decision', 3 *EC Competition Policy Newsletter* (October 2001). This decision attracted vigorous criticism from US officials. See W. J. Kolasky, *North Atlantic Competition Policy: Converging Toward What?,* BIICL Second Annual International and Comparative Law Conference, London, England, 17 May 2002; *United States and European Competition Policy: Are There More Differences Than We Care to Admit?* (10 April 2002); *International Convergence Efforts: A U.S. Perspective,* before the International Dimensions of Competition Law Conference (22 March 2002); *Conglomerate Mergers and Range Effects: It's a Long Way from Chicago to Brussels* (9 November 2001). See also Commission Press Release IP/01/855 of 18 June 2001 ('Commissioner Monti dismisses criticism of GE/Honeywell merger review and rejects politicisation of the case'). There was also a great deal of controversy surrounding the adoption of the clearance decision in the EC in the *Boeing/McDonnell Douglas* case. See Commission Decision of 30 July 1997, *Boeing/McDonnell Douglas,* COMP M.877, OJ 1997 L336/16. The Commission eventually cleared the case after the reported intervention of US President Bill Clinton.

exemption. This does not mean, however, that efficiency considerations should play no role under an Article 82 analysis. As the goal of competition law is to promote economic efficiency, efficiency considerations cannot be excluded from the analysis carried out under Article 82. Efficiencies should be taken into consideration in order to distinguish abusive behaviour that should be banned from legitimate behaviour which should be tolerated. As in the case of Article 81, Article 82 analysis should be grounded on rigorous economic analysis. Rigid and formalistic positions should be avoided.

Unfortunately, Article 82 analysis is probably the area of competition law where the decisional practice of the Commission and the case law of the European Courts are the least in line with economic theory. The core of the problem comes from the fact that the Commission and the European Courts tend to apply *per se* prohibitions to various forms of conduct carried out by dominant firms. From a general point of view, economic analysis allows little space for *per se* analysis, as the assessment of conduct should depend on the circumstances of the case. Moreover, as will be seen below, *per se* prohibition of certain types of conduct is sometimes unjustified, as such conduct may have welfare-enhancing effects.

Price discrimination is one category of conduct where the EC's *per se* approach appears to be unjustified. It is covered by Article 82(c) of the Treaty, which considers as one form of abuse 'applying dissimilar conditions to equivalent transactions with other trading parties, thereby placing them at a competitive disadvantage'. Economists tend to distinguish between different types of price discrimination.[137] First-degree price discrimination arises when a firm is able to discriminate perfectly between consumers. This situation is, however, extremely unlikely to arise in practice. Second-degree price discrimination occurs when a firm sells different units of output at different prices, although consumers buying the same amount of the goods pay the same price. The most common example of this form of price discrimination is the granting of volume rebates. Third-degree price discrimination arises when a firm segregates consumers into distinctive groups characterized by different elasticities of demand. Ramsey pricing is a classic form of third degree price discrimination.[138] For reasons of space, I will focus hereafter only on second degree price discrimination and, more specifically, on the highly problematic issue of loyalty rebates.[139]

---

[137]   See Bishop, Walker, *supra* n. 2, at 195.
[138]   On Ramsey pricing, see Geradin, Kerf, *supra* n. 4, at 28–9.
[139]   See J. Kallaugher, B. Sher, 'Rebates Revisited: Anti-Competitive Effects and Exclusionary Abuse under Article 82', 25(5) *European Competition Law Review* (2004), p. 263; L. Gyselen, *Rebates: Competition on the Merits or Exclusionary Practice?*, paper presented at the 8th EU Competition Law and Policy Workshop,

The Commission and the European Courts have tended to take a hostile stand on loyalty rebates granted by dominant firms. In *Hoffman-La Roche*, the Commission found that the firm's discount scheme was an abuse because these discounts were conditional on the customers obtaining all or most of their requirements from Roche and because the discounts were not based on 'the differences in costs borne by Roche in relation to the quantities supplied'.[140] In *Michelin I*, the Commission found that Michelin's rebates based on a previous period's purchases by an individual dealer were abusive.[141] The Commission stated that 'with the exception of short-term measures, no discount should be granted unless directly linked to a genuine reduction in the manufacturer's costs. The compensation paid to Michelin tyre dealers must be commensurate with the tasks they perform and the services they actually provide, which reduce the manufacturer's burden'.[142]

Pursuant to these two Commission decisions, which were subsequently confirmed by the ECJ, in order not to be declared abusive, discounts must be based on cost savings. This means that all discount schemes not based on such savings should be subject to a *per se* prohibition, an approach unanimously criticized by economists as overly simplistic. Indeed, it is not possible to determine in advance whether a given rebate scheme will be pro- or anticompetitive. This can only be determined through a market effects test. Unfortunately, in two recent cases, the Court of First Instance (CFI) held that under Article 82 there is no need for the Commission to show an anticompetitive effect. In *British Airways*, the CFI held that

> for the purposes of establishing an infringement of Article 82 EC, it is not necessary to demonstrate that the abuse in question had a concrete effect on the markets concerned. It is sufficient in that respect to demonstrate that the abusive conduct . . .

European University Institute, June 2003; R. O'Donoghue, 'Over-regulating Lower Prices: Time for a Rethink on Pricing Abuses under Article 82 EC', in Ehlermann, Atanasiu (eds), *European Competition Law Annual 2003: The Abuse of a Dominant Position Under EC Competition Law* (forthcoming, Hart Publishing, 2005) (paper presented at the 8th EU Competition Law and Policy Workshop, European University Institute, June 2003); OECD, *Loyalty and Fidelity Discounts and Rebates*, DAFFE/COMP(2002)21; D. Ridyard, 'Exclusionary Pricing and Price Discrimination Abuses under Article 82 – An Economic Analysis', 23(6) *European Competition Law Review* (2002), p. 286.

[140]   Commission Decision 76/642/EEC of 9 June 1976, *Vitamins*, Case IV/29.020, OJ 1976 L223/27, recital 22, upheld by Court of Justice of 13 February 1979, Case 85/76, *Hoffmann-La Roche v Commission*, [1979] ECR 461.

[141]   Commission Decision 81/969/EEC of 7 October 1981, *Michelin*, Case IV/29.491, OJ 1981 L353/33, recital 54, upheld by Court of Justice of 9 November 1983, Case 322/81, *Michelin v Commission*, [1983] ECR 3461.

[142]   Ibid.

tends to restrict competition, or in other words, that the conduct is capable of having, or likely to have such an effect.[143]

In *Michelin II*, the CFI followed the same line, declaring that conduct can be abusive if it 'tends to restrict competition or, in other words, that the conduct is capable of having that effect'.[144] The CFI is thus content to consider that, to the extent that loyalty rebates can have an exclusionary effect, they must be subject to a *per se* prohibition rule, independently of the need to show whether the rebates in question do have a negative impact on competition.

In sum, the Commission and the European Courts' approach to loyalty rebates is clearly over-inclusive and risks condemning rebate schemes that do not harm competition. Loyalty rebates thus provide a clear example of why *per se* rules should be avoided by the Commission and the European Courts. They do not provide the degree of flexibility that is required by economic analysis, pursuant to which it is not the nature of conduct but its practical effect on competition that should determine its compatibility with EC competition rules. As we have seen in Part IV, one of the main trends in the application of Article 81 is the shift from a form-based approach to an effects-based approach. It is submitted that a similar approach should be pursued with respect to the application of Article 82.

From that standpoint, an important issue is whether a dominant firm can assert an efficiency justification for conduct that would otherwise be abusive. Although, as mentioned above, there is no exception system under Article 82 of the Treaty, it is generally considered that conduct that would normally be prohibited as an abuse can be regarded as legitimate when it is 'objectively justified'.[145] Efficiency considerations can represent an objective justification.

To take the example of loyalty rebates again, it is generally recognized that there are circumstances where such rebates can generate a range of economic benefits. O'Donoghue provides three examples.[146] Firstly, loyalty rebates can be efficiency-enhancing in industries characterized by high fixed costs and low marginal costs. In such industries, loyalty rebates 'allow the seller to

---

[143]   Court of First Instance of 17 December 2003, Case T-219/99, *British Airways plc v Commission*, not yet officially reported.

[144]   Court of First Instance of 30 September 2003, Case T-203/01, *Manufacture française des pneumatiques Michelin v Commission*, [2003] ECR II-4071.

[145]   See Court of Justice of 29 April 2004, Case C-418/01, *IMS Health GmbH & Co. OHG v NDC Health GmbH & Co. KG*, not yet officially reported; Court of Justice of 26 November 1998, Case 7/97, *Oscar Bronner GmbH & Co*, [1998] ECR I-7791; Court of Justice of 6 April 1995, Joined cases C-241/91 P and C-242/91 P, *Radio Telefis Eireann and Independent Television Publications Ltd v Commission*, [1995] ECR I-743.

[146]   See *supra* n. 139.

recover fixed costs more efficiently than normal quantity discounts'. Secondly, fidelity rebates may increase the overall level of inter-brand competition by encouraging buyers to concentrate all their purchases by buying from just one seller. Finally, efficiencies may arise when the effect of loyalty rebates is to reduce the cost of production.

Tying is another example of conduct which, although it is generally severely reprimanded by the Commission and the European Courts because of its potential foreclosure effects, can in some cases be justified by efficiency considerations.[147] Firstly, a great number of products are efficiently tied. For instance, there is no need for antitrust intervention when consumers are willing to buy assembled products, such as laced shoes, strung tennis rackets, radios or cars. Mandating the unbundling of all consumer products would be grossly inefficient and would clearly reduce consumer welfare.[148] Tying may also be justified by the need for producers to assure the quality of their products. Indeed, customer use of low quality complementary products or services may damage the reputation of the producer's brand and lead to lower sales.[149]

This does not mean, however, that the Commission and the European Courts will necessarily be receptive to efficiency claims made by dominant firms. In the case of loyalty rebates, for instance, the efficiencies outlined above have been systematically rejected in the case law. In *Michelin II*, the CFI stated that 'according to settled case-law, discounts granted by an undertaking in a dominant position must be based on a countervailing advantage which may be economically justified'.[150] But the quantity rebate system would only be compatible with Article 82 EC 'if the advantage conferred on dealers is justified by the volume of business they bring or by any economies of scale they allow the supplier to make'.[151] None of the efficiencies pointed out above has thus been accepted by the CFI or the ECJ.

In some cases, dominant firms will not try to justify their conduct by the fact that they *generate* efficiencies, but by the fact that their conduct is necessary to *protect* their efficiencies. The need to protect their incentives to invest and thus compete dynamically in the long run is, for instance, often invoked

---

[147]   Generally, on tying, see M. Dolmans, T. Graf, 'Analysis of Tying Under Article 82 EC: The European Commission's Microsoft Decision in Perspective', 27 *World Competition* 225 (2004); Ch. Ahlborn et al., *The Antitrust Economics of Tying – A Farewell to Per Se Illegality,* available at http://aei-brookings.org/admin/pdffiles/phpsp.pdf.

[148]   Van den Bergh, Camesasca, *supra* n. 5, at 279–81.

[149]   Ibid.

[150]   See *Michelin II, supra* n. 144, at recital 100.

[151]   Ibid.

by dominant firms refusing to give access to 'essential facilities'.[152] By contrast, access seekers will generally argue that obtaining access to these facilities is necessary for them to compete on a downstream market. From an economic standpoint, the mandatory access debate can be framed around a tradeoff between *ex ante* and *ex post* efficiency.[153] On the one hand, requiring a dominant firm holding an essential facility to share such a facility with one or several competitors will stimulate competition in downstream markets, thus promoting *ex post* (allocative) efficiency.[154] On the other hand, mandatory sharing may reduce the returns to the facility holder and thus decrease its *ex ante* incentives to invest and compete dynamically.[155]

Interestingly, this tension is at the core of the *Microsoft* case and, in particular, in the part of the decision of the Commission dealing specifically with interoperability problems.[156] On the one hand, in its complaint to the Commission, Sun Microsystems argued that, by refusing access to interoperability information, Microsoft was leveraging its market power in the PC operating systems market in order to monopolize the work group server market. On the other hand, during the proceedings, Microsoft justified its refusal to provide that information, some aspects of which were protected by intellectual

---

[152]   Generally, on the essential facilities doctrine, see B. Doherty, 'Just What Are Essential Facilities?', 38 *Common Market Law Review* 397 (2001); J. Temple Lang, 'The Principle of the Essential Facilities Doctrine in European Community Competition Law – The Position Since Bronner', 1 *Journal of Network Industries* 375 (2000); D. Ridyard, 'Essential Facilities and the Obligation to Supply Competitors and Access to Essential Facilities', 17 *European Competition Law Review* (1996), p. 438; J. Temple Lang, 'Defining Legitimate Competition: Companies' Duties to Supply Competitors and Access to Essential Facilities', in B. Hawk (ed.), *Fordham Corporate Law Institute* (1995), p. 245.

[153]   For an excellent discussion of this trade-off, see Elhauge, *supra* n. 9, at 295–6.

[154]   In economic terms, perfectly competitive markets maximize consumer welfare by promoting allocative efficiency (making the goods consumers want in the quantities valued by society) and productive efficiency (producing goods at the lowest possible costs) as well as dynamic efficiency (stimulating innovation and technological change). In the presence of non-perfectly competitive markets, a tradeoff may have to be made between these different forms of efficiencies.

[155]   See Elhauge, *supra* n. 9 at 297 ('If property rights are restricted to allow sharing and imitation, then a necessary cost will be a reduced incentive to invest and invent.').

[156]   Commission Decision of 24 March 2004, *Microsoft*, Case COMP/C-3/37.792, available at http://europa.eu.int/comm/competition/antitrust/cases/decisions/37792/en. pdf. For a discussion of this case, see D. Geradin, 'Limiting the Scope of Article 82 of the EC Treaty: What can the EU learn from the U.S. Supreme Court's Judgment in Trinko in the wake of Microsoft, IMS, and Deutsche Telekom?', 41(6) *Common Market Law Review* (2004), p. 1519.

property rights, on the ground that it needed to 'protect the outcome of billions of dollars of R&D investments in software features, functions and technologies. This is the essence of intellectual property right protection. Disclosure would negate that protection and eliminate future incentives to invest in the creation of intellectual property.'[157] This argument was essentially used by Microsoft as an 'objective justification' for its refusal to share interoperability information with its competitors.

To respond to this argument, the Commission engaged in a balancing process between Microsoft's interests in protecting its investment in IPRs and the benefits (in terms of innovation) that would be derived from requiring Microsoft to give access to the information requested by its competitors and it concluded that:

> [a] detailed examination of the scope of the disclosure at stake leads to the conclusion that, on balance, the possible negative impact of an order to supply on Microsoft's incentives to innovate is outweighed by its positive impact on the level of innovation of the whole industry (including Microsoft). As such, the need to protect Microsoft's incentives to innovate cannot constitute an objective justification that would offset the exceptional circumstances identified.[158]

The interesting aspect of the above passage is that the Commission in fact agreed to examine Microsoft's argument that mandatory access would have a negative impact on its incentives to invest and, thus, on dynamic efficiency. The Commission, however, rejected Microsoft's defence on the ground that the possible negative impact of an order to provide access on Microsoft's incentives to innovate was outweighed by its positive impact on the level of innovation of the whole industry. Here, the efficiency defence raised by Microsoft was thus considered, but rejected.

In sum, the above developments suggest that, although not completely excluded, efficiency claims will receive a less favourable welcome under Article 82 proceedings than in Article 81 proceedings. There are several reasons for that. First, Article 82 does not contain an exception that specifically refers to efficiencies as a cause of justification, as is the case with Article 81. Second, Article 82 applies to firms that hold a dominant position. As we have seen in the context of Article 81, the Commission will generally be suspicious when efficiencies are claimed by firms holding market power. Firms subject to Article 82 are always in that situation. Finally, the welfare effects of conduct by dominant firms are often ambiguous and thus are not often easily justifiable under efficiency considerations.

---

157 See Decision of the Commission, *supra* n. 10, at recital 709.
158 Ibid. at recital 783.

2 Efficiency Considerations under Sector-specific Regulation

Over the last 15 years, the Commission has been progressively opening network industries to competition.[159] Network industries cover economic sectors that operate on the basis of network infrastructures, such as telecommunications, electricity, gas and rail networks, and so on. These industries are different from other industries, as their network infrastructures usually exhibit natural monopoly features.[160] Another feature of these industries is that incumbent operators will usually maintain significant market power in the years following liberalization.[161] It is thus not possible to create competitive markets in network industries overnight. Liberalization is usually a long and painstaking process.[162]

Efficiency considerations have played an important role in the liberalization of network industries. The major driver for market opening reforms was the view that State monopolies were inefficient. These monopolies were able to impose supracompetitive prices through restrictions of output (thereby harming allocative efficiency) and did not have the right incentives to produce at the lowest possible costs and engage in innovation (thereby harming productive and dynamic efficiency). Proponents of the liberalization process thus argued that market opening reforms were needed to stimulate the performance of these sectors. In these historically monopolistic sectors, competition would become the vehicle for performance enhancement.

As incumbent operators will usually retain high market shares and continue to own essential facilities, controlling market power is of central importance in network industries. The aim of such control should be to prevent both exclusionary and exploitative abuses. This can be achieved through two complementary tools.[163] First, as we have seen above, Article 82 of the Treaty can be used to prevent dominant firms from abusing their market power at the expense of their competitors (exclusion) or their consumers (exploitation). In recent years, Article 82 has frequently been applied in the telecommunications, postal services, energy, and transport sectors.[164] Second, market power

---

[159]   See Geradin (ed.), *supra* n. 3; J. L. Buendia Sierra, *Exclusive Rights and State Monopolies under EC Law*, Oxford University Press (1999).
[160]   For a discussion of the concept of a 'network', see N. Economides, 'The Economics of Networks', 16 *International Journal of Industrial Organization* (1996), p. 673.
[161]   See D. Geradin, *The Opening of State Monopolies to Competition: Main Issues of the Liberalization Process,* in Geradin (ed.), *supra* n. 3, pp. 181–2.
[162]   Ibid.
[163]   On the interface between these two tools, see Geradin and Kerf, *supra* n. 4.
[164]   See Geradin (ed.), *Remedies in Network Industries: EC Competition Law vs. Sector-specific Regulation*, Intersentia (2004).

can also be controlled through sector-specific legislation.[165] Although liberalization is sometimes referred to as a 'deregulatory' process, it is in fact a regulatory-intensive process. The significant number of sector-specific directives that have been adopted by the EC in support of liberalization bears witness to that aspect. In the developments that follow, I will try to determine the extent to which efficiency considerations have been taken into account in sector-specific regulation.

From a general standpoint, it is useful to draw a distinction between regulatory measures that are designed to promote and/or protect competition in network industry markets and those designed to regulate the market segments displaying natural monopoly features and that thus cannot be opened to competition.

The first set of measures, which can be referred to as pro-competition measures, are based on the central vision that competitive markets will increase economic welfare and that thus the competitive process must be enhanced or, when competition is already burgeoning, protected. Several approaches can be taken to pursue that objective. First, competition can be enhanced through the adoption of measures reducing switching costs. This is, for example, the case of number portability requirements in the telecommunications sector.[166] Allowing customers to retain their telephone number when they decide to switch operators contributes to enhancing competition between the incumbent and new entrants. Second, competition can be protected by adopting measures designed to prevent incumbents from leveraging their market power in one segment in order to extend it to one or several other market segments. For instance, measures that provide for accounting separation between monopolistic and competitive segments aim at preventing anti-competitive forms of cross-subsidization.[167] The objective of these measures is thus to promote economic efficiency through the enhancement or the protection of competitive market structures.

The second category of measures is designed to regulate market segments where no competition is possible due to the presence of natural monopoly features. These measures can be designed to protect end users (for example,

---

[165] Ibid.

[166] See Article 30 of Directive 2002/22/EC of the European Parliament and of the Council of 7 March 2002 on universal service and users' rights relating to electronic communications networks and services (the 'Universal Service Directive'), OJ 2002 L108/51.

[167] See Article 13 of Directive 2002/21 of the European Parliament and of the Council of 7 March 2002 on a common regulatory framework for electronic communications networks and services (the 'Framework Directive'), OJ 2002 L108/33. Generally on cross-subsidization, see L. Hancher, J. L. Buendia Sierra, 'Cross-subsidisation and EC Law', 35 *Common Market Law Review* 901 (1998).

retail price controls) or competitors (for example, third party access measures) in which case they also have a pro-competition element. Indeed, ensuring competitors' access to essential facilities is one of the ways by which competition can be stimulated in downstream markets.[168] Although no competition is possible on such naturally monopolistic market segments, preventing incumbents from abusing their market power by refusing access or by imposing excessive access prices is a way to allow competition to take place on potentially competitive markets. The economic efficiency rationale discussed above is thus also present with respect to access regulation. This form of regulation may, however, generate tensions between the different forms of efficiencies identified in the first part of this chapter. Regulatory authorities setting an access price will often face conflicting goals. On the one hand, setting an access price that is low will stimulate entry and thus competition in the downstream market. This will in turn contribute to allocative efficiency and thus consumer welfare.[169] On the other hand, setting a low access price might have the effect of discouraging investments, especially when the incumbent is not compensated for its costs.[170] This might in turn affect productive and dynamic efficiency. The types of tradeoffs faced by competition authorities in essential facilities cases are thus also faced by regulatory authorities in access pricing cases.

There is another reason why efficiency considerations play an important role with respect to the measures designed to regulate bottleneck segments. The choice of an access pricing methodology will also impact the incentives of the bottleneck holder to be efficient. For instance, one advantage of opting for a forward-looking long-run incremental cost (LRIC) – as opposed to a backward-looking cost-based – pricing methodology when regulating interconnection rates in telecommunications is that, while the latter methodology compensates the incumbent on the basis of its actual costs and thus gives it no incentives to reduce such costs, the former methodology will not compensate the incumbent for its actual costs. It rather compensates on the basis of the costs of a benchmark efficient firm, thereby giving it incentives to be efficient and reduce the actual costs that it incurs in providing interconnection.[171] The same remark can be made with respect to the regulation of retail prices. Here again, the choice of a retail price methodology will impact the incentives of the dominant supplier to be efficient. For instance, while price regulation based on a rate-of-return methodology provides weak incentives for cost controls since all costs are covered in the prices, a price-cap methodology

---

168   See Geradin, *supra* n. 161, at 183 et seq.
169   See Geradin and Kerf, *supra* n. 4, at 34–45.
170   Ibid.
171   Ibid.

provides strong incentives to reduce costs because the firm retains the benefits of lower than expected costs for the period during which prices are fixed.[172]

The above developments thus show that efficiency considerations take a central role in sector-specific regulation. Firstly, the central objective liberalization seeks to achieve is to promote economic efficiency through the creation of competitive markets in network industries. Such regulation is thus rooted in efficiency considerations. Moreover, the various mechanisms chosen to price infrastructures or services in which there is no competition will impact the incumbent's incentives to be efficient.

VI CONCLUSIONS

Efficiencies are playing an increasingly important role in the assessment of restrictive agreements and mergers under Article 81(3) of the Treaty and the Merger Regulation respectively. There is thus a clear recognition of the 'efficiency defence' in these two areas of EC competition law. The Commission is not, however, ready to recognize any type of efficiency as a defence. Clearly, the burden of proof is on the parties invoking efficiencies as a justification for a given agreement/transaction. The various guidelines we have examined above also provide for a series of principles that need to be complied with for a given set of efficiencies to be taken into account. The principle that claimed efficiencies must 'outweigh' the negative effect of restrictions of competition contained in an agreement requires a balancing of the pro- and anticompetitive effects of an agreement. Clearly, this balancing test will not always be easy to carry out and, as noted above, will generally leave an important margin of discretion to the competition authorities and the courts asked to examine the agreement.

Efficiencies should also be taken into consideration in the context of abuse of dominance cases. Indeed, the ECJ has recognized that conduct by dominant firms that would otherwise be considered as abusive is legitimate when it can be objectively justified. Economists have shown that, in certain circumstances, conduct such as price discrimination, tying, and so on, can have pro-competitive effects. The problem, however, comes from the fact that the Commission and the European Courts consider that certain types of conduct, such as loyalty rebates, should be subject to a *per se* prohibition. The rigidity of such a test is at odds with economic theory, according to which it is not the nature of the conduct but its effects on the competitive structure that should be determinative. It is suggested that this problem should be considered by the Commission in its current internal review of Article 82 of the Treaty.

---

[172]   Ibid. at 25–34.

Efficiency considerations also play an important role in the sector-specific regulation applicable to network industries. The market-opening reforms pursued in these sectors are based on the idea that competition will enhance the performance of the market players by forcing them to be more efficient. Indeed, state monopolies in network industries were characterized by a high degree of inefficiency and a low degree of consumer satisfaction. Moreover, the various tools used to control the access prices of monopolistic infrastructures and the retail prices in non-competitive market segments will usually contain an efficiency component.

Comment: A short note on the generation of efficiencies in the context of the 'constitutional' principles of European competition law

Gustavo Ghidini*

The subject matter of this workshop stimulates, *inter alia*, a reflection on the position and role of the generation of efficiencies in the framework of the 'constitutional' principles of EU competition law.

First of all, of course, we must consider the paradigm of Article 81(3) of the EC Treaty – a basic paradigm which I assume (and as I will later try to argue) embodies a balance of interests which basically informs the whole process of anticompetitive assessment – from the earlier Treaty-based cartel law to the subsequent Merger Regulations.

Now, Article 81(3) tells us precisely that an agreement that produces substantial, long-lasting efficiencies, even if they also benefit users (as indeed they must in order to be relevant), cannot be authorized if it is likely to eliminate competition from a substantial portion of the relevant market. Thus, Article 81(3) sets a double hierarchy between different general interests: a) the interest in preserving workable actual competition is foremost, and prevails over the – also general – interest in the generation of efficiencies, be they connected to superior productive, distributive or technological performance; b) in turn, the interests of the parties to the agreement are placed a step below those of consumers – the only 'guaranteed' social group. Further, how strongly the hierarchy is set may be seen from the fact that, even where the prospective efficiencies can be deemed to be long-lasting, the restriction to competition, however substantial or 'insubstantial', can only be tolerated for a limited time.

Bon gré, mal gré, this is the normative pattern. Accordingly, all economic analysis-based reflections can be regarded as a very useful contribution to a

---

* Professor, Libera Università Internazionale delle Scienze Sociali (LUISS) Guido Carli, Rome.

realistic and reasonable interpretation/application of competition law *in so far as* they do not contradict (or ignore) – as sometime happens – the normative paradigm, and the related basic hierarchy of relevant interests/values.

As already indicated, I also believe that such a basic hierarchy permeates merger control, and it does so even under Regulation 139/2004 of 20 January 2004.

First of all, and preliminarily, the Merger Regulation confirms and restates the positive role of efficiencies (be they allocative or dynamic) in the overall appraisal of concentrations, as a possibly compensating factor for a merger's anticompetitive effects. (I refer to long-term efficiencies, the only ones legally relevant.)[1] Thus, the Regulation confirms and restates a development initiated several years before, that is, the repudiation of earlier assessments of efficiencies as a cause or evidence of an incompatible dominance. The foundations of such a shift can be traced back to the Commission's 'Notes on Council Regulation (EEC) 4064/89' of 1998, which stated that 'technical and economic progress' as mentioned in Article 2(1)(b) of Regulation 4064/89, 'must be understood in the light of the principles enshrined in Art. 85(3) of the Treaty'. This obviously implied a positive evaluation of efficiencies, since Article 85(3) – now Article 81(3) – regards the promotion of technical and economic progress as a ground for exemption and definitely not as evidence of anticompetitiveness. This approach, confirmed in the 2002 Draft Horizontal Merger Guidelines which accompanied the concomitant issuance of a *Proposal for a revised merger regulation*,[2] was restated in Regulation 139/2004.

All this is beyond question. The most important and perhaps controversial point is the normative subordination of the generation of efficiencies to the preservation of an effective although restricted competitive physiognomy of the market concerned by the merger. Professor Geradin has quite rightly recalled the Commission Notice of 28 January 2004 (Horizontal Merger Guidelines), which states that it is 'highly unlikely that a merger leading to a market position approaching that of a monopoly . . . can be declared compatible with the common market on the ground that efficiency gains would be sufficient to counteract its potential anti-competitive effects' (para. 84).

Thus, the basic balance of interests, the basic hierarchy originally set in Article 81(3), is confirmed: efficiencies can compensate for anticompetitive effects provided that these do not eradicate effective, albeit reduced competition.

The continuity is also within the Merger Regulation. Diverging here a bit

---

[1]   See Commission of 25 February 1991, *Aerospatiale*, OJ 1991 C 59, 13; Commission, 'Guidelines on the appraisal of horizontal mergers', OJEC 2004 C 31, 5, at no. 88.

[2]   See OJ 2003 C20/4.

from Professor Geradin's analysis, I believe that a 'market position approaching that of a monopoly' is the substantial equivalent of a dominant position that can cause lasting damage to competition.[3] Historically it has been the basic legal criterion for assessing a merger's incompatibility with the Common market – and I believe it still is. Indeed, a substantial continuity seems to emerge, first of all in the full and literal preservation in Regulation 139/2004 of the criteria for merger appraisal listed in Article 2(1)(a) of the 1989 text, as well as in the confirmation, in Regulation 139/2004, of the pivotal role of dominance.[4] A pivotal role, yes, whereas the room for a direct assessment of a 'significant impediment to effective competition' in cases where there is no dominance, is strictly limited to cases which according to experience are exceptional, that is, cases of anticompetitive effects stemming from the adoption of parallel, albeit not collusive behaviour among oligopolists.[5] This provision was inserted, as is well known, to fill the alleged 'gap' of enforcement of anticompetitive effects of mergers that exist even in the absence of a recognizable situation of joint dominance. The sharply restricted room for such an assessment to only that case – *exclusively* to that case (the German text says '*ausschliesslich*') – confirms *ex contrariis* the continuity of the basic European reference to the criterion of dominance. This, by the way has always implied, quite clearly – literally! – a dual test: an assessment of dominance and ('recte': qualified by) a further assessment of its impact ('as a result of which . . .') on competition.

Thus, the limited derogation to the traditional dominance criterion cannot reasonably be construed as signalling an abandonment of the latter – an abandonment also opposed, if I may recall, by the vast majority of large continental firms, as expressly stated by the European Round Table of Industrialists' response to the Commission's Green Paper on the revision of the Merger Regulation.

Thus, although constantly evolving towards more flexible, economic analysis-based criteria of assessment of pro- and anticompetitive long-term effects (as demonstrated by, *inter alia,* the merely indicative role assigned to market shares in the evaluation of the degree of market concentration), we should by no means rush to conclude that we are 'now' walking on a Chicagoan path whereby the Commission should approve a merger-to-monopoly provided only that economic analysis suggests that a *de facto* monopoly would probably not allow the merged entity to impose artificial price or quantity restrictions.

---

3   Cf. Article 2(1)(b) and recital 5 of Regulation 4064/89.
4   See Articles 2(2) and 2(3), also in conjunction with recitals 26 and 29.
5   See Merger Regulation 139/2004, recital 25, last part.

That continuity, confirming the basic 'constitutional' hierarchy of Article 81(3) as reflected also in the Merger Regulation, extends to the requirement that efficiencies, in order to be relevant, accrue also to consumers. More than this: the accrual of such benefits is *causally linked* to the preservation of an *actual* competitive market physiognomy, an actual competitive pressure, including structural features. Even in 2004, in the Horizontal Merger Guidelines, the Commission states that: 'the incentive on the part of the merged entity to pass efficiency gains on to consumers is often related to the existence of competitive pressure from the remaining firms in the market and ["and", not "or"] from potential entry'.[6] Thus, the European approach continues to privilege the maintenance of competitive market features, and is quite reluctant to rely merely on the potential for future entry, while in the 'meantime' consumers are deprived of any effective alternatives, and thus freedom of choice. (By the way, the European scepticism for the capacity of potential competition alone to virtuously discipline the behaviour of firms enjoying significant market power is also at the root of the uniquely European idea of attributing a 'special responsibility' to dominant firms in order to prevent 'abuses' of such power.)

The European approach seems consistent with economic experience showing that: a) mergers often generate short-term efficiencies which in the long term vanish, and with them, consumer benefits (as Professor Tesauro recently argued, 'we assess efficiencies over years, Americans over six months'); b) once actual competition has been backed into a corner, its revival can be much less easy than the 'optimistic', 'pro-dominant firm' Chicagoan approach suggests. May I just point out that recently, Professor F. M. Scherer cooled down the apologetic enthusiasm for the 'rapid erosion' of dominant positions in the US, by recalling that '[i]t took *seventy-five years* for the pricing power of the United States Steel Corporation . . . to erode sufficiently that independent pricing could be seen . . . it took roughly *fifty-five* years for Japanese entry to undermine the price and product leadership of General Motors'.[7] And to those who object that 'things are different in the new economy, in the ICT sector usw', the great scholar replies:

> Intel and Microsoft enjoyed near-monopoly positions for two decades in personal computer microprocessors and operating systems respectively. There is *no indication* that a serious challenge to Microsoft's position has materialized. In micro-processors, Intel's position was *first* challenged seriously when Advanced Micro Devices ('AMD') leaped ahead technologically with its Athlon processor *in the year 2000*. Whether AMD will be able to sustain its competitive challenge remains to be seen.[8]

---

6   Horizontal Merger Guidelines, *supra* n. 1, at no. 84.
7   F. M. Scherer, 'Some Principles for Post-Chicago Antitrust Analysis', 52 *Case Western Reserve L.Rev.* 5, 10 (2001) (emphasis added)
8   Ibid.

Even upon further consideration I do not believe that the 'European' approach should be abandoned. If we accept that efficiencies can justify even the achievement of monopoly or quasi-monopoly positions (leaving aside the pseudo exception of the so-called 'failing firm' defence, the real justification for *Newscorp/Telepiù*),[9] would not this dangerously affect the already troublesome process of liberalization of public utilities which is going on throughout European countries? After all, if we do not mind the giant and simply want it to behave, why do we not just keep the one we have and make it toe the line by means of some regulatory blows when needed?

(By the way, will it really toe the line?)

Besides its economic rationale, the EU approach to both the merger control as a whole and the role of efficiencies may also be traced back to two distinct, essentially political factors, or values, which significantly affected the imprint of EU competition law, and which are briefly worth recalling.

The first factor is the idea of reconciling competitive efficiency ('a high degree of competitiveness') with a wider realm of social welfare, with the goal – enshrined in Article 2 of the Treaty on European Union and explicitly recalled by both Regulation 4064/89 and Regulation 139/2004 – of a 'balanced and sustainable development' of economic activities. This goal, which is far from simple rhetoric, has a profound historical–political (and therefore also juris–political) meaning. Indeed, the EU's competitive ethos is intimately intertwined with the goal (which also inspired the post-war European adhesion to the *soziale Marktwirtschaft*) of creating the economic texture for the reduction/elimination of both the creeping social inequalities and economic conflicts among Member States.

Furthermore, the driving principles of EU competition law may also be historically linked to strong reasons of 'democratic efficiency'.[10] I am referring to the 'libertarian motivations' developed by the so-called Ordoliberal school founded in Freiburg, Germany (*before* the country's rebirth) and championed by lawyers such as Franz Boehm and Hans Grossman-Doerth and economists such as Walter Eucken. They considered competition law to be more than an instrument to foster economic efficiency, but rather as a policy tool meant to preserve 'economic pluralism'. For them – recalls David Gerber – it was not sufficient to protect the individual from the power of government, because governments were not the only threats to individual freedom. Powerful economic institutions could also destroy or limit freedom, especially economic freedom. Thus, they

---

9   Commission of 2 April 2003, OOMP/M.2876.
10   Giuliano Amato, *Il potere e l'antitrust*, Bologna 1998, at 95.

supported the dispersion of not only the political power, but economic power as well.[11]

This legacy is still alive. As emphasized above, it is enshrined in the *present* normative hierarchy of constitutional interests pursued by European antitrust law, whereby efficient economic outcomes on the one hand are prized provided they effectively translate into consumer benefits, and on the other, however positive and worthy, can never justify the elimination of competition: *because* such elimination cannot lastingly benefit consumers – and citizens.

---

[11]   D. Gerber, *Law and Competition in Twentieth Century Europe – Protecting Prometheus*, Oxford 2001.

Index

absolute territorial protection 122, 123, 327, 329
abuse 26, 28, 229, 275, 277
abuse of collective dominance 91
abuse of dominance 207, 234, 355
abuse of dominant position 71, 75, 76, 107, 171, 204, 205, 206, 207, 208, 210, 211, 213, 214, 215, 216, 305, 306, 315
abuse of domination 207, 209, 215, 216, 218, 219
abuse of economic dependence 207, 216, 217, 218, 219, 220
abuse of market power 10, 11, 201–23, 279
abuse of power 234
abuse of purchasing power 218
abusive behaviour 111, 14, 118, 119, 212, 221, 229
abusive clauses 220
abusive de-linking 218
abusive practices 281, 302
abusive prices 124
abusive pricing policies 212
Academic Society for Competition Law (ASCOLA) 3, 201
access regulation 231, 243, 248, 249, 250, 252, 253, 354
active sales 91, 101
agency 86, 102, 108–9, 110, 277, 278, 282, 283, 284, 285, 286, 287, 289, 295, 343–4
agent 95, 102, 103, 129, 137
agreements between firms 26, 27, 92, 146, 305, 319
agreements of minor importance 46, 70, 92, 160
airline alliance 128, 130, 138–41, 144, 147, 150–52, 156, 166
airlines 29, 126,153, 167
alliance 126–7, 129, 133, 134, 135, 140–41, 150, 152, 153, 166–7

allocation of resources, best 204, 222, 223, 279
allocative efficiency 23, 48, 315, 316, 318, 350, 352, 354
anticompetitive agreements 75, 303, 306, 309
anticompetitive behaviour 116, 204, 206
anticompetitive effect 64, 69, 95, 112, 113–15, 309, 318, 320, 321, 329, 332, 335, 336, 342, 343 344, 358, 359
anticompetitive practices 153, 207, 208, 209, 218, 228, 273
anticompetitive strategies 209
antitrust 18, 20, 23–5, 30, 36, 37
antitrust enforcement 25, 28, 29, 37, 47, 76
antitrust law 13, 21, 22, 24, 25, 203, 235, 277, 278, 301, 362
antitrust legislation 19, 169
antitrust policy 22, 266
antitrust rules 28, 39, 64, 272, 284
a posteriori control 206, 209, 228
a posteriori penalties 188
a priori control 206
audience share 176, 193, 194, 196
audiovisual sector 170, 172, 177, 178, 179, 180, 182, 185, 189
audiovisual services 176
authorization regime 72
automobile industry/sector 126, 139, 149, 196
automotive sector 131

block exemption 55, 56, 65, 76, 90, 92, 93, 94, 162
block exemption regulations 33, 85, 91, 162, 194, 320, 321, 326, 330, 336
broadcasting 176, 195, 189, 283, 289
broadcasting rights 182
broadcast rights 186

cable network markets 185
Canada 28, 29, 35
cartel 5, 20, 21, 22, 24, 25, 26, 29, 63,
    72, 98, 167, 221, 228, 235
cartels 206, 221, 228
cartelization 24, 25, 282
Chicago school of economics 30, 31, 33,
    93, 95, 124, 203, 204
client-specific investment 328
'code sharing' 127, 129–30, 151, 167
collaboration 26, 157, 158, 163, 164,
    235
collective dominance 79, 91
collective restraints 228
collusion, tacit 79
collusive cooperation 144
combined media sector 194
commercial feasibility 129
commercial freedom 43, 45, 93, 122,
    125
commercialization agreements 323, 324,
(EC) Commission policy 31–2, 129
Commission's Guidelines 32–3
common carrier 248–50
common carrier model 267, 268
Common market 27, 41, 49, 50, 80, 230,
    340, 358–9
Community competition law 34, 76, 208
Community competition policy 11
community public interest 72
competition 18–37, 202, 204, 278, 279,
    280, 281, 285, 291
competition authorities 7, 21, 46, 48, 71,
    72, 76, 91, 106, 144, 148, 151,
    152, 178, 183, 187, 190, 200, 222,
    286, 287, 306, 307, 309, 313, 354
competition law 17, 27–8, 30, 34, 37, 39,
    41, 47, 48, 49, 53–4, 71–82,
    157–8, 185–90, 191, 192, 202,
    203, 205, 206, 207, 219, 220, 300,
    307, 313, 361
competition policy 4–5, 11, 37, 40, 41,
    47, 51, 112, 154, 167, 203, 217,
    263, 265, 270, 273
competition rules 9, 13, 26, 28, 30, 34,
    149, 200
competitive market structure 192, 194,
    314
competitive process 40, 49, 51, 226, 332,
    353

competitive strategy 206
competitor 33, 34, 55, 56, 62, 66, 80,
    277, 286, 288, 304, 337, 350, 351
concentration 49, 79, 80, 126, 128, 147,
    157, 166, 168, 195, 204, 305, 306,
    308, 339
concentration strategies 164
concerted practices 4, 46, 72, 326
consumer benefits 335, 360
consumer welfare 23, 30, 33, 46, 99,
    152, 278, 314, 316, 317, 343, 349,
    354
contestable markets theory 145, 204
contractual freedom 214, 215
contractual inequalities 216
control of abuses 89
control of market concentration 206, 210
control of market dominance 314, 315,
    345
convergence rule 73
cooperation 74, 126, 132, 134, 136, 139,
    140, 141, 142–4, 149, 150, 153,
    157–9, 164, 167, 269–70, 322
cooperation agreements 29, 47, 135–42,
    168, 321, 322
cooperative agreements 142, 168, 321
cooperative networks 133, 134, 135–8,
    157, 158, 159, 160, 162, 163, 164
co-opetition 127, 143, 144–5, 155, 159,
    160, 166
cost-benefit analysis 247, 263, 268
cross-license 57, 60, 62, 63, 68,
cross-media checks 194
cultural diversity 170, 171, 196, 318
cumulative effect 89, 221
customer allocation 57, 325
customer restrictions 59, 94

dealer 97, 98, 122, 123–4, 347
decartelization plan 24, 25
decentralisation 71, 76, 204, 205
demand side 227, 228
de minimis 70, 161, 162
dependency 227
deregulated sectors 288
deregulation movement 242, 243, 295,
    298
deregulatory process 353
direct effect 75
discriminatory practices 217

distortion of competition 169, 225
distribution 45, 102, 264, 322, 327,
    328–9, 334
distribution agreements 44, 110
distributor 6, 91, 102, 103, 217, 327–9
dominance 49, 79, 80, 90, 112–15, 227,
    228, 314, 315, 358, 359
dominant enterprises/undertakings 8,
    104, 105, 106, 107
dominant firm 303, 304, 308, 309, 313,
    316, 345, 346, 347, 348, 349, 350,
    352, 355
dominant position 8, 34–6, 49–50,
    79–81, 106, 182, 186, 193, 204,
    205, 206, 207, 208, 210, 214, 216,
    227, 230, 307, 340, 349, 360
downstream market 87, 149, 231, 243,
    248, 249, 250, 251, 253, 254, 267,
    316, 349–51, 354
dual pricing 103
dynamic competition 271
dynamic efficiency 145, 150, 315, 316,
    318, 351, 352

EC Competition law 27, 30, 34, 90,
    313–18, 329, 355, 357, 361
École de Nice 276, 288
economic activity 197, 292
economic analysis 112, 113, 146, 205,
    216, 223, 225, 227, 313, 320, 329,
    346, 348
economic approach 33, 45, 46, 81, 86,
    110, 117, 161, 184, 325
economic concepts 185
economic effects 32, 106, 111
economic efficiencies 30, 65, 205, 206,
    222, 225, 313, 315, 318, 327, 339,
    346, 353, 361
economic freedom 45, 270, 271, 278,
    293
economic integration 317
economic liberty 268–9
economic objectives 307
economic pluralism 361
economies of scale 34, 41, 47, 135, 242,
    318, 320, 324, 328, 333, 349
effective competition 49, 50, 51, 122,
    158, 251, 254, 266, 341
effects-based approach 87, 99, 110, 348
effects' doctrine 28, 29

efficiency 47, 48, 99, 223, 284, 308, 318,
    322, 331, 332, 333, 334, 336, 358,
    360
efficiency claims 14, 32, 168, 273,
    314–15, 319–21, 341, 345,
efficiency defence 47–51, 168, 335, 355
efficiency gains 33, 47, 50, 65, 90, 150,
    152, 163, 168, 270, 338, 341, 358
electricity fields 192
electricity industry/sector 263, 264, 272,
    273, 352
electronic communications 187, 302,
    303, 305, 306, 307, 309
end consumers 101, 270
energy sector 261–2, 293, 294
enforcement activity 72, 73, 74
enforcement system 71, 72
environmental policy 225
essential facilities 148, 155, 303, 316,
    350, 352, 354
essential facilities doctrine 213–15, 230,
    231, 267, 269, 304
essential networks 306
European Community 26, 27, 31, 40,
    231
European competition authorities 78,
    151, 309
European competition policy 17, 38, 42,
    111, 117, 118, 120
European industry 41, 42, 51
European market 38, 47, 242, 317
European school of competition law 224,
    226, 230
ex ante access regulation 252
ex ante control 188
ex ante mechanism/intervention 278,
    302, 303
ex-ante notification 147
excessive prices 229
exclusive distribution 85
exclusive purchasing 85
exclusivity contracts 189
ex post control 188, 209, 278
ex post mechanism 278, 302

fair share 48, 316, 322, 334, 338, 343
field-of-use restrictions 59–62, 66
financial markets 283
fixed price 94, 97, 99
floating shares 185

France 175, 177, 193, 197, 210, 214, 220, 254, 276, 288, 289
franchise agreements 85
franchising 159, 160
free competition 40, 219, 226, 296
freedom/liberty of expression 170, 171, 199
freedom of speech 171, 172
free market competition 172, 173
free-rider 112, 327, 329
free-riding 97, 100, 123–4, 329
French law 171, 181, 184, 188, 189, 207, 208, 211, 218, 228, 288
functional and plurivalent enterprise 185

'Gate keeper' 187
German system/law 88, 123, 169, 208, 228, 260
Germany 24, 25, 26, 95, 253, 257, 258, 259, 361
global competition 39
global economy 121, 124
global market 127, 132–5, 136, 150, 155, 157
globalisation 133
globalisation of competition 158
governmental power 20
'gray' license restrictions 69
group exemption regulations 43, 46
group of companies 185, 251, 256

hard-core list 66, 67, 69, 99, 110, 123
hard-core restrictions 46, 55, 56, 57, 60, 65, 86, 88, 91, 92, 93, 94, 115, 117, 123, 323
high price level 121
'hold-up' problem 328
horizontal agreements 13, 47, 88, 119, 319, 320, 321, 323, 325, 328, 331, 340, 342
horizontal cartels 98
horizontal cooperation 74, 126, 127, 131, 146, 160, 344
horizontal cooperation agreements 47, 140, 146, 322, 344
horizontal cooperative networks 163
horizontal mergers 32, 48–51, 187, 340, 342, 343, 344
horizontal network 138–9
horizontal (non-binding) control 74–5

horizontal restrictions 320, 321, 330, 331

individual examination/assessment 86
industrial economics, modern 119
industrial policy 41, 47, 225, 233, 308, 318
infrastructure competition 243, 244, 251, 253
innovation 39, 133, 204, 234, 235, 247, 249, 270, 318, 323, 337, 341, 351
integrated reseller 102
integration 41
intellectual property 7, 54, 70, 215, 123, 316, 351
interbrand competition 90, 93, 96, 99, 327, 349
inter-firm horizontal cooperation 126
internal market 39, 40, 41, 101, 308, 318
international antitrust enforcement cooperation agreements 29
inter-network competition 250, 251, 253
inter-party competition 148, 150, 154, 166
intrabrand competition 93, 96, 99, 100
intra-network competition 243, 244, 250, 251, 253
intra-sector regulation 171, 190
investment 235, 242, 328
Italian electricity sector 263
Italy 170, 173, 194, 263–72

joint production agreements 163
joint ventures 82, 131, 140, 149, 150, 157, 164, 167, 169, 308, 309
'just-in-time' system 149

Laker antitrust litigation 29
large market power 90, 113
'Law and Economics' school 203, 205, 206, 221, 223, 224, 225
legal exception system/principle 72, 76, 81
liberalisation process 111, 291, 293, 296, 352, 361
licence agreement 56, 58, 337
'Lisbon Strategy' 17, 18, 31, 38
low-market-share restraints 67
low-priced products 102
low pricing 234

mandatory licences 189
mandatory notification 179
mandatory waiting period 188
manufacturer 60, 96, 98, 101, 103, 123, 347
marginal costs 227, 315, 348
market competition 119, 172, 173, 194, 254, 275, 336
market concentration 204, 206, 359
market dominance 49, 50, 113, 114, 118, 119, 121, 123, 163, 228, 313, 314, 315, 345
market failure 241, 326, 328, 331
market impairment 211
market integration 10, 31, 32, 41, 42, 89, 99, 124, 242, 252, 256, 314, 318
market power 35, 46, 47, 69, 85, 87, 90, 113, 119, 162, 204, 227, 234, 300, 306, 307, 315, 316, 317, 319, 320, 323, 325, 335, 337, 351, 352
market segmentation 101, 103, 105, 124, 125
market share 32, 46, 87, 88, 184, 193, 359
market-sharing agreement 321
market share threshold 87, 90, 93, 110, 112, 119, 123, 167, 337
market specific 339
maximum prices 118
media 170, 182, 191, 195, 262
media concentration 13, 191, 192, 196, 198
media control rules 174, 187
media merger 183, 190
media operators 195
media pluralism/plurality 196, 198, 199, 200
media sector 171, 173, 179, 194, 197, 198, 199
media-specific legislation 193, 194, 199
merger 313–15, 341, 342, 343
merger law 9, 13, 48–51
merger control 47, 48, 78, 87, 167, 168, 174, 175, 177, 181, 183, 184, 185, 318, 319, 320, 361
merger referral 79,
merger reform 71, 78
(EC) Merger Regulation 32, 35, 40, 48–51, 147, 168–9, 197–9, 342–3, 358–9

minimum price 97, 99
minimum resale price 97, 122, 123
modernization (reform) 32, 36–7, 71–8, 86, 110, 205, 339
mono-media concentration controls 194
monopolist enterprises 275
monopolistic markets 8, 192
monopolization 35, 36, 234, 282
monopoly 242, 248, 249–50, 296
monopoly control 235
monopoly power 36, 235, 288
most favoured customer clause 92
motor vehicle distribution 305
multimedia 175, 176,
multi-party licensing 64

national authorities 72, 73, 74, 75, 76, 77, 91
national competition agencies 258
national courts 52, 75, 330, 336
national enforcement system 72
national judges 72, 75, 76, 77
national monopoly 242, 243, 250, 252, 256, 304
national regulatory authority 303
natural monopoly 241, 242, 248, 249, 281, 352, 353
negative market effects 161
network industries 242, 248, 249, 250, 251, 253, 263, 314, 315, 345, 352, 356
networks 37–42, 126–8, 135, 137–42, 146, 148, 150, 166
network sectors 242, 248, 252
networks of distribution 221
New institutional economics approach 244–5, 246–7, 263
new products 33, 125, 133, 134, 231, 315, 320
non-collusive oligopolies 79, 80
non-competition values 233
non-competitors 57, 58, 337
non-cooperative oligopolies 81
normative theory of regulation 246
notifications 76
notification system 72, 330
notification, voluntary 188

oligopolies 168
oligopolistics markets 81

operators 173
optimal allocation of resources 205

parallel trade 102, 104, 105, 125
passive sales 57, 92, 101
patent 28, 58, 63–4
perfect competition 119, 204, 315
per se approach 102, 346
per se prohibition 94, 329, 346, 347, 348
per se rules 115–18, 321, 348
personal computers 236
pharmaceutical products 101, 103, 104,
        125
Portugal 131, 132, 183
postal services 261, 262
power
    economic power 19, 20, 22, 361
    governmental power 20
    private power 20
practices restricting competition 218,
        219
predatory pricing 33
'pre-notification' consultation process 78
press 170, 172, 175, 181, 194
press sector 177, 179, 185
price collusion 96
price-cutters 95
price differentiation 102, 104, 254
price discrimination 346
price-fixing 66, 95, 123, 321, 324
private enforcement 34
private market regulation 163, 164
private parties 68
privatization 183, 287, 290, 291, 295–6,
        298
procedural system/rules 76, 77, 78, 169
procedure 77
pro-competitive behaviour 116
pro-competitive benefits 60, 86
pro-competitive effects 106, 321, 331,
        332, 335
production agreements 323, 324
productive efficiency 49, 315, 317, 318,
        352
productivity 18, 19, 39, 41
profit neutrality 64
public authorities 301
public interest 20, 72, 246, 247, 269,
        278, 281
public regulation 205

public sector 285
public undertaking 297, 309
purchasing agreements 324

quantity fixing 115

rebates 314, 349
    loyalty rebates 346, 347, 348
    volume rebates 346
reciprocal control 73, 74
refusal to deal 96, 234
refusal to sell 117, 218
regionalisation 133
regulated industries/sectors 248, 276,
        277, 281, 282, 283, 284, 299
regulation 278, 279, 280, 281, 291, 295,
        298, 300, 302, 307
regulation of competition 202, 203, 209
regulation, positive theory of 246
regulatory agency/bodies/authorities 286,
        287, 302, 303, 305, 306, 354, 370
regulatory approach 85, 242, 245, 252,
        253
regulatory measure 226, 265, 299, 353
regulatory power 196, 278
regulatory system 278, 284
relevant market 44, 45, 46, 129, 148,
        149, 152, 209, 210, 214, 320, 327,
        331, 344
remedies 8, 72, 36, 326
re-regulation 298
resale price maintenance 94, 95, 96, 98,
        99, 115, 117, 118, 122, 329
research and development (R&D) 40,
        316, 322, 336, 341, 351
research and development (R&D)
        agreements 119, 146, 162, 163,
        167, 321, 323
reseller, independent 91, 102
restraint of competition 45, 161, 162,
        228, 280
restraint of trade 160, 280
restriction of economic freedom 45
restrictions of competition 40, 42, 43,
        44, 45, 127, 161, 202, 323, 336,
        338–9, 355
restrictive agreements 42, 72, 73, 107,
        313, 315, 319, 321, 334, 338, 340,
        343, 345
restrictive practices 218, 220, 221, 228

retail 93
retailer 91, 95, 124, 218
risk allocation 63, 108
rivalry 40, 50, 142, 227, 228, 229, 335
rule of reason 68, 69, 93, 99, 115–17,
    161, 164
running royalties 55, 62–4, 66, 68

scientific progress 204
sector-specific agencies 259
sector-specific regulations/law 175, 179,
    181, 184, 186, 188, 191, 193, 195,
    241, 242, 243, 244, 247, 251, 252,
    254, 256, 257, 302, 315, 353,
    356
securities 184
selective distribution agreement 44
servicing 127
settlement 35, 36
Sherman Act 20, 21, 22, 23, 26, 29, 36,
    37, 96, 234, 235, 281
significant impediment to effective
    competition 48, 158, 168, 359
significant market power 85, 195, 251,
    256, 304, 307, 327, 352, 360
Single European market 317, 329
sliding scale 325, 334, 339, 342, 343,
    344
social policy 225
spare parts 127
specialisation agreements 162, 163, 167
state monopolies 172, 290, 314, 352, 356
state-owned enterprise 298
static competition 271
strategic alliance 128, 139, 140, 146,
    147, 151, 157, 158, 159, 160, 163,
    164
strategic collusion 144
strategic competition policy 38–42,
    45–6, 51
strategic network 139–40, 159
'substantial lessening of competition'
    test 79
substitutability, absence of 214
supplier 19, 87, 91, 95, 102, 103, 131,
    139, 150, 217–18, 227, 262, 324,
    349
supply side 227
Switzerland 121–2, 125, 254
system coherence 291

system of undistorted competition 216,
    226

technological development 158
technological innovation 249
technology transfer agreements 336, 337
Technology Transfer Block Exemption
    Regulation (TTBER) 54, 58, 65
telecommunications 186, 192, 209, 214,
    215, 231, 243, 244, 248, 250, 253,
    262, 273, 277, 283, 354
telecommunications sector 180, 254,
    283, 289, 293, 298, 352, 353
telephone service market 234
television 171, 172, 173, 176, 181, 194,
    195
television sector 185
territorial exclusivity 91, 92, 100, 103,
    105
territorial protection 102, 105, 115, 117,
    122, 123, 327, 329
territorial restrictions 94, 105
territorial segmentation 102
third-party competition 150, 154, 166
transaction costs theory 145
transmission network 264, 265, 267, 269
treble damage 22, 28, 29
tying agreements 91, 314

undistorted competition 9, 216, 226,
    230
uneven bargaining power between
    contracting parties 228
unfair contractual terms 228, 229
unfair trading practices 205, 206
United Kingdom 89, 194, 242, 280
upstream market 267, 273
uranium litigation 28

vertical agreement 90, 95, 98, 112, 114,
    115, 116, 118, 124, 146, 319, 320,
    326–8, 331
vertical cooperation 74
vertical integration 35, 102, 136, 159,
    186, 188, 248, 267
vertical merger 115
vertical network 131, 138
vertical territorial market segmentation
    124
vertical relations 27, 216, 220–22

vertical restraints 13, 85, 86–8, 89, 92,
        93, 100, 105, 106, 107, 110,
        111–12, 121, 162, 326–7
vertical restrictions 123, 320, 325–9,
        330, 331

welfare economics approach 244,
        247
welfare losses 116
welfare standard 314, 316, 343